Baldur von Schirach

Baldur von Schirach

Nazi Leader and Head of the Hitler Youth

Oliver Rathkolb

Translated by John Heath

Frontline Books

Translated and edited with the kind support of the Future Fund of the Republic of Austria, the National Fund of the Republic of Austria for Victims of National Socialism and the Faculty of Historical and Cultural Studies of the University of Vienna.

First published in Great Britain in 2022 by
Frontline Books
An imprint of
Pen & Sword Books Ltd
Yorkshire – Philadelphia

Copyright © Oliver Rathkolb 2022
Translation © John Heath 2022

ISBN 978 1 39902 095 4

The right of Oliver Rathkolb to be identified as Author of this work has been asserted by him in accordance with the Copyright, Designs and Patents Act 1988.

A CIP catalogue record for this book is
available from the British Library.

All rights reserved. No part of this book may be reproduced or transmitted in any form or by any means, electronic or mechanical including photocopying, recording or by any information storage and retrieval system, without permission from the Publisher in writing.

Typeset by Mac Style
Printed in the UK by CPI Group (UK) Ltd, Croydon, CR0 4YY.

Pen & Sword Books Limited incorporates the imprints of Atlas, Archaeology, Aviation, Discovery, Family History, Fiction, History, Maritime, Military, Military Classics, Politics, Select, Transport, True Crime, Air World, Frontline Publishing, Leo Cooper, Remember When, Seaforth Publishing, The Praetorian Press, Wharncliffe Local History, Wharncliffe Transport, Wharncliffe True Crime and White Owl.

For a complete list of Pen & Sword titles please contact

PEN & SWORD BOOKS LIMITED
47 Church Street, Barnsley, South Yorkshire, S70 2AS, England
E-mail: enquiries@pen-and-sword.co.uk
Website: www.pen-and-sword.co.uk

Or

PEN AND SWORD BOOKS
1950 Lawrence Rd, Havertown, PA 19083, USA
E-mail: Uspen-and-sword@casematepublishers.com
Website: www.penandswordbooks.com

Contents

Note on the Translation		vi
Introduction		vii
Chapter 1	From Bull Run to the Grand Duchy and Court Theatre	1
Chapter 2	Influences and Ruptures	10
Chapter 3	High Tea with Herr Hitler	16
Chapter 4	Moving Forwards!	28
Chapter 5	A Useful Lad, Able and Clever	41
Chapter 6	Raised for Revolution	64
Chapter 7	My Gau, My Vienna	73
Chapter 8	The "Special Action"	99
Chapter 9	Slave Labour	109
Chapter 10	"Viennesed"	118
Chapter 11	Neither a Commander Nor a Hero	142
Chapter 12	A Cranach for the *Reichsleiter*	160
Chapter 13	I Alone Bear the Guilt	172
Chapter 14	I Believed in Hitler	190
Selected Bibliography		202
Notes		209
Index		238

Note on the Translation

In order to combine readability and terminological accuracy, titles and offices of the so-called "Reich" are given in English followed by the German in parentheses, unless historiography in English tends to use the German, in which case this volume follows suit, followed by an English rendering in the first instance.

Most German terms appear in italics unless they are commonly used in English too or form part of quotations. The reader will also note that some German terms appear in quotations marks, reflecting the author's conscious decision to distance himself from the National Socialist vocabulary, questioning its accuracy or legitimacy.

For German source material that has already appeared in English, the published translations have been used, with the exception of Henriette von Schirach's memoirs, since some cited passages were omitted from the English version. Unless stated otherwise, all other translations of German sources are the translator's own.

Introduction

Hitler's *Reichsjugendführer* (Reich Youth Leader) Baldur von Schirach was probably the greatest young hope of the National Socialist terror regime. "Führer" Adolf Hitler had a lot to thank him for, especially the media-savvy staging of German adolescents' mass mobilisation in the Hitler Youth (*Hitlerjugend*, HJ) and the League of German Girls (*Bund Deutscher Mädel*, BDM). It didn't take long for him to bring the entire system of youth organisations in Nazi Germany under the ideological control of the regime. Despite the bloody war of aggression and the persecution of Jews and other victim groups throughout Europe, as *Reichsleiter* and *Gauleiter* (Reich leader and regional leader) of Vienna he accelerated the exuberant promotion of high culture from 1940 onwards, quickly winning over the elites and many artists. With their characteristic obedience to authority, the Viennese were soon enamoured with the anti-democratic nationalist traditions he imported from Weimar. While his sometimes controversial contemporary art exhibitions brought him into conflict with the Berlin central departments and Adolf Hitler, plans to replace him could not be pushed through. Schirach had already become one of the central satraps of National Socialism and had at his disposal a skilful propaganda machine. At the same time, however, Baldur von Schirach is also representative of an aristocratic-bourgeois elite that aligned itself with National Socialism. But for a few exceptions in the military resistance, this class promoted the movement and ultimately supported the regime until its total collapse.

Schirach's father, as the director of the Grand Duchy and Court Theatre in Weimar, was a member of a bourgeois German nationalist elite in the town of Goethe and Schiller, a town that had also honoured Nietzsche and Liszt but had already become German nationalist, anti-democratic and in many ways nationalist-anti-Semitic prior to the First World War. This elite saw in the Weimar Republic its arch-enemy. It was in Weimar of all places that the National Assembly spent months discussing and finally determining the new democratic constitution from February 1919 onwards; this only intensified its rejection by the traditional elites and played a large role in shaping Baldur von Schirach's authoritarian and extremely nationalist understanding of politics. Yearning for a return to the monarchy was soon replaced by the search for a new, strong nationalist dictatorship – from 1925–26 onwards, Hitler became a saviour figure for the Schirachs.

While Baldur von Schirach briefly met Hitler twice in 1925, he soon came to project a particular reverence onto the former private, who had not been an officer but had nevertheless received the Iron Cross First Class. This veneration of Hitler as a veteran of the First World War clearly reflects Schirach's formative experiences growing up in a family of officers. He joined various anti-democratic and nationalist youth defence groups before becoming a member of the NSDAP and the SA at the age of eighteen. His father, formerly the cavalry captain (*Rittmeister*) of a prestigious regiment of the imperial Guards Cuirassiers in Berlin, soon followed him in joining the NSDAP and becoming a founding member of the anti-Semitic Militant League for German Culture (*Kampfbund für Deutsche Kultur*).

After a meteoric rise in the National Socialist German Students' League (*Nationalsozialistischer Deutscher Studentenbund*) from 1927 onwards, Baldur von Schirach became a member of Hitler's inner circle. In 1931 he advanced to *Reichsjugendführer*, directly under the highest level of SA leadership. He married Henriette, the daughter of Hitler's wealthy personal photographer Heinrich Hoffmann, thereby cementing an even closer connection to the "Führer". He artfully made use of his propaganda skills, landing his first great marketing hit with the pictorial volume *Hitler wie ihn keiner kennt* (*Hitler as No One Knows Him*), which he edited together with his father-in-law: Schirach made Hitler familiar to both a bourgeois and a more common public. He became the youngest member of the *Reichstag* in 1931, the NSDAP being the parliamentary group with the highest proportion of aristocrats, and surprised Hitler with a Reich Youth Party Congress in Potsdam attended by 70,000 enthusiastic participants.

By 1936, Schirach had already recruited around six million adolescents to the Hitler Youth – always with the trick of adolescent self-administration but with clear ideological, National Socialist goals, which were partially communicated in playful form, but always in disciplined and controlled structures. The Hitler Youth increasingly received rights enabling it to function as an instrument of surveillance in the schools.

But Schirach wanted more, striving for total control of the adolescent education system and schools. However, he lost this battle with the education bureaucracy. His transfer to Vienna was already the beginning of his political demise, but to the mounting ire of Propaganda Minister Goebbels, with whom he had originally had an amicable relationship, Schirach built up a cultural empire, courting Richard Strauss and his Jewish daughter-in-law Alice as well as the writer Gerhart Hauptmann.

The extent to which Schirach actually warned Hitler about attacking the Soviet Union or war with the USA will be debated, as will the conflict between Hitler and Henriette von Schirach at the Berghof concerning the brutal deportation of the Jews from the Netherlands. At the same time, Schirach boasted about deporting the Viennese Jews ("I have made Vienna free of Jews"), much to the annoyance of Goebbels, who feared negative international reactions. Schirach also announced he would make Vienna "free of Czechs" – and indeed the Gestapo began to keep files to that end.

Schirach certainly had political ambitions far beyond his *Gau* (administrative region of the Reich): for instance, in 1941 he skilfully used the propaganda campaign surrounding the 150th anniversary of the death of Wolfgang Amadeus Mozart to propagate a "European ideology" under German leadership in an effort to legitimise in the long term the occupation of large swathes of Europe, an occupation he sought to underpin with cultural hegemony. Here he intensified his old contacts with the Italian Fascist youth leaders and organised European youth congresses and journalists' meetings. Ultimately, Hitler wanted to have Schirach replaced, since the latter did not wish to defend Vienna as a bastion. However, the "Führer" didn't dare take this measure, since Schirach had a firm hold on the city in terms of cultural policy and ultimately did switch very swiftly to the course of military defence. Schirach escaped from the Red Army at the last minute, not without ensuring his art treasures, many of them stolen from Jews, were moved westwards from his "Aryanised" villa on the Hohe Warte hill in Döbling from 1944 onwards.

Employing a skilful defence strategy during the Nuremberg trials in 1946, he escaped the threat of execution, his aristocratic-bourgeois and partly American origins proving an advantage along with his willingness to accept responsibility for his role as *Reichsjugendführer* while also downplaying its importance as an ideological and military preparatory organisation. His memories and reflections of 1967 concerning the causes and consequences of National Socialism, the role of Hitler and other National Socialist actors, and the Shoah (Holocaust) and anti-Semitism are subjected to critical inspection, using both his original interview transcripts and new source material in addition to extensive studies – not least in Vienna's only surviving *Gau* Press Archive.

The central question remains: to what extent is the usually suppressed ideological prehistory of German society in the Empire and its aristocratic-bourgeois elites prior to 1914 an essential factor explaining the potency and duration of the National Socialists' unjust regime? The initial turbo-globalisation, industrialisation and internal European migration saw, besides the innovation of early Modernism, a boom in anti-Semitic racial and conspiracy theories that exploded in aggressive fashion after the end of the First World War. Its elite protagonists, including Carl von Schirach, his intellectual and artistic circles and his son Baldur, then permanently attacked parliamentary democracy and the Weimar Republic with all they had. This intensive erosion emanating from bourgeois right-wing conservative networks was a central precondition for the success of the NSDAP before and after 1933. The demon of Weimar that had made Goethe and Schiller its political prisoners and misused them for its murderous ideologies is an important prerequisite for Hitler's appointment as Reich chancellor (*Reichskanzler*). He was long idolised by members of the 'old' imperial and bourgeois elites, as demonstrated by his early visit to the Schirach residency in 1925. The system's rapid stabilisation after the National Socialists came to power despite many clear breaches of the law and acts of terrorism cannot be understood without this other cultural history of the German Empire of which the Schirachs are symbolic.

Unlike examinations of the National Socialist regime's key decision-makers and Hitler's satraps such as Heinrich Himmler, Joseph Goebbels, Hermann Göring and Albert Speer, studies on Baldur von Schirach are shaky and somewhat patchy. The first comprehensive biography, *Baldur von Schirach, Hitlers Jugendführer* (*Baldur von Schirach, Hitler's Youth Leader*) by Michael Wortmann, appeared in 1982 as the basis of a doctoral thesis, and the revisionist retort by Schirach's former press officer

Günter Kaufmann in 1993 was quite rightly largely ignored. Stefanie Hundehege's doctoral thesis of 2017, *Writing the Nazi Movement. The Poetry of Baldur von Schirach*, focusing on Schirach as a poet and literary figure, is still unavailable, but excerpts can be read in the form of articles.

Nevertheless, there is not a single study on the National Socialist period in Vienna from 1940–45 that does not touch on Baldur von Schirach – be it with respect to the Hitler Youth or the evacuation of children to the countryside, or in the recent study of National Socialist art theft. A recent prior study on the "Aryanisation" of works of art and the role of Baldur and Henriette von Schirach has been produced by Theresa Sepp within the framework of the Central Institute of Art History in Munich.

On the basis of the many years I have spent researching National Socialist cultural and anti-cultural policy since my book *Führertreu und gottbegnadet* (Loyal to the Führer and Divinely Gifted) (1991) and drawing on recent studies in the framework of the full-text digitalisation of Schirach's entire National Socialist *Gau* Press Archive, I have attempted to provide a critical examination not only of Baldur von Schirach but also of his family background from the Weimar years onwards. I also consider the period after 1945.

The question of Baldur von Schirach's guilt – ultimately central to the present and the future – is re-qualified. To this end I use hitherto unseen documents and insights into the extent of his knowledge about the Shoah – as early as 1942 – and his hitherto unreflected role in the brutal persecution of so-called "asocial" people (*Asoziale*) in Vienna from 1940 onwards.

One of Schirach's grandchildren, the former defence lawyer and world-renowned writer Ferdinand von Schirach, provided his own answer with unmistakable clarity in *Der Spiegel* in 2011:

> What my grandfather did is something quite different altogether. His crimes were organised, they were systematic, cold and precise. They were planned at a desk, there were memoranda on them, discussions, and he repeatedly made his own decisions. The deportation of the Jews from Vienna was his contribution to European culture, he said at the time. Such a statement renders all further questions, all psychology superfluous. Sometimes a person's guilt is so great that everything else is irrelevant. Of course, the state itself was criminal,

but that does not excuse people like him, since they themselves created this state. My grandfather did not break through a thin ceiling of civilisation; his decisions were not an accident, not a coincidence, not negligence.[1]

I would especially like to thank two people for their support in the realisation of this book project: Dr Johannes Sachslehner, who as a successful non-fiction writer in the field of contemporary history and an experienced editor had the initial idea and assisted with its realisation and the editing of the illustrations throughout, and Agnes Meisinger, who combed through the manuscript and proofs with a critical eye, offering corrections and asking many important questions. Special personal thanks are due my wife, Dr Lydia Rathkolb, who made the intensive work and research periods possible while always keeping me grounded in real life.

In the course of the research, I received assistance from many colleagues, most notably Daniela Ebenbauer, Dr Wolfgang Form, Jutta Fuchshuber, Michael Hetz, Johann Kirchknopf, Dr Andreas Kranebitter, Dr Petra Mayrhofer, Dr Christoph Mentschl, Renate Moszkowicz, Prof. Dr Bertrand Perz, Dr Hans Petschar, Prof. Dr Peter Roessler, Prof. Markus Stumpf, Prof. Sybille Steinbacher, Christine von Unruh and Prof. Dr Kerstin von Lingen. Ford E. Robertson, Marie Schwieterman Robertson and Agnes Meisinger offered helpful perspectives on the manuscript.

For an important background discussion I thank the retired lawyer Dr Klaus von Schirach and Ferdinand von Schirach, who allowed me to access the preliminary study he initiated, the *Vorstudie zur Rekonstruktion des Kunst- und Kulturguts* (Preliminary Study in Reconstructing Artistic and Cultural Property) reconstructing the artistic and cultural property of Baldur and Henriette von Schirach.

Chapter 1

From Bull Run to the Grand Duchy and Court Theatre

The Schirach Family on their Way to Weimar

Baldur von Schirach was an omnipresent figure throughout the "Third Reich". The youth movement of the 'brown revolution' bore his signature. In his own mind, he actually considered himself a revolutionary – as a bustling brown-shirt 'fixer', bonded to his revered Adolf Hitler for better or for worse. He had been catapulted to the pinnacle of politics by a remarkable meteoric rise in the shadow of the "Führer": Baldur von Schirach, born 1907, became a member of the NSDAP in 1925, at age of eighteen. From 1927 onwards, he wore the brown shirt of the SA, the "movement's" *Sturmabteilung*. In 1928, the young man from Weimar, beyond the political sphere a writer of clumsy poetry, took on the position of *Reichsführer* of the National Socialist German Students' League, became *Reichsjugendführer* in 1931, and *Jugendführer* of the German Reich in 1933 in his capacity as a secretary of state. He was able to establish himself in the inner circle of power despite the fact that to the long-serving party members, the "iron eaters" from the *Freikorps* and beer cellars, he seemed something of an "errant aristocrat".[2]

For a long time, he was highly appreciated by Hitler and Goebbels too, since he presented the "Führer" as they liked to see him: "as the father of his loyal and beloved people".[3] Hitler's image was to a large extent the work of his young paladin Schirach. Shortly after serving briefly on the Western Front, in August 1940 Baldur von Schirach was sent by Hitler to Vienna as *Reichsstatthalter* and *Gauleiter*. He nevertheless remained NSDAP *Reichsleiter* for Youth Education and tasked with overseeing the Hitler Youth, and retained supreme responsibility for National Socialist youth policy, even after his deputy Artur Axmann became *Reichsjugendführer*. Hitler's plan was that Schirach would win over the hearts of the Viennese, a role the latter interpreted in the most peculiar manner: while the 'Viennese culture' he promoted enjoyed great success on the stages of the city's concert halls and theatres and he made great efforts to prove himself on the level of European diplomacy, the wagons rolled out of Aspang station to the death camps in the East and those men and women who dared resist the National Socialist terror regime died at the Regional Court gallows. While Schirach did not wish to see the bloody work of the executioner, he was happy to announce that the city had become "free of Jews" under his aegis. When he was supposed to defend Vienna against the advancing Red Army in the spring of 1945, he soon demonstrated he was not up to the task, leaving 'his' Hitler Youth to counter the Russian tanks. His less heroic flight from the battle for Vienna led to the gloomy isolation of a prison cell in Berlin-Spandau via the dock at the Nuremberg trials ...

Three-quarters American

If we consider the extant autobiographical sources on Baldur von Schirach, their overlaps are just as important as their omissions and proven departures from the historical facts. A comprehensive authorised autobiographical document is the official nine-page self-portrait he penned when appointed *Reichsstatthalter* and *Gauleiter* in Vienna on 8 August 1940.[4] Some of it matches the data assembled by Schirach's autobiography *Ich glaubte an Hitler* (I Believed in Hitler) (1967), ghostwritten by two journalists who interviewed him.[5] The document of 1940 does not mention a word about his mother's American background, however.

His father, Carl Baily Norris von Schirach (1873–1948), had been a US citizen before joining the Guards Cuirassiers in Berlin. In 1908 he left military service and was appointed general director of the Grand Duchy and Court Theatre in Weimar. Baldur's great-grandfather Karl Benedikt von Schirach (1790–1864) had emigrated to the USA in 1855, and his grandfather Friedrich Karl von Schirach (1842–1917) became a major in the US Army. Friedrich Karl married the American Elisabeth Baily Norris (1833–73) from Baltimore, Maryland. Baldur von Schirach's mother, Emma Middleton Lynah Tillou (1872–1944) was also from the USA, from Chestnut Hill, a suburb of Philadelphia. In his tabular CV of 1940, he also omitted to mention that until the age of six he had grown up in an exclusively English-speaking environment and went to school a year later than he was supposed to in order to become fluent in German in preparation.

In 1939, Max von Schirach, a cousin of Baldur's, published an extensive family history,[6] complete with details of their connections to the USA. This clearly didn't fit with National Socialist propaganda however, since the official long CV from the National Socialist era doesn't mention the family's close ties to the USA. It was only in his memoirs that he dared to relate more about his American family members.

Nor was there any mention of his parents' entirely aristocratic-hegemonial circumstances. The Schirachs' luxurious lifestyle was also a bone of contention within the family, as evident in a letter of 1897:

> Madame Filou, as Hermann[7] calls her – her surname is Middleton Tillou – did not make a favourable impression, despite being attired in a fragrant summer suit with fine embroidery and being a grande dame, comme il faut. Well, Karl isn't any better either and no longer makes an effort in the company of dukes, princes, counts and barons as far as his manners are concerned. Sport, racing and expensive horses are otherwise pretty much all he is interested in, and although he has a fair fortune, around 200,000 dollars, he will soon be shot of it.[8]

Baldur von Schirach's father, Carl Baily, after taking his *Abitur* (final exams at the grammar school) in Lübeck, became an officer in the regiment of the Gardes du Corps No. 1, headed by Kaiser and King Wilhelm II. While visiting relatives in the USA, he met his later wife Emma Middleton Lynah Tillou, whom he married in Chestnut Hill in 1896.

On her mother's side, she came from one of the richest families in the Southern states, owners of several plantations. Emma's great-grandfather Henry Middleton (1717–84), for instance, owned twenty plantations with a total 200 square kilometres and around 800 slaves. He was a successful cotton and rice planter, exporting around 83 million tons of the latter in 1770,[9] but he was also a committed politician. Middleton held several offices, ultimately becoming one of the most important figures in anti-British politics in the colonies. He was elected South Carolina's representative in the First Continental Congress, of which he was president in 1774–75.

Henry's first-born son Arthur Middleton (1742–87), who like his father was a member of the First Continental Congress, inherited the property Middleton Place from his mother and together with other delegates from South Carolina signed the United States' Declaration of Independence in the Congress in 1776. During the War of Independence he spent some time in British captivity.

Henry Middleton, known as the "Colonial Gentleman", had impressive gardens built by slaves in 1741 on a bow in the Ashley River, 12 miles upstream from Charleston. Today it is one of the oldest in the USA and a National Historic Landmark.[10] His grandson, Henry Middleton (1770–1846), was governor of South Carolina from 1810 to 1812 and served as the US ambassador to the tsar's court in St Petersburg from 1820 to 1830.[11]

In 1865, towards the end of the Civil War, the Middleton family's grand buildings, the gardens and the cotton plantations were destroyed by General Sherman's Union troops and all the slaves were freed. Further destruction was caused by an earthquake in 1886. A wing of the three-storey main house remained intact; today it serves as a museum.

Quite in the spirit of these family traditions, in Weimar Carl von Schirach had a stately home with a housekeeper, a cook, a "silver servant" and other staff.[12] In contrast, Baldur's grandfather Friedrich Karl, known to his family only as "Fritz", led a rather spartan existence as a former officer who had fought for the North in the American Civil War under the name Frederick C(harles) von Schirach. As a first lieutenant he was severely wounded in the second battle at Bull Run, Virginia, on 29 August 1862 and only survived due to the partial amputation of his right leg.[13] He served in the guard of honour as the murdered US President Abraham Lincoln lay in state in 1865; he had a job keeping mourners from attempting to cut off a piece of the shroud.[14] A year later, he re-entered active service with a leg made of cork, and in 1867 he was made a captain "for gallant and meritorious services during the war". He retired in 1870 and received the title Major Retired, US Army in 1904. A hero of the Northern states who remained an American citizen throughout his life, he married Elizabeth Baily Norris in St Paul's Church in Chestnut Hill in 1869. Elizabeth was the daughter of the successful railway pioneer Richard Norris, who had become famous for his legendary locomotive, the George Washington. In February 1871, Friedrich Karl von Schirach returned to Germany with his family. His wife Elisabeth died in 1873, shortly after the birth of their son Carl, in Wiesbaden.

In his autobiographical sketch of 1940, Baldur von Schirach only briefly describes his childhood and adolescence in Weimar. These years would play a key role in his defence at the International Military Court in Nuremberg in 1946, however, although he completely reinterpreted the ideological influences to which he was exposed.

To understand why he actively sought to get close to Adolf Hitler and National Socialism so soon, it is necessary to take a closer look at the contradictions in his versions of events and his recollections. They show that the ideological influences had already firmly taken root before he met Hitler in person in 1925. Let us thus examine his personal milieu in Weimar in greater detail.

Baldur von Schirach was born at home at Blücherstrasse 17 in Berlin-Kreuzberg on 9 May 1907 before the family moved to Weimar. The apartment was close to his father's workplace, the barracks of the Guards Cuirassiers Regiment at Tempelhofer Feld, where Carl Baily Norris was a first lieutenant (*Oberleutnant*) and later a *Schwadrons-Chef* before retiring as a cavalry captain (*Rittmeister*). He had begun his military career in the First Baden *Leib-Dragoner-Regiment* (dragoon regiment of the local ruler) in Karlsruhe.

His mother Emma enjoyed Berlin, as Schirach relates in his memoirs;[15] Kaiser Wilhelm II used to converse with her in English at receptions. He writes that she later found Weimar "confined and provincial" in comparison to Berlin, but especially hated the stiff ceremony at the grand ducal court, from which there was no escape – her father was, after all, the grand ducal chamberlain. As such, he often had to attend official events in the traditional court garb consisting of dark-green tails, knickerbockers, a dagger and a bicorne, a "masquerade" that became a source of great entertainment to the three children Rosalind, Karl and Baldur.

The daily routine in the Schirach family's stately household followed strict rules – including high tea at 5 p.m. Notably, Baldur von Schirach's memoirs do not relate much more about his family life. His wife too, Henriette von Schirach, only shares fragmentary impressions of the prosperity she enjoyed in the house at Gartenstrasse 37, today's Abraham-Lincoln-Strasse in Weimar. For instance, in American captivity she recalled the dress shirt worn by her father-in-law.[16] Their son Richard was later able to piece together the scant information about this high-aristocratic lifestyle in his book *Der Schatten meines Vaters* (My Father's Shadow).

A more precise examination of the performances under the aegis of theatre director Carl von Schirach till the end of the monarchy or the abdication of Grand Duke Wilhelm Ernst and the former's release in January 1919 show that he programmed a conservative repertoire and, as an amateur thespian primarily employed as an officer, was not really cut out for the post. Even then, he had close contact with the right-wing conservative-nationalist literary critic Adolf Bartels, who, like the Schirachs' ancestors, was from Schleswig-Holstein. Although Bartels had not gained any academic qualifications, having rather idled through university, in 1905 he was appointed an honorary professor by Grand Duke Wilhelm Ernst. With his literary history *Die Deutsche Dichtung der Gegenwart. Die Alten und die Jungen* (German Poetry of Today. The Old and the Young), first published in 1897 and enjoying several print runs, he was considered the most important representative of German nationalist and anti-Semitic literary criticism, although he had been rather philo-Semitic during his student days. During the Nuremberg trials, it was the self-same anti-Semitic, dilettante attempt at literary criticism Baldur von Schirach described as key reading that had shaped his youth.

As early as 1906, Bartels had prevented a "celebration of the Jewish poet"[17] Heinrich Heine in Weimar. He was a protagonist of *Heimatkunst* (homeland art) and his 'literary history' made a "pure distinction" between "Germans and Jews"; his catalogue of Jews and poor literary figures included Thomas Mann – a judgment Baldur von Schirach would not share, incidentally.[18] During the First World War, Bartels voiced German nationalist attitudes, served on the advisory board of the influential anti-Semitic *Deutschvölkischer Schutz- und Trutzbund* (German Nationalist Protection and Defiance Federation), and as a member of the circle led by Pastor Friedrich Andersen and the Bayreuth lay theologian Hans von Wolzogen he actively supported "German Christianity", which strived for the 'cleansing' of Jewish influences "alien to the people".

Bartels' disciple and secretary in 1922–23 was Hans Severus Ziegler (1893–1978), who as an early National Socialist (membership number 1317) was deputy *Gauleiter* of Thuringia from 1925 to 1931 and became director general of the Weimar National Theatre in 1933. As early as

1924, Ziegler publicly propagated National Socialist ideas and established the weekly newspaper *Der Völkische*, which later became the daily *Der Nationalsozialist*. This pioneering Nazi with a doctorate in German philology – Ziegler had written his thesis on *Friedrich Hebbel und Weimar* – was an important contact for Carl von Schirach and his son Baldur. Carl von Schirach's predecessor as director in Weimar was the equally conservative nationalist Hippolyt von Vignau (1843–1926). Thirty years his senior, Vignau had also been a Prussian officer, a major, and had run a large salon[19] in Berlin as well as the Dessau Court Theatre. Schirach was eventually mentioned as a potential successor and was indeed appointed director. Rumour has it that a certain Cavalry Captain (*Rittmeister*) von Stechow helped his comrade from the Gardes Cuirassiers Regiment land the job.[20] When the new theatre boss was presented to the press, to underline Schirach's musicality mention was made of his younger brother Friedrich Wilhem, a composer in Munich, and Carl's experience as an assistant to director Max Martersteig at the Cologne *Stadttheater* (City Theatre).[21] The claims of musicality were not far off the mark; Carl von Schirach was a keen violinist.

Before Carl von Schirach took up his new post in October 1909, cultural policy in Weimar was already anti-Modernist. For instance, before 1914, Harry Graf Kessler, director of the Grand Ducal Museum of Arts and Crafts from 1903 to 1906, and the Belgian architect and designer Henry Van de Velde, who had run the arts and crafts school he had built since 1908, had called for a modern "model theatre building"[22] as an alternative to the backward-looking Court Theatre. Court Theatre director Vignau, who had sought to officially ban the critical reporter Dr Otto Francke from delivering his "unwelcome" reports[23] on new construction plans as early as 1900, succeeded in blocking the modern concept. The new theatre building, designed by the architect Max Littman, who built the Munich *Hofbräuhaus* beer hall, ultimately reflected the aesthetic and cultural policy ideas of the conservative cultural elite, who openly criticised museum director Graf Kessler's Jewish provenance. There was no appreciation for Kessler's great achievement of bringing modern art and architecture to sleepy Weimar with its population of 33,000.[24]

In 1909, Schirach's father was already an active supporter of Bartels' nationalist project, the National Festival for German Youth, which opened with a performance of Friedrich Schiller's *Wilhelm Tell*. Bartels cobbled together verses that left no one in any doubt about the ideological aims of the National Festival, which were wholly in the Bismarckian tradition:

Ihr Söhne aller deutschen Stämme, hört!
Haltet des Deutschen Reiches heil'gen Bund!
Begraben sei die alte deutsche Schande,
Seid einig im geeinten Vaterlande![25]

[You sons of all German tribes, hark! Keep the German Reich's holy union! Let the old German shame be buried, be as one in the united fatherland!]

Schirach senior remained an important figure in the Weimar Art Society after being released as director general of the former Grand Duchy and Court Theatre in January 1919, and was also appointed to the board of the German Shakespeare Society.[26] Like many members of the aristocracy and the upper bourgeoisie, he belonged to a class of self-proclaimed educated citizens who were disappointed with both the Weimar Republic and the provisional state government of the Free State of Saxe-Weimar-Eisenach, and had already propagated anti-democratic and nationalist ideas, rejecting and indeed aggressively opposing Modernism in art and culture both prior to and during the First World War. Hence the first concrete decisions to ban politically undesirable plays in April 1927 can be traced back to Carl von Schirach's initiative as a member of the management committee and the board of the German Shakespeare Society.[27] He enjoyed an important stage for cultural policy activities in the form of his chairmanship of the Weimar Art Society, whose members included the above-mentioned German philologist Hans Severus Ziegler, who enthusiastically furthered his own career with his newspaper *Der Nationalsozialist*.[28] Eventually, however, Schirach senior and Ziegler fell out – probably for personal reasons: "Unfortunately I cannot comply as I would like to due to Dr Ziegler's tiresome concessions to the party. Since he should actually be summoned before an honorary council and thrown out of the Society of Artists."[29] Ziegler considered himself the "oldest party member among all leading theatre people".[30]

However, Carl von Schirach followed the same nationalist line as Ziegler. For instance, in May 1929, he brusquely rejected the invitation to become a member of the new Franz Liszt Society: "As a matter of principle, apart from the German Shakespeare Society, I would only like to be considered a member of the Militant League for German Culture, of whose board I am a member. The experience of the war and particularly the post-war years means that every development [...] on any foundation other than a purely nationalist one seems futile to me."[31] For Schirach, this society was too international and some of the proposed members were also of Jewish origin. The Militant League for German Culture, on the other hand, clearly pursued anti-Semitic and racist aims.

Chapter 2

Influences and Ruptures

The Fight Against Communism and Democracy and the Search for a 'Strong Man'

For their second son, Baldur, the Schirachs chose an education that was considered particularly modern and progressive: after attending the renowned *Wilhelm-Ernst-Gymnasium* in his home town[32] from Easter 1916 to March 1917, the boy Baldur was sent to the "Forest Pedogogium" on the Hexenberg hill outside Bad Berka, approximately 10 kilometres south of Weimar. A new world opened up for the son of an aristocratic family who up to that point had enjoyed tender care; a spartan, simple life combined with the experience of camaraderie, responsibility, fulfilment of one's duty and an enterprising spirit. The boys' school uniform consisted of "short Lederhosen, blue linen jackets and scarlet berets", which were a "red rag" to the village youth; when they went to village shops, the pupils were often greeted with a hail of stones – for Baldur a "wonderful adventure".[33] A brief description of the Forest Pedagogium on the Hexenberg can be found in the *Militär-Wochenblatt. Unabhängige Zeitschrift für die deutsche Wehrmacht* (Military Weekly. Independence Newspaper for the German Army), which in 1917 carried an advertisement mainly targeting children from officer families: "One-year option, Realschule, Gymnasium, Realgymnasium, educational school of the Godesberg type: teachers and house parents, a doctor and educators work hand in hand educating youth in all-round proficiency, furthering the backward, caring for and strengthening the strong. Own farm and livestock breeding ensure sufficient meals."[34] Incidentally, the Hexenberg was named after a woman who was burnt at the stake at this site in 1673 after being found to be a 'witch'.

The Bad Berka Forest Pedagogium, founded by the teacher Dr Emil Endemann in 1911, consisted of several log cabins and ran until 1922. It was inspired by Hermann Lietz's ideas on the family principle of the

Evangelical Pedagogium in Bad Godesberg,[35] according to which the teachers lived with the pupils as "house parents" in their own homes. The use of "prefects", i.e. older pupils who could also mete out punishments, was ultimately intended to underpin an authoritarian educational regime. In 1910, Lietz described the system thus:

> We strictly implement the institution of prefects, who have supported us in our work as educators and thereby grow up independent and showing self-control, becoming earnest and conscientious in the fulfilment of their duty and caring for smaller pupils; they have to ensure order and quiet in the dormitories, work and bicycle rooms, the gymnasium and the workshops, and it is their responsibility to ensure that the relevant rules are followed. The latter enable everything to be determined in the smallest detail and [enable the pupils to] get used to a firm, orderly way of life.[36]

Hermann Lietz himself was not shy of beating pupils, although corporal punishment was not officially part of the educational repertoire. A German nationalist who rejected every notion of peace during the First World War, in 1917 he announced with pride that all of his pupils fit for service had joined the German Fatherland Party (DVLP – *Deutsche Vaterlandspartei*) that had been newly formed in the September of that year and would strive to establish a *Führer* state under military control. With the introduction of the 'Aryan principle' from 1903 onwards, Lietz's concept clearly showed early tendencies towards the racist, German national education of an elite. His pupils were largely children from the upper classes, many of whom had had difficulties or failed to pass at other schools. In the case of Baldur von Schirach, however, there is no indication he encountered such problems. In his autobiography he provides no specific details about his schooling or educational successes.

While there are no materials or recollections concerning the situation at the Bad Berka Forest Pedagogium, the nationalistic, anti-democratic line stipulated by Lietz is extremely well documented. Schirach, however, never subjected it to critical reflection; his portrayal was, rather, utterly positive. Hermann Lietz's strategy was opposed to the drill-like cramming practised in schools in the cities, but his concept was ultimately heavily influenced by an Evangelical Christian, strict and spartan worldview that glorified both the Wilhelmine Empire and German nationalism and was dominated by anti-Semitic, anti-capitalist and Darwinist ideas.[37]

A quick look at his brochure *Des Vaterlandes Not und Hoffnung. Gedanken und Vorschläge zur Sozialpolitik und Volkserziehung* (The Fatherland's Plight and Hope. Thoughts and Proposals on Social Policy and National Education), published in 1919 by the Verlag des Waisenheims an der Ilse, an orphanage press, should suffice to demonstrate that Lietz was already writing about the 'question of race' and anti-Semitism in the context of the strengthening of the German nation, including measures involving 'racial hygiene'. Hence it is no coincidence that he was also repeatedly cited during the National Socialist period.

In 1934, Alfred Andreesen, his successor as director of the Lietz schools, proclaimed somewhat grandly that "everything Lietz strived for in his longstanding struggle" had been "condensed in a great political desire in National Socialism".[38] In 1935, Baldur von Schirach echoed this sentiment in connection with the publication of Lietz's memoirs, which Alfred Andreesen had republished[39] and supplemented with letters and reports: "I see in Lietz our people's purest and most fruitful educational figure."[40]

While Schirach himself makes no mention of Lietz's ideological background – or abyss – in his autobiography, he quite openly documented the anti-democratic environment with its loyalty to the *Kaiser* that prevailed at the Bad Berka Forest Pedagogium. As an eleven-year-old, he raised a flag quickly put together by the boarding school's seamstresses in the colours black, red and gold above one of the wooden huts. The flag actually commemorated the revolution of 1848, and would become the flag of the Weimar Republic. He received a reprimand from headmaster Emil Endemann, who pointed out that Schirach's father had also been ousted by the "Reds". The young Schirach swiftly removed this "revolutionary flag" from the roof, since in this environment the preferred colours were still the black, white and red of the *Kaiser*.[41]

Baldur von Schirach adapted quickly, joining his fellow boarders in throwing snowballs at mounted troops of the provisional *Reichswehr*. Some 6,000 men were supposed to protect the Weimar National Assembly, i.e. the 423 deputies (including, for the first time, thirty-seven women) working on the new constitution.[42]

The time Schirach spent in the boys' boarding school on the Hexenberg became the central narrative of his adolescence, both in his autobiography of 1967 and his long opening statement during the main session of the Nuremberg trials in 1946. He artfully ensured that the principles of the reform pedagogue resonated with his time in office as head of the Hitler Youth:

> That is actually the place where this idea of youth self-leadership first developed within me [sic] while I was a small boy. For when I arrived at this rural boarding school I was an eleven-year-old child. There was a small room in this house, it was called the fledgling coop. In this room there lived a very small boy by the name of von Wolzogen and a little von Herff. And I was told, you're the room senior and have to make sure they wash properly in the morning and keep their ears clean etc.
>
> The youth self-leadership, the self-administration of youth within the school community, the relationship between adolescents and educators, du, not Sie [addressing educators using the informal instead of the formal pronoun], the same thing I later introduced for the entire youth. Those are its origins. Not in the Wandervogel [hiking movement], as much as the Wandervogel [movement] probably influenced the rural boarding schools. But I actually had nothing to do with the Bündnische Jugend.[43]

In his very first statement in the main session of the Nuremberg trial on 23 May 1946, Schirach emphasised the influences he had experienced during his childhood and adolescence:

> I joined my first youth organization when I was 10 years old. I was then just the age of the boys and girls who later on entered the Jungvolk. That youth organization which I joined was the so-called "Young German League," (Jungdeutschland Bund), which Count von der Goltz had founded, a Boy Scout organization. Count von der Goltz and Haeseler, impressed by the British Boy Scout movement, had formed Pathfinder [*Pfadfinder* – O.R.] units in Germany, and one of these Pathfinder organizations was the Jungdeutschland Bund just mentioned. It played an important part in the education of German youth until about 1918 or 1919.

> Much more significant in my development, however, was the time which I spent in a country boarding school (Waldpädagogium). This was an educational institution directed by an associate of the well-known educator, Hermann Lietz. [...]
>
> Lietz' idea was to give youth an education in which they have in the school an image of the state. The school community was a miniature state and in this school community was developed a self-administration of youth. I only want to point out in passing that he, too, was applying ideas which long before him had been developed by Pestalozzi and the great Jean Jacques. All modern education, of course, goes back somehow to Rousseau, be it a question of Hermann Lietz or the Boy Scouts, the Pathfinder movement or the German Wandervogel movement. At any rate, that idea of self-administration of youth in a school community gave me my idea of the self-leadership of youth.
>
> My thought was to attract the younger generation in school to ideas that Fröbel had originated 80 years before. Lietz wanted to win over youth from early school days onward.
>
> I may perhaps mention very briefly that when in 1898 Lietz began his educational work, the British Major Baden-Powell was being surrounded by rebels in a South African town, and was training youngsters to scout in the woods and with this laid the groundwork for his own Boy Scout movement, and that in that same year, in 1898, Karl Fischer from Berlin-Steglitz founded the Wandervogel movement.[44]

During the session, Schirach quite clearly attempted to portray all the youth organisations he had belonged to as similar to the *Pfadfinder* in order to cast doubt on the uniqueness of the National Socialist path leading to the militarisation of children and adolescents. In fact, however, the *Jungdeutschlandbund* he joined at the age of ten was intended from its very inception in 1911 to prepare urban youth for military defence. Its founder, Baron Colmar von der Goltz, planned a "people's war", i.e. a war the civilian population were to continue themselves after the end of regular military conflicts and battles.[45] To this end, a great many sporting and terrain games were held in collaboration with municipalities and sports clubs. It can be assumed that Schirach's membership of this right-wing conservative youth association, which numbered 750,000 members in 1914,[46] was the work of his authoritarian father.

The total and emotional rejection of the Weimar Republic with which the young Schirach grew up had an even stronger subjective impact due to the suicide of his beloved elder brother Karl Benedikt, known as "Buddabu", who took his own life at the Rossleben Evangelical boarding school. There is no indication that Baldur von Schirach's parents tried to help him through this difficult time: the dreadful news of Karl's suicide was brought to him by the housekeeper in Gartenstrasse, Frau Junghans, who, "dressed all in black and teary-eyed", came to take him home from Bad Berka.[47]

It is hardly surprising, then, that in looking back on his youth – he was only twelve at the time – Baldur von Schirach interpreted the suicide of the nineteen-year-old *Abitur* pupil on 28 October 1919 as a reaction to the end of the monarchy and a despairing act against the new democratic circumstances that placed his family in a precarious position. Karl, who presumably wanted to become an officer of the *Badisches Leib-Dragoner-Regiment* and whom Baldur describes in his memoirs as a "universal genius" with "extraordinary scientific talent", allegedly left a suicide letter explaining he did not want to survive "Germany's misfortune". The twelve-year-old pupil felt the need to follow in his brother's footsteps – quite in the spirit of the later cult of the dead cultivated by the Hitler Youth: "With Karl's death I had lost more than a brother. For me he was a person to whom I looked up and whom I wanted to emulate. Aged twelve, I took his place. I had taken up a legacy that demanded of me a special love of the fatherland."[48] Baldur's son, Richard von Schirach, has revealed this depiction to be a myth, almost completely deconstructing it with extensive research.[49] He reports there was no indication Karl was actually personally devastated by the defeat of the Empire as Baldur von Schirach thought so obvious.

Subjectively however, the twelve-year-old may well have interpreted and experienced it as such. The "three-quarters American" became a "nationalist German".[50] It probably wasn't a coincidence his parents quickly brought him home from the Forest Pedagogium. Perhaps they were worried about their second son. Incidentally, it is remarkable that Baldur von Schirach writes about his older brother Karl, but only mentions his successful sister Rosalind (1898–1981) in passing; nine years his senior, she would go on to have a successful musical career as an opera singer.[51]

Chapter 3

High Tea with Herr Hitler

From the *Knappenschaft* to the SA

The twelve-year-old who felt duty-bound to continue his brother's legacy first had to go to school, however. But is that what he did? There is a lack of precise information on the young Baldur's day-to-day school life after he returned to Bad Berka from Weimar. It seems reasonable to assume he received home schooling. According to his own account, he finished *Realgynasium* (grammar school with a focus on modern languages and the natural sciences) at Museumsplatz 3 in Weimar as an external pupil. At least, he names this school on today's Rathenauplatz as where he took his *Abitur* at Easter 1927.[52]

In his memoirs and an *SA-Führer*'s questionnaire of 1932 he is more precise with regard to his political activities. For instance, he even mentions his membership of the *Knappenschaft* (literally 'knaves'), a youth division of the Prussian League (*Preußenbund*), in Weimar.[53] The Prussian League, or to be more precise, the League of the Faithful to the Kaiser (*Bund der Kaisertreuen*), was a conservative nationalist organisation founded in 1913 that was close to the German National People's Party and demanded the restoration of the monarchy after 1918.[54] This 'youth defence league' had been forbidden by the Ministry of the Interior as early as 30 September 1922, with reference to clause 1 of the Ordinance for the Protection of the Republic. In Thuringia, it was a subsidiary organisation of the Young German Order (*Jungdeutscher Orden*).[55] In his autobiography, a disappointed Schirach relates a brief encounter with General Ludendorff, who marched a *Knappenschaft* formation on Weimar's airfield on 20 July 1924, whereafter he criticised the young boys' lack of military discipline. Even if the pseudo-uniforms worn by the *Knappen* were not particularly impressive – "grey windcheaters and breeches, as headwear skiing caps made of grey canvas, 'Hitler caps' they were called, since on 9 November 1923 a man named Adolf Hitler had marched at the head of similar columns to the Munich Feldherrnhalle"⁵⁶ – the *Knappen* had expected more attention from the legendary field marshal of the Great War. Ludendorff, with an "enormous, square double chin, grumpy, unmoved, dismissive, frowning", did not even bother to greet the boys. In Schirach's succinct assessment, he no longer had anything to say to the young generation.⁵⁷

In his book *Hitler-Jugend* of 1936, Schirach explicitly distanced himself from this organisation and claimed he had had to leave his "cherished defensive formation" together with many other members because he had given a speech in support of Adolf Hitler.⁵⁸ What is certain is that his boss Hans Severus Ziegler also joined the National Socialists. Incidentally, Ziegler's mother was, like Schirach's, an American; she was from the same family as the German-American music publisher Gustav Schirmer. In 1930, Hans Severus Ziegler became an aide to the Ministry of the Interior and Public Education in Thuringia led by Wilhelm Frick; the NSDAP only had two members of parliament but supported the marginal bourgeois majority.

Harald Sander's itinerary of Hitler's travels⁵⁹ precisely reconstructs the date of the visit to Weimar and provides an approximation of the events. On Sunday, 22 March 1925, having departed from Munich, Hitler had arrived at the Saale station, whence a party member drove him to Weimar via Isserstedt. The *Knappenschaft* had also assembled to meet him, and included the seventeen-year-old Baldur von Schirach, who initially took more interest in the "Führer"'s' car than in the man himself: "And then came Hitler. That is, at first I didn't notice him at all. For suddenly a car drove up, the likes of which I had hitherto only seen in pictures, a Mercedes Kompressor, with spoked wheels. The latest thing. I was so fascinated I scarcely took note of the men getting out of this marvel."⁶⁰

At 16.30 in the Schiesshaus, packed to its capacity of one thousand, Hitler gave his first speech in Weimar. Hans Severus Ziegler briefly introduced the speaker, then gave the floor to Hitler – for the young schoolboy Baldur von Schirach, who with his fellow members of the *Knappenschaft* acted as security, it was a key experience that would shape his fate: "I don't recall details of this Hitler speech. I only know that I paid attention at the sound of his voice. It was a completely different voice to those I had previously heard from speakers – from teachers, priests, officers or politicians. The voice was deep and raw, resonant like a cello. Its accent, which we considered Austrian – in reality it was Lower Bavarian – seemed alien here in Central Germany and it was that which made you listen."[61] Schirach too was unable to escape this characteristic voice – he considered Hitler's speech in the hall of the Weimar Schiesshaus the strongest he ever heard from the "Führer".

Hitler gave another speech that evening at the Erholung ('Recreation') clubhouse at Goetheplatz number 11. In between, he rested at the personal residence of Hans Severus Ziegler at Johann-Albrecht-Strasse 15 (today's Kantstrasse). At Ziegler's request, the house was guarded by the *Knappen* Baldur von Schirach and his friend Hans Donndorf, an apprentice at Deutsche Bank. The two boys were in luck: when Ziegler and Hitler left the flat after about an hour, they suddenly found themselves standing before the "Führer": "Hitler gave us a long handshake, looking at us firmly."[62] An unforgettable moment – if his memoirs are to be believed, the intensive eye contact with his new idol put the seventeen-year-old in a "patriotic-poetic mood" to which he felt compelled to lend immediate expression: he ran home and poured his feelings into glowing verses:

Ihr seid viel Tausende hinter mir, und ihr seid ich, und ich bin ihr.
Ich habe keinen Gedanken gelebt, der nicht in euren Herzen gebebt.
 Und forme ich Worte, so weiß ich keins, das nicht mit eurem Wollen eins, denn ich bin ihr, und ihr seid ich, und wir alle glauben, Deutschland, an dich.[63]

[You are many thousands behind me, and you are me, and I am you.
I haven't lived a thought that hasn't trembled in your hearts.
 And while I form words, I don't know of one that isn't at one with your desires, for I am you, and you are me, and we all believe, Germany, in you.]

The next day, Hitler visited the above mentioned nationalist-anti-Semitic writer Adolf Bartels at Liszstrasse 11 and went to see the Goethe and Schiller House, the Baroque Widow's Palace and the State Library. According to Baldur von Schirach's version of events, it was in the Goethe House that Hitler made his famous comment, "You know, Dietrich Eckart wrote poems as good as Goethe's."[64] The writer and aggressive anti-Semite was the editor of the agitating paper *Auf gut deutsch* (a title punning the phrase 'to be frank' with the idea of good German-ness), a "Weekly Paper for Law and Order" in which he could give his abstruse anti-Semitic and nationalist ideas free rein and fought the Weimar Republic with his own slogan of "Germany, awaken!" In 1920, he also took over as editor-in-chief of the *Völkischer Beobachter* (Nationalistic Observer), the newspaper of the NSDAP party organ. He died shortly after the Hitler putsch on 26 December 1923, having been temporarily remanded in custody. Hitler, who was also heavily indebted to Eckart financially, dedicated the first volume of *Mein Kampf* to him.[65]

Schirach's verses of 22 March 1925 caused a sensation however: Ziegler, to whom he showed his poem, promptly printed it in his rag *Der Nationalsozialist*, and other National Socialist papers reprinted it. This resulted in a letter from Munich, from a "certain Rudolf Hess": "Herr Hitler has read your poem in the Gau and sends as thanks the enclosed photograph with a personal dedication."[66] The heroic, patriotic, passionate tone Schirach had adopted clearly pleased Hitler; the pathos-filled murmurings of the grammar school boy with a gift for poetry were clearly a perfect fit with his own rhetoric. Incidentally, the poem Schirach retrospectively labelled, rather accurately, one of his "many bad poems",[67] was set to music by Gerhard Pallmann[68] and found its way into several songbooks, including those intended for schools. The photograph of Hitler Schirach had received from the NSDAP headquarters was taken by the Munich photographer Heinrich Hoffmann, with whom he would have a close personal and professional relationship a few years later. Schirach put it in a silver frame and placed it on his desk. The enthusiasm for the man with the moustache, about whom Ziegler fed him further information, continued to grow; even his parents couldn't stop his almost cultic veneration.[69]

Half a year later, on Wednesday, 28 October, Hitler paid another visit to Weimar. He had soon realised that the town of Goethe and Schiller was a good hunting ground for the NSDAP's campaign trail. This time he travelled by car from Nuremberg. He again spoke in the private Erholung bar, this time to an audience of 800, before taking in Lortzing's opera *Der Wildschütz* (*The Poacher*) at the National Theatre – and not, as Baldur von Schirach recalled, *The Valkyrie* from Wagner's *Ring* cycle.[70] This time Hitler stayed in a better hotel, the Hohenzollern at Weimar railway station, and after a brief meeting Ziegler had arranged with Carl von Schirach and his son Baldur at the National Theatre, he visited the former general director at his home in the rented villa at what was then Gartenstrasse 37. They drank tea and spoke about theatre and music. Hitler, who was accompanied by Rudolf Hess, had the typical musical layman's ability to rattle off performances in Vienna, which impressed the retired theatre boss, who had also directed operas himself. The "Führer", wearing his blue 'standard suit' with a white shirt and black tie, had since learnt to behave elegantly in 'well-to-do' circles: he had brought flowers for Frau Schirach and kissed her hand; he "listened attentively, didn't interrupt anyone. It was an entirely informal teatime".[71] The "agitator of the Munich beer halls" who had climbed out of the trenches of the Great War was received by the "exclusive patrician".[72]

The utterly pleasant guest also had a few words for his host's son: "He asked me what I wanted to do. At the time, I had another year and half before the Abitur and then intended to study [at university]. Hitler said, "If you study, then come to me in Munich."" These were words that would shape Schirach's life.[73]

It was typical of Baldur von Schirach that despite the positive impression Hitler had made on Carl von Schirach with his knowledge of opera, he was mainly influenced by his mother's assessment, which she voiced in English: "How well he behaves" and "At least a German patriot".[74] Moreover, during his visit Hitler had admired her precious Empire furniture from her endowment.

The ideology of National Socialism had also taken root in the conservative nationalist Carl von Schirach's worldview, and hence the former Prussian guardsman joined the NSDAP, becoming member number 48505 on 6 December 1926.[75] Twelve years later – now director of the German Theatre in Wiesbaden – on the occasion of his sixty-fifth birthday he received the laudation from the Reich Ministry for Public Enlightenment and Propaganda (*Reichsministerium für Volksaufklärung und Propaganda*): "Von Schirach is, as party member no. 48505 and a holder of the Golden Badge of Honour, the third-oldest party member among the German theatre directors (after *Staatsrat* Dr Ziegler in Weimar and director Robert Rode in Trier)."[76]

It is not clear when his son finally left the *Knappenschaft*; his departure from "my old youth league" probably took place before the *Abitur*. His former comrades interpreted his support for Hitler as a "betrayal of the purely nationalist [*völkisch*] cause".[77] According to his version of events, the *Knappenschaft* acted as stewards for the NSDAP and other right-wing parties and groups to prevent attacks by communists. While Schirach's autobiography not does mention any such incidents, it proudly lists his services to right-wing conservative nationalist speakers such as General Ludendorff, the *Stahlhelm* (Steel Helmet) leaders Franz Seldte and Theodor Duesterberg, or the media magnate Alfred Hugenberg.[78] The latter was a member of the German National People's Party (*Deutschnationale Volkspartei*), supporting and controlling the right-wing-oriented press and cooperating with the NSDAP.

After joining the NSDAP shortly after his eighteenth birthday on 29 August 1925 (member number 17251), Baldur von Schirach, like his father Carl, was assigned to the local group for Weimar/Thuringia, where he had applied to join the *Gau* Society Office (*Gaugesellschaftsstelle*), which he described as a "modest premises in one of the cheapest residential areas". The monthly party subscription amounted to 80 *Pfennig*; the main task of the new recruit, who 'firmly' believed Hitler would take power in Germany, was to distribute pamphlets. Since he had joined the NSDAP before his father, he received the Golden Badge of Honour for long-serving party members on 10 March 1933; Carl von Schirach received his on 2 March 1934.

In 1925, the grammar school boy Schirach also became a member of the SA in Weimar, although for reasons unknown he was listed as on leave in 1926 before reappearing in the SA (*Sturm* 1) documents in Munich in 1927. He took his *Abitur* at Easter 1927, having already made a decision on his future: he would continue to follow the "Führer": "Only one thing was certain: I wanted to go to Munich, since that was where Hitler was."[79] That was probably the end of his musical ambitions too – since 25 September 1923, Schirach had studied classical piano under Hermann Oschmann as a guest pupil at Weimar State Music School, today's University of Music Franz Liszt, without showing any great commitment, as he conceded in his memoirs. According to his student record, he was de-registered from classes on 31 July 1926.[80] The memoirs of pianist Bruno Hinze-Reinhold, then rector of the Music School, describe his father Carl von Schirach as an "arrogant man" who later received the Golden Party Badge. His "ill-fated" son Baldur, who would play such a "shameful" role in the Nazi era, made a somewhat "deaf" impression, but was already writing "provocative poems".[81]

The young SA man's first great challenge was the Second Reich Party Congress of the NSDAP in Weimar in July 1926. Schirach "sped" back and forth on his bicycle between the railway station and the town, between mass billets in public houses and private accommodation to meet the demands of the participating party members. The stage of the National Theatre provided him with his experience of the ritual of "consecrating the flag": "Hitler consecrated the flags and standards of newly formed SA units by touching the new cloth with the blood flag. For us young people, it was a sacred act. In those moments, Hitler seemed more to us than a politician."[82] Schirach also recalled the appearance of the bald-headed "Jew-hater" Julius Streicher, who bombarded his audience with a slew of anti-Semitic slurs and threats – which Schirach retrospectively described as an "embarrassing incident". The good citizens of Weimar had only shaken their heads "disconcertedly", but the Nuremberg *Gauleiter*'s rabid performance was unable to shake Schirach's "youthful faith". He had only considered it a "cosmetic error", since "National Socialism – for me that meant Hitler, the comradeship of the like-minded, the community of high and low, rich and poor".[83]

Two key questions arise here, questions Baldur von Schirach would also address in his memoirs. How was Adolf Hitler able to win over former political and cultural elites from the Empire who continued to live a bourgeois–conservative, elitist lifestyle? Some, like Carl von Schirach, for instance, soon joined the NSDAP and put their name to an openly anti-Semitic and anti-modern nationalist cultural organisation, the Militant League for German Culture (*Kampfbund für deutsche Kultur*), thereby displaying visible and sustained support for the NSDAP's claim to authoritative interpretation of national culture, an issue that was so important to the upper echelons of German society.

Carl von Schirach was one of the fifty-four signatories of the founding call to create the Militant League for German Culture – an initiative that drew on the racist National Socialist ideologue Alfred Rosenberg and would become an important network for preparing the cultural hegemony of the NSDAP after 1933. Further signatories were Adolf Bartels, the publishers Hugo and Elsa Bruckmann, who had made their political salon in Munich available to Hitler and other NSDAP functionaries, but also Winifred Wagner and Eva Chamberlain, the widow of the anti-Semitic nationalist ideologue Houston Stewart Chamberlain.[84]

In his memoirs, Baldur von Schirach does not dodge the issue of the anti-democratic tendencies of said elite prior to 1918, recounting the arguments with which they justified their stance and their fear of losing their position in society or of a communist or socialist takeover. However, if we examine Carl von Schirach's professional career more closely, we cannot speak of a social demise, since after he was released by Weimar's Grand Duchy and Court Theatre in 1919, he won a legal battle with the state of Thuringia, securing a pension. His private life was also devoid of significant setbacks: Carl von Schirach retained a box at the theatre, and his family household continued to be able to afford a housekeeper and servants on the level typical of the ruling classes.

Weimar's fear of un-German Modernism set in well before the rise of the NSDAP; before 1914 it had led to the success of anti-Modernism, as demonstrated by the above debate about the modern model theatre Harry Graf Kessler designed for Weimar.

Radical anti-Semitic polemics and ridicule of democracy prevailed prior to 1914. Towards the end of the First World War, in 1917, these authoritarian and radical tendencies intensified. Long before the Treaty of Versailles placed Germany under an extreme economic and above all psychological burden, said networks, to which Carl von Schirach also belonged, opposed the peace. The establishment of a parliamentary democracy, which Carl von Schirach and many in the same milieu had vehemently rejected before 1919, named the "Weimar Republic" to boot, seemed to challenge their claim to be the sole representatives of German Neoclassicism in the town of Goethe and Schiller. Hence it was no coincidence, but an expression of this anti-democratic, authoritarian development in Weimar's cultural networks that the National Socialists were able to participate in government in Thuringia before 1933. Harry Graf Kessler,[85] the former voluntary director of the Museum of Arts and Crafts, took a clear stance against the Thuringian Public Education Ministry's decree of April 1930. Entitled "Against Negro Culture", the decree stated, "For years almost all areas of culture have increasingly displayed the influences of alien races with the potential to undermine the moral powers of German national traditions. A prominent place is taken here by productions which, like jazz band and drum music, negro dances, negro song and negro pieces, represent a glorification of negrodom and are a slap in the face to German cultural sensitivities. Preventing these subversive manifestations wherever possible is in the interests of the preservation and reinforcement of German national traditions. A legal foundation to this end is provided by the provisions of clauses 32, 33 a, 52 paragraph 2 of the Trade and Commerce Regulations."[86]

Ultimately, it was one of the very first National Socialists and the later director of Weimar's National Theatre, Hans Severus Ziegler, who initiated the exhibition on "Degenerate Music" in 1938–39.[87] This exhibition agitating against representatives of modern music – most of them of Jewish provenance – was staged as part of the Reich Music Days in Düsseldorf, imitating the 1937 exhibition on 'Degenerate Art'. The exhibition "Degenerate Music" was then held in Weimar, Munich and Vienna.

"I read it and became an anti-Semite"

During the Nuremberg trials, Schirach named three books he claimed had shaped him – against the wishes of the presiding judge, who was not interested in such background information: *Grundlagen des 19. Jahrhunderts* (The Foundations of the Nineteenth Century) by the "Bayreuth thinker", as Schirach called him, Houston Stewart Chamberlain, Adolf Bartels'[88] *Weltgeschichte der Literatur* (World History of Literature) and Henry Ford's *The International Jew*. He immediately qualified Bartels' work by saying that while it didn't contain any "explicitly anti-Semitic tendencies", anti-Semitism was the main thread running through it. He asserted that the work that had had the most decisive influence on him and his companions was Henry Ford's *The International Jew*: "I read it and became anti-Semitic. In those days this book made such a deep impression on my friends and myself because we saw in Henry Ford the representative of success, also the exponent of a progressive social policy. In the poverty-stricken and wretched Germany of the time, youth looked toward America, and apart from the great benefactor, Herbert Hoover, it was Henry Ford who to us represented America."[89] Here, Schirach again used the same strategy of re-interpretation he had employed when discussing the right-wing conservative and in some cases anti-Semitic youth defence leagues; he compared them to British general Baden-Powell's Boy

Scouts. He omitted that Baden-Powell's Boy Scouts were not a British nationalist, but an international youth movement; in 1929, for instance, 50,000 scouts from some seventy-two countries took part in the world jamboree in England.[90] While Baden-Powell's military experience meant that in some respects the Boy Scouts displayed paramilitary structures such as learning to track or relay messages, the organisation was not characterised by the aggressively nationalist and racist fundamentals actively communicated to adolescents within said German associations by active or retired military men. Nevertheless, to this day debate rages concerning the extent of militarism and pacifism originally intended by Baden-Powell, whom Michael Rosenthal accused of anti-Semitism.[91]

In Nuremberg in 1946 or later, in his memoirs of 1967, Schirach himself failed to recognise that anti-Semitism and racial doctrine had been deeply rooted in the German elites prior to 1914 and was especially prevalent in the ranks of the army and the officer corps. For instance, Kaiser Wilhelm II maintained intensive correspondence with the British writer and cultural philosopher Houston Stewart Chamberlain,[92] who was, as is well-known, Richard Wagner's son-in-law, and he made the two volumes of his anti-Semitic, racist work of 1899, *The Foundations of the Nineteenth Century*, compulsory reading for senior teacher training and teachers' seminars.[93] Written in the metropolis of the Habsburg Empire after he moved from Dresden to Vienna in 1896–97, the work became a key reference work[94] for the National Socialist movement's discussion of racial theory and German nationalism. This 1,200-page tome was already a hit with educated citizens well before 1914; conspiracy theories explaining the alleged international dominance of world Jewry were lapped up just as eagerly as Chamberlain's search for the 'original Aryan' or the 'original Germanic'.

Adolf Bartels' two-volume literary history was also completed before 1914. Entitled *Geschichte der deutschen Literatur* (History of German Literature), it was first published in 1901–02 and enjoyed large print runs until 1940. In 1906, Bartels had already aggressively polemicised against a monument to Heinrich Heine in Hamburg.[95]

In 1910, Bartels, whom Kurt Tucholsky would later call the "clown of today's German literature" and a "pogromic idiot staggering through the labyrinth of German literature",[96] became chairman of the German National Writers' Union (*Deutschvölkischer Schriftstellerverband*). After 1914, he pushed through the use of racial criteria in the 'pure distinction' between writers as Jews and non-Jews.[97] At the first public meeting of the Leipzig German Students' Union (*Deutscher Studentenverband Leipzig*), which he had co-founded, he agitated against the 'secret rule of Jews' and attacked both Liberals and Social Democrats, whom he considered to be parties supported or established by them.[98] In the *Deutsche Biographie*, Walter Goetz provides a concise analysis of Bartels' works: "The 'Geschichte der deutschen Literatur' and the 'Einführung in die Weltliteratur' [*Introduction to World Literature*] (3 volumes, 1913) show him to be a one-eyed partisan of the racial principle and anti-Semitism; from then on, most of his many works are not scholarship but propaganda for purely nationalist literature."[99]

He had already proven a pronounced anti-Semite in his publications before 1914, as demonstrated by the pamphlets *Heine-Genossen. Zur Charakteristik der deutschen Presse und der deutschen Parteien* (Heine Comrades. On the Characteristics of the German Press and the German Parties, 1907), *Judentum und deutsche Literatur* (Jewry and German Literature, 1912) or *Deutsch-jüdischer Parnaß* (German-Jewish Parnassus, 1912).

In his memorandum *Der Siegerpreis* (The Victor's Prize) during the early stages of the First World War in August 1914, he called for the permanent occupation of Poland and western Russian and "out-posts on the Daugava and the Dnieper and on the Black Sea".[100]

The Weimar National Socialist, Hitler Youth regional leader and friend of Baldur von Schirach's, Rainer Schlösser (1899–1945), who would go on to have a career as Reich dramaturg (*Reichsdramaturg*) under Goebbels, offered a precise description of Adolf Bartels' role for National Socialist literature policy: in his "examination of literature", Bartels had "anticipated the National Socialist principle".[101]

In his article "Professor Bartels' Bücher" ("Professor Bartels' Books") in the German newspaper *Die Zeit*, Volkhard Knigge, director of the Buchenwald and Mittelbau-Dora Memorials Foundation in Weimar, clearly and unequivocally shows the reciprocal relationship between the originally nationalist–racist anti-Semitism[102] and National Socialism: "The anti-Semitism of Bartels was not a matter for truncheon-wielding fanatics, but a scholarly-based cultural prerequisite for well-read, fatherland-loving patriots. The Weimar message went, 'Anyone who is not an anti-Semite in our era is not a good German either.'"[103]

Schirach's claim that he had read Bartels' and Chamberlain's anti-Semitic writings but only became a Nationalist anti-Semite after reading Henry Ford's book *Der internationale Jude. Ein Weltproblem* (Leipzig 1922) cannot be true. Racist anti-Semitism was well established, especially in Schirach's Weimar environment, and had formed a dangerous political conglomerate with conservative nationalist anti-democratic positions from the time before 1918. It wasn't a coincidence that Hitler gained such early acceptance in Weimar, including in the circles of the bourgeois elite represented by the Schirachs, whose young progeny became a glowing admirer. Adolf Bartels, who was on familiar terms with the Schirachs, is also said to have given their son Baldur private tuition – presumably on the history of German literature.[104]

Chapter 4

Moving Forwards!

Schirach's Rise as Student Leader

Adolf Hitler may have invited the schoolboy Baldur to Munich, but he wasn't waiting for him. Hence Schirach had to renew contact with the "Führer" – which proved to be a somewhat difficult undertaking. Rudolf Hess gave the pushy student seeking an appointment with Hitler short shrift, and even Elsa Bruckmann's attempts to help him failed. Schirach recognised he would have to confront Hitler with a new mission if he was to win him over. And then there were his studies, which he organised wholly in line with his own predilections and interests. His first digs in Munich were in the Franz-Joseph-Strasse in Schwabing, a "proper student flat".[105]

According to Schirach's own entries in an SA leader's form of 13 March 1931,[106] he spent four semesters in Munich studying German, English and art history; records at Ludwig Maximilian University (LMU) say five semesters – from the summer semester of 1927 to the end of the summer semester of 1929.[107] The only subject listed by the student register is German, which must have been his main focus. The records in the LMU archive tell us nothing about his performance in exams. As his memoirs relate, Schirach only saw his studies as something of a sideline; his priority was already his party work for the National Socialist movement.[108]

He remembered lectures on English literature by Max Förster, an internationally renowned expert on Old English philology, and art history by Wilhelm Pinder. The art historian from Kassel was an expressly nationalist scholar[109] who openly propagated strengthening the German nation by retaking "Eastern abodes" conquered by Slavs and lectured on "German *Bluterbe* [blood heritage] and historical heritage". As early as 1930, Pinder publicly attacked the curator of the Pinakothek museum, August Liebmann Mayer, as an "art Jew". Mayer was dismissed in 1933; after fleeing to France, in 1944 he was deported to the Auschwitz extermination camp, where he was murdered. After the National Socialists came to power, Pinder openly campaigned for the movement and Adolf Hitler, but never became a member of the NSDAP, despite applying.

According to his memoirs, Schirach also attended the Goethe seminar taught by Hans Heinrich Borcherdt, an associate professor of modern German literature who had also been head of Munich's Institute for History of Theatre since 1926. Like Baldur von Schirach's father, he was not only the son of an officer, but also joined the anti-Semitic Militant League for German Culture, albeit not until 1931. In 1937, NS university functionaries still considered Borcherdt a supporter of the Bavarian People's Party (*Bayrische Volkspartei*) married to the "daughter of a Bavarian minister from the days of the [old] system".[110]

Finally, there were no reservations about him, and he even received permission to travel in order to speak on "German idealism's idea of the state" to Vienna's *Deutscher Klub* (German Club), an elite network of National Socialists, German Nationalists and anti-Semites, on 2 March 1937.[111] In 1942, Borcherdt was appointed a full professor in Königsberg.

Incidentally, Schirach junior claimed somewhat arrogantly that as a member of Weimar's Shakespeare Society he already knew every English scholar of renown in Germany.[112]

In his memoirs, Schirach also names impressive scholars he got to know in the salons of *Geheimrat* (Privy Councillor) Frick's family and especially in the Bruckmanns' salon. They included, for instance, the Romance scholar Karl Vossler, the historian Hermann Oncken and the Egyptologist Wilhelm Spiegelberg, whose political leanings should also be briefly outlined.

Vossler, an important Romance specialist, is the great exception in this list. For instance, in 1926–27 he advocated as rector that equal status be granted to Jewish student fraternities and had the black, red and gold imperial banner, so reviled by right-wing conservatives and National Socialists, raised at celebrations.[113] In 1930, he went so far as to publicly ask, "How will we rid ourselves of the disgrace that is anti-Semitism?"[114] He was forced into retirement by the National Socialist regime in 1937. Schirach presumably met Vossler in the salon hosted by *Geheimrat* (Privy Councillor) Josef Schick, who like Schirach's father was an active member of the German Shakespeare Society.¹¹⁵ Schick himself had spent two years studying in England and was an outstanding mathematician with a *Habilitation* (a German post-doctoral qualification required to lecture at a university) in English. He taught at the LMU from 1896 until his retirement in 1925. A well-travelled scholar, he had also taught at Columbia University in New York in 1911–12 and was married to an Englishwoman. Despite his advanced years – he was born in 1859, in Risstissen near Ulm – he volunteered to fight in the First World War and was thoroughly German nationalist in his convictions.¹¹⁶ Schick lived at Ainmillerstrasse 4 in Munich and invited the young Baldur von Schirach to various meetings at his home.

For instance, in his *Revolutionstagebuch 1919* (*1919: Diary of a Revolution*), Viktor Klemperer wrote about how he and his wife Eva Schlemmer, a concert pianist, called on Schick, whose lectures he had attended in 1902. However, since only his wife Mary Schick, née Butcher, was at home, the two women got talking; Frau Schick asked, "... whether we really thought the English wanted the war? They were no more bloodthirsty than the Germans or the French – nobody, no, nobody had this murdering on their conscience other than the Jews, the only ones who had profited from it. Speechless, we looked at the old lady in shock; she took it to be empathy and continued to preach the sisterly bond between all female hearts."¹¹⁷ Klemperer, an accomplished Romance scholar who had converted to Judaism, registered the Schicks' anti-Semitism as early as 1919, then. The historian Hermann Oncken, on the other hand, might have been for the fatherland and a National-Liberal member of the Baden parliament from 1915 to 1918, but like Vossler he had little to with the anti-Semitic nationalist and anti-democratic circles Schirach moved in. Oncken's reputation was that of a "republican by reason". Nevertheless, like many others he voted for Austria's "annexation" before 1933 and nearly moved to the University of Vienna for that reason in 1923.¹¹⁸ In Berlin in 1929, he held a speech commemorating the ten years of the Weimar constitution.¹¹⁹ Oncken attempted to build bridges between social democracy and the bourgeoisie, but also between the Empire and the Weimar Republic. He sought to win over the students for the Republic as the democratic nation state via a kind of "organic connection" between "the German past and the German future".¹²⁰ After 1935, he clashed with the National Socialists, whose anti-Semitic, racist version of history he rejected, and was forced to retire as a result.[121]

The final interesting personality from Schirach's university days was the German Jewish Egyptologist Wilhelm Spiegelberg, who had converted to Protestantism and had been head of the Egyptology department in Munich since 1923.[122] He is the only scholar of Jewish provenance to be mentioned in Schirach's memoirs. Spiegelberg, who died after an operation in 1930, considered himself completely assimilated and was "appalled" by the "conspicuous, often provocative affectations of some Jews" in the street and complained about the make-up and "over-the-top" garb worn by Jewish women.[123]

Baldur von Schirach's intellectual network in and beyond Ludwig Maximilian University in Munich reinforced the basic Weimar dialogue's tendency to display anti-Semitism, German Nationalism and an anti-democratic stance despite the above two exceptions of Oncken and especially Vossler. It is hard to imagine Schirach was really impressed with the latter.

But an even more important factor for the development and reinforcement of the political networks in his family and the Weimar environment were the intensive contacts the young Nazi careerist cultivated in the salon hosted by Elsa and Hugo Bruckmann.[124] Elsa Bruckmann, born in Traundorf near Gmunden in Upper Austria in 1865, was the daughter of the former Royal Bavarian Ulan officer Prince Theodor Cantacuzène and hence a descendant of an old Greek Byzantine princely dynasty. Her mother, Countess Caroline Deym von Střitež, was descended from the Bohemian-Austrian *ancienne noblesse* – in 1893–94, the "princess" was a guest of the Jewish Todesco family in Vienna, where she met the young "boy" Hugo von Hofmannsthal.[125] She maintained what was at times close contact with him until 1924; she would later dismiss her infatuation with the poet as "flirtation".

Else Bruckmann married the bourgeois Munich art book publisher Hugo Bruckmann in 1898, at the age of thirty-three. In January 1899, she opened her Munich salon in the new building of the Bruckmann press at Nymphenburgstrasse 86 with a reading by Chamberlain. Elsa Bruckmann was a very well-read woman with an eye for art; the evenings in her salon – held at the Prinz-Georg-Palais townhouse at Karolinenplatz 5 from 1909 onwards – became a kind of networking meetings for artists, writers, theatre people and scholars, but also for politicians and anti-Semitic and German nationalist ideologues such as Chamberlain. Her colourful horde of guests included such renowned personalities as Rainer Maria Rilke, Heinrich Wölfflin, Rudolf Kassner, Hermann Graf Keyserling, Karl Wolfskehl, Ludwig Klages, Harry Graf Kessler, Alfred Schuler, Georg Simmel, Hjalmar Schacht and her nephew Norbert von Hellingrath, all of whom competed with each other in searching for the direction and guiding principles of Modernism in the first phase of turbo-globalisation. During the First World War, this hub of bourgeois networking radicalised the aggressive German nationalism and anti-Semitism that had existed before 1914: the onus was placed on the search for a strong man who could lead Germany, but also Europe, out of its crisis and insignificance. That, it was hoped, would also provide the final answer to the question of Modernism. Hence it was no coincidence that Hugo Bruckmann was an early admirer of the Italian Fascist dictator Benito Mussolini – as was, incidentally, Hugo von Hofmannsthal, briefly. Hofmannsthal ultimately developed his own authoritarian world of ideas with the model of a "conservative revolution", which he introduced during a speech in Munich in 1927.

On 23 December 1924, in the Bruckmanns' spacious dwelling at Karolinenplatz 5, Else Bruckmann first introduced Adolf Hitler to her bourgeois society guests, only two days after his release from prison following his failed putsch attempt. The publisher's wife would later enthusiastically recall, "Now Adolf Hitler stepped towards me – in short Bavarian uniform and a yellow linen jacket: simple, natural, knightly and bright-eyed!"[126]

In this cultural environment – Elsa and Hugo Bruckmann had meanwhile received the representative NSDAP membership numbers 91 and 92 – Baldur von Schirach managed to do more than deepen his personal acquaintance with Adolf Hitler. He later moved from his student flat in Franz-Josef-Strasse in Schwabing to a more comfortable apartment at the Bruckmanns' at Leopoldstrasse 10, where they had moved their salon from Karolinenplatz in early 1931. From his new home in the third storey of this spacious building constructed during the country's late nineteenth-century entrepreneurial boom, he enjoyed a view of Munich's *Siegestor* (triumphal arch).

The Bruckmanns knew Baldur von Schirach's uncle, the retired *Rittmeister* Friedrich Wilhelm von Schirach, who had to give evidence at the trial of Hitler and Ludendorff after their failed putsch attempt. As district leader (*Bezirksführer*) of the Munich branch of the Fatherland Leagues (*Vaterländische Verbände*), he had information on Reich State Commissar (*Reichsstaatskommissar*) Gustav von Kahr's plan to march to Berlin and the arrest of General Ludendorff.[127] Friedrich, who died the same year, 1924, was well known in Munich – also as a composer.

A chance meeting with Hitler in November 1927 – before the pending elections for the "General Student Committees" – became the trigger for Schirach's career as a student representative: after some to and fro, the "Führer", who had taken his young disciple with him to a discussion in the flat at Thierschstrasse 41, allowed himself to be persuaded to speak to students in the festive hall of the Hofbräuhaus – on the condition that the room was "full". Schirach was as good as his word: on 21 November 1927, the hall was "so packed out that the students were sitting on the tiled stoves".[128] Hitler was forced to keep his promise and spoke on "The path to freedom and bread". His appearance was a triumph, and from that point on Schirach enjoyed Hitler's favour: he was the man who had brought the students to him. Having initially been sceptical about them, in 1930 Hitler would write in the Nazi weekly paper *Die Bewegung* (The Movement): "Nothing gives me more faith in the victory of our idea than National Socialism's successes at the universities."[129]

In February 1928, Baldur von Schirach became university group leader (*Hochschulgruppenführer*) of the National Socialist Students' League (*Nationalsozialistischer Deutscher Studentenbund*, NSDStB) in Munich as well the leader of an SA unit. In July 1929, he took on the leadership of the NSDStB. Moreover, in the same year he also founded the *Akademischer Beobachter* (Academic Observer), a magazine that was wrapped up in December 1929 and replaced with the weekly newspaper *Die Bewegung*, which was also short-lived (being disbanded in May 1931).[130]

These bare facts concerning his party career do not relate the severe conflicts between Wilhelm Tempel (1905–83), who founded the NSDStB in 1926 and had taken on its leadership on the Reich level, and Schirach, who led the Munich NSDStB University Community (*Hochschulgemeinde*, HGM), which had gone through three HGM leaders in the short time since its inception.[131] While the law student Tempel and his group were more interested in activism and saw themselves as a "youth and defence movement" that did little beyond a few mass gatherings, Schirach sought to make the barely visible HGM an "intellectual focal point of Munich's academic life". To this end, he had new club facilities with a reception room and a library set up, complete with sleeping quarters for himself, accommodation for three other HGM functionaries and a "ladies' room".[132] This was all part of a massive strategic conflict, however, since Schirach – like the party leadership – wanted to broaden the NSDAP's reach and appeal to bourgeois circles. The group around Tempel, on the other hand, targeted proletarian or petty bourgeois and less economically successful strata. This strategy also involved the founding of the "Militant League for German Culture" in May 1928, whose proponents included Schirach's father and the Bruckmanns. Tempel attempted to get rid of Schirach, removing him from his position. However, Schirach already enjoyed not only Hitler's support, but also that of Alfred Rosenberg and Joseph Goebbels, and had himself elected the new *Reichsführer* of the NSDStB in July 1928.[133] Since the factions were marked by massive internal divisions, Schirach won the election by a slight majority, gaining six of the seventeen votes, while four delegates voted for the leader of the Dresden university group, Herbert Knabe. Hitler is alleged to have sought to push through the Kiel representative Dr Joachim Haupt, intending for Schirach to serve merely as his deputy, but Haupt only received three votes.[134] Tempel himself had been too strong in advocating the positions of the left-wing Otto Strasser faction, who were a thorn in the side of both the Munich party headquarters and Goebbels in Berlin. Hitler's actual goal at this point was already to take power with as broad a social basis as possible, including bourgeois circles.

As well as turning the student movement towards conservative bourgeois classes, Schirach, himself not a member of a duelling (i.e. fencing) fraternity (*Korporation*), attempted to open up the NSDStB towards these traditional student bodies.

Despite his very fortunate and slender victory in being elected student leader, Schirach took a short break from politics in 1928 in order to travel to the USA with his mother, accompanying her on visits to relations in Philadelphia and New York, where he even received an offer from his uncle Alfred E. Norris to work for his bank in Manhattan.[135] Schirach had long since become enamoured with politics, however, and despite the NSDAP's meagre results at the *Reichstag* election of 20 May 1928 – the party gained only 2.6 per cent of the vote and twelve seats – he remained a supporter of Adolf Hitler.

Overall, the NSDStB was initially rather unsuccessful under Schirach's leadership: in 1933, only 4.8 per cent of students had joined the league.[136] At some elections, however, the organisation did register gains – over 50 per cent at the universities of Greifswald and Erlangen in 1929–30, for instance, or a remarkable 33 per cent in Kiel.[137]

But Schirach soon demonstrated he wasn't really interested in classical university politics; rather, he sought to win over the students as a group of voters for the NSDAP. To this end, he organised a large event introducing Hitler to academic circles. In the meantime, he had already gained some experience as a speaker himself, and was certainly already showing the trappings of a "diva": at some events there were "conditions for Schirach meetings": "It must be ensured that after his speech, Party Member von Schirach cannot be asked questions by every party member who feels like it [...] Party Member von Schirach must always be put up in a hotel. Accommodation in private quarters requires express prior agreement."[138]

Despite the ideological proximity, many duelling fraternity old boys, who fundamentally rejected political parties in general, kept their distance from the NSDAP leadership. There was often conflict with Schirach too, since he wasn't a member of a fraternity. Schirach was nevertheless increasingly able to attract students who were; in 1929, the NSDStB had members in 170 fraternities. In 1930–31, the NSDStB gained absolute majorities at eleven universities and became the strongest faction at ten.

Between the autumn of 1930 and the spring of 1931, there was then a massive conflict in Munich, not only between the city's fraternities and Schirach, but also with the NSDAP Reich leadership: Wilhelm von Holzschuher, secretary of the NSDAP's inquiries and arbitration committee, was a member of the Corps Franconia duelling fraternity and refused a fellow member's challenge. By his own account,[139] Schirach himself was also challenged to a duel after criticising the organisation. He claims he accepted, but insisted on pistols.

At the same time, his later wife, Henny Hoffmann, sought to intervene by directly asking Hitler to prevent the duel from taking place.

Schirach, however, stopped the publication of Hitler's ban on duelling in the *Völkischer Beobachter*, the NSDAP's main newspaper, in order to save face before the armed fraternity members. Ultimately, the skirmish was put to bed on the highest level by the intervention of Hitler and his deputy Rudolf Hess.[140] Schirach received a conditional sentence of six months' imprisonment, however, since he had breached paragraph 201 of the penal code on "Acceptance of a challenge to a duel with deadly weapons". This absurd interlude and the state's response are a revealing example of the backward-looking discussions in the Weimar Republic that ultimately served as a distraction from its own problems and the NSDAP's aim to take total control. At the same time, they are symbolic of the attempt to win over the traditional elites, such as the fraternities, to National Socialism.

There was still strong internal resistance however, culminating in a memo signed by thirty-one groups severely questioning Schirach's character and organisational skills. This intrigue was led by his deputy, Reinhard Sunkel (1900–45), the NSDStB's Reich organisational leader (*Reichsorganisationsleiter*). Hitler, however, valued Schirach's ability to attract new bourgeois voters and win support among the students, and thus gave him his unequivocal backing at the student leaders' assembly:

> Since Party Member von Schirach has been in charge of the Student League, he has given it inestimable service in the sense that in times of general depression and stagnation there has always been this great drive: we are moving forwards!
>
> When the theorists say the NSDAP is a superficial party, then I can only answer: you're just a theorist. It's a pitched battle, not studies in war economy. We haven't got time to train leaders who are highly educated, for we find ourselves in a giant surge ... Party Member Schirach has understood what is needed: the grandiose mass movement alone ... Herr Sunkel,[141] now I'm the old dog from the front who sticks up for his comrade and defends him against whatever is thrown at him![142]

After this speech at the fifth leaders' meeting of 2 May 1931,[143] the criticism from Berlin drummed up by Reinhard Sunkel was finally crushed; the "rebel" Sunkel was expelled from the NSDStB.

Schirach had not only frozen out Sunkel and neutralised him with his appointment to organisational leader, but also claimed the success of his second rival, the Hamburg agronomist Walter Lienau (1906–41), as his own. Although he was an NSDStB functionary, Lienau had been elected chairman at the fourteenth German Students' Conference in Graz. Schirach reported this coup to Hitler, claiming it had only come about because he had refrained from standing himself. In reality, Schirach wouldn't have stood a chance of being elected without a fraternity connection. Lienau, on the other hand, had been an active member of the Isaria München fraternity in Kösen.[144] At the time, the NSDStB only had 4,000 members, but 60,000 voters among the approximately 120,000 members of the German student body.[145] Lienau also sought to get rid of Schirach, seeing him as competition; he complained to Hess, and on 22 October 1931 even applied to have him expelled[145] before withdrawing from university work himself. This, then, was the complexity of the various intrigues within the National Socialist student organisations, which Schirach had the skill to exploit for his own benefit, however.[146]

A Duel that Never Took Place

Schirach survived yet another political conflict that nearly ended in a duel, this time of his own making and with an old friend from his Weimar *Knappenschaft* days, of all people: Hans Donndorf. On New Years' Eve 1929–30, Schirach had visited and slept with a certain Elfriede M., the woman Donndorf, now an SA man and employed in the administration of the Grand Ducal Treasury, wanted to marry. Schirach responded to the serious allegations levelled at him by his old schoolmate with a cynical, condescending letter:

> You seem to be angry because the little girl you revered as the Madonna is a quite common little tart. That you so unjustly transform this disappointment of yours into a grudge against me is very foolish. It was after all her business and a matter for her conscience whether she was faithful to you or not. You weren't engaged to her, so there was no barrier between her and myself. I wouldn't like to create the impression with this letter that I attach any greater significance to the episode. For me the little girl (I've even forgotten her name!) was an amusing trifle. I hope for you too that you might become sufficiently mature that one day you can laugh about it as heartily as I can.[147]

Donndorf thereupon called Schirach a "Jew boy"; in turn, Schirach challenged him to a three-bullet duel, which was banned by the party, however. Donndorf sought his revenge with a party tribunal at which an old acquaintance from Weimar, Hans Severus Ziegler, deputy *Gauleiter* in Thuringia from the Weimar network, testified against Schirach. Without elaborating further, he said that their relationship was clouded by "a number of motives", ultimately accusing Schirach of abusing his powerful position in the party in "absurd fashion".[148] In the end, Schirach, who had sought to bring a "declaration of disrepute" against Donndorf, was forced to settle, since he was also accused of cowardice by party members for his conduct at a meeting at the University of Jena after it had allegedly been stormed by the Communist youth; they claimed he had fled via the back door.

In retrospect, all these reproaches and rumours are hard to verify, but taken together they demonstrate that during this early stage of his career, Schirach displayed a confident or even imperious manner and led a lavish lifestyle – despite stating on an SA leaders' form that he was reliant on "expenses" from the SA or the NSDAP. Even then, he still drove a Mercedes-Benz 8/38 – although it isn't clear whether it was the four-door saloon or the five-seater special cabriolet.

During his student days in Munich, Baldur von Schirach lived, as outlined above, in a three-room flat at Leopoldstrasse 10,[149] at the home of Hugo Bruckmann, who was also a major in the Reserve. In 1933 he was registered at Königinstrasse 31,[150] where he occupied the ground floor of the villa-like house owned by the successful East Tyrolean genre and historical painter Franz Defregger. The building had been designed by Georg Hauberrisser, the architect of Munich's New City Hall. On the first floor, the painter Carl Theodor von Piloty had had an opulent apartment housing small replicas of his great museum paintings – such as the famous "Seni Before Wallenstein's Corpse", which Adolf Hitler also admired in Schirach's flat, which also housed copies of Piloty. The "Führer" eventually bought one of these reproductions himself.[151]

The Fighter and Victim

Baldur von Schirach also liked to portray himself as a persecuted National Socialist. For instance, he used his arrest following an anti-Versailles demonstration at the University of Cologne to stylise himself as a victim of the Weimar Republic. He had only been convicted, he claimed, because he had fought against France (by which he meant the Treaty of Versailles). He skilfully used his appearance before the court – the state prosecutor had demanded a four-month prison sentence – to attack the Republic: "It is within your power to detain me and lock me up for four months, but that won't change my struggle, which is also a struggle of young Germany. When these four months are up, I will again make the fight against Versailles the cause of the German university movement, and nothing will be able to stop me."[152] After eight days in solitary confinement, Schirach received a three-month suspended sentence. A year later, on 13 April 1932, the *Tagblatt* daily newspaper in Linz still reported on this trial of July 1931 in order to show how the SA could put judges under pressure. In 1931, after Cologne's *Rheinische Zeitung* exposed the trial, all available SA men were ordered to sit in the public gallery in civilian clothing in a demonstration of power.

Here Schirach displayed the typical behaviour of many young men of his generation who had not served in the First World War but had been exposed to the propaganda: they were constantly looking for a fight – here specifically the "fight against France". In Schirach's case, the extent of his conviction is telling: when the Hamburg *Gauleiter* Albert Krebs, who had served at the front, pointed out an error in Schirach's version of the war, Schirach patted him on the shoulder and self-assuredly told him, "No, dear Doctor Krebs! It was just as I said!"[153] In his 1959 book on the early days of the NSDAP, Krebs wrote that Schirach was too young and an "overeducated intellectual and aesthete"[154] who had yet to decide where he stood ideologically within the NSDAP.

The constant yearning to repeat the First World War and experience it for himself is evident in the poems Schirach wrote during this period; they seek to create a metaphysical connection between the post-war generation and the fallen:

Als wir noch Kinder, dröhnten die Kanonen,
und manches Kinderlachen brach entzwei,
kam eine Meldung von den Todeszonen:
"Dein Vater starb, damit die Jugend frei!"

Wehe dem Sohn, der das je kann verwinden
Und nach so großem Preis vom Kampfe schwieg!
Wir wollen unsres Daseins Sinn verkünden:
Uns hat der Krieg behütet für den Krieg![155]

[When we were but children, the canons droned, and many a child's laugh split in two when a message came from the death zones: "Your father died so youth might be free!"

Woe betide the son who can ever get over it and remained silent after the fight's great price! We'll announce the meaning of our existence: the war spared us for war!]

Baldur von Schirach emerged from the conflicts outlined above strengthened, having received Hitler's unequivocal and, as such, unusually firm support. Hitler usually let his functionaries compete for his favour, often delaying his decisions on personnel.

A decisive factor behind his gaining Hitler's assistance was surely that Schirach had connections to the salonnière Elsa Bruckmann, who to Goebbels' annoyance had a strong influence on the party chairman.[156]

Chapter 5

A Useful Lad, Able and Clever

Schirach's Battle for Supremacy in the Nazi Youth Movement and Development of the *Führer* Myth

Baldur von Schirach was not happy playing second fiddle and worked tirelessly to rise up the ranks. As early as 1929, bolstered by the NSDStB's move to embrace right-wing *Bündische Jugend* organisations and the fraternities, he went up against the first *Reichsführer* of the Hitler Youth, Kurt Gruber (1904–43), attempting to replace him with a trusted ally. Hitler's response was typical of his approach to such power struggles; he wanted to see which of his followers would prove the strongest. By founding the School Children's Leagues (*Schülerbünde*), Schirach sought to create competition to the Hitler Youth, at least among younger adolescents. Schirach emerged the early victor following intensive efforts and a speaking tour of nineteen universities.

In Joseph Goebbels, he also gained an important ally in the highest echelons of the party hierarchy. On 7 August 1928, with the battle between Gruber and Schirach at its fiercest, the Berlin *Gauleiter* enthusiastically wrote in his diary:

> The Hitler Youth is now well under way. As is the Students' League, with whose *Reichsleiter* v. Schirach I had a long discussion yesterday. A fine chap. Nobleman. Able and clever.[157]

A year later, on 4 July 1929, Goebbels appeared at an assembly in Hamburg with Schirach as his opening speaker and was appointed an honorary member of the Students' League during the festivities that followed.[158] A few days after this Hamburg event, Hitler himself spoke at an assembly of the NSDStB in Berlin. His speech, which lasted an hour, was a "damning indictment of the system", Goebbels noted.[159] Hitler's propaganda boss was so taken with Schirach that he planned to write a volume of poetry together with him, the National Socialist poet Heinrich Anacker and the *Kampfzeit* illustrator Hans Schweitzer.[160] Entitled *Der unbekannte S.A. Mann. Ein guter Kamerad der Hitlersoldaten!* (The Unknown SA Man. A Good Comrade of Hitler's Soldiers!), the book was ultimately published anonymously. It included a call to destroy democracy:

> Stand up, you young aristocrats of a new working class! You are the gentry of the "Third Reich"! What you sow with your blood will blossom as a splendid harvest! Clench your fists! Tighten your foreheads! Perform and work. The battle will decide the new aristocracy! Smash the equality of democracy blocking the young working class's path to historical completion. Democracy is suicide of the head and the first. Protest against equality! Resist being placed on the same level as every idiot![161]

Drawing on the myth of the "Unknown Soldier" of the First World War, the aim was to create a new myth of the unknown SA man who fought to the death against democracy and for National Socialism without demanding any reward or giving a thought to his own safety.

Schirach's further meetings with Goebbels in 1930 took place with a young seventeen-year-old by his side: "Henny Hoffmann, the daughter of Hitler's private photographer and personal friend Heinrich Hoffmann". They had got to know each other in the spring of 1930 in the editorial office of the Students' League magazine. Henriette, who assisted with the magazine's dispatch and the distribution pamphlets on a voluntary basis, later recalled, "One day, a young man in a light suit came running up the stairs whistling Yankee Doodle; he had just returned from America, he was the boss, the publisher and editor, the leader of the Students' League, a speaker at the Asta [*sic* – AStA] elections and actually a philology student, twenty-three years old, Baldur von Schirach."[162] They soon grew close as the young "boss" told her about America over coffee and apple cake – Goebbels, who constantly harassed women, described "little Hoffmann" as "a charming thing".[163] One evening, they took in a "Romantic concert" with works by Schumann and Schubert.[164] In January 1933, a few days before Hitler took power, their first child was born: their daughter Angelika Benedikta.

It was through Henriette Hoffmann that Schirach developed a close personal relationship with Hitler – even closer than via his Weimar connection or the Bruckmanns' salon. Politically too, Schirach backed the right horse early on: he was for Hitler and against Gregor Strasser, the NSDAP's powerful *Reichsorganisationsleiter* (Reich organisational leader) whose social-revolutionary and anti-capitalist ideas Hitler rejected. Goebbels already considered Schirach a "useful lad".[165] On 31 March 1932, Baldur von Schirach and Henriette Hoffmann married. Adolf Hitler and the head of the SA, Ernst Röhm, were witnesses to the marriage, and the reception was held in Hitler's private apartment in Munich.

In his attempts to make himself indispensable to Hitler's circle, the ambitious and enterprising student leader clashed with Ernst "Putzi" Hanfstaengl, chief foreign press officer to the "Führer". As Hanfstaengl later reported in his memoirs, Schirach, who had applied to be his "adjutant" in 1930 but had been turned down due to his "flippant manner",[166] had scant regard for the division of roles: "Another rather strenuous test for me was Baldur von Schirach, who took it upon himself to arrange for Hitler to talk to Englishmen and Americans, serving as an interpreter, or interfering in my conversations with foreigners in order to drown out my deliberately moderate portrayals with the fury of his youthful radicalism." For instance, Hanfstaengl mentions a conversation with the British conservative Robert Boothby, a confidant of Winston Churchill's; Schirach went so far as to say, "And we students don't want any Jews as teachers!"[167] If Hanfstaengl is to be believed, Schirach also had a hand in his later dismissal as chief foreign press officer: "An even more direct warning came from a respected member of the party. She and her family were increasingly outraged by Baldur von Schirach's manner. So one day she plucked up the courage and sought me out to tell me that Schirach had had too much to drink one time and had told her to keep her distance from me; I was on the black list and would soon be removed."[168]

In 1932, ahead of the ultimately successful *Reichstag* elections of 31 July,[169] Schirach produced a very successful propaganda book together with his father-in-law Heinrich Hoffmann, "photo reporter to the NSDAP *Reichsleitung*" (Reich leadership). Featuring hundreds of Hoffmann's photographs and texts and captions by Schirach, it had a sustained impact in bringing Hitler to broad swathes of the population.

Hitler wie ihn keiner kennt. 100 Bilddokumente aus dem Leben des Führers (Hitler as No One Knows Him. 100 Pictorial Documents from the Life of the Führer) became one of the most important brochures depicting Hitler and enjoyed several print runs. According to the imprint, 420,000 copies had been produced by 1935.

There followed further lavishly illustrated propaganda brochures with introductions by Baldur von Schirach, such as *Der Triumph des Willens. Kampf und Aufstieg Adolf Hitlers* (Triumph of the Will. Adolf Hitler's Struggle and Rise, 1933), *Jugend um Hitler* (Youth Around Hitler, 1935) or *Hitler in seinen Bergen* (Hitler in His Mountains, 1935). In the autumn of 1932, the publisher of these illustrated brochures, the Berlin contemporary history press Wilhelm Andermann, also founded its own book community, the "Brown Book Ring" (*Der braune Buchring*), which had grown to 70,000 members by 1938, thereby creating an additional market.[170]

Schirach moved in Henny Hoffmann's circle of contacts from the spring of 1930 onwards, exploiting her private connection to Hitler. As early as 1931, he managed to rise above the den of intrigue that was the students' movement and the Hitler Youth. Schirach claims that a decisive moment for his future career was a private dinner with Hitler in October 1931. He had invited the *Führer* round to his apartment; his memoirs[171] relate two different versions of this meeting that would become a landmark for his rise in politics – ultimately, he claims, this dinner led to his appointment as *Reichsjugendführer* on 30 October 1931. Schirach was thus rewarded for his untiring work and was able to persuade Hitler that his rival Kurt Gruber wasn't the right man to mobilise young Germans, despite various successful marches by the Hitler Youth. Hitler himself had his doubts as to whether the Saxon proletarian Gruber had it in him to become a sufficiently prominent figure for the Hitler Youth throughout the Reich. On the whole, the NSDAP in Saxony was "nationalist-revolutionary" in orientation.[172] Gruber saw the roots of the Hitler Youth in the working-class environment, in direct competition with Social Democrats and Communists: "Those who today still [...] demonstrate as Marxists do so either out of stupidity or habit [...] Today, another army is marching on the streets: the brown battalion of the National Socialist liberation movement. Productive German working youth who have recognised their national [*völkisch*] and racial strength and are prepared to take to the streets to break the hegemony of the *Untermenschen*."[173]

Despite the NSDAP's success in the *Reichstag* elections on 14 September 1930, when they became the second-largest parliamentary group with 107 seats and 6.4 million votes, the *Bündische Jugend*[174] retained 50,000 members, while the Hitler Youth only had 18,000.[175] After his appointment to *Reichsjugendführer*, Schirach was made a group leader (*Gruppenführer*) of the SA. Gruber's resignation had been announced on 29 October 1931; the social revolutionary had been promoted sideways to the NSDAP *Reichsführung* (Reich Leadership). Initially, however, Schirach would not take on direct leadership of the Hitler Youth; rather he received a new position as *Reichsjugendführer* within the SA leadership and answered to the Supreme SA Leadership (*Oberste SA-Führung*). For the time being, both the Hitler Youth and the NS Schoolchildren's League remained under the leadership of Theodor Adrian von Renteln, a Baltic German who had lived in Germany since 1917 and succeeded Gruber.

Berlin *Gauleiter* Joseph Goebbels' enthusiasm for Schirach wasn't diminished however. On 22 November 1931 he noted in his diary: "Schirach is here. Noble, brave lad. And full of spirit, of good character."[176]

In 1932, the Hitler Youth, despite having grown to 40,000 members, remained a small youth league compared to the two million members of junior sporting associations, the one million children and adolescents in Catholic youth associations or the 600,000 members of Evangelical Protestant youth organisations – even the Young Communist League (*Kommunistischer Jugendverband*, 55,000), the *Bündische Jugend* (70,000), the Young Socialist Workers (*Sozialistische Arbeiterjugend*, 90,000) and the Young Trade Unionists (*Gewerkschaftsjugend*, 400,000) had more members, at least on paper.[177]

In the course of 1932, Schirach strengthened his private and political relationships with Hitler and other high-ranking NSDAP functionaries. It was no coincidence that Schirach's first apartment in Munich was at Schellingstrasse 29, where he had set up the office of the National Socialist Students' League. Other renters in 1932 were Theodor Adrian von Renteln and Kurt Gruber.[178] Close by, in the rear courtyard of Schellingstrasse 50, the NSDAP had established its Reich offices, opposite the editorial office and printing house of the *Völkischer Beobachter*. Hitler's favourite restaurant, the Osteria Bavaria, was at number 62.[179] Thanks to his aristocratic and upper-bourgeois background, Schirach knew the importance of logistical proximity to the wheelhouse of political power.

It was in the Students' League office that he first met his future wife, Henny Hoffmann, whom he considered the embodiment of feminine chic: a "chestnut" bob, make-up that was unusual for the time, fashionable sweaters, short, tight skirts, silk stockings and high heels – Hitler's young acolyte was captivated.[180]

It was through Heinrich Hoffmann, Hitler's friend and photographer with a near-monopoly on portraits and photographs, most of them staged in private settings, that Schirach finally got to know Henny better. It was also through Hoffmann, a highly skilled photographer with the best international training and connections and a high-profile clientele, that Shirach met another "beauty" – Eva Braun, who ran Hoffmann's postcard department and would later become Hitler's lover.

After their wedding on 31 March 1932 and a skiing holiday in Tyrol, Schirach and his young wife moved into a luxurious apartment at Königinstrasse 31 by the English Garden, which they were able to afford due to the support of the wealthy Heinrich Hoffmann.

Just twelve days after the wedding, Hitler met Schirach in his apartment – to talk about the Röhm affair: a copy of his intimate correspondence with fellow homosexual medic Dr Karl-Günther Heimsoth had been leaked to the Social Democrat publicist Helmuth Klotz, who had published it. Hitler still sought to hold on to Röhm, who had excellent contacts to right-wing conservative and bourgeois party circles. Schirach could hardly help solve the "problem", Röhm having just been a witness at his wedding. Heimsoth, who had supported the rights of homosexuals via his publishing activities, mysteriously disappeared in March 1934 after the Gestapo had remanded him in "protective custody".

In May 1932, Hitler made the twenty-five-year-old Schirach the NSDAP *Reichsleiter* for youth education (*Reichsleiter für Jugenderziehung*). In June, he took on the leadership of the Hitler Youth and resigned from the Students' League, which had never really interested him. On the one hand, he sought to strengthen the members' emotional bond by integrating elements of the *Bündische Jugend*'s youth work into the Hitler Youth, while on the other hand he imported the brutality of street battle; the Hitler Youth repeatedly stewarded NSDAP events and played an active role in demonstrations.[181] In 1932, twenty-one members of the Hitler Youth died during such activities – Schirach took the opportunity to write texts and speeches cultivating a new myth of the blood sacrifice. A typical example might be the following poem he wrote commemorating the fifteen-year-old Herbert Norkus, who had been beaten up and stabbed to death by young Communists while distributing National Socialist pamphlets in Berlin-Moabit on 24 January 1932:

Mein Herz brennt heiß und Deine fahle Hand und Deine Stille stört mir jede Stunde, und Deine Augen, die ich nie gekannt, sind stets vor mir. Ich bin von Dir gebannt, Du Ewiger. Du sprichst mit stummem Munde.
O bleib mit mir, Geläuterter, im Bunde und quäle mich, dass ich nichts andres weiss, als Deine Größe bis zum tiefsten Grunde in Not und Kampf und mit der Todeswunde. Und was ich tue, sei auf Dein Geheiss [...]182

[My heart burns hot and your pallid hand and your silence disturbs all my hours, and your eyes which I never knew are always before me. I am captivated by you, you eternal one. You speak with mute mouth. Oh stay in league with me, purified one, and torment me so that I know no other than your greatness to the very fundament in need and battle and with the fatal wound. And may whatever I do be your bidding [...]]

To mark the third anniversary of his murder, 24 January 1935, Schirach gave a memorial speech at a flag consecration ceremony for the "young German people" in Marienburg in East Prussia, calling for selflessness and loyalty as the basic virtues of National Socialist youth.[183]

Despite his young years, following the resounding success in the *Reichstag* elections on 31 July 1932, Schirach was entrusted with one of the NSDAP's 230 seats. The party had become the strongest in the history of the Weimar Republic, gaining 37.3 of the vote, just seventy-five seats short of an absolute majority. The Social Democrats (SPD) received 21.6 per cent, the Communists (KPD) 14.3 per cent. Incidentally, the SDAP had the highest proportion of aristocrats among the members of parliament and a further eleven of aristocratic provenance, including Schirach, while the German National People's Party (DNVP) had only nine.[184] The Prussian *Landtag* (diet) also contained ten aristocrats from the NSDAP.

48   Baldur von Schirach

Schirach made no bones about his rejection of parliamentary democracy. Even before the elections, in a speech of 31 May 1932 to thousands of NSDAP supporters in the Graz industrial hall, he employed a dramatic depiction of the murder of the Hitler Youth member Herbert Norkus to announce the political aim in uncertain terms: forming a coalition government was to be "just the beginning. The real end is: National Socialist dictatorship".[185] He closed with quite untypical remarks clearly tailored to his Catholic audience in Styria: "It isn't the living and the dead who are fighting with us, but God in heaven. This God will see to it that we will be able to say we aren't Austrians, not Germans of the Reich, not Sudeten Germans etc., we are the German peoples."[186]

"You are the coming people": the Reich Youth Day in Potsdam

Despite the election triumph of 31 July, the NSDAP was in rather poor shape financially in 1932; it couldn't even afford another Reich Party Congress. Schirach, who in his function as student leader had already surprised Hitler with one large-scale event at the University of Munich, proposed holding a "Reich Youth Day" in Potsdam in its stead.

In Schirach's apartment, Hitler himself had already designed the obligatory badge to be earned by participants in NSDAP mass events, and Schirach had simply changed the inscription to "NS Reich Youth Day 1932". Hitler was initially sceptical, but Schirach attempted to finance the event via extensive promotional measures and the sale of badges and other paraphernalia. The poster was designed by the most renowned commercial artist of the day, Ludwig Hohlwein[187] from Munich, who had already provided illustrations for the anti-Semitic front soldiers' league *Der Stahlhelm* (The Steel Helmet) around 1930.[188]

A few weeks before the mass event in Potsdam, Schirach visited Hitler in the apartment he had permanently rented in the old Berlin Kaiserhof hotel since 1932 to discuss the programme in person. Hitler had moved into a permanent suite on the top floor; his room overlooked his political target: the Reich Chancellery (*Reichskanzlei*). Schirach's enterprising father-in-law Heinrich Hoffmann, as always seeking to get close to Hitler, had also taken residence in the hotel.[189]

Schirach kept his word: on 1 October 1932, between 50,000 and 70,000 adolescents from the Hitler Youth and the League of German

Girls (BDM) filled the Luftschiffhafen (Airship Bay) stadium in which the giant Zeppelins had once landed. Potsdam had become a cauldron of battle songs and Hitler Youth refrains; drums and the pipes of the musical processions even drowned out the noise of the many lorries and buses that gradually blocked access to the town. Schirach's deputy and Hitler Youth organisational leader Karl Nabersberg had his work cut out trying to keep track of everything that was going on. Ultimately, the organisational chaos and deficient logistics proved irrelevant; the nocturnal illumination worked perfectly, and they succeeded in creating a total mass experience. As part of the opening ceremony, Schirach made some introductory remarks before Hitler began his speech to excessive cheering. In a display of skilful rhetoric, Hitler summarised the central principles of his aims to instrumentalise Germany's youth:

> Germans must learn again to feel like one people beyond status, confession and social class. Our people fell from its proud height because it forgot everything, and in the National Socialist movement you, my German boys and girls, shall relearn to feel like brothers and sisters of one nation. You shall seek and find German commonality beyond professions and social classes, over everything that threatens to tear you apart [...]
> National Socialist youth education shall benefit not a party, but the prosperity of the entire German people, as indeed the National Socialist movement shall one day be Germany, and self-sacrificing German youth's unanimous affirmation of the idea of National Socialism provides clear proof of this. Let the others mock and laugh, one day you will be Germany's future.
> You are the coming people and with you rests the completion of that which we are fighting for today ...
> National Socialism formed a "people's community" ["Volksgemeinschaft"] that begins with the child and ends with the aged. Nobody can silence this tremendous symphony of Germany life.[190]

This concept of a "people's community" beyond class boundaries was the foundation of a totalitarian rule that culminated in the bloody Second World War, the genocide against Jews and the persecution and annihilation of other victim groups – without broad resistance within German society.

In his memoirs, Schirach described his role in setting up the First Reich Youth Day in Potsdam in 1932 and constructing the "Führer" myth as follows: "Thus I participated out of honest conviction in the development of the Führer myth for which the German people was so receptive. This boundless, almost religious veneration, to which I contributed just as much as Goebbels, Göring, Hess, Ley and many others, reinforced in Hitler himself the belief that he was in league with providence." At the same time, Schirach qualified his responsibility by describing Hitler as "an essentially kind man who has to force himself to be hard". [191]

It is in this context that we must again point to Schirach's role as a publicist and propagandist of the "Führer" myth, a role that has been largely underestimated since 1945; together with his father-in-law Heinrich Hoffmann he framed the iconography of the "Führer" with short, polished texts, lending expression to the Hitler myth piece by piece, photo by photo. According to the Zeitgeschichte Verlag press, there were some 400,000 copies of the photo album *Hitler as No One Knows Him* in circulation by 1940. By 1943, a total of 260,000 copies of *Youth Around Hitler* had been produced, in addition to 200,000 copies of *Hitler in His Mountains* by 1942. While the NSDAP had not been as successful in the *Reichstag* elections of 6 November 1932 as it had been in the June, losing 4.2 per cent (two million votes), it remained the strongest party, with 33.1 per cent, followed by the SPD with 20.4 per cent, a slight loss (of minus 1.2 per cent).

The Communists, in third place, gained 2.6 per cent to take 16 per cent of the overall vote. Schirach had long since supported Hitler in his heated internal exchanges with NSDAP Reich organisational leader Gregor Strasser, who pursued a pronounced anti-capitalist and social revolutionary course and repeatedly sought both ideological and strategic conflicts with the "Führer". Strasser nevertheless remained a passive, marginal figure as Hindenburg appointed Hitler Reich chancellor (*Reichskanzler*). In coordination with the incumbent chancellor of the Weimar Republic, Kurt von Schleicher, Strasser had already attempted to secure some posts in the government ministries for the NSDAP, but Hermann Göring, Joseph Goebbels and ultimately Hitler too put all their eggs in one basket and set their sights on the chancellorship. Robert Strasser, whom Kurt von Schleicher had offered to make vice-chancellor, completely withdrew from politics; Robert Ley took over his remits on 8 December 1932.

Ultimately, Strasser didn't dare split the National Socialists' hold on the *Reichstag* into a left wing led by himself and a right wing with Hitler, Göring and Goebbels at its core.

Schirach, on the other hand, had a good relationship with Robert Ley: back in the days of the "struggle", the Cologne *Gauleiter* Ley had got thousands of NSDAP members to demonstrate before the court when Schirach was sentenced and spent eight days in custody.

After Hitler was appointed Reich chancellor of a coalition government with the Centre Party (*Zentrumspartei*), Vice Chancellor Franz von Papen and just two other ministers from the NSDAP, Schirach organised a donation from an unknown industrialist in order to buy the building at Kronprinzenufer 10 in Berlin for the *Reichsjugendführung* (Reich Youth Leadership). Munich was no longer of any interest to Schirach now Hitler had moved to Berlin; as a skilled networker, he realised the importance of keeping close to the central decision-makers in the NSDAP.

From January 1933 onwards, Schirach's magazine *Wille und Macht. Führerorgan der nationalsozialistischen Jugend* (Will and Power. The Führer's Organ of the National Socialist Youth) appeared twice a month; its editorial office was soon based at Kronprinzenufer 10. According to the publishers, 60,000 copies went out in 1938. From 1937 on, a magazine was published by the NSDAP's central press, Franz Eher Nachf. GmbH, edited by the *Reichsjugendführung*: *Der Pimpf. Nationalsozialistische Jungenblätter* (The *Pimpf* [member of the *Jungvolk*; literally "rascal"]. National Socialist Boys' Digest) a magazine that had already appeared since 1935 under the title *Morgen* (Morning). Some 46,000 copies were printed in 1937 and 120,000 in 1939. Due to the war, the publication stopped on 1 September 1944. Another editorial office in the villa on the Kronprinzenufer was responsible for *Jugend am Pflug* (Youth By the Plough), the official organ of the *Reichsjugendführung* and the Reich Nutritional Estate for Rural Youth Issues (*Reichsnährstand für Landjugendfragen*) until it was disbanded in 1935. The magazine *Das deutsche Mädel* (The German Girl), formerly *Die Mädelschaft* (The Girl's Group [referring to the smallest unit within the BDM]) was also based in Schirach's building, as was *Musik in Jugend und Volk* (Music Among the Youth and the People) and *Die Spielschar. Zeitschrift für Feier- und Freizeitgestaltung* (The Play Horde. Magazine for Celebratory and Leisure Activities).

As *Reichsjugendführer*, Schirach headed a publishing company that was able to influence various areas ranging from youth work to youth music. His main interest, however, was the "leading organ" *Wille und Macht*. After Strasser's resignation, this soon brought him into conflict with Goebbels, who controlled all internal propaganda. For instance, in 1934 the Catholic Hitler Youth leader Hermogenes Ziesché from Breslau criticised Ernst Graf zu Reventlow's article "Die Bedeutung der religiösen Frage für Jugend und Arbeitertum" ("The Issue of Religion's Importance for Youth and Workers")[192] in issue 15 of *Wille und Macht*. Reventlow voiced radical anti-clerical theories and wanted German youth to grow up free from the Church's influence. Ziesché went so far as to assert that such arguments would allow Jewish liberal ideas to gain ground again. Goebbels disliked the anti-clerical debate within the Hitler Youth, purely for strategic reasons,[193] even fearing the pope might intervene on other issues.[194] Hence he sought to rein in both Schirach and Rosenberg. With the Saar Referendum looming, he demanded, "The battle for the Saar has begun. We will win it. But Schirach and Rosenberg has [*sic*] to hold back on the confession issue. Until it's in the bag."[195]

Relations between Schirach and Goebbels were spoilt not only by this strategic debate on the Catholic Church, but also by a very private matter. Goebbels suspected Henriette von Schirach of asking Hitler to intervene in his affairs with other women.[196] His wife, Magda, had then received an appointment with the "Führer", and complained to him about her husband.

After Hitler was appointed Reich chancellor, Schirach intensified his promotion of the Hitler Youth; along with the usual trips and camps, he offered dedicated leisure programmes recruiting for the Flying, Reconnaissance, Motorised and Mounted Hitler Youth special units.

But change was also accelerated in the traditional youth organisations by use of force: on 5 April 1933, Schirach had the offices of the Reich Committee of German Youth Leagues (*Reichsausschusses der Deutschen Jugendverbände*) in Berlin occupied by a unit of the Hitler Youth. At Hitler's suggestion, on 10 June 1933 the *Reichstag* then granted Schirach new special powers as "Reichsjugendführer of the German Reich": "The Reichsjugendführer of the German Reich heads all male and female youth leagues, as well as the youth organisations of adult leagues. Founding youth organisations requires his permission."[197]

By the directive of 23 June 1933 and following Schirach's instructions, all youth organisations were retroactively dissolved from 17 June – from the Free Horde of the German Nation (*Freischar Junge Nation*) and the German Scouts Association (*Deutscher Pfadfinderbund*) to the abovementioned Reich Committee of German Youth Leagues. The Reich Committee became the Youth Leaders' Council (*Jugendführerrat*), headed by Schirach.[198] Within just short of two years, all the remaining youth organisations were disbanded, in line with the maxim Schirach had already pronounced after the NSDAP had banned all other parties in July 1933: "Just as the NSDAP is now the only party, the Hitler Youth must be the only youth organisation."[199]

As a member of parliament, Schirach supported all the manoeuvres by Hitler and the NSDAP in the *Reichstag*. Following the *Reichstag* fire of 27 February 1933, which the NSDAP had immediately sold as a Communist conspiracy, thousands of Communists and Social Democrats had been arrested and their basic rights suspended by the "Reich President's Directive for the Protection of the People and the State". Despite the wave of terror and the new elections on 5 March 1933, a majority government was formed by the NSDAP, with 43.9 per cent of the vote, and the DNVP, with 8 per cent. However, they no longer possessed a two-thirds majority. The enabling act of 24 March 1933, the "Law Remedying the Plight of the People and the Reich", sought to finally do away with the parliament as a legislative body. The KPD's eighty-one members of parliament had already been imprisoned or had gone underground; only the ninety-four SPD delegates voted against this "total" enabling act that transferred all law-making powers to Hitler.

In retrospect, for Schirach this law marked the end of the Weimar Republic and the beginning of totalitarian rule.[200] Like all other "brownshirt" *Reichstag* delegates, after the referendum Schirach enthusiastically participated in a rendition of the "Horst-Wessel-Lied", a battle song written by a well-known Berlin SA *Sturmführer* who had died after being shot by a Communist in 1930. The lyrics were sung to a nineteenth-century navy melody. The song soon became a second national anthem without even being officially recognised as such by the *Reichstag*:

Die Fahne hoch! Die Reihen dicht geschlossen!
SA marschiert mit ruhig festem Schritt
Kam'raden, die Rotfront und Reaktion erschossen,
Marschier'n im Geist in unser'n Reihen mit.

[The flag flying high! The ranks closed tight! March, SA, with calm firm steps, comrades, the Red Front and the reaction shot, march with us in spirit in our ranks.]

This song was quite consciously created as a counterweight to the "Internationale", the battle song of the socialist workers' movement whose lyrics were first written as early as 1871 before being set to music by the Belgian socialist and composer Pierre Degeyter in 1888. At the same time, the "Horst-Wessel-Lied" was also symbolic of the further marriage between the NSDAP and the state.

Political songs had been an important representational tool in the development of the mass parties since the second half of the nineteenth century and played an equally important role in the marches and party work of the NSDAP, the SA and the Hitler Youth.

Schirach also used his political position to further his ambitions as a writer, producing many song lyrics and propaganda pieces. His central themes were uncompromising readiness for battle, disdain for death and absolute loyalty to the "Führer" symbolised by loyalty to the flag. These motifs also shaped the lyrics he wrote for the song of the Hitler Youth flag, published in 1933:

1. Vorwärts! vorwärts! schmettern die hellen Fanfaren,
Vorwärts! Vorwärts! Jugend kennt keine Gefahren.
Deutschland, du wirst leuchtend stehn,
Mögen wir auch untergehn.
Vorwärts! vorwärts! schmettern die hellen Fanfaren,
Vorwärts! Vorwärts! Jugend kennt keine Gefahren.
Ist das Ziel auch noch so hoch,
Jugend zwingt es doch!
Unsre Fahne flattert uns voran.
In die Zukunft ziehn wir Mann für Mann.
Wir marschieren für Hitler durch Nacht und durch Not

Mit der Fahne der Jugend für Freiheit und Brot.
Unsre Fahne flattert uns voran. Unsre Fahne ist die neue Zeit.
Und die Fahne führt uns in die Ewigkeit!
Ja! Die Fahne ist mehr als der Tod![201]

[1. Forwards! Forwards! blare the clear fanfares, forwards! Forwards! Youth knows no danger. Germany, you will stand radiant even if we should perish. Forwards! Forwards! blare the clear fanfares, Forwards! Forwards! Youth knows no danger.
May the goal be so very high, youth nevertheless conquers it! Our flag flutters ahead of us. We march into the future man by man. We march for Hitler through night and need with the flag of the youth for freedom and bread. Our flag flutters ahead of us. Our flag is the new age. And the flag leads us into eternity! Yes! The flag is more than death.]

With its melody by the renowned film composer Hans-Otto Borgmann, the battle song of the Hitler Youth was first used in the propaganda film *Hitlerjunge Quex* (Hitler Youth Quex).[202] Shortly before it premiered, Joseph Goebbels edited the script himself in order to increase its propaganda impact: "Afterwards, at home, H. Junge Quex. Very strong in parts. But there is too much talking. The dialogues are completely untrue. I shall cut some more."[203] After a successful premiere, the film became a box office hit, as Goebbels noted in his diary, praising himself for his – ultimately very minimal – alterations: "Hitlerjunge Quex a great success in the UFA-Palast. After my changes it almost seems like a new film. Hitler, Göring, everyone there. The audience is completely enraptured."[204]

The film is a prime example of how skilfully National Socialist propaganda used a variety of media to manipulate its audience, fusing moving pictures, music and text to a single entity with a clear basic ideological message. Schirach was at the centre of the film, not only as a writer, but also as its "patron", as the film poster with prominent actors such as Heinrich George shows.

The film hit cinemas in September 1933 and was intended to be watched by the entire Hitler Youth. Again, the protagonist, based on Herbert Norkus, was a martyr from the days of battle before 1933. In the future too, the Hitler Youth would be called on to follow his example and show total readiness to do battle – without regard for their own lives.

During their probationary period as a "Pimpf", boys had to learn the song of the Hitler Youth flag by heart. It was also used in all official processions and celebrations, and had to be sung by the League of German Girls too.

It is remarkable, however, that the remaining oppositional youth, persecuted with draconian measures, used the same melody for a song mocking not only the song itself, but also the "Führer" Baldur von Schirach:

Brüder, Brüder, laßt uns die Flammen bewahren,
Brüder, Brüder, wehret den stumpfen Barbaren,
Nirgends laßt den Baldur ran,
Daß er nichts zertrampeln kann.
Laßt ihn trügen, werben mit lockenden Klängen,
Laßt ihn lügen, hetzen, drohen und bedrängen,
Steht er heut auch noch so hoch,
Einmal kippt er doch.
Unser Baldur flattert uns voran,

Unser Baldur ist ein dicker Mann,
Wir marschieren trotz Schirach, durch Nacht und Verbot,
Und wir schern uns den Teufel um Neid und Verbot.
Unser Baldur flattert uns voran,
Unser Baldur meint die neue Zeit,
Doch wir halten uns wachsam und trotzig bereit,
Unser Bund gilt uns mehr als der Tod.[205]

[Brothers, brothers, let us preserve the flames, brothers, brothers, repel the dull barbarians, never let Baldur in so he cannot trample everything to pieces. Let him deceive, woo with enticing sounds, let him lie, agitate, threaten and harass, as high as he stands today, one day he will fall. Our Baldur flutters ahead of us, our Baldur is a fat man. We march despite Schirach, through night and bans, and we don't give a damn about envy and bans. Our Baldur flutters ahead of us, our Baldur thinks it's the new age, but we remain vigilant and defiantly prepared. Our league means more to us than death.]

Singing such parodies was a dangerous undertaking and could result in persecution by the Gestapo. But this pastiche mocking Schirach could not stop his political rise within the National Socialist movement. Like other writers with National Socialist leanings – including Hanns Johst, Hans Friedrich Blunck, Hans Baumann, Curt Langenbeck or Hans Grimm – Schirach benefited from the politically motivated large print runs of his books and texts. While he reported in detail on Hitler's royalties from *Mein Kampf* and his various fees for articles,[206] he kept quiet about his own royalties from his many publications[207] and texts, which are also difficult to reconstruct completely due to the paucity of sources. The large print runs and his father-in-law's business sense would certainly suggest he earned substantial sums as a writer and editor. Since he listed his occupation as a "writer", he may have also claimed the tax benefits for creative artists.

At the same time, in 1933 Schirach proclaimed the image of a new German youth "that does not want profit, not self-interest, but does service and makes sacrifices for the community [...] Not a youth with new rights – a generation of hard fulfilment of its duty".[208]

Neither Hitler, to whom the Hitler Youth swore their allegiance, nor Shirach lived according to this motto; rather, they led a life of luxury and made a significant fortune from their political functions – Hitler much more so than Schirach, of course.

Hitler himself whipped up the youth movement bearing his name during the Nuremberg party conference of 1935: in her skilfully shot and edited propaganda film *Triumph des Willens* (Triumph of the Will), director and mountain film exponent Leni Riefenstahl documented this party event as a perfectly staged mass rally, here too preferring an exaggerated pathos. On the morning of 14 September 1935, with 54,000 members of the Hitler Youth in the Nuremberg stadium, the "Führer" took the opportunity to secure their allegiance in the coming fight, making his famous programmatic statement: "In our eyes, the German boy of the future must be slim and lissom, as swift as greyhounds, as tough as leather and as hard as Krupp steel."[209]

Hitler had already used this metaphor, often cited today, in *Mein Kampf* to describe his idea of the ideal party warrior, although there the military aspect was emphasised more clearly.[210] In Nuremberg, Schirach merely gave the welcoming speech preparing the audience for the appearance of the "boss"; in this respect, he largely resembled the figure in the satirical song.

Nevertheless: by implementing the comprehensive ideological reorganisation and centralisation of the youth movement and crushing all opposition in this sphere, Schirach made a significant contribution to stabilising National Socialist rule. A particularly important aspect – and one which is usually overlooked – is the strong emotional connection to Hitler that Schirach's speeches and texts repeatedly communicated to the members of the Hitler Youth.

In 1975, the American writer and philosopher Susan Sontag noted in her essay "Fascinating Fascism", a response to Leni Riefenstahl's book of photographs of the Nuba in Sudan and the publication *SS Regalia* by Jack Pia:

> Fascist aesthetics include but go far beyond the rather special celebration of the primitive to be found in *The Last of the Nuba*. More generally, they flow from (and justify) a preoccupation with situations of control, submissive behavior, extravagant effort, and the endurance of pain; they endorse two seemingly opposite states, egomania and servitude. The relations of domination and enslavement take the form of a characteristic pageantry: the massing of groups of people; the turning of people into things; the multiplication or replication of things; and the grouping of people/things around an all-powerful, hypnotic leader-figure or force. The fascist dramaturgy centers on the orgiastic transactions between mighty forces and their puppets, uniformly garbed and shown in ever swelling numbers. Its choreography alternates between ceaseless motion and a congealed, static, "virile" posing. Fascist art glorifies surrender, it exalts mindlessness, it glamorizes death.[211]

Sontag astutely describes the mechanisms used in the pathos-filled heroic staging of the Hitler Youth rallies. The ultimate aim of these mass experiences was total subordination to the "Führer" and a willingness to lay down one's life for the National Socialist ideology – a message Schirach, too, repeatedly used in the hero cult he built around the "flag" of the NSDAP and the "martyrs" of the Hitler Youth who had died in the street battles before 1933.

In everyday life, however, Schirach also tried to reinforce the impression of apparently independent self-organisation, although the Hitler Youth – like other NSDAP organisations – was closely connected to the SA and the party leadership. This enabled the adolescents to feel special; Hitler Youth functionaries were equal to their older comrades in the party. The motto "Youth leads youth" held only within the confines of a prescribed, narrow ideological corset, however.

This psychological mobilisation is a key element stabilising Nazi rule. Incidentally, it also had an impact within the same age group in Austria. The NSDAP was considered a youthful movement. In Germany, its membership had grown to 3.5 million by 1935.[212] In Austria, the NSDAP had been banned since 12 June 1933 due to bloody acts of terrorism and the failed putsch attempt of July 1934, in which the authoritarian Federal Chancellor Engelbert Dollfuss was killed. The party nevertheless continued to gain new members, especially from younger sections of the population.

In 1935, Hitler's rule was secure, the opposition having been liquidated. Now the National Socialists could continue to expand their power. They had recently reintroduced General Military Service (*Allgemeine Wehrpflicht*), thereby removing the last of the restrictions imposed by the Treaty of Versailles with which the Allied powers had sought to prevent Germany's military revival after the First World War. And Hitler followed through on his speech to the country's adolescents in Nuremberg: in 1936, the Hitler Youth was declared the only legal youth organisation in Germany, and membership became compulsory in 1939. From that point on, almost eight million adolescents from the age of ten marched in uniforms, drilled in schoolyards, took part in rifle practice and saluted the flag – with the sole aim of becoming "as swift as greyhounds, as tough as leather and as hard as Krupp steel". If war broke out, they were to kill and – if fate so decreed – die for the "Führer".

The day 1 December 1936 marked the pinnacle of Baldur von Schirach's political career thus far: when the "Law on the Hitler Youth" came into force, as "youth leader of the German Reich", he was tasked with implementing the education of German youth in its entirety within the Hitler Youth. He now headed a Supreme Reich Authority (*Oberste Reichsbehörde*) with a headquarters in Berlin and answered directly to the "Führer" and Reich chancellor.[213]

Paragraph 2 of this law unequivocally established totalitarian ideological aims: "Beyond the parental home and school, German youth in its entirety is to be educated within the Hitler Youth physically, mentally and morally in the spirit of National Socialism and to serve the people and the "people's community" ["Volksgemeinschaft"]."[214] In one fell swoop, the Hitler Youth now comprised around six million members and Schirach was able to implement a comprehensive National Socialist education programme. Some local Hitler Youth leaders (*Gebietsführer*) had their reservations however, both in the run up to the legislation and thereafter. They feared they had been transformed overnight from an elite youth organisation whose members were selected and enrolled on a voluntary basis into a kind of "mass state youth".[215] Formally, the Hitler Youth remained a sub-group of the NSDAP, but in practice it morphed into a compulsory state youth organisation under the party's ideological control. Schirach had virtually become a secretary of state with the power to issue decrees. While membership of the Hitler Youth did not become compulsory until March 1939, for Schirach the "progress" was quite obvious: at the Hitler Youth leaders' congress in Königsberg in 1937, he declared that the Hitler Youth law represented a "new chapter in the educational history of humanity".[216]

Schirach also skilfully resisted the attempts by other Nazi organisations such as the National Socialist Reich League for Physical Exercise (*Nationalsozialistischer Reichsbund für Leibesübungen*, NSRL), the German Labour Front (*Deutsche Arbeitsfront*, DAF) or the Reich Labour Service (*Reichsarbeitsdienst*, RAD) to influence his youth work.[217] The massive rise in members saw the growth of a Hitler Youth administration with five offices in Berlin employing over 1,000 staff in twelve specialist offices and nineteen leadership departments. In 1936, the Hitler Youth bureaucracy, equivalent in size to a ministry, managed to organise almost 95 per cent of children born in 1926 – i.e. almost all ten-year-olds – in the *Jungvolk* or the *Jungmädel*. Three-quarters of all potential adolescents and children had already been gathered in the Hitler Youth.[218]

Another remarkable aspect of this phase around 1935–37 is the attempt by the Hitler Youth leadership to maintain as much distance from the *Wehrmacht* as possible, despite close contacts and a prominent liaison officer with connections to the supreme command in the form of Lieutenant Colonel Erwin Rommel. In keeping with the principle of

German youth's self-education, the military were not to take on direct responsibility for the Hitler Youth's paramilitary training. Instead, this was the sole preserve of the HJ leaders. They themselves would then create the basis for its members' subsequent basic military training as soldiers. The main aim was to ensure that future young recruits were already firmly aligned with the NSDAP's ideology: "We will not be putting a military weapon, a 98 rifle,[219] a machine gun [...] in any young person's hands. That is not youthful. We don't want a youth oriented towards killing. [...] [T]hey must only be trained to defend the country. But weapons belong only in the hands of men."[220]

As part of the *Reichsführer* camp of 1937 in Weimar, a treaty was negotiated between Rommel and Hartmann Lauterbacher, the Hitler Youth *Stabsführer* (staff leader) and Schirach's deputy. Schirach rarely bothered himself with such arduous formal details. Although Lauterbacher had thoroughly rejected Rommel's draft, the experienced military strategist was able to trick Schirach into signing his version. Schirach was then only able have the treaty amended after Lauterbacher took the matter to Hitler, who sharply criticised Schirach.[221] As a result of this breach of trust, Rommel was released as the liaison officer between the Hitler Youth and the *Wehrmacht*.

In 1941, this insistence on independence from the *Wehrmacht* would undergo a radical transformation however: the erstwhile Office for Physical Training (*Amt für körperliche Ertüchtigung*) was renamed the Office for Defence Training (*Amt Wehrertüchtigung*), and education, leisure activities and propaganda thenceforth worked towards ensuring adolescents were fit for service and battle.[222]

In the meantime, Baldur von Schirach, who had sent the members of the Hitler Youth and the BDM on a successful mission collecting donations for the youth organisation, had already earned enough in publishing royalties and from his political functions to buy Schloss Aspenstein in Kochel am See in March 1936. This stately property was 65 kilometres from Munich and relatively close to Adolf Hitler's mountain residence, the Berghof. Prior to that, Henriette and Baldur von Schirach had lived in a hunting lodge they owned in Urfeld am Walchensee.

Lashes for Manfred von Brauchitsch

Kochel am See was the scene of a veritable scandal in March 1936, when the renowned and highly popular motor racer Manfred von Brauchitsch and his brother Harald insulted Schirach's wife in the bar of the Hotel Post und Jäger, allegedly shouting in a drunken state, "While the Reichsjugendführer drives around, his wife amuses herself here in her own way."[223] The next day, Henriette von Schirach stormed into the hotel, slapped Manfred von Brauchitsch's face and demanded an apology. Schirach learned of the incident ten days later and went round to the Brauchitsch brothers' Berlin apartment with some Hitler Youth leaders. Schirach told them they were not "men of honour, since they had insulted a decent German woman".[224] When Manfred von Brauchitsch proposed Schirach take "satisfaction by weapon", Schirach rejected the idea of duelling with pistols and "disciplined" the brothers there and then with a dog whip. Brauchitsch's mother had already been locked in her apartment. In order to bring legal proceedings, the brothers' lawyer, Dr von Birckhahn, asked the *Reichstag* president to revoke Schirach's immunity, to no avail.

Not only does this skirmish document Schirach's regressive ideas of honour, but, tellingly, it did no harm to his reputation within the NSDAP whatsoever. Schirach was at the height of his power within the party – in January 1936, Hitler consulted propaganda minister Goebbels on whether the *Gauleiter* of Munich, Adolf Wagner, or Schirach should succeed Bernhard Rust as Reich minister for science, education and public enlightenment.[225] Hitler was unhappy with Rust, criticising his conflict with Robert Ley, the leader of the DAF.

Schirach, on the other hand, had forged strong ties with Ley via the Hitler Youth's Reich Vocational Games (*Reichsberufswettkämpfe*), which also met with Goebbels' approval. For instance, he wrote in his diary on February 1935, "Sportpalast H.J. Reich Vocational Games opened. Fine German work. Schirach speaks well. Ley's old dream. I am in great form. The youth exults. I soar. An invigorating evening. I am blissfully happy. How enjoyable it is to speak before the youth."[226]

Some 500,000 youths had taken part in the first Reich Vocational Games in 1934 in Berlin. The organisational work was headed by *Obergebietsführer* (Supreme Regional Leader) Artur Axmann and Robert

Ley for the DAF. Schirach thus gained a very public media stage that enhanced the visibility of the concept of the National Socialist "people's community" in the context of young people's employment.

In 1935, the UFA *Tonwochenschau* news bulletin proclaimed, "A million German boys and girls take part in the Reich Vocational Games, opened by the Reichsjugendführer in the A.E.G. transformer factory."[227]

In turn, Adolf Hitler used these events for propaganda purposes by staging a reception for the winners in the Reich Chancellery.

Chapter 6

Raised for Revolution

The Hitler Youth Targets Schools

The Reich Law on the Hitler Youth of 1 December 1936 made it the organisation's leadership mission to establish themselves as a third educational authority along with parents and school. Before the law came into force, teachers had already been instructed to help recruit pupils to the *Jungvolk* and the Hitler Youth.[228] In August 1933, for instance, Bernhard Rust ordered schools in Prussia to keep two afternoons a week free for Hitler Youth service. This even applied to the fourth year in primary school – in Thuringia, this meant a dedicated free period every Wednesday and Saturday evening.

At the same time, Schirach himself propagated a completely new type of Hitler Youth leader, demanding in a speech in Weimar's National Theatre in 1936: "The Jugendführer and educator of the future will be a priest of the National Socialist faith and an officer of National Socialist service."[229]

Despite several public displays of cooperation, the conflict between Rust and Schirach exploded in January 1937 when Hitler entrusted Ley and Schirach with the task of organising Nazi schools. The two of them quickly designed the new Adolf Hitler schools, circumventing the influence of the state education authority. Rust was incandescent and protested vigorously.[230] Schirach and Ley coolly replied that these schools were the preserve of the Hitler Youth. In October 1941, Hitler, prompted by Schirach, ruled that the final exams at the Adolf Hitler schools were equal to qualifications at the state high schools. The plan was to have one Hitler school for every *Gau*, although ultimately, there would only be twelve of them. Their aim was to educate "political, economic and administrative" leadership cadres from the group aged twelve to eighteen.[231]

Using his Hitler Youth publishing channels, in 1938 Schirach skilfully launched a campaign presenting the Hitler Youth as the only force of 'real reform' to the school system while heralding a "new order of questions of total education".²³² Schirach almost managed to bundle all educational authorities; a few months before the start of the war in 1939, representatives of the *Wehrmacht* demanded "a uniform orientation of the entire education system around the country's defence". Moreover, as early as 1938 Göring had announced the "utmost pooling of all forces for the fortification of Germany".²³³

Indeed, after the invasion of Poland, those close to the Council of Ministers for the Defence of the Reich (*Ministerrat für die Reichsverteidigung*) discussed appointing Schirach Reich education minister (*Reichserziehungsminister*), although it was unclear whether or not that would include the university sector. But Schirach had underestimated the potency of the Nationalist Socialist Teachers' League (*Nationalsozialistischer Lehrerbund*), which rejected the Hitler Youth's criticism of insufficiently ideological teachers as strongly as the Reich Ministry for Education. At the same time, the Hitler Youth became increasingly vehement in its calls for new ideological teachers, and Schirach propagated "youth's responsibility for itself in school".²³⁴

Ultimately, the war prevented such radical reform, since even the ideologists in the Hitler Youth, such as Supreme District Leader (*Obergebietsführer*) Helmut Stellrecht, recognised the strength of the teaching apparatus of the Reich Ministry for Education and the NDSAP leadership did not wish to provoke conflict in this field during the war.

Regional empirical studies in the German Reich also show that the original conflict between the Hitler Youth and the teachers faded as the war drew on, and was much stronger in the university sector than in primary and secondary education.²³⁵ In many cases, community struggle was ordered – for instance the extended relocation of children and adolescents from urban bombing targets to rural areas from 1940–45, under the auspices of the Hitler Youth, which in turn was supported by the teachers.

At the same time, the Hitler Youth leaders fuelled the strong trend of denunciation among the German population, which was ultimately responsible for 60 to 80 per cent of Gestapo arrests – for instance when questionnaires were handed out to grammar school pupils or apprentices to establish whether parents, teachers or employers were hindering participation in Hitler Youth duties.²³⁶ For many teachers, the fanatical

Hitler Youth leaders in particular constituted a dangerous group of spies, as demonstrated by People's Court (*Volksgericht*) proceedings from 1944.

The New Diplomacy of the Hitler Youth Leader

Baldur von Schirach was extremely keen for the Hitler Youth to have an international presence and ties with other youth organisations throughout Europe. Even before the National Socialists took power, the Italian Fascist youth movement led by Renato Ricci, the *Opera Nazionale Balilla*, had planned a tour of Germany for 200 to 300 boys aged fourteen to seventeen.[237] In 1933, the trip eventually went ahead with more than 400 "Avantguardisti", with extensive newspaper coverage. Schirach cautiously maintained ties with Italy. On 1 May 1935, formerly Labour Day but now the "National Holiday of the German People", he organised the opening celebrations in the form of a mass event with speeches by Hitler and Goebbels on Berlin's Sportfeld. An Italian delegation headed by Ricci took part in this display of power by the Hitler Youth, a performance that even impressed Propaganda Minister Goebbels, no stranger to success: "Ricci and Schirach picked me up at home in the morning. I'm still so tired. But we have the best of conversations. Then to the Sportfeld. An overwhelming picture. 150,000 participants. And a great atmosphere. First Schirach and I speak. Then comes the Führer and receives a rapturous reception. He very much speaks to the hearts of the youth. A splendid and moving celebration."[238]

Discussions were taken up once more in 1934 in the initial planning stages of the Olympic Games in Berlin connection. Hartmann Lauterbacher, *Stabsführer* of the *Reichsjugendführung*, finalised the negotiations with Ricci over closer bilateral collaboration between the two countries' youth organisations. The most prestigious element of this agreement was the Hitler Youth trip from Berlin to Rome from 15 to 25 September 1936 following the Berlin Olympics; some 450 youths from twenty-five regions paraded before Benito Mussolini. During this visit, Schirach spoke with Mussolini, Foreign Minister Galeazzo Ciano, Minister Dino Alfieri and Youth Leader Ricci. While Ricci and Schirach were primarily worried about the other's youth movements putting theirs in the shade, they were also very interested in cooperating more closely as fascist, central youth organisations. In the course of subsequent negotiations, a "German–

Italian Institute for Youth Leadership" was founded in Rome in order to align Italy's young Fascists more closely with the German model. In terms of propaganda, the centrepiece, befitting the proclamation of the Berlin–Rome Axis – was a parade by 12,000 Balilla youths during Hitler's visit to Italy in June 1937. Hitler heralded the future with a martial speech: "It is a delightful feeling to know that in Italy, just as in Germany, a country is constructed with defence and weapons [...]. Another thing that connects us: youth that has ideals and is prepared [...] to die for them."[239]

In previous years, the National Socialist had also cultivated peaceful ties with England via youth organisations: the then German ambassador to London, Joachim von Ribbentrop, even arranged for Hartmann Lauterbacher, Schirach's deputy, to meet with the inventor of the Boy Scout movement, Robert Baden-Powell, whom Lauterbacher invited to meet Hitler. Baden-Powell was quite open to discussions, as the British secret service MI5 documented: "Lauterbacher's visit was a success, especially his interviews with Baden-Powell leading to removal on [sic] bar on wearing uniforms in Germany for English groups."[240] MI5 also placed individual Hitler Youth cycling group trips to England under observation, even noting who invited them to dinner, as documented for the Spalding Rotary Club.[241] It remains unclear whether they were actually sent as spies to make precise notes on the lie of the land and bridges and rivers encountered on their cycling tours, as the *Daily Herald* claimed in May 1937, citing a German-language newspaper in Prague.[242] Even the friendly government in Hungary was irritated by such "trips" by German adolescents, complaining about "these secret observation services". Schirach denied this was the aim in 1935 after receiving a note from Foreign Minister Konstantin Neurath asking him to inform Hitler himself about the Hungarians' grievances.[243]

From 1936 to 1938, contacts with France were intensified in order to underscore the peaceful intentions of Hitler's Germany – far too much for Propaganda Minister Goebbels' liking; he intervened in 1938, objecting, "There is too much blather about German–French understanding. Especially by Schirach and the H.J. I'm having it stopped somewhat."[244]

Schirach himself travelled a great deal between 1936 and 1938 in his capacity as *Reichsjugendführer*, retrospectively focusing on his meetings with Fascist dictator Benito Mussolini in the Palazzo Venezia in Rome on 22 September 1936 and Kemal Atatürk in Turkey in 1937.[245] He reported on the latter meetings to Hitler, and Goebbels enthused, "Veritable marvels. Schirach has been received especially warmly by Kemal Atatürk. The Führer thinks Turkey wants better relations with us again. I can only confirm that. The game with Moscow is only a matter of expediency."[246]

Prior to his trip to the Near East, Schirach spoke with Bulgarian prime minister Georgi K'oseivanov in Bucharest on 27 November 1937. His memoirs do not mention his visit to Athens on 29 November and a meeting with Greek dictator Ioannis Metaxas, however, despite the fact that he took with him gifts and decorated the leader of the National Youth Organisation *(Ethniki Organosis Neoleas,* EON) and Crown Prince Paul with gold medals.[247]

In an audience with Kemal Atatürk lasting one-and-a-half hours, the Turkish dictator was primarily eager to hear about the Hitler Youth, by Schirach's account. In fact, however, Ankara, like King Ghazi in Baghdad, pursued concrete geostrategic interests. In a report to Goebbels, published by the British newspaper *News Review*, Schirach claimed to have made clear during his visit to Iraq in 1937 that all those German citizens in Arabian countries who were critical of Hitler's government had to be thrown out. At the same time, he dangled the prospect of German money and weapons.[248] There was diplomatic outrage in Paris when, following the *Reichsjugendführer*'s stopover in Damascus, an "Arabic club was formed with German money, with the aim of stirring up the Arabic population against French mandate rule".[249]

It is impossible to verify whether a bureau for the "culture of thoughts" modelled on the Reich Ministry for Public Enlightenment and Propaganda was really established after Schirach's visit to Reza Shah in Iran.[250] After a meeting with Minister of Culture Hekmat, his visit in December 1937 certainly received plenty of coverage in the Persian press, and Iranian adolescents used the Hitler salute at official ceremonies.[251] The day after Schirach returned to Berlin, Iranian newspapers published reports under the headline "The West and the East". The message was clear: Great Britain and France, the countries of the "old West", required a rebirth after the Persian model that had returned the Persians to their Aryan roots. Only Germany represented the true West. This was evident in the Germans' economic, technological and military strength, whereas the old West was characterised by false ideas such as enlightenment, liberal capitalist democracy and communism.[252]

Schirach did not mention any of this exchange in his memoirs. His former press officer, Günter Kaufmann, also merely related that Schirach could quote the Persian poet Firdusi.²⁵³ What he didn't mention was that Firdusi was repeatedly used to document the close connection between Nazi Germany and the ancient cultures of the Orient. For instance, a celebration of Firdusi was held in Berlin in 1934, with speeches by Schirach, Alfred Rosenberg, Berlin's lord mayor Heinrich Sahm and the Reich student leader Andreas Feickert.²⁵⁴

Schirach declared 1938 the "Year of Understanding" for the Hitler Youth. The *Reichsjugendführer*'s overseas bureau had planned for fifty-two international camps, 345 group visits abroad, ski camps, sports events and exchanges for that year.²⁵⁵ As the representative of the overseas bureau, Lauterbacher had skilfully organised this network; in 1942, it was active in Italy, Hungary, Romania, Bulgaria and Slovakia, but also in occupied countries such as France, the Netherlands, Norway, Denmark and the so-called "Reichskommissariat Ostland" in the Baltic states and western parts of Byelorussia.

After using intermediaries to seek contacts with England and France, in 1938 Schirach was already planning a kind of umbrella association for comparable youth organisations. His Italian connections would prove particularly useful here. In June 1938 he met with Mussolini's son-in-law and Italy's foreign minister Ciano, with whom he got on well, and Achille Starace, the Fascist Party secretary, in order to negotiate more intensive collaboration.²⁵⁶ The Reich Party Congress in Nuremberg hosted youth delegations not only from friendly states such as Italy, Bulgaria, Hungary, Romania and Spain, but also from Greece, Turkey, Yugoslavia, Finland, Iran, Iraq, Denmark and Portugal. Schirach's "travel policy" was, then, certainly fruitful. Cooperation with the Office of Foreign Affairs included funding, and "Delegates of the Jugendführer of the German Reich" (*Beauftragte des Jugendführers des Deutschen Reiches*) were also appointed.

In July 1938, he met with Yugoslav prime minister Milan Stojadinović and Prince Regent Paul of Yugoslavia in Bled. Against the background of the "annexation" of Austria and the forthcoming takeover of Czechoslovakia, this meeting was of great strategic importance. Yugoslavia emphasised its friendly relations with Germany – even if the *Wehrmacht* were to march through Hungary.²⁵⁷ In 1939, Schirach also travelled to Bucharest for the holiday celebrating the Romanian state youth.

The close ties to Italy cooled off appreciably when Ricci was replaced as youth leader by Achille Starace, a brutal party functionary who had spent some time as number two to Mussolini and had already committed war crimes in Abyssinia. Despite two meetings with Schirach in 1938, there was no longer any real cooperation.

Meanwhile, the Hitler Youth, now a mass movement, was faced with increasing organisational problems that would completely spiral out of control when war broke out in 1939; juvenile crime rose significantly with the war and blackouts, in terms of both individual offenders and gangs.[258] At a conference dedicated to youth issues, the Council of Ministers for the Defence of the Reich (*Ministerrat für die Reichsverteidigung*) attempted to establish the root causes and develop solutions, but Schirach was increasingly excluded from the decision-making process.

In this situation, Hitler approved Schirach's request to volunteer for the *Wehrmacht*, and hence the *Reichsjugendführer* joined the Infantry Demonstration Regiment (*Infanterie-Lehrregiment*) in Döberitz, west of Berlin, in December 1939. The Hitler Youth leadership's business was now overseen by the man who had already ensured organisational order and calm: Hartmann Lauterbacher. A native Tyrolean from Reutte and a trained apothecary, Lauterbacher had first been involved in National Socialist youth work in 1923, in Kufstein.[259] He continued his political career in Brunswick and was appointed Hitler Youth *Stabsführer* and deputy *Reichsjugendführer* in 1934. Lauterbacher also took care of the Hitler Youth's international contacts and intensified relations with the *Opera Nazionale Balilla*. In 1936, he also became a member of the *Reichstag* and increasingly emerged as a competitor to Schirach, in part due to his good connections abroad. Schirach sought to prevent the successful organiser from gaining more influence over the Hitler Youth in his function as *Reichsführer*, and so on 5 April 1940, without informing his deputy, he wrote directly to Hitler, requesting that Lauterbacher be released for military services "in accordance with his wishes". Schirach also wanted the relatively young Hitler Youth leader Artur Axmann, who had enrolled in the infantry in November 1939, to be given leave and installed as a probationary *Reichsjugendführer* at the age of twenty-seven.[260] Schirach himself had already turned thirty-three, Lauterbacher thirty-one. Schirach practically sent Lauterbacher to the *Wehrmacht* by press release, immediately publicising Axmann's return. Axmann was appointed on 3 May, Lauterbacher joining the *SS-Leibstandarte* "Adolf Hitler" as a recruit in Berlin-Lichterfelde.

A Hero in France

On 10 May 1940, Germany attacked France. Schirach's unit participated in the breach at Sedan and within eight weeks Private von Schirach had become a lieutenant. Shortly thereafter he received the Cross of Honour Second Class. According to Schirach's own account, he convinced Hitler that his motorised infantry regiment, "Grossdeutschland", led by Lieutenant Colonel Gerhard Graf von Schwerin, had been deployed at the head of the successful advance.

Schirach's memoirs are extremely reticent when it comes to specific wartime experiences. They only depict the heavy British artillery fire covering the retreat of the British Expedition Corps at Dunkirk, then the retreat of his own regiment after heavy losses and their subsequent deployment in breaching the Weygand Line.[261] Initially, Schirach was a signaller with the Fourth Company; later, he was the leader of a machine gun squad. The CV he presented upon becoming *Reichsstatthalter* in Vienna contains a more detailed description of his military career; he was not shy to embellish it with heroic deeds.[262] However, although the First Battalion of the Grossdeutschland motorised infantry regiment was involved in two massacres of black African soldiers in the French army ("Tirailleurs") and their officers,[263] Schirach made no mention of this.

The *Wehrmacht* did not take well to his brief deployment on the Western Front, nor to his swift promotion and decoration, as transcripts of eavesdropped conversations between prisoners of war demonstrate:

Well! What they get up to. Your Gauleiter BALDUR and [*sic*] SCHIRACH. The man is a soldier for half a year, and has his E.K.2 and is a lieutenant. The man speaks to German youth and is Reichsjugendführer. I mean, if he had gone to the front and had earned, say, a Knight's Cross, in honest fashion by destroying ten or twelve tanks, then he can show himself at the front and say, he is a model [*sic* – "to"?] German youth and what have you and you'd certainly have to follow him. But this way, my word, the devil knows how he's conned his way into getting the E.K.2, on the Western

Front, has advanced to lieutenant within half a year and then cleared off, the story being he is 'indispensible'. I guarantee everyone can be replaced and this greenhorn, my word, he still needs replacing as Gauleiter in your OSTMARK.[264]

In the late June, Hitler called Schirach to his Tannenberg headquarters outside Freudenstadt in the Black Forest to tell him he was needed for a new mission; he was to go to Vienna as *Reichsstatthalter*.[265] What Schirach's memoirs do not mention is that the dismissed Josef Bürckel, Minister Hans Heinrich Lammers, Hitler's secretary Martin Bormann and *Gauleiter* Robert Wagner were also present, as photographs demonstrate. Schirach attempted to imply it had been an exclusive meeting; in fact, other appointments were made.

Chapter 7

My Gau, My Vienna

Gauleiter and *Reichsstatthalter* in Vienna, 1940–45

My Gau, my Vienna – in my future life, that will be the object of my thoughts and studies, my cares and my loyalty. It is here that I see my new life's work.

Baldur von Schirach in his inaugural address, 10 August 1940

Schirach's wife Henriette, now a mother of three, could hardly believe her luck: "I confess that I forgot about the whole war at the idea of being able to live in Vienna", she recalled in her memoirs.[266] Her greatest concern: choosing a new abode in the metropolis of the "Ostmark", as Austria had been renamed. Hitler had recommended Prince Eugen's Belvedere palace, while the City of Vienna suggested the imperial Hofburg palace. The Schirachs, however, opted for the spacious villa at Hohe Warte 52–54, where his predecessor Josef Bürckel had lived. Surrounded by a large garden, it promised to be the right home for the family.

From Schirach's perspective, the new task in Vienna ultimately amounted to a political setback. The man who had always done his utmost to be close to Hitler and the nerve centre of the NSDAP and had thus moved the Hitler Youth administration from Munich to Berlin now found himself pushed to the periphery of the Reich. His promotion to the position in Vienna was a clear sign he had become less important politically. As *Reichsjugendführer*, he had lost the battle for supremacy over the entire school sector to Education Minister Rust, probably because he was no longer able to get through to Hitler directly during the decisive days when war broke out. On 6 September 1939, Goebbels had written in his diary: "Schirach will now take over the schools and Rust will form a pure science ministry. It would be best if he retired altogether."[267]

A second new problem was a direct consequence of the war: the rise of juvenile crime. After the *Wehrmacht*'s first campaigns, it had become clear that the Hitler Youth was not able to keep all adolescents under control in this extreme situation. Mass conscription to the *Wehrmacht* and blackout orders created a climate fostering juvenile indiscipline, often a protest against the war and the regime.

This situation was compounded by organisational deficiencies and the fact that almost 90 per cent of Hitler Youth leaders had been conscripted; many of them had been killed in the first months of the war. The constant ideological propaganda with the Hitler Youth's cult of the dead, its fallen martyrs and a hero's death for the "Führer" had claimed its toll. At internal conferences on juvenile crime, headed by Reinhard Heydrich, the chief of the *Sicherheitspolizei* (Security Police) and the *Sicherheitsdienst* (Security Service, SD), by commission of *Reichsführer-SS* Heinrich Himmler and Hermann Göring, Hartmann Lauterbach also conceded that "regular HJ service was completely impossible".[268] Initially, however, the leadership elite led by the Prussian premier, Field Marshal Göring, was on the whole rather helpless, resorting to radio announcements addressing German youth. *Reichsleiter* Alfred Rosenberg, the "Führer's Delegate for the Entire Intellectual and Ideological Education of the NSDAP" (*Beauftragte des Führers für die gesamte geistige und weltanschauliche Schulung und Erziehung der NSDAP*), was supposed to organise well-known speakers for these propaganda broadcasts. Ultimately, this enabled him to get at least a temporary hold on the Hitler Youth's ideological work, something Schirach had hitherto always been able to prevent. Rosenberg thus accelerated "education work for war". In March 1940, Schirach was even forced to agree to this in writing. The *Reichsjugendführer*'s ambitious plans to establish a "Reich Institute for National Socialist Youth Work" (*Reichsinstitut für Nationalsozialistische Jugendarbeit*), still one of his projects in September 1939, were consigned to the past.

Obergebietsführer (Supreme Regional Leader) Helmut Stellrecht, whom Schirach had forced out of the *Reichsjugendführung*, was a *Stabsleiter* under Rosenberg. Schirach was nevertheless at least able to receive Hitler's written assurance that as *Reichsleiter* he would retain sole responsibility for the German Youth Movement and function as a kind of supervisor for the Hitler Youth leadership as "Delegate for the Inspection of the Entire Hitler Youth" (*Beauftragter für die Inspektion der gesamten Hitler-Jugend*).[269] A cryptic addition was "also in the state sector".[270] Whether that allowed him to retain control of education remains uncertain. As mentioned above, he was at least able to push through Artur Axmann as his successor in the Hitler Youth's executive. At the same time, it was also announced that Hartmann Lauterbacher, Schirach's former deputy as *Reichsjugendführer*, had been appointed deputy *Gauleiter* of "Süd-Hannover-Braunschweig" and Josef Bürckel, the former *Gauleiter* and *Reichsstatthalter* of Vienna, had been made head of the civilian administration in occupied Lorraine. On 1 July 1940, Robert Wagner, also present at the "Führer's" Tannenberg headquarters, was appointed *Reichsstatthalter* and *Gauleiter* of Alsace.

As Reich commissar for the reintegration of the Saarland (*Reichskommissar für die Rückgliederung des Saarlandes*), the previous *Gauleiter* and *Reichsstatthalter* in Vienna, Josef Bürckel, had perfectly prepared the popular referendum on Austria's "annexation" in April 1938. He had been appointed Reich commissar for the reintegration of Austria into the German Reich (*Reichskommissar für die Wiedereingliederung Österreichs in das Deutsche Reich*) on 23 April 1938. Hitler's philosophy in appointing him had been simple: he wanted someone who "even at risk of making himself unpopular" would go "to work with radical resoluteness and without Viennese botchery".[271] In March 1939, Bürckel had taken on the position of *Reichsstatthalter* as well as *Gauleiter* of Vienna and commissar for the defence of the Reich (*Reichsverteidigungskommissar*) in Defence District XVII (*Wehrkreis XVII*). The son of a baker from the southern Palatinate, he was not well received in Vienna however. "This man was completely foreign to us in blood and mind. His ways and even his voice were also completely repugnant to us", the Christian trade unionist and vice mayor of Vienna Lois Weinberger wrote in his memoirs.[272]

Bürckel was particularly brutal in going after Jews, but also those NSDAP functionaries who were considered to be corrupt and embroiled in intrigue and, moreover, had had a bad reputation in Berlin prior to 1938 due to their constant in-fighting. Furthermore, the Austrian NSDAP had also failed in the attempt to launch a putsch against the authoritarian Dollfuss regime, during which the chancellor had been murdered. Hence the mood among many illegal members of the party was correspondingly negative. After discussions during his visit to Vienna on 14 June, Goebbels noted, "Had a long chat with our people. Bürckel is making bad mistakes here in Vienna. A little Palatinate schoolmaster as the successor to the

Habsburgs. That's not enough. The people here are a little unhappy. And rightly so."[273]

Bürckel's task: driving out the Jewish population as quickly as possible via anti-Semitic propaganda; enforcing the state-controlled seizure of property for the benefit of the German Reich; and crushing any oppositional groups from the Dollfuss–Schusnigg regime. He was also to sniff out and crush the few Social Democrat and Communist resistance networks that remained after the chancellors' dictatorships. While the literature speaks of a "Vienna model",[274] I would use the term 'Bürckel model', in which many Austrian National Socialists played a leading role as 'Eichmann men'.

On all leadership levels, Bürckel mainly used National Socialists and experts from the Reich's initial territories (the "Altreich") and employed a firm hand in reorganising the quarrelling NSDAP, for which he received more criticism than for the racially motivated, meticulously organised looting raids. It was here that Schirach went to work, seeking to better integrate the NSDAP's formerly Austrian functionaries and members.

It is remarkable how Schirach presented himself to the Viennese in the context of increasing aversion to party members from the "Altreich": in the biography he compiled for the press, now held in the *Gau* Press Archive in Vienna, he focused on his encounter with Hitler in Weimar in 1925. He also claimed that at the age of sixteen he had experienced the Beer Hall Putsch attempt in Munich in November 1923, which is far from the truth. In fact, his uncle, Friedrich Wilhelm, played a marginal role in the events in Munich. The biography goes on to label Schirach "the Führer's youngest aide" before emphasising his achievements in "revolutionising the youth" and presenting his successes as *Reichsjugendführer* – under the headline "From 40,000 to 10 million members". Almost as much space is dedicated to his literary activities under the heading "Singer and Warrior". "It was no time for literary figures, for poets with no connection to reality or Romantic singers"; rather, what was required was "political poetry" in which the "language of the people" was manifested. Schirach also cleverly mentioned that he had published the poetry anthology *Die Fahne der Verfolgten* (The Flag of the Persecuted), a collection of poems by Austrians who had joined the Hitler Youth illegally.

After a detailed description of his relatively brief time at the front (see Chapter 6), he closed the piece with a clear challenge to the previous regime under Bürckel and declared it his goal to secure "second place" for Vienna within the "new European order". To this end, he also cited Hitler's famous statement from 1938, which in no way reflected the "Führer's" political goals, however: Vienna was not to play a particularly important role among the German cities – quite the contrary:[275]

```
Wie sagte doch Adolf Hitler ?

   "Diese Stadt ist in meinen Augen eine Perle.
    Ich werde sie in jene Fassung bringen,die
    dieser Perle würdig ist, und sie der Obhut
    des ganzen Deutschen Reiches, der ganzen
    deutschen Nation anvertrauen."。
```

[How did Hitler put it? In my eyes, this city is a pearl. I will get it into a state worthy of this pearl, and entrust it to the care of the entire German Reich, the entire German nation.]

After Hitler appointed him *Reichsstatthalter* and *Gauleiter* of Vienna on 7 August 1940, Baldur von Schirach arrived in Vienna and initially took on the role of *Gauleiter* in the Councillors' Hall (*Ratsherrensaal*) in the City Hall. On 10 August, in the Konzerthaussaal (the hall of the Konzerthaus), he was inaugurated as *Reichsstatthalter* of Vienna, with intensive press coverage.[276] The front page of the Vienna edition of the *Völkischer Beobachter* feted him as the successful "Jugendführer", as a "fighter and revolutionary" who had to deal with two pressing problems: the artistic and the social. The article alluded to Bürckel's failure with both issues, which would be solved by the "artist and socialist", as Schirach was labelled.[277]

"My Gau, my Vienna – in my future life, that will be the object of my thoughts and studies, my cares and my loyalty. It is here that I see my new life's work."[278] These were the words with which Baldur von Schirach opened his inaugural speech in the Konzerthaus. He sought to stress the idea of the "Volksgemeinschaft" (people's community) and the importance of the workers for National Socialist Germany. He also declared his "love for this blessed and gifted city with its immeasurable cultural treasures, its proud past and even prouder present".[279]

The handing over ceremony was conducted by the "Führer's" deputy Rudolf Hess, whom Schirach had known since Hitler's visit to his father's house in Weimar. On the one hand, the young Schirach admired Hess as an officer who had served on the front and as a fighter pilot during the First World War, while on the other hand he considered him a "herbal apostle" whose "favourite subjects" were "naturopathy, yoga and health food".[280] Indeed, the "Führer's Deputy" Hess had very little real political influence – when Poland was invaded on 1 September 1939, Hitler named Göring as his first-choice successor in the event of his death, followed only then by Hess. In his very first confidential political speech to *Gauamtsleiter* (regional office leaders) and *Kreisleiter* (district leaders), in the *Gauleiter*'s room in the former parliament building on 14 August, Baldur von Schirach made it clear he would be pursuing a different policy to his predecessor Josef Bürckel, both with respect to his own position and that of the NSDAP in Vienna. He declared he saw the *Reichsstatthalter*'s headquarters on the Ballhausplatz as something of a historical site. He also demonstrated this during later visits to the Ballhausplatz by other NSDAP politicians, telling them he was sitting in the same room Metternich had sat in, next to the hall that had hosted the Congress of Vienna in 1814–15.[281] He declared the parliament building the NSDAP's "Gauhaus" in which he would work on party affairs. At the same time, he announced that he would only fill two staff positions with aides from the "Altreich" – a critical sideswipe at Bürckel, who had taken several "Altreich German" aides with him to Vienna. He addressed unpopular subjects such as housing and coal,[282] and also demanded that criticism of the causes of negative developments in the social and economic spheres be communicated to him directly.

As early as 14 April 1939, Thomas Kozich, the former vice-mayor of Vienna, had informed the "Führer's" office of the reasons for the housing shortage of between 120,000 to 130,000 apartments: there had already been 70,000 too few in 1938, which posed a problem with respect to the 15,000 members of the NSDAP who had fled the Dollfuss and Schuschnigg regime for the "Altreich" before 1936 and now intended to return with their families.[283]

Since the war of aggression meant there were no substantial housing construction programmes, Schirach inherited this problem and Hitler had his secretary, Martin Bormann, tell him in November 1941 that "your job in Vienna [is] not creating new residential quarters, but 'cleaning up' the existing conditions. First, in connection with Reichsführer-SS Himmler, all Jews are to be deported as soon as possible, then all Czechs and other 'alien peoples' ['Fremdvölkischen'] who 'hinder' a uniform political orientation and the shaping of opinion in the Viennese population."[284] Hitler thought this inhumane coercive measure would free up 400,000 to 500,000 apartments for the "Volksgemeinschaft".

Schirach's closest aide in the press sector was *Gebietsführer* Günter Kaufmann, the former head of the *Reichsjugendführung*'s press and propaganda office, whom he made his personal advisor. He also brought Walter Thomas to Vienna. Hitherto head dramaturg of the Städtische Bühnen (Municipal Theatres) in Bochum, Thomas would now serve as his personal aide for all cultural issues.[285] His first choice for this role had been *Reichsdramaturg* Rainer Schlösser, but Goebbels refused to let him go to Vienna.

Along with these new internal signals, he also intensified bilateral contacts. His first visit was to nearby Pressburg (today's Bratislava) in Fascist Slovakia, where he was presented with a public square named "Baldur-von-Schirach-Platz" in his honour on 19 October 1940.[286] He also visited an old acquaintance, Fascist Italy's former youth leader Renato Ricci, now the Italian minister of corporations, and welcomed Joseph Goebbels at Vienna's Ostbahnhof railway station on 26 October 1940.

Goebbels had already sent Schlösser to Vienna in September 1940 to scope out the cultural sector. Schlösser was critical of Bürckel's legacy, but Schirach always praised his predecessor in public. Goebbels wrote in his diary: "Dr Schlösser reports on Vienna: he is glad to be able to return to Berlin soon. Schirach has to proceed very carefully in personnel issues. He very loyally respects the rights of our ministry. [Heinz] Drewes intervenes a little [too] much in the Vienna music scene. He has yet to understand the difference between leadership and administration. Those who want to lead must keep away from the trifles of administration, or they lose the clarity of leadership. Schlösser fulfils the task I have given him with the utmost precision. Vienna is still full of intrigues and departmental vanities. To this end, Schirach has to eradicate the terrible legacy of Bürckel, who left without a single friend in Vienna."[287] Goebbels was subsequently very optimistic, writing that collaboration with Schirach would now work well.[288]

Goebbels, who was very satisfied with the decision to send Schirach to Vienna, had already spoken with Kaufmann in Berlin about his work as head of the Reich Propaganda Office (*Reichspropagandaamt*), itself under Goebbels's command: "He [Kaufmann] is very able and intelligent, but still a little too young. In Vienna he will have a very broad range of duties to fulfil. In particular, he should remove the friction between Berlin and Vienna. He is probably the right man for it. He knows Schirach well, and me fairly well too. He should start, then."[289]

The *Reichspropagandaminister*'s first visit to Schirach, from 16 to 28 October 1940, was all very friendly. Goebbels was visibly enthused when Schirach told him he was sitting in Metternich's old room – although where exactly this room was remains unclear to this day. Goebbels also admired the marble hall in which the Congress of Vienna had taken place and called the "corner" in which "Dollfuss was shot dead" a historical room.[290] In fact, Dollfuss had bled to death on a sofa, since the Nazi putschists had prevented him from receiving medical assistance.

At Kaufmann's inauguration, Goebbels even declared that the Reich Theatre Weeks would now only take place in Vienna. He was just as taken with a Tchaikovsky concert by Wilhelm Furtwängler, the Vienna Philharmonic and the pianist Emil von Sauer as he was with a performance of *Don Giovanni* at the Vienna State Opera staged by Goebbels's new appointment as director, Heinrich Karl Strohm. He was also pleased with his souvenirs, the original score to Johann Strauss's waltz "Frühlingsstimmen" ("Voices of Spring"), a gift from Schirach, and two costume designs by Alfred Roller. The only thing that displeased the all-powerful propaganda minister was Furtwängler's wish to succeed Peter Raabe as president of the Reich Chamber of Music (*Reichsmusikkammer*).

Schirach cleverly used the diverse offerings in the fields of art and culture to impress his guests. Here he could make a much better impression due to his background and upbringing in Weimar, which helped him mend the fissures that had developed between members of the NSDAP from the former Austria and those from the "Altreich" while raising Viennese self-esteem. At the same time, it was also about self-presentation.

Overall, in his first speeches in Vienna Schirach tried to make it clear he had taken note of the criticism of Bürckel's regime on all levels. Hitler himself got his information about the increasing antipathy towards Bürckel, including in NSDAP circles, from a friend of his beloved Eva

Braun, Marianne (Marion) Schönmann, née Petzl (1899–1981).[291] Hailing from Munich and a member of the NSDAP since 1931, "Frau Marion" often visited the Berghof and was also acquainted with Erna, Heinrich Hoffmann's second wife. Her aunt was Luise Perard-Petztl, a famous singer in Vienna and Munich, and her uncle, Dr Arthur Zimmer, was a general practitioner in Vienna. Frau Schönmann repeatedly complained about Bürckel.[292]

A year later, Schirach continued this strategy of showing understanding for his fellow party members in Vienna, unlike Bürckel. In another speech to political leaders, on 5 October 1941, he did this by expressing open criticism of the "disgusting and poor" behaviour of "some Altreich Germans here in this city". He received a "long" ovation when he added, "This city has nothing to learn in this respect; rather, it sets an example. It's political philistines that come here and think they can teach the Reichsgau Wien how you stick with the Führer. These people are, however, isolated cases."[293]

The *Erweiterte Kinderlandverschickung*

On 29 September 1940, Baldur von Schirach was sworn in as *Reichsstatthalter* of Vienna by Hitler in Berlin. Hitler took this opportunity to entrust him with the overall leadership of a programme Martin Bormann had already communicated to all *Gauleiter* in a top secret circular of 27 September, with the aim of sending "the youth from the areas that repeatedly have night-time air raids, on a voluntary basis, to the other areas of the Reich".[294]

The idea of sending children to rural areas was not only to keep them safe from British bombing raids; with the children far away from school and their parents, it would be possible to intensify their re-education along the lines of National Socialist ideology. The *Erweiterte Kinderlandverschickung* ("Extended Relocation of Children to the Countryside", KLV) programme was introduced in October 1940 in the cities of Berlin and Hamburg, which were under the greatest threat of air raids.

In his memoirs, Schirach claimed to have already invented the KLV in 1933. The fact is, however, that children had already been evacuated during the First World War, by the *Reichszentrale Landaufenthalt für Stadtkinder e.V.* (Reich Centre for Urban Children's Rural Stays), from 1916/17 to 1918. Church organisations such as Caritas also played a role here. From 1933 on, the National Socialist People's Welfare (*Nationalsozialistische Volkswohlfahrt*, NSV) sent children to rural areas for six weeks' free recuperation, accompanied by the corresponding propaganda. In 1940, one of the achievements they reported was that 150,000 children had been brought to "rural foster parents" in 1933, while some 350,000 had availed themselves of the opportunity in 1940.[295]

With Schirach's appointment, HJ functionaries took over the overall organisation of the KLV; exceptions were made for children under ten, who remained the remit of the NSV. The programme was headed by the HJ *Stabsführer*, Helmut Möckel, who had also been in charge of building HJ homes since 1937. While the children were initially sent to foster parents, sometimes together with their mothers, increasingly they were accommodated in purpose-built KLV camps, where they would receive provisional schooling in collaboration with the National Socialist Teachers' League (*Nationalsozialistischer Lehrerbund*). What many children have forgotten is the KLV leaders' censorship of correspondence with their parents and the permanent ideological indoctrination by the HJ. The daily schedule was structured accordingly, the core subjects being taught exclusively by teachers increasingly infiltrated by the HJ: "7.00 wake-up call, washing, making the bed, housework, health check; 8.00 flag ceremony or morning roll call; 8.15 breakfast; 8.45–13.00 lessons; 13.00–15.00 lunch, bed rest or leisure time; 15.00–18.00 Hitler Youth service with sport, craftwork, picture book presentation, singing, music, terrain games, hiking etc. An afternoon in the home is held once a week. Otherwise the afternoon and the time after dinner is filled with schoolwork, cleaning and repair hours, and reading and writing hours. 21.00 lights out, ensuring a night's rest of ten hours. On Sundays, [HJ] morning services take place."[296]

After the initial plans were conceived, Schirach became involved mainly with the propaganda effort in order to publicise the programme, which was not without its detractors among the German population. For instance, he held a large press conference in Berlin on 31 March 1941 and an exhibition on "Youth in the Reich" at the Berlin National Gallery on 12 January 1942. What this propaganda didn't mention was that sending children privately to relatives remained just as important and that the

NSV programme continued to run. Around a third of children were sent to KLV camps controlled and organised by the Hitler Youth. Many of them were in the occupied protectorate of Bohemia and Moravia; towards the end of the war, they were mainly in the "Alpengau" and "Donaugau" (Alps and Danube administrative regions) and in Bavaria. In 1944, some 850,000 children and adolescents, boys and girls, lived in KLV camps, where they were taught by 6,800 teachers, under the ideological and organisational control of 4,500 HJ camp staff and BDM leaders. A further 13,000 administrative workers and 2,100 doctors, 1,000 medical assistants and 850 nurses were involved in the campaign.[297] The shortage of HJ leadership staff ultimately prevented a genuinely intensive indoctrination of the children and adolescents beyond the compulsory activities. At the same time, however, it led to excessively tough physical training. The teachers were in control of lessons while the HJ and BDM were in charge of the extracurricular activities.

Schirach's "European Youth Association" and the Idea of a European Hitler Youth

In the late summer of 1942, a mischievous joke did the rounds in Vienna: "Do you know why the tanks on the Volga aren't getting anywhere? – Well, they've had to give up their petrol for Baldur's children's party."[298] The joke gives us a clear picture of what people really thought of the *Reichsstatthalter*'s idea of holding a "European Youth Congress" (*Europäischer Jugendkongress*) and founding a "European Youth Association" (*Europäischer Jugendverband*). Schirach's general cultural advisor Walter Thomas, who compared the events to the "Parallel Action" in Robert Musil's novel *Der Mann ohne Eigenschaften* (*The Man Without Qualities*), was later scathing in his recollection of the pompous preparations: "The impact of this vast machinery sent tremors into the furthest-flung offices of the state and municipal administration and the transport department. For weeks the city shook in the vortex of this gigantic apparatus."[299]

Schirach, however, did not let any of this criticism stop him. He and Axmann steadfastly used their old international networks of Fascist youth organisations throughout Europe. He sought to remain visible in the field of international politics, much to the displeasure of Foreign Minister Joachim von Ribbentrop and the Office of Foreign Affairs. During the

Hitler Youth's winter games in Berlin and Garmisch-Patenkirchen in the late February and early March of 1941, the *Reichsstatthalter* of Vienna and Artur Axmann were already planning to establish a Fascist youth umbrella organisation. The aim was ultimately to deepen National Socialist claims to rule and power in Europe so that they were not simply reduced to military occupation or alliances. The old pre-1939 networks were thus renewed.[300]

Schirach first announced his idea to launch a "European Youth Association" with Fascist Italy and twelve other countries at the fifth HJ summer games in Breslau on 28 August 1941 after Axmann had done the groundwork during discussions with Mussolini in Rome. A year later, between 14 and 18 September 1942, this association was actually formed in Vienna, although it was a loose federation; it neither had an impact on the internal procedures of the national youth organisations nor did it amount to a pan-European union.[301] The official events of the "Congress of Vienna Operetta", as Walter Thomas polemically referred to the Youth Congress, all took place in the *Gauhaus*.

It was impossible to overlook the fact that the foundation of the European Youth Association was accompanied by constant jostling for equal status between the Italian and the German functionaries. It was thus eventually decided to have a joint presidency, held by *Reichsjugendführer* Artur Axmann and the commander general of *La Gioventù italiana del littorio*[302] (GIL), Aldo Vidussoni. Schirach and Minister Ricci were instated as joint honorary presidents.[303]

The head of the Finnish delegation, Probst V. Louhivuori, summed up the association's central common aim: "The view of Europe's youth is being lit up by the harsh reality of war. This and also the brotherhood in arms, consecrated in blood, guarantees that out of the ongoing war there will rise a new Europe which – after the wounds occurring in the war have healed, will offer its peoples a peaceful and happier homeland."[304]

The other representatives also agreed to a military alliance. The new president of the Youth Association, Spanish state youth leader José Antonio Elola-Olaso, pointed to Emperor Karl V as representative of the alliance between Spain and the Holy Roman Empire, and the Japanese imperial emissary Sakuma invoked the "heroic spirit of the Japanese people" and the "Samurai spirit" that would reach its climax in "dying for the people and the fatherland". A high-ranking official of the Ministry of Education in Brussels, the Flemish writer Filip De Pillecyn, pointed to "Flemish youth's struggle for the new educational ideals", and a Dutch professor by the name of Captayn declared in no uncertain terms that Dutch youth, "who professed National Socialism [...]", were looking for "a new worldview". Tido J. Gašpar, the head of the Slovakian propaganda office, also supported the ideal of a community.[305] The national head of Hungarian military youth training, Field Marshall Lieutenant Vitéz Alois von Béldy, underscored the central importance of military national education, while Piero Barlani Dini of the GIL general command pointed to Benito Mussolini's and Adolf Hitler's call to the youth to "conscientiously take up the bloody and holy fight to defend themselves and civilisation".[306] The other allies of the National Socialist regime, such as the Bulgarian state youth, the Brannik, or the Hlinka Youth in Slovakia and representatives of youth organisations from Denmark, Croatia, Norway and Wallonia, argued with similar goals.[307] Portugal, the "Protectorate of Bohemia and Moravia", Latvia and Estonia had sent observers. However, Schirach was unable to attract the leading representatives of the National Socialist regime to Vienna. Nevertheless, Reich Organisational Leader Ley and five *Gauleiter* – Bracht, Hanke, Jury, Bohle und Uiberreither – took part in the opening ceremony, during which Schirach stressed "national consciousness as duty of honour" and declared "youth's new ideal: duty".[308]

At the same time, he launched a racist and anti-Semitic agitation offensive, blaming Jewry for the crisis besetting Europe and above all Germany after the end of the First World War:

> Only those who experienced the terrible time of the Jewish-communist unrest can have any idea of the fate of the youth of the World War. Béla Kun in Hungary, the Munich Soviet Republic of the Jews Eisner and Levine-Nissen, the communist gangs of murderers of a Max Hoelz in Central Germany characterise the development we found ourselves in back then. It was officers of the World War, Freikorps fighters and national heroes who put an end to this spectre. What they did, they accomplished out of a sense of duty to their peoples by obeying the mission of their conscience. Jewry, however, took possession of all instruments serving to influence public opinion, the press, radio and film, and moreover infiltrated all governments of the European states.

For the whole of Europe, the post-war period was an epoch of unscrupulous Jewish moneymaking, a boom time for Jewish trafficking. Back then, Jewry attempted with all available means to spoil the healthy youth. All ideals that are sacred to our continent were publicly besmirched, ridiculed and dismissed as out of time! The corrupt gazettes were full of the Jewish phrase "There is no more stupid an ideal that that of the hero". Instead, boundless freedom in sexual enjoyment was preached to the youth. The greyer everyday life became, the more radiant became the nightlife. The American film and the American revue, created over there by Jews, imported over here by Jews, endlessly appealed to the senses of teenage youth, spoiling them and pulling them into the maelstrom of chaos from which they no longer returned to their nation. Wherever the Jew has tried to corrode a people's national substance, he has done it by arousing the basest instincts, by propagating an untamed greed for sex and disparaging all moral and ethical breeding.

National consciousness is our duty of honour.

What used to sound in the valleys of Provence and to this day has remained the exalted song of Europe and thus its cultured peoples, the song of courtly love as the expression of that higher emotion that distinguishes us from Jews and North American jazz band Negroes can never be understood by people of the Jewish mind. Ethos is alien to the Jew.

The ancient world, that which we understand as Greece and Rome, the Italian Renaissance, German Classicism and Neoclassicism, is so opposed to the Jewish world of feeling that we must quietly profess in these circles: every Jew at large in Europe is a danger to European culture. If one wished to confront me with the accusation that I have deported tens of thousands upon tens of thousands of Jews to the eastern ghetto from this city that was once the metropolis of Jewry, I must answer that I consider it an active contribution to European culture. If you say to me, how can you banish Herr Israel Loewenstein to the ghetto of the east, that means a terrible punishment for this man who has sold over a hundred German books and is thus to be called a pillar of culture, I must retort that for me it would not be a punishment if I were expelled from a foreign country in order to live in another place together with German compatriots or in a purely

German community. I would strive with all means to participate in a transport that leads me as a German to my German brothers.

Can you imagine an Italian, a Hungarian, a Romanian, a Finn, a Slovak, a Croat thinking differently? Is not for all of us – and by this, I mean all nations that do us the honour of gathering here today – our awareness of belonging to our own people's [*völkisch*] community so strong that we would see it virtually as a duty of honour to share happiness and sorrow with the other members of our people, even if we had to give up a lawyer's office or a factory abroad for it? We are simply determined by our national character. The Jew however is international.[309]

I have quite deliberately chosen this long quotation to emphasise the world of anti-Semitic thought in which Schirach developed his ideas of youth and cultural work. He quite openly justified the policy of deporting Jews and declared it the future basis of the new, National Socialist Europe, a Europe without Jews. From a military perspective, the *Wehrmacht* seemed undefeatable, its troops having just reached the Volga south of Stalingrad, while the Africa Corps and Italian troops were 10 kilometres before Egypt's El Alamein.

At the same time, the General Secretariat for the Foundation of the European Youth Association (*Generalsekretariat für die Gründung des Europäischen Jugendverband*) also sought to further mobilise girls for the indirect war effort with an exhibition on "The German Girl in the War" ("Das deutsche Mädel im Kriege").[310] All forces were to be assembled; "total war" was already becoming evident.

And Schirach was already planning for the time after the war: the new Europe was to be under the hegemony of Nazi Germany. This basic premise required justification: national sovereignty within a National Socialist ideological framework. This included anti-Semitism and the destruction of parliamentary democracy, liberalism and Enlightenment thought, to be replaced by the *Führer* principle, dictatorship and nationalistically racist "people's communities" ("Volksgemeinschaften") – excluding Jews and Roma.

At the closing rally in Heldenplatz square, at around 9 p.m. on 18 September 1942[311] and in the presence of the former youth leader Renato Ricci, head of the National Socialist Party Organisation (*Parteiorganisation*)

Robert Ley and SA Chief of Staff Lutze, the new honorary president of the European Youth Association, *Reichsleiter* Baldur von Schirach, declared, "For Adolf Hitler we live, for Adolf Hitler we fight!"

After the official events, many of the approximately 10,000 adolescents spilled into Vienna's lively nightlife. Carl Diem, the former chief organiser of the Berlin Olympics, was openly critical of what went on "behind the scenes" of the militarily correct facades to the HJ events – something that was overlooked by most newspapers, and has also been largely neglected by scholarship:

> Two wagons of flowers, one wagon of geese rolled from Holland to Vienna to 'replace' the youth leaders. The mannequins were invited to dance and the brothels were given police security for the high-ranking guests, but due to the high price of the pleasures [it is said that] there was dissension; no one had a coupon and stamp book for that. For a week, the participants fully enjoyed themselves. The sparkling wine flowed, the geese sizzled [...] Notwithstanding the insults between Hungarians, Romanians and the German middlemen.[312]

Ultimately, the Berlin central offices had disapproved of the meeting before it took place: Ribbentrop tried to prevent foreign statesmen and diplomats from participating, and Goebbels blocked reporting on the conference – at least beyond Schirach's sphere of influence in Vienna. At the ministers' conference of 18 August 1942, he then declared that "the Pimpfe have been wallowing in useless waffle. The minister says the conference in Vienna seemed like a youth carnival."[313]

The propaganda minister also vented his anger with the European Youth Congress to Schirach's close confidant Günther Kaufmann, who complained about the obstruction policy pursued by the Office of Foreign Affairs (*Auswärtiges Amt*): "However, I also let Kaufmann know very forcefully that the new Europe will not be brought about by the blathering of youth leaders in Vienna, but by the fight of the German Wehrmacht, which has reached its dramatic pinnacle."[314]

Goebbels recognised, however, that Schirach had touched on an important subject for ensuring Nazi Germany's dominance over Europe, and hence the propaganda minister also explained his ideas on how to channel the discussion. He considered "two possibilities for Europe's new order, the pan-European, which of course we reject, and the formation of central power that will attract the other states with magnetic force".[315]

While Schirach's concept was along these lines, for Goebbels it was too diffuse and ultimately did not concentrate sufficiently on Nazi Germany via the Italian axis. In Berlin, Schirach was accused of adopting ideological elements of the *Bündische Jugend*[316] and envisaging democratic structures, which was by no means the case, however. On the contrary, he had agreed, for instance, that every nation had a vote and would not be able to hold an annual congress for thirteen years. This equality did not go down well with Hitler and Goebbels, for here Schirach was *de facto* advocating the concept of a "Europe of nations".[317]

Hitler's telegram in response to the greetings from Schirach and Ricci was taciturn in comparison with Mussolini's somewhat flowery phrasing. Around the same time, Hitler had also had Martin Bormann put his chief ideologue Alfred Rosenberg in his place after the latter had mentioned Schirach's event in Vienna and was planning an exhibition on the 'fight for Europe'. Bormann communicated Hitler's firm "No" in a telegram: "the fuehrer has also been precisely informed about the planned exhibition 'fight for europe', he is of the opinion that even quite abstract topics that broach or warm up the topic of europe must be most undesirable to us. Churchill would certainly make use of the topic and content of such an exhibition against germany in no small measure [...]."[318]

If Bormann had known that despite the ban on Rosenberg's Europe exhibition, Schirach had commissioned an exhibition of "European Documents" in the State Hall (*Prunksaal*) of the Austrian National Library on Josefsplatz, it would have been the perfect scandal. With some 200 rare charters and unique books, some brought from the depositories outside of Vienna, where they were kept safe from air raids,[319] the National Library and the State Archive presented a Habsburg history of Europe with elements of greater German or Prussian history, such as a Gutenberg Bible or a letter from King Friedrich II to Emperor Joseph II. In the *Gauhaus*, i.e. the parliament building on the Ring, Professor Drobil and the sculptor Josef Franz Riedl erected a monumental sculpture of "Europe".

The Office of Foreign Affairs not only sought to obstruct the congress, but also ensured Reich Foreign Minister Ribbentrop intervened via

Bormann and Lammers, with a highly classified communiqué by Undersecretary of State (*Unterstaatssekretär*) Martin Luther to envoy Emil von Rintelen dated 14 September 1942.[320] This message, marked "Secret. Personal", also mentioned Schirach by name and criticised Bormann for not having done something about the former's foreign policy escapades. With the European Youth Congress, Schirach had finally pushed things too far, however, and the Reich Foreign Ministry skilfully defended its hegemonial power even against the interests of the party by having Bormann and Lammers read the riot act to the various *Gauleiter* and especially to Schirach

The Hitler Youth's European activities were subsequently banned and by the "Führer's" order of 4 November 1942, all HJ foreign delegates were recalled. The Youth Association no longer pursued any activities to speak of; it seems opposition was too strong or the Office of Foreign Affairs took over initiatives in the field of European politics.

It is probably no coincidence that the files from Schirach's main office held by Vienna's State Archive (*Staatsarchiv*) contain an order from Hitler from this time stating that

> in cultivating relations between states, party offices must never forget that the tenets and knowledge of National Socialist ideology correspond to the essence of German blood and hence cannot be transposed onto foreign peoples [...] Hence the NSDAP and its organisations do not have a European or worldwide mission to fulfil. The domain of foreign policy is not suitable for experiments and personal endeavours.[321]

There were still some isolated instances of contact with Italy in 1943 in relation to a follow-up congress in Italy, but there would never be a second international event. On 8 December 1942, a meeting of the Youth and Family Consortium (*Arbeitsgemeinschaft "Jugend und Familie"*) was held in Madrid, but only around half the nations attended.[322]

After that, Schirach's *Gau* Press Archive only contains one further reference to the European Youth Association: at a reception for Walloon youth leaders given by Schirach and *HJ-Hauptsturmführer* Hans Lauterbacher in late February 1944, the *Reichsleiter* reminded his guests that the association had been formed in Vienna "in awareness of the common fate, comradeship and equality of the youth of the national peoples of our continent". The Walloon youth leaders were looked after by Hans Lauterbacher, who had helped organise the meeting in 1942 and was now in charge of the local leadership of the HJ in Vienna and the related "war tasks of the Hitler Youth".[323] Hans Lauterbacher was the brother of Hartmann Lauterbacher and had most recently seen action on the Eastern Front in 1943, as part of the SS division *Leibstandarte Adolf Hitler*.

A second international initiative under Schirach's patronage is documented for early December 1941: the head of the Reich press, Otto Dietrich, gave an anti-Semitic speech deriding the "Jewish abuse of the news" in England, France and the USA, announcing before press representatives from Germany, Italy, Hungary, Romania, Bulgaria, Slovakia and Croatia the foundation of a Union of National Journalists' Associations (*Union Nationaler Journalistenverbände*) and an "Institute for Research on the International Press" (*Institut zur Erforschung des internationalen Pressewesens*).[324] The *Völkischer Beobachter* in Vienna proudly ran the headline "New press era in the new Europe" – at the same time, a clear message was communicated by the presidium of the new Union, which had made Maximilian du Prel, head of the NSDAP Party Press Office (*Amt Parteipresse der NSDAP*), its general secretary: the Union "sent its special greetings to all those journalists who stand at the front, weapon in hand in the fight against the democratic and Bolshevik world enemy. The responsible journalists who have banded together in the Union see in these editor-soldiers the valiant champions of their journalistic ideals."[325]

The reduced National Socialist idea of Europe was thus clearly defined – Nazi Germany, Italy and the Axis states formed the "new Europe". Ultimately, it was not about a free professional press, but propaganda for victory in the war. As early as April 1942, some 300 journalists from fifteen countries were accepted into the Union in Venice, Spain and occupied Norway.

The same year, Schirach then made prestigious venues available for these international activities, and hence the Union of National Journalists' Associations convened in Palais Schönborn, the former Palais Batthyány, at Renngasse 4 in the centre of Vienna. The president of the Union was *SA-Obergruppenführer* Wilhelm Weiß, editor-in-chief of the *Völkischer*

Beobachter. Around the same time, an Institute for Newspaper Studies (*Institut für Zeitungswissenschaften*) was established at the University of Vienna.[326]

These two "European" associations quickly became intertwined. Giuseppe Tassinari heralded the European Youth Association's inaugural event with the headline "Youth and press in one front", claiming that "the anti-Bolshevist and anti-democratic press of the new Europe, which believes in victory and is fighting for more social justice, finds its better part in the youth".[327]

This union of "editor-soldiers" was subsequently able to win over the Office of Foreign Affairs, and hence at the second conference in Vienna in 1943 a telegram of support was read out by Paul Schmidt, Foreign Minister Ribbentrop's close aide and translator. This time, the anti-Semitic agitation was voiced by the chief press officer of the royal Bulgarian press service, Envoy Serafimoff, who pointed out that the Bulgarian press had been "free of Jews" for almost a hundred years.[328]

The European Youth Association also responded predictably swiftly, making its logo an allegory of Europe riding a bull. In a joint statement, they attacked the USA under the headline "Europe's youth's answer to Roosevelt", with brief propaganda statements by the youth movements from Belgium (both the Flemish and the Walloon representatives), Croatia, the Netherlands, Norway and France.[329]

The Crafty Turncoat: Colin Ross

Baldur von Schirach had already met the renowned travel writer, filmmaker and speaker Dr Colin Ross (often spelt Roß) in 1933.[330] Ross travelled the world with his wife, Dr Lisa Ross (née Peter) and their children, daughter Renate (born 1915) and son Ralph Colin (born 1923), reporting on his adventures using all available media.[331] Between 1910 and 1945, he published around 1,200 newspaper and magazine articles, wrote thirty-five books, made six films and gave several talks.[332] He had served in the military as a one-year volunteer in the Bavarian Field Artillery, after which he began to study engineering and hut-building in Berlin before finally opting for national economics and history in Munich and Heidelberg.

He made his name as a journalist with his reports from the Balkan War between the Ottoman Empire and Bulgaria in 1913, and after a sojourn in the Mexican Civil War in 1913 he continued his journalistic career during the First World War, not only publishing, but also serving as a first lieutenant (*Oberleutnant*) on the Russian front, where he was wounded. He subsequently worked for the propaganda department of the Supreme Army Command (*Oberste Heeresleitung*). In 1918–19, with the revolutionary turn from the Empire to the Weimar Republic, he tried his hand as a military advisor at the highest level. After a brief stint in the Executive Council (*Vollzugsrat*) of the Workers' and Soldiers' Soviets (*Arbeiter- und Soldatenräte*) and a failed attempt to build a career in the young republic, he emigrated to South America, launching his journalistic career as a travel writer, initially via newspaper articles on South America. He also had great success as a travel filmmaker, shooting with a Bamberg-Askania camera; one of his notable successes was *Mit dem Kurbelkasten um die Erde* (Around the World With a Movie Camera, 1926). Some of his films were produced by the German UFA studios and were well received by the public. He had taken a stance against the political parties and parliamentary democracy as early as 1919, but following a trip through Switzerland, France, Spain and Great Britain in September 1931, he published very subtly formulated totalitarian political ideas in his book *Der Wille der Welt* (The Will of the World). Shortly before Hitler took power, in an unpublished manuscript, on which his wife Lisa also worked, he was already developing specific ideas of a totalitarian, national German dictatorship, but also expressed his hopes for a pan-Europe dominated by Germany and France.[333] The NSDAP played a leading role in his vision, but he hoped a unified party uniting all political wings would establish a national dictatorship. In November 1933, he reported from Chicago to his political mentor, the retired general and geopolitical expert Karl Haushofer, who made him acquainted with the NSDAP elite, that he was striving for a "world philosophy of National Socialism".[334]

Colin Ross met with Schirach in 1933, and they were next-door neighbours in Munich from 1945 onwards. In 1937, Ross worked on a German–French exchange with the Hitler Youth, in which his fourteen-year-old son, Ralph Colin, also participated. Both Hitler and French president Albert Lebrun received the respective groups of twenty-one adolescents from Germany and France.

At Schirach's invitation, Ross took part in the *Reichsführer* Congress (*Reichsführertagung*) in Weimar in 1937, and in his newspaper article on the event he went so far as to compare Schirach with Goethe, albeit indirectly:

> "I feel it is as if the old Goethe were standing at the palace window looking down on us", said Baldur von Schirach.
> "No, for me it's the young Goethe", says the pretty girl next to him heading Germany's Mädelschaft [the smallest unit of the BDM – O.R.] ...
> "They're both right", I am compelled to think, the man and the girl. They are among us, the old and the young Goethe.[335]

Around this time, he also reported on Buchenwald concentration camp, justifying the strict incarceration of political opponents, calling it a "political necessity".[336]

A year later, in 1938, Ross met the new foreign minister, Joachim von Ribbentrop, and tried to persuade him to support the German-American societies, arguing that the "racial idea" was becoming increasingly important in the USA too. He also attempted to win diplomatic and financial support for a tour of America he was planning. Ernst Wallenberg, the former editor-in-chief of the *B.Z. am Mittag* (Berlin Midday Newspaper) who as a Jew had been forced to flee Germany for the USA, described Ross – in my opinion most accurately – as a political opportunist:

> This man rides always with the wind, and he changed from democracy in 1918 to communism, denying his officers qualification, emphasising the same in 1932, changing from hundred percent pro-jewish to hundred percent antisemitic, as you will see by this impudent article about New York. [337]

In several talks, Ross cannily defended National Socialism and Adolf Hitler, and justified the anti-Jewish policy of the "Third Reich". He was even able to obtain an appointment with Hitler in the New Reich Chancellery for 12 March 1940 in order to present to him his geopolitical ideas on the basis of his book *Unser Amerika* (Our America).[338] In a marketing coup, he had his visit to the "Führer" announced in the newspapers.[339] Completely overestimating the interests and opportunities of the German immigrants, he believed the German organisations in the USA represented an influential lobby. At the same time, he tried to divert Hitler's strategic focus on Great Britain to the USA; his theory was that intensified immigration by Jews from Germany and Europe would strengthen anti-Semitism in America. Meanwhile, he thought, Germany should accept the US's sphere of influence in the West and give off the right signals to ensure that the US would accept German domination of Central Europe. In this conversation, Hitler also hinted that in his inhumane conception, he actually considered the "Jewish question" a "problem of space" and that he thought there was not sufficient available for the then policy of deportation and ghettos.[340] This was a clear statement by Hitler indirectly signalling the next step, the Shoah, which Ross did not realise at the time, however.

Even Goebbels was enthusiastic after speaking with Ross about his North African tour in 1942, describing him in his diary as a "very astute and objective observer".[341] He rejected Ross's assessment that the USA's military strength would decide the war. For Goebbels, it would be decided by the campaign against the Soviet Union, but he wanted to use Ross more for National Socialist propaganda in neutral countries. A few weeks later, at *Reichsstatthalter* Schirach's invitation, Ross spoke to the political *Führerkorps* (Leader Corps) in Vienna, presenting Africa as "Europe's supplementary space" and a "reserve of raw materials and space".[342] He also attacked the USA and Roosevelt and again spoke of the danger the USA posed to Nazi Germany.

At Schirach's European youth congress of 1942, Colin Ross spoke at the Academy of Sciences on 16 September on the subject of "Tomorrow's World", changing his geostrategic thesis. Now the threat to the National Socialist "Greater Europe" was not from the Asian peoples such as the Japanese or the Chinese, but from the "peoples of the Central Asian steppe, the Bolshevists".[343] His usual anti-Semitic polemic against the USA and his racist, hierarchical ideas were stressed by the Vienna edition of the *Völkischer Beobachter*:

> Colin Roß [sic] then characterised the essence of the triangle Roosevelt–Churchill–Stalin as exponents of materialism, touched

on the fateful role of Jewry in this context and continued, "The new world is dawning like the new day. It will bring a natural hierarchy of the races and peoples and, in its framework, of the groups and individuals. The emergence of this hierarchy can already be clearly recognised as fate today. It is this from this that follows the course of British world rule and the failure of the attempt to replace it with Bolshevist or American [rule]."[344]

Ross increasingly saw himself as a propaganda warrior of National Socialism. The death of his son Ralph Colin during the invasion of the Soviet Union in 1941 did nothing to change this: the young soldier was struck by lightning. The same year, Colin Ross joined the NSDAP. In 1943, he became the head of the Office of Foreign Affairs' America Committee. On 23 July 1943, he presented his "Campaign Plan for the Ideological War" (*Feldzugsplan für den ideologischen Krieg*).[345] He repeatedly portrayed himself as an ideological pioneer of National Socialism and ultimately interpreted the war as an ideological conflict.

According to Schirach, in 1944 Ross had privately discussed the persecution and annihilation of Jews with him after Schirach seemed to sense the extent of the genocide against Europe's Jewish population following the Posen conference of *Reichsleiter* and *Gauleiter* and Himmler's speech at this meeting. In 1946, during the Nuremberg trials, he claimed that Ross wanted to develop a memorandum on the emigration of all Hungarian Jews and discuss its submission to Hitler with Foreign Minister Ribbentrop – a claim for which there is no written evidence, however.

In the interviews with Jochen von Lang, Schirach presented a different version, again referring to his alleged conversation with Ross in 1944: he proposed that all Jews in the area under German rule be "offered [...] to the American president" via the Red Cross.[346] In his memoirs, Schirach then gave a third response to Himmler's speech of 1944. Ross was outraged, saying, "We must take control of the Führer's person, the man is crazy."[347] According to Schirach, his one-to-one attempts to persuade Göring to organise a coup failed.

Shortly before Germany capitulated, Ross, like Hitler, Goebbels and many other Nazi functionaries, saw suicide as the only way out. On 29 April 1945, he and his wife took cyanide capsules in the Schirachs' wooden hut in Urfeld am Walchensee, where they had lived after their apartment in Munich's Königstrasse was destroyed. He then shot his wife and himself. Presumably he feared retribution by Allied soldiers.[348] The physicist Werner Heisenberg, the Nobel Prize winner of 1932, and his wife Elisabeth, who had also taken refuge in Urfeld and were friends of the Rosses, took leave of the dead:

> The bodies are stretched out in the living room in which we had visited them on occasion, wrapped in canvas up to their faces. Colin Ross's face looks very angular and yet calm and peaceful. This face made a deep impression on me, but in general this time is so full of tension and events that even death no longer moves me much.[349]

The private meetings that took place between Ross and Schirach from 1933/34 on are not well documented. As far as the portrayal of the Ross family in Henriette von Schirach's memoirs is concerned, they display what one might call strategic gaps in her memory with respect to their close personal ties, for instance regarding the alleged origins of Ross's wife Lisa. Whether Baldur von Schirach deliberately perpetuated the false rumour that she was of Jewish descent can only be presumed, not proven. Schirach was certainly fascinated by worldly and clearly racist ideological assessments voiced by Colin Ross, who always enthused about the superiority of the "white race" in his various pieces of travel writing. In his speeches and texts about the USA, German immigration took on a disproportionately important and positive position, as outlined above. This portrayal too perfectly fitted the family history of the Schirachs, who wished to be known as Germans despite the fact that several family members had emigrated to the USA.

Katharina Dobbs, Schirach's Secret Lover

Everyone who might have known about her discreetly remained silent, but she existed nevertheless: his lover. She can be traced via the memoirs of the Holocaust survivor and director Imo Moszkowicz (1925–2011), the son-in-law of the Styrian *Gauhauptmann* (*Gau* governor) Armin Dadieu, who made her acquaintance in South America after the war:[350]

> There was no way of knowing that in Chile I would encounter the former adjutant to Hermann Göring[351] and the former lover of Baldur

von Schirach. Katharina Dobbs played Marion and was a thoughtful friend who later called me to Brazil to found the German-language artists' theatre pro Arte São Paulo, which I then ran.

Katharina Dobbs, born in Rottenmann in Styria on 7 December 1920, was the daughter of Käthe Dobbs, née von Kaler Laurenheim, and her first husband, William Dobbs, who died in 1926. Her mother had studied acting at Vienna's Reinhardt Seminar in 1931–32. In 1934, Käthe married the administrator (*Verwaltungsrat*) Wilhelm Künstler, a qualified engineer from Aussig an der Elbe, after appearing in the Burgtheater and playing a supporting role during the Salzburg Festival.

Between 1941 and 1943, her daughter, Katharina Dobbs, studied acting at the State Academy of Music and Performing Arts (*Staatsakademie für Musik und darstellende Kunst*) in Vienna.[352] In 1943, she won a bit part as Countess Clementine von Roggenbühl in the film version of Richard Billinger's play *Gabriele Dambrone* and made her debut at Linz's Landestheater in August 1943 as Hero in Franz Grillparzer's *Des Meeres und der Liebe Wellen* (*The Waves of the Sea and of Love*). After the premiere, the music reporter,[353] who attested to her "unpretentious and internalised acting and expressive performance", referred not only to her education at the "Schönbrunn Seminar" and the Ackermann School in Berlin, but also to the fact that she had been a "full-time BDM leader". In 1943, the young actress spent a lot of time in Berlin, where she took an exam at the *Reichstheaterkammer* (Reich Theatre Chamber) and played Janthe in the same play by Grillparzer at the Berlin State Theatre. In 1944, she temporarily lived in Pfullingen, at Klostergarten 28. After 1945, she surfaced at Tübingen's Städtisches Schauspielhaus (Municipal Theatre), now under the name of Katharina Dobbs. In 1945 she bore a son, Christoph, to her first husband Egon Keutmann, adjutant to *Reichsmarschall* Hermann Göring. On 28 February 1948, she arrived in Buenos Aires by ship.[354] At this point she was already divorced, however. She later married two more times and died in Cologne.[355]

Further confirmation of Imo Moszkowicz's tip that Katharina Dobbs was Baldur von Schirach's lover came to light in a conversation with Christine von Unruh. The fact is that her acting career took on a very steep trajectory during the final phase of National Socialism – everything indicates that the aspiring actress enjoyed benevolent support behind the scenes.

Chapter 8

The "Special Action"

The Deportation and Murder of Vienna's Jewish Population

As head of the civil administration entrusted with dealing with the housing shortage, Baldur von Schirach undoubtedly knew all about the deportation of Vienna's remaining Jews. At a private dinner for the governor general of the Polish territories, Hans Frank, in Hitler's Berlin apartment on 2 October 1940, at which Schirach, *Gauleiter* Koch and Martin Bormann were also present, Frank reported on the Jewish policy in the "Generalgourvenement" (General Governate). The minutes of the meeting, taken by Martin Bormann, established that Schirach "remarked that he still had more than 50,000 Jews in Vienna whom Dr. Frank would have to take over. Party Member Dr. Frank said this was impossible."[356] In the end, he was overruled during this conversation and had to take in more Jews from Vienna.

Two months after this meeting, Hitler gave one of his very few direct orders with respect to the persecution of Jews: on 3 December 1940, the head of the Reich Chancellery, Reich Minister Heinrich Lammers, informed Schirach of the deportation order. Schirach himself had already been keen to get on with it, as demonstrated by Lammers' correspondence.

The documents put before Schirach during the Nuremberg trials also prove that his office received a constant flow of information about the deportation and murder of Vienna's Jewish population, including from Reinhard Heydrich. His response was that he had not taken note of the documents in question, or he would have signed them:

> MR. DODD: Now take a look at Document 3921-PS, which becomes USA-872. Now this is a communication concerning the evacuation of Jews, and it shows that 50,000 Jews were to be sent to the Minsk-Riga area, and you got a copy of this report as the Commissar for the Defense of the Reich, and if you will look on the

last page you will see an initial there of your chief assistant, the SS man Dellbrügge, and also the stamp of your own office as having received it.

VON SCHIRACH: I can only see that Dr. Dellbrügge marked the matter for filing. It shows the letters "z.d.A." to the files.

MR. DODD: And he did not tell you about this report concerning the Jews? Even though you had been talking to Hitler about it? That they were being moved out of your area? I suppose your chief assistant did not bother to tell you anything about it. Is that what you want us to understand?

VON SCHIRACH: Yes.

MR. DODD: Now then, take a look at another document which will shed some light on this one. It is USA-808, already in evidence. It tells you what happened to the Jews in Minsk and Riga, and this was also received in your office if you recall. Maybe it is not necessary to show it to you again. You remember the document – that is one of those monthly reports from Heydrich wherein he said that there were 29,000 Jews in Riga and they had been reduced to 2,500, and that 33,210 were shot by the special unit, and "Einsatz" group. Do you remember that?

VON SCHIRACH: During the last 2 days I looked at these monthly reports most carefully. The bottom right-hand corner of the cover of these monthly reports – and I want to make this categorically clear – bears initials something like "Dr. FSCH.," that is Dr. Fischer's initials. At the top the reports are not initialed by me, but by the Government President, with the notation that they should be put into the files. If I had read them …

MR. DODD: I am not suggesting that you had your initials on any document like this, but I am claiming that these documents came into your organization and into the hands of your principal assistant.

VON SCHIRACH: But I must point out that if they had been submitted to me, then there would have been on them the notation, "submitted to the Reichsleiter," and the official submitting them would have initialed this notation. If I myself had seen them, then my own initials would be on them with the letters "K.g.," noted.

MR. DODD: Yes. I want to remind you that the date of that report is February 1942, and I also want to remind you that in there as well Heydrich tells you how many Jews they had killed in Minsk.[357]

According to Wilhelm Bienenfeld, a survivor from the Council of Elders of the Jewish Community of Vienna (*Israelitische Kultusgemeinde Wien*), it was clear that Schirach knew full well what was going on:

> That Schirach must have known about all these orders is already evident in the fact that people went to him to intervene, albeit almost always without success. At any rate, it is certain that all the measures in the area of emigration to the West and the deportations to Poland were only begun under Schirach and were conducted under his aegis. I consider it a matter of course that he had to know about these measures because every child in Vienna saw and knew; the transport of Jews to Poland took place quite openly in public. The carts stood before the houses while the designated people conducted the transport. Every passer-by saw this. How the people then fared in Poland and what happened to them was also known in Vienna. Of course, people tried to alleviate the fate of those sent away by intervening, all the way up to the Reichsstatthalter. The truth is, however, that we could not get through to the Reichsstatthalter because of course he refused to speak to Jews.[358]

In his memoirs, Schirach corrected his assertion during the Nuremberg trials that he had first heard about the genocide against the Jews from Colin Ross,[359] pointing to Himmler's second Posen speech before the *Reichsleiter* and *Gauleiter* of 6 October 1943, although he wrongly dated it to 29 May 1944.[360] Here, Himmler made no bones about the murder of European Jewry in its entirety:

> I ask you really to only hear what I say to you in this circle and never to speak about it. We were faced with the question: what is the situation with the women and children? – I have decided to find a

perfectly clear solution here too. Namely, I did not consider myself authorised to exterminate the men – that is, to kill them or have them killed – and allow the avengers in the form of the children to grow up for our sons and grandsons. The difficult decision had to be made to make this people vanish from the face of the earth. For the organisation that had to carry out the mission, it was the hardest we had to date. [...] I considered it my duty to speak to you openly as the supreme decision-makers, as the supreme dignitaries of the party, of the political order, of this political instrument of the Führer, and tell you what was done. – The Jewish question in the countries occupied by us will be dealt with by the end of this year. Only a few remaining individual Jews who have gone into hiding will be left.[361]

In fact, Schirach had already learnt of the genocide campaigns during a speech behind closed doors by the *Gauleiter* of the "Wartheland", Arthur Greiser, to the *NS-Führerkorps* (Leader Corps) of the Vienna *Gau* on 12 May 1942. This speech in the Great Assembly Hall of the *Gauhaus* in Vienna took almost an hour and forty minutes. Ten days earlier, Greiser had reported to Himmler that around 100,000 Jews had been killed under his remit.[362] Here I quote for first time from Greiser's previously undiscovered speech, held in the *NS-"Gaupresse"-Archiv* at the library of the Department of Contemporary History at the University of Vienna:[363]

The "Special Action" 103

Nun werden Sie mit Recht fragen, warum heute in dem Ghetto und auch ausserhalb, nur mehr so wenig Juden sind, und da sage ich Ihnen als Nationalsozialist : Diese Frage kann ich in einem solchen Kreis nicht im einzelnen beantworten. Ich kann sie nur dahingehend beantworten, dass die Juden selbstverständlich auch weniger werden, bis auf die 45.000, die tatsächlich arbeiten – und die Wiener Juden, die wir in der Zwischenzeit bekommen haben, die haben auch bereits den Arbeitseinsatz gesehen. Ich kann Ihnen versichern, dass Ihre ehemaligen Mitbürger dieser schönen Stadt in der Zwischenzeit sehr gut gelernt haben, Strohschuhe – das sind Postenschuhe für unsere Wehrmacht – und andere schöne Dinge zu machen. Ein Teil von ihnen wollte durchaus nicht im Ghetto bleiben, weil es ihnen dort nicht gefallen hat und wollten sich mit ihrem Judengott besser stellen und aussöhnen, und wir haben auch dazu die Hand geboten und haben........(Grosse Heiterkeit und starker Beifall)

[Now you will quite rightly ask why there so few Jews left today in the ghetto and outside it too, and here I say to you as a National Socialist: I cannot answer this question in such a circle in detail. I can only answer by saying that the Jews there are of course becoming fewer [in number], down to the 45,000 who actually work – and the Viennese Jews we have received in the meantime, they too have already been put to work. I can assure you that your former fellow citizens of this beautiful city have in the meantime learnt very well to make straw shoes – these are sentry shoes for our Wehrmacht – and other nice things. Some of them did not want to stay in the ghetto at all, because they didn't like it there, and they wanted to be better situated and make their peace with their Jew god, and we gave them a hand with that and … (Great amusement and strong applause)]

In his Vienna address, Arthur Greiser left no one in any doubt that of the 800,000 Jews originally interned in the Litzmannstadt ghetto, only the 45,000 slaves were to remain alive. In the first part of his speech, he had already unequivocally given the reasons for the subjugation and persecution of the approximately 3.6 million Poles. A few days earlier, he had written to Himmler to propose killing 35,000 Poles infected with tuberculosis after confirming the "special treatment" of around 100,000 Jews.[364] Himmler rejected his proposal, however.[365]

While Schirach mentions a disconcerting speech by Greiser in interview with the journalist and writer Jochen von Lang, the transcript of the previously unpublished speech documenting the loud laughter and strong applause of the *NS-Führercorps* tells a different story: the party members in Vienna were most entertained by Greiser's cynical performance. Nor is there any evidence supporting his claims that he verbally instructed Dellbrügge to reduce the capacity of the deportations, since the death transports from Vienna towards Minsk and Izbica continued without interruption.[366] Between November 1941 and October 1942, a total of 10,000 were deported in ten transports from Vienna to the village of Maly Trostinets outside Minsk, under agonising conditions, before being shot in the nearby Blagovchina woods or murdered in gas cars. Only seventeen survived. More Austrians were killed here during the Shoah than at any other site. In 2019, a monument bearing the names of the victims was erected as the result of a Viennese private initiative led by Waltraud Barton. This initiative took more than ten years to push through.

Baldur von Schirach's closest colleague in the administrative sector was Vienna's government president *SS-Brigadeführer* (Brigadier) Hans Dellbrügge (1902–82), a lawyer from the Reich Ministry of the Interior who had gained experience as *Hauptabteilungsleiter* (chief departmental leader) in the *Reichskommissariat Norwegen* (Reich Commissariat for Norway) in 1940. In 1944, Dellbrügge wrote to the head of the Reich Security Main Office (*Reichssicherheitshauptamt*) Ernst Kaltenbrunner requesting Hungarian Jews for "essential war work in the city of Vienna". Mayor Hanns Blaschke, also an *SS-Brigadeführer*, intervened and persuaded Kaltenbrunner to send "several evacuation transports" to Vienna/Strasshof:

> [...] At the moment it is a question of four transports with approximately 12,000 Jews. They will reach Vienna within the next few days.
>
> According to previous experience it is estimated that 30 percent of the transport will consist of Jews able to work, approximately 3,600 in this case, who can be utilized for the work in question, it being understood that they are subject to removal at any time. It is obvious that these people must be assigned to work in large, well-guarded groups, and accommodated in secured camps, and this is an absolute prerequisite for making these Jews available.
>
> The women and children of these Jews who were unable to work, and who are all being kept in readiness for a special action and therefore one day will be removed again, must stay in the guarded camp during the day too [...][367]

The term "special action" ("Sonderaktion") used in this communiqué represented an SS code word for the murder of women and children who were unfit for work. After Berlin had given the green light, in the summer of 1944 a total of 15,011 Jewish men, women and children were moved from the Debrecen "wagon loading hub" to Strasshof. The journey to the Marchfeld took several days and was hell for the people crammed into the cattle wagons. There were 80 to 100 men to a wagon with nothing but two buckets: one containing water, the other for nature's call. The terrors of the journey were followed by those of the "transit camp" (*Durchgangslager*, DULAG) in Strasshof. The wooden barracks were packed, there wasn't sufficient food and the sick had to lie on the ground in the open air. After the war, the doctor Charlotte Wieser told the People's Court (*Volksgericht*) in Vienna about the terrible conditions:

> When we arrived in Strasshof, we were immediately driven into the disinfection [unit]. Since all of our clothes and our entire belongings were taken away, we had to march around stark naked before the SS all day.[368]

As Dellbrügge and Blaschke had planned, the *Gau* labour office (*Gauarbeitsamt*) sent the Hungarian Jews to various companies, commercial enterprises and farms as a labour force. Strasshof, which would be liberated by the Red Army on 10 April 1945, became a hub for the "distribution" of Hungarian Jewish forced labourers. Only around 3,000 survived the nightmare.

While in Nuremberg Schirach could not remember reading the reports on the murder of Jews, his memory was very precise concerning a statement by *Reichsführer-SS* Heinrich Himmler in the late March of 1945. On the morning of 28 March 1945, Himmler had arrived in Vienna by chartered train to make sure everything was in order. He gathered the officers of the *Waffen-SS* in the police headquarters (*Polizeipräsidium*) for a final roll call, urging them to continue to "trust" in the "Führer" and to stand to the last man. Secretly, however, the *Reichsführer-SS* had another aim in mind: he was already thinking about negotiating with the Western Allies; to this end, he needed hostages. And so he summoned Franz Ziereis, the commandant of Mauthausen, and the heads of Mauthausen's individual sub-camps in the Vienna region and instructed them to collect all remaining Jews within their jurisdictions – this applied particularly to the Hungarian Jews who had been put to work building the fortifications of the "South-east Wall" (*Südostwall*). This was the name Nazi propaganda gave to a system of defences that were supposed to run from the White Carpathians to the River Drava. Construction began in 1944; tens of thousands were put to work: civilians pressed into duty, most of them senior citizens; members of the Hitler Youth, foreign workers; prisoners of war; and Hungarian Jewish forced labourers. At the trial, Schirach cited Himmler relatively accurately, claiming he had said, "I want the Jews now employed in industry to be taken by boat, or by bus if possible, under the most favourable food conditions and with medical care, *et cetera*, to Linz or Mauthausen." He claims Himmler told Franz Ziereis, "Please take care of these Jews and treat them well; they are my most valuable assets."[369] What Schirach didn't mention was that concurrently, the order remained to prevent any Jews from falling into hands of the Red Army alive.[370] Himmler's order thus had terrible consequences: thousands died on the death marches to Mauthausen.

Although Schirach had often bragged about deporting Vienna's remaining Jews in 1942, in Nuremberg in 1946 he held Hitler, Himmler, the SS and the Reich Security Main Office (*Reichssicherheitshauptamt*) solely responsible. At the same time, he again claimed that he had instructed his adjutant or an assistant, such as General Cultural Advisor

(*Generalkulturreferent*) Walter Thomas, to intervene by contacting the responsible *SS-Hauptsturmführer*, Alois Brunner, "so that possibly an exception might be made for these persons". He said he had not been able to do any more, since he had assumed this transport was in the "interests of Jewry".[371]

If we consider individual cases, these interventions of Schirach's seem somewhat ambivalent. For instance, the Burgtheater actress Margarethe Dux, née Bernhuber, attempted to persuade Schirach's general cultural officer, Walter Thomas, to prevent the deportation of her Jewish stepmother, Fanny Dux. "Liquidator" Alois Brunner[372] was outraged at the request, but let Schirach decide whether she should remain in Vienna or be forced to "move place of residence"[373] to the Theresienstadt ghetto. Fanny Dux, a teacher, was ultimately deported to Theresienstadt, where she died in 1943 aged sixty-five.

In another case, the conductor Josef Krips, stigmatised as a half-Jew and banned from performing, approached Schirach at the recommendation of SS man and chairman of the Vienna Philharmonic Wilhelm Jerger, requesting permission to leave the country in order to continue his career abroad. Schirach rejected the request, however, and referred Krips to the Reich Chamber of Culture (*Reichskulturkammer*).[374] Other efforts to intervene on Krips' behalf were also in vain, despite being made by the NSDAP member Franz Schütz, who had "Aryanised" the Academy of Music and Performing Arts (*Akademie für Musik und darstellende Kunst*), and the conductor Clemens Krauss, held in particularly high regard by Hitler. Josef Krips had to work in a munitions factory until the end of the war and gave private classes for singers to make ends meet.

Although Schirach was patron of the Vienna Philharmonic, he did not lift a finger to prevent the deportation of five retired and highly regarded members of the orchestra – Armin Tyroler, Viktor Robitschek, Max Starkmann, Moritz Glattauer and Julius Stwertka. Chairman Jerger, an SS man who had himself been an illegal member of the NSDAP, wrote to Schirach's general cultural officer Walter Thomas requesting that the artists be made exempt from deportation – without success.[375] All five were deported and became victims of the Shoah.

There is only a single case in which there is evidence of a great effort on the part of Schirach: that of Alice Strauss, née Grab-Hermannswörth, the Jewish daughter-in-law of the then most important living German composer, Richard Strauss. On 12 November 1941, she had already completed her application for a German passport in Vienna, where she lived with her husband. The *Reichsstatthalter* in Vienna wrote to the Reich Minister of the Interior on 12 January 1942 seeking an "exemption approval for Frau Alice Sara Strauss", meaning her passport would not be stamped with a red "J" stigmatising her as a Jew.[376] His request was turned down just four days later, since Hitler did not wish for there to be any exemptions from the Nuremberg Laws. The attempt by local Government President Hans Dellbrügge to obtain an identification card for Alice Strauss without the letter "J" in Vienna was also unsuccessful. Their children, Richard and Christian, however, had been exempted by order of the "Führer" on 22 April 1941. In January 1944, Franz and Alice Strauss were arrested by Gestapo officers and interrogated in Hotel Metropol, the feared Gestapo headquarters in Vienna. They were released two days later after Schirach intervened (via Walter Thomas).[377] In his memoirs, Walter Thomas recalled how Richard Strauss suffered under the terror against his family, who were treated as if they were "lepers".[378]

Richard Strauss was eternally grateful to Schirach for his extensive support and described him in conversation with Klaus Mann, son of Thomas, as "an unusually decent chap".[379]

Chapter 9

Slave Labour

A Visit to Mauthausen Concentration Camp and Economic Measures

Baldur von Schirach's ambition was not just limited to continuing his foreign policy plans from his time as *Reichsjugendführer* on the European level; he also attempted to make his role in Vienna more important by establishing economic networks. This area in particular is usually dealt with in cursory fashion by the literature on Schirach, but it is an important factor. Schirach himself ignored the subject in his memoirs. The main instrument for his Central European economic strategies was the South-eastern European Company (*Südosteuropa-Gesellschaft*, SOEG) founded by his predecessor Josef Bürckel on 10 March 1940. Under the patronage of Reich Economics Minister Walther Funk, the SOEG was dedicated to the "maintenance and expansion of the economic and cultural relations between Germany and the South-eastern European States, with a particular focus on the interests of the Ostmark and the City of Vienna".[380] It received starting capital of one million Reichsmark, some of it from the fortune[381] of the German Club (*Deutscher Klub*), an anti-Semitic, German nationalist and ultimately National Socialist elite network disbanded in 1938,[382] but also from other sources.

In the early years, Schirach used the Vienna Autumn Trade Fair in particular to pass public comment on issues relating to economic policy and to invite well-known personalities to Vienna. One such figure was Walther Funk, who gave a major speech in the *Konzerthaussaal* (Konzerthaus Hall) on 1 September 1940. Schirach clearly signalled that he sought to raise Vienna's economic importance – alluding, in this respect, to the city's significance for the Habsburg Empire, but only indirectly, since the monarchy was anathema to the National Socialists: "Due to the laws of its natural location, this city has always strived for a large economic region, booming when there were no barriers to its urge for activity, sinking into misery when the gate to the South-east was slammed shut or the north-western road to the empire's centre was closed."[383]

In Berlin's Hotel Kaiserhof, Vienna's mayor Hermann Neubacher had already stressed the super-regional importance of the Vienna Trade Fair and the participation by Turkey, Italy, Switzerland, the Netherlands, the Nordic states and Hungary, Romania and Bulgaria.[384] Taking up this line, the *Reichsstatthalter* claimed to be making a contribution to the "coming Europe", exploiting the coincidental presence of foreign guests; the Autumn Fair of 1940 began with hectic negotiations coinciding with the Second Vienna Award (*Zweiter Wiener Schiedsspruch*), the Hungarian delegation being led by Prime Minister Count Pál Teleki and Foreign Minister Count István Csáky, the Romanian by Foreign Minister Mihail Manoilescu. In discussions with the German foreign minister, Ribbentrop, and his Italian counterpart, Ciano, a solution was sought for competing Romanian and Hungarian territorial claims. Schirach did not play a role in the secret negotiations, but he made sure he was seen around the meetings. In this Second Vienna Award, signed by the delegations on 30 August in the Belvedere palace, Germany and Italy forced Romania to give up 43,492 square kilometres of its important north-eastern territories to Hungary. Mihail Manoilescu suffered a heart attack while signing.

This was not the only instance of Schirach taking the opportunity for discussions and receptions when foreign politicians used Vienna as a stopover. He also met with the Bulgarian minister of agriculture, Ivan Bagrianoff, on 5 and 11 October 1940. At the Spring Trade Fair of 1941, Schirach brought an old close friend from the party to Vienna, the *Reichsorganisationsleiter* and head of the DAF, Robert Ley, with whom he had founded the "Adolf Hitler Schools" in 1937. He hosted Ley on 2 March.

The first economic project Schirach had organised by the SOEG related to the Protectorate of Bohemia and Moravia. After initial discussions in Prague between Schirach and *Reichsprotektor* Baron von Neurath, the German Economic Society (*Deutsche Gesellschaft der Wirtschaft*) held a large conference in Bohemia and Moravia in December 1941. This networking meetings was opened by Reich Economic Minister Walther Funk, Deputy *Reichsprotektor SS-Obergruppenführer* Reinhard Heydrich and *Reichsleiter* Baldur von Schirach.[385] State President Emil Hácha and members of the "Protectorate Government" also participated in Prague Castle's Spanish Hall.

In his speech, Schirach not only put Vienna at the centre of economic policy in the Danube and Southern European region, but also declared that the Reich Industrial Group (*Reichsgruppe Industrie*) and the Central European Economic Conference (*Mitteleuropäischer Wirtschaftstag*, MWT, an association furthering the interests of the leading German companies, banks and economic associations) were in charge of "conducting the entire industrial planning for South-eastern Europe". In "agreement with these offices, the society [i.e. the SOEG]' had "formed a committee for economic planning to which all the scientific institutes, economic organisations etcetera belong under the leadership of the South-eastern Europe Society".[386]

This announcement, however, concealed a severe conflict between the MWT and the SOEG.[387] After the Vienna Autumn Trade Fair of 1941, Schirach, together with Funk, had already planned to force the MWT to disband and be subsumed by the SOEG. The Office of Foreign Affairs rejected this plan too. Ulrich Hassell in particular considered the SOEG "practically useless" and tried to fend off this attack by "the party".[388] Hassell, a conservative former diplomat and a member of the NSDAP since 1933, would later join the military resistance of July 1944, for which he was executed. He was a member of the board of the MWT and an opponent of the National Socialist policy of persecuting and annihilating the Jews.

Hassell took a very dim view of Schirach:

Schirach [...] (who has dishonesty written all over his face, incidentally) plays the generous benefactor [...] The food was brought from a hotel, with the result that we were sitting at the table in torment for two-and-a-quarter hours and Schirach ended the dinner in despair before the cheese [course]. At the reception in the City Hall [...] Schirach acted like a sovereign with the daughter of "Reich Drunkard" Hoffmann [...] But he later sat next to his good lady wife like a little bourgeois.[389]

At the Vienna Autumn Trade Fair with its exhibitions from thirteen nations, Schirach signalled that he would pursue an Eastern and South-eastern European economic plan. Also present at this well-publicised meeting were Reich Finance Minister Lutz Graf Schwerin von Krosigk and Undersecretary of State Major General (*Generalmajor*) Adolf von Schell, Bulgarian Minister of Agriculture Dmitri Kuscheff, Finnish Trade Minister Väinö Tanner, Greek Economics Minister Hatzimichalis, Croatian Minister for Forestry and Mining Ivica Frković and Slovak Economics Minister Gejza Medrický. The Vienna edition of the *Völkischer Beobachter* ran the headline: "Vienna Trade Fair – proof of our confidence. Ceremonial opening by Reichsleiter Baldur von Schirach".[390]

In 1942, however, this strong international economic strategy came to an end, perhaps in part because Schirach and his team of organisers behind all these events were concentrating entirely on the European Youth Congress.

After the assassination of Heydrich, with whom he sought to cooperate closely in the economic sphere, Schirach once again took up Hitler's ideas on deportation of 1940–41. He chose a speech to members of the German Labour Front in the Vienna Konzerthaus on 6 June 1942 for his big publicity coup. He began by accusing the "hoarders and food racketeers" of endangering the economic military successes before specifically attacking the "asocials of all classes and strata of our people" who had participated in these dealings, claiming that it had mainly been "Jewish and Czech elements".[391]

Schirach then became even clearer in his attack:

When I came here in 1940, I told our Führer that I consider my main task to be making this city free of Jews. This evening, I can tell you that in the autumn of this year, 1942, we will experience the celebration of a Vienna purified of Jews (sustained thunderous applause). Now, as far as the Czechs in this city are concerned, I would like to declare the following: the bullets that hit our comrade Heydrich have also injured us, for this bullet was meant for all of us. Hence I give my subordinate offices of the state and the party the order after the complete evacuation of the Jews to remove all Czechs (The stenographer could not catch the last word due to the rising and sustained thunderous applause).

I do not know whom these murderous knaves have chosen to be their next victim. Perhaps they have selected me. (Cries: boo!) I can only tell you: one cannot destroy me, for I am a generation (rapturous applause) and just as I will make this city free of Jews, I will also make it free of Czechs! (sustained rapturous applause).[392]

A day later, at a meeting of Vienna's councillors, Schirach repeated his deportation proposal. But the public debate on the planned deportation of Vienna's Czechs was quickly forbidden by Bormann and Goebbels, and all *Gauleiter* were instructed not to discuss the "Czech question" either at internal events or in public.[393]

In 1939 – a year after Austria's "annexation" – 56,284 Viennese still stated their mother tongue was Czech despite the extremely German nationalist, racist propaganda and the idea of the National Socialist "Volksgemeinschaft". Some 13,500 even declared themselves to be of Czech nationality.[394]

As Schirach's general cultural officer Walter Thomas later reported in his memoirs, the *Reichsstatthalter* himself was a little uneasy at his speech of 6 June. The day after, Schirach invited some artists to his Hohe Warte villa, where they "chatted about French painting and modern poetry". When his guests had left, he still had one question for his cultural officer:

"What are they saying in artistic circles about my speech yesterday …?" I remained silent. The evening before, actor friends had vented their outrage at the speech. "Now, don't be scared! They're all cursing me, are they?" – "They're horrified!" – "I knew it …" He paced up and down a little. Studying a sculpture on his desk next to Rodin's "Thinker", he said, "Yes, these artist gentlemen! If you say something and they don't understand the background to it, they slate you. How 'often' must the politician say something even if he feels completely differently! … But it's fine that way!"[395]

Schirach clearly wished to imply that the severity of his words had been a political strategy. This is also reflected by the evidence given by adjutant Gustav Höpken in Nuremberg on 28 May 1946, who pointed out that immediately after his speech, Schirach had instructed his press officer, Günter Kaufmann, to phone through "every point in the speech, especially to the DNB Berlin headquarters". Schirach had also remarked that he had "every reason to make a concession to Bormann on this point".[396]

In the context of the SOEG at least, from 1942 onwards Schirach was no longer able to influence decision-making processes in the field of economic policy, not least due to Albert Speer's central armament policy. Despite all sorts of plans and utopian goals, in reality the SOEG was probably nothing more than a "Viennese breakfast and speeches club without economic impact", as the then MWT president, Tilo Wilmowsky, who was imprisoned in Ravensbrück concentration camp after 20 July, would put it in 1945. And even the director of the SOEG, August Heinrichsbauer, a "fellow combatant" of Funk's, thought that at the end of the day, the society was "pie in the sky".[397]

From 1940–41 onwards, a central element of the economy, including in the "Ostmark", was the exploitation of forced and slave labourers from Mauthausen concentration camp and its satellite camps. As outlined above, forced labour was also performed by Hungarian Jews and prisoners of war, and other foreign workers came from friendly foreign states such as Bulgaria and Slovakia.[398]

Schirach himself visited Mauthausen and the Gusen satellite camp at the invitation of the *Gauleiter* of "Oberdonau", August Eigruber, on 16 February 1943, during an agricultural conference in Linz.[399] A prisoner from the crematorium detail described the visit; Schirach also "had a look at" the crematorium:

> I know that Baldur von Schirach also had a look at the crematorium. We had to clear up and clean everything beforehand. To burn the bodies, 5 coffins were brought, the release notes were completed and the urns readied. In the presence of Schirach, the bodies were burnt, the ashes were placed in the relevant urns and then soldered as per the regulations. It was all very hygienic, Schirach found. He wasn't shown the gas facility. That day, bodies that had died normal deaths were burnt.[400]

During the Nuremberg trials, Schirach recalled that he had already taken a look at Dachau concentration camp in 1935. It had been more dressed up for him than during his Mauthausen visit, although he had been shown more than other visitors of comparable standing. He also dated his Mauthausen visit to 1942, not 1943:

VON SCHIRACH: [...] And I should now like to give you my first impressions. The camp area was very large. I immediately asked how many internees there were. I believe I was told 15,000 or 20,000. At any rate, the figure varied between 15,000 and 20,000. I asked what kind of internees were imprisoned there and received the reply I was always given whenever I inquired about concentration camps – namely, that two-thirds of the inmates were dangerous criminals collected from the prisons and penitentiaries and brought to work in the camp; that the remaining third was allegedly composed of political prisoners and people guilty of high treason and betrayal of their country, who, it is a fact, are treated with exceptional severity in wartime.

DR. SAUTER: Did you, in this camp, convince yourself as to the nature of the treatment meted out to the prisoners, accommodations [*sic*], the food situation, *et cetera*?

VON SCHIRACH: I witnessed one food distribution and gained the impression that, for camp conditions, the food ration was both normal and adequate. I then visited the large quarry, once famous and now notorious, where the construction stone for Vienna had been quarried for centuries. There was no work going on at the quarry since the working day had come to an end, but I did, however, visit the works where the stone was cut. I saw a building with an exceptionally well-equipped dental clinic. This clinic was shown to me because I had questioned Ziereis about the medical assistance afforded in the camp. I would add that, during this visit, I asked in general the same questions which I had been used to ask [*sic*] during all my visits to the camps of the youth organizations – that is, questions pertaining to food, medical aid, the number of people in the camp, *et cetera*.

I was then taken to a large room in which music was being played by the prisoners. They had gathered together quite a large symphony orchestra, and I was told that on holiday evenings they could amuse themselves, each man according to his own tastes. In this case, for instance, the prisoners who wished to make music assembled in that room. A tenor was singing on that occasion – I remember that particularly.

I then inquired about the mortality rate and was shown a room with three corpses in it. I cannot tell you here and now, under oath, whether I saw any crematorium or not. Marsalek has testified to that effect. I would not, however, have been surprised if there had been a crematorium or a cemetery in so large a place, so far removed from the city. That would be a matter of course.

DR. SAUTER: Herr Von Schirach, during this official visit under the guidance of Camp Commandant Ziereis, did you discover anything at all about any ill-treatment, or atrocities, or of the tortures which were allegedly inflicted in the camp? You can answer the question briefly – possibly with "yes" or "no."

VON SCHIRACH: Had that been the case, I would of course have endeavored to do something about it. But I was under the impression that everything was in order. I looked at the inmates, for instance, and I remember seeing, among others, the famous middle-distance runner Peltzer, who was known as a sexual pervert. He had been punished because he had, on innumerable occasions, freely committed sexual offenses against youths in his charge in a country school.

I asked Ziereis, "How does one ever get out of these concentration camps? Do you also release people continuously?" In reply he had four or five inmates brought to me who, according to him, were to be released the very next day. He asked them in my presence, "Have you packed everything, and have you prepared everything for your release?" – to which, beaming with joy, they answered, "Yes."[401]

One of the aspects that were not mentioned during Schirach's trial was his aggressive policy concerning "asocials". A football match soon gave him his opportunity: on 17 November 1940, the crowd whistled their dislike of him when the Vienna club Admira played Schalke 04 in the Prater Stadium. Admira supporters also pelted his car with stones and slashed his tyres – which doubtlessly came as a shock to a *Reichsstatthalter* used to discipline and subordination. The windows of the German champions' team bus were also smashed, and 200 so-called "asocials" were subsequently arrested.[402] The newspapers made no mention of the incidents in their match reports, the *Völkischer Beobachter* merely giving

A dashing captain of the Guards: father Carl Baily Norris von Schirach transferred from the imperial military to the Court Theatre in Weimar.

Schirach's paternal grandmother Elizabeth Baily von Schirach, née Norris

Schirach's paternal grandfather, US Civil War veteran Friedrich Karl von Schirach, the hero of Bull Run.

One of the founding fathers of the United States: Arthur Middleton was a signatory to the Declaration of Independence in 1776. Oil painting by Benjamin West, ca. 1771.

An important landowner and influential politician: Henry Middleton helped determine South Carolina's fate. Oil painting by Benjamin West, ca. 1771.

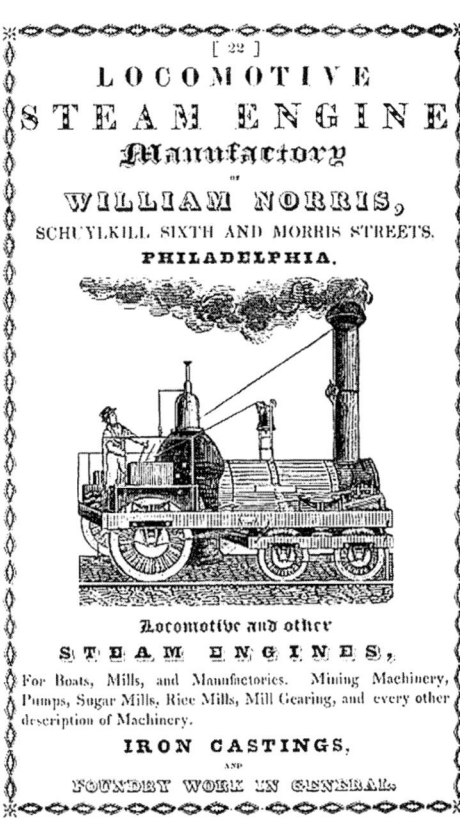

Schirach's great-grandfather built locomotives; William Norris's factory in Philadelphia supplied engines to Europe too.

Schirach's sister Rosalind von Schirach was nine years his senior and embarked on a career as an opera singer after the First World War.

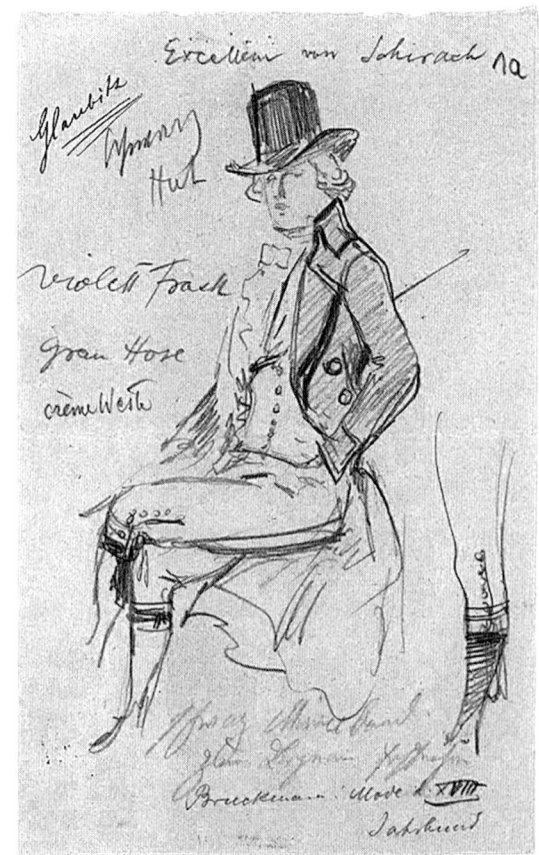

Tails, dagger, knickerbockers and bicorne: Baldur's father Carl von Schirach in his grand ducal chamberlain's "costume". Drawing, Hauptstaatsarchiv Weimar, Landesarchiv Thüringen.

"Beloved fatherland, reawaken, that God may again be with us!": nationalist anti-Modernism mobilised the youth against the Weimar Republic. Promotional postcard of the Young German Order, designed by "Bruder [Brother] Zickerow".

The youth were to be equipped for a potential war: General Field Marshall Baron Wilhelm Leopold Colmar von der Goltz formed the Young Germany League in 1911.

The writings of Weimar's Jew-hating Adolf Bartels (pictured) played a large role in Schirach's ideological orientation as a National Socialist.

An important cornerstone of Schirach's defence in Nuremberg in 1946: he claimed that reading Henry Ford's anti-Semitic polemic *The International Jew* made him an anti-Semite.

A professor Schirach later recalled from his student days in Munich: the English specialist Josef Schick.

Another professor Schirach recalled from Munich: Wilhelm Spiegelberg.

Together with his father-in-law Heinrich Hoffmann, Schirach worked on the image of the "Führer", with no little success: hundreds of thousands of copies were printed of the volume *Hitler wie ihn keiner kennt. 100 Bild-Dokumente aus dem Leben des Führers* (Hitler As No One Knows Him. 100 Pictorial Documents from the Life of the Führer), with an introduction by Baldur von Schirach, and similar works such as *Hitler in seinen Bergen* (Hitler in his Mountains), pictured here.

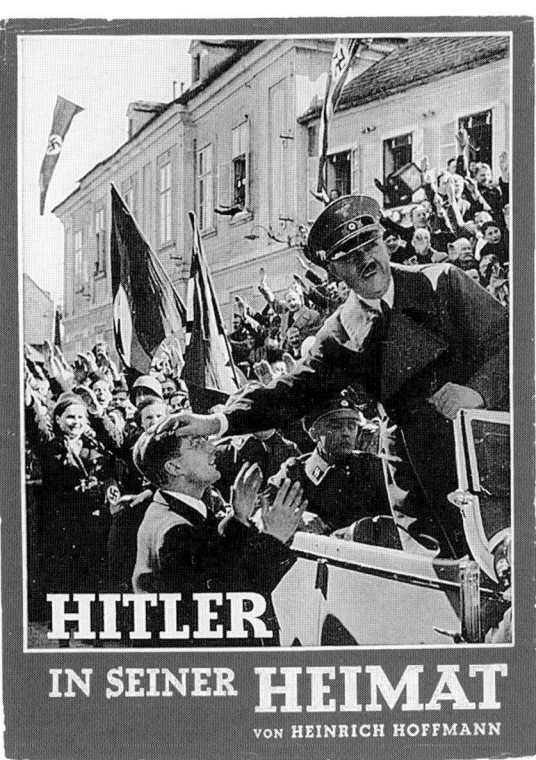

Hitler in seiner Heimat (Hitler in His Homeland)

Jugend um Hitler (Youth Around Hitler)

The "total mass experience": the "First National Socialist Reich Youth Day" on 1 October 1932 in Potsdam's Luftschiffhafen (airship bay) Stadium was a great triumph for Baldur von Schirach, despite organisational errors.

A still from the HJ propaganda film *Unsere Fahne flattert uns voran* (Our Flag Flutters Ahead of Us).

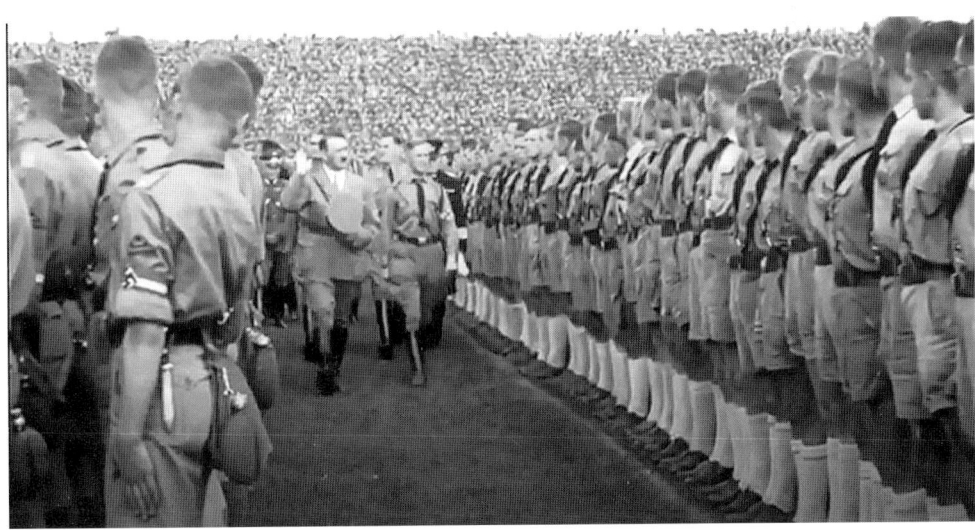

"Führer", flag and fatherland: the Hitler Youth's totalising ambitions are publicly celebrated, always in the presence of Schirach. Stills from the HJ propaganda film *Unsere Fahne flattert uns voran* (Our Flag Flutters Ahead of Us), produced in 1934.

The brochure *Das Reich Adolf Hitlers* (Adolf Hitler's Reich), a *Bildbuch vom Werden Großdeutschlands* (A Picture Book of Greater Germany's Becoming), edited by Baldur von Schirach in his capacity as *Reichsjugendführer*.

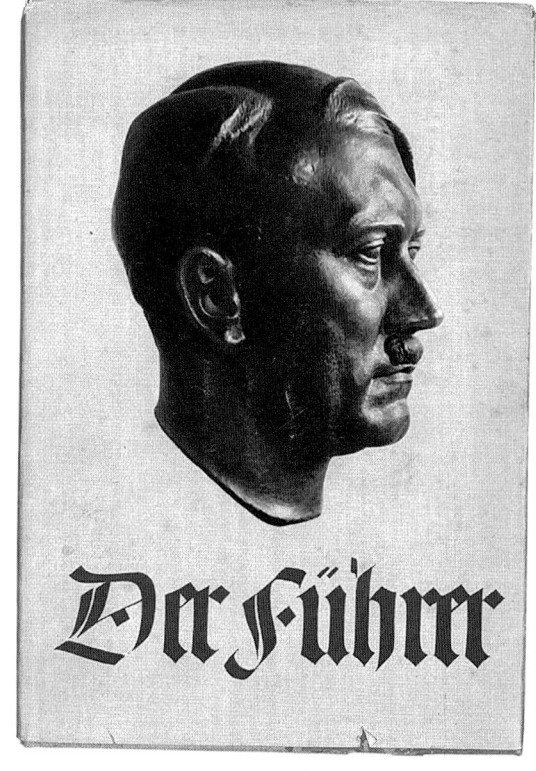

Another book edited by Baldur von Schirach: *Der Führer* by Eberhard Wolfgang Möller (1938).). Möller was *Gebietsführer* (area leader) in the *Reichsjugendführung* (Reich Youth Leadership); his book displeased Alfred Rosenberg, while Schirach publicly praised the work in 1939 as an "unforgettable and immortal epic".

The Hitler Youth magazine *Wille und Macht* (Will and Power), edited by Baldur von Schirach.

Poster for the premiere of the propaganda film *Hitlerjunge Quex* on 11 September 1933. Schirach had taken on "patronage" of the film's production.

Poster for the BDM Reich Games of 1934.

"As swift as greyhounds, as tough as leather and as hard as Krupp steel" – almost eight million adolescents marched, trained and worked for the ideal stipulated by Hitler and executed by Schirach. Poster for the Reich Vocational Games of German Youth, 1934.

The youth of Vienna are still keen to obtain the new *Reichsstatthalter*'s autograph.

They departed on good terms: Schirach and his predecessor as *Reichsstatthalter*, Josef Bürckel, who was unable to win over many people in Vienna.

Die Übergabe des Reichsgaues Wien an Baldur von Schirach

In festlicher und eindrucksvoller Feier vollzog am vergangenen Wochenende der Stellvertreter des Führers, Reichsminister Rudolf Heß, die Uebergabe der Aemter des Reichsstatthalters und Gauleiters von Wien an den Reichsjugendführer Baldur von Schirach und sprach dem scheidenden, zu neuen Aufgaben berufenen Gauleiter Joseph Bürckel, der in Würdigung seiner Verdienste um diese Stadt zum Ehrenbürger von Wien ernannt wurde, den Dank des Führers für sein vorbildliches Wirken aus.

Wien, die Stadt, in der der Führer seine Jugend verlebte, das ewige Bollwerk deutscher Kultur an der Ostgrenze des Reiches, ist in der Person des neuen Reichsstatthalters und Gauleiters aufs neue mit der deutschen Jugendbewegung, die mit Stolz des Führers Namen trägt, verbunden, deren kultureller Sendung sich auf dem Boden dieses alten deutschen Kulturzentrums neue Kräfte erschließen werden.

Oben: Die Jugend Wiens grüßt den Stellvertreter des Führers ◆ Links von oben nach unten: Der Stellvertreter des Führers verliest die Handschreiben des Führers an den scheidenden und an den neuen Gauleiter ◆ Nach dem scheidenden Gauleiter hielt Baldur von Schirach seine Antrittsrede, die ausklang in den Worten: „... eines wird uns in unserer Arbeit miteinander untrennbar verbinden: Die Liebe zu dieser gesegneten und begnadeten Stadt mit ihren unermeßlichen kulturellen Schätzen, ihrer stolzen Vergangenheit und ihrer noch stolzeren Gegenwart." ◆ Der Stellvertreter des Führers verläßt nach der feierlichen Kundgebung mit Reichsstatthalter Gauleiter Baldur von Schirach und Gauleiter Bürckel das Konzerthaus ◆ Rechts: Reichsstatthalter und Gauleiter Baldur von Schirach dankt in der 5. Ratshermsitzung dem scheidenden Gauleiter Joseph Bürckel für seine Verdienste um die Stadt ◆ Aufnahmen: Presse-Hoffmann

Schirach, the good-looking young Nazi the Viennese soon called "Baron" due to his feudal attitude, knew what they wanted to hear from him, and hence in his inaugural speech he spoke of his "love for this blessed and gifted city" and its "proud past and even prouder present". At this point, he preferred to remain silent about what he was planning to do to one section of its population. *Wiener Illustrierte*, 31 August 1940.

"Europa's new youth marches": while the Holocaust and the National Socialists' war of aggression were claiming their many victims, Schirach celebrated the foundation of the "European Youth Association". Berlin's reaction to the *Reichstatthalter*'s ambitious "parallel action" was to hush it up. *Wiener Illustrierte*, 16 September 1942.

Schirach in statesman's pose: meeting *Falange* leader Pilar Primo de Rivera on 13 September 1942.

The young actress Katharina Dobbs, born in Rottenmann, Styria, in 1920, was allegedly the *Reichstatthalter*'s lover for some time. Henriette von Schirach was said to have known about her husband's affair. The photo was taken in Argentina.

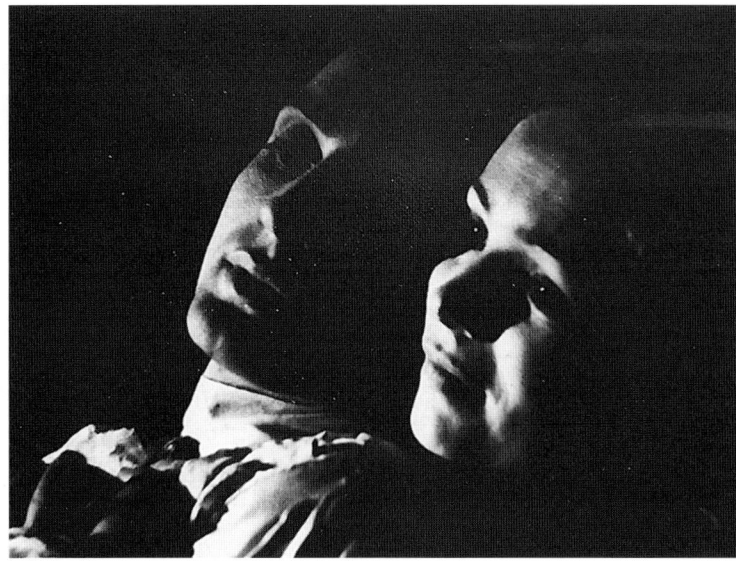

Katharina Dobbs in the role of Marion in Büchner's drama *Dantons Tod* (Danton's Death) at the Teatro Marconi in Buenos Aires.

Katharina Dobbs in Graz, 1946/47.

One of Hitler's very few instructions concerning the persecution of the Jews: Hans Heinrich Lammer's communication to Schirach of 3 December 1940 was important evidence in Nuremberg in 1946.

```
                          Abschrift!

Der Reichsminister und Chef              Berlin W 8, den 3.12.40
     der Reichskanzlei                   Voßstr.6.
     Rk. 789 B g
                              Geheim!
An
     den Reichsstatthalter in Wien
     Herrn Gauleiter von S c h i r a c h
                         Wien

              Sehr verehrter Herr von Schirach!

      Wie mir Reichsleiter Bormann mitteilt, hat der Führer auf
einen von Ihnen erstatteten Bericht entschieden, daß die in dem
Reichsgau Wien noch wohnhaften 60 000 Juden beschleunigt, also
noch während des Krieges, wegen der in Wien herrschenden
Wohnungsnot ins Generalgouvernement abgeschoben werden
sollen. Ich habe diese Entscheidung des Führers dem Herrn Gene-
ralgouverneur in Krakau sowie dem Reichsführer SS mitgeteilt
und darf Sie bitten, gleichfalls von ihr Kenntnis nehmen zu
wollen.
                                            Heil Hitler!
                                         Ihr sehr ergebener
                                            gez.Dr.Lammers
Abschriftlich:
1. an  ::-::  Dr.Dellbrügge  ::-::
2. Reg.Präs. J u n g
```

"Development work" and "urgent tasks for the future": in his cynical speech to the "Leadership of the Reichsgau Wien", Artur Greiser, *Gauleiter* of the "Warthegau", did not pass up the opportunity to mention the genocide committed against the Jewish population. *Kleines Blatt*, 14 May 1942.

Aspang railway station in Vienna's Third District. It was from here that the trains departed for the ghettos and death camps.

Nowhere did more Austrians die in the Shoah than in the Blagovchina woods outside Maly Trostinets, near Minsk. The memorial commemorates the ca. 10,000 victims.

59. Jahrgang Nr. 37

Wien, 11. September 1940

Preis 20 Pf.

Wiener Illustrierte

Reichswirtschaftsminister Funk und Reichsleiter Reichsstatthalter Baldur von Schirach

auf dem Rundgang durch das Ausstellungsgelände nach der Eröffnung der Wiener Herbstmesse 1940

Aufnahme: PBZ-Essel

Reich Minister for Economic Affairs Walther Funk (left) and *Reichsstatthalter* Baldur von Schirach during the opening of the Vienna Autumn Trade Fair, 1940. *Wiener Illustrierte*, 11 September 1940.

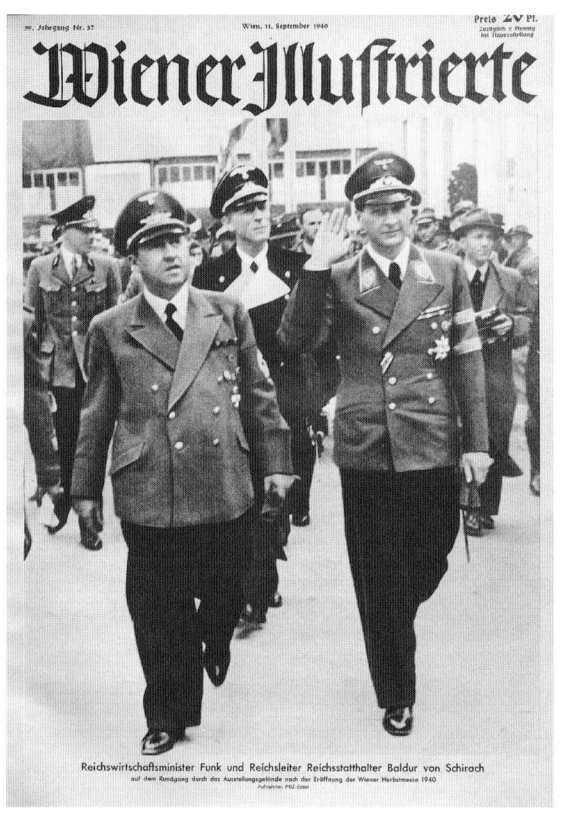

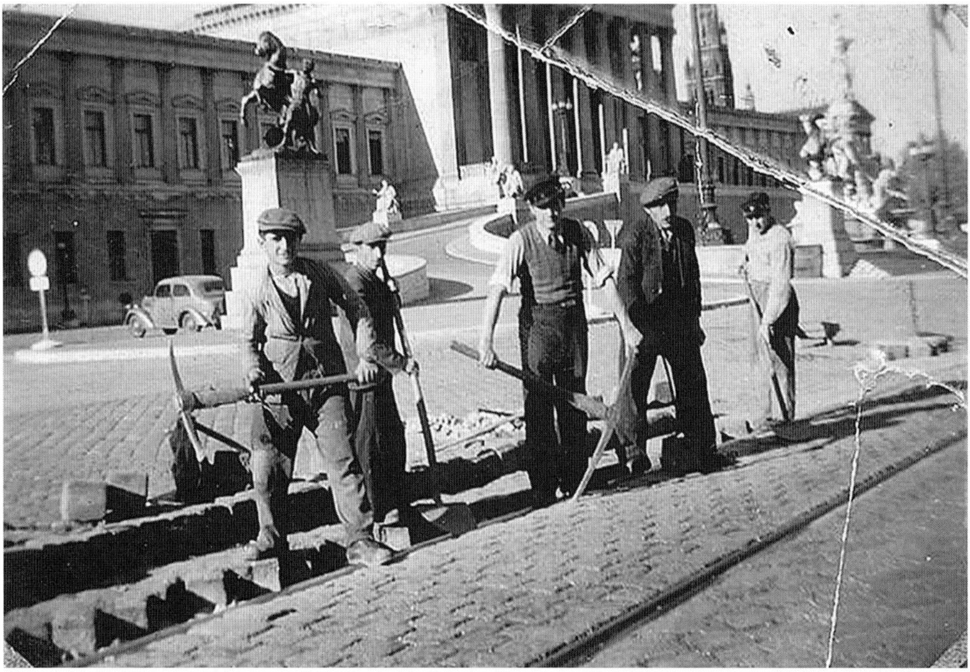

Polish forced labourers during road works before the *Gauhaus*. The *Schaubild der Woche* (Weekly Illustrated) teaches everyday racism: Polish forced labourers are to remain shunned.

Congress of the South-eastern Europe Society in Prague, December 1941: *SS-Obergruppenführer* Reinhard Heydrich, Reich Minister for Economic Affairs Walther Funk and Baldur von Schirach enter the Spanish Hall in Prague Castle.

The article in the *Neues Wiener Tagblatt* that would cost journalist Aurel Wolfram his job: the idea of Vienna as a "refuge of the German soul" did not go down well with Berlin.

During an extensive speech in the Burgtheater on 6 April 1941, Schirach announced, "Vienna's new position obliges us to [perform] cultural achievements of the extraordinary kind." *Kronen-Zeitung*, 8 April 1941.

Goebbels and Schirach became joint patrons of the Mozart Week of the German Reich from 28 November to 5 December 1941.

A star-studded cast was on show during the Grillparzer Festival Week: Paula Wessely as Hero and Paul Hubschmid as Leander in *Des Meeres und der Liebe Wellen* (*The Waves of the Sea and of Love*). *Wiener Illustrierte*, 15 January 1941.

Schirach's deputy, Karl Scharizer. Born in the Mühlviertel, he told one of Martin Bormann's spies that "Party Member" von Schirach "somehow lives in a different world".

Oscar Fritz Schuh's staging of the opera *Johanna Balk* by Rudolf Wagner-Régeny triggers protests by the "old warriors" and the first glitch in relations with Berlin. The work premiered at the Vienna State Opera on 4 April 1941.

Neues Wiener Tagblatt

Nr. 79 — Dienstag, 3. April 1945 — 79. Jahrgang

Die Stunde Wiens ist gekommen

Männliche Worte

Unter schwersten Blutopfern ist es den Bolschewisten gelungen, nun auch im Südosten des Reiches über die Grenzen zu dringen und bis nach Steinamanger, in das westliche Raabtal und in den Raum des Neusiedler Sees vorzustoßen. Die Feindnähe ist nun spürbar, das Antlitz der Stadt hat sich in den letzten Stunden gewaltig verändert, die Schwere der Stunde, die vor uns liegt, die Pflicht zur Verteidigung der Stadt, die der Reichsverteidigungskommissar proklamiert hat, stehen in jedem Antlitz geschrieben. Die Stunde ist ernst, der Krieg tritt nun jedem Wiener, jeder Wienerin persönlich gegenüber, und jeder hat sich mit ihm auseinanderzusetzen. Ein Ausweichen ist unmöglich, ein Nachgeben bedeutet den sicheren Untergang.

Aber es ist ja nicht das erstemal, daß die Bevölker dieser Stadt dem Kriegsärm ins Angesicht sieht, Worte wenig. Wenn ich mit meinen Männern mit dem Verteidigern dieser schönen, alten Stadt zugesellte, so geschieht dies mit dem festen und unverbrüchlichen Vorsatz, alles nur Menschenmögliche zu tun, dieses Bollwerk des deutschen Südostens unseres undeutschen Vaterlandes zu erhalten.
Mehr zu versprechen, wäre vermessen. Der Kampf wird hart, der Erfolg schwer.
Sie, meine Wiener und Wienerinnen, kennen den Feind aus früheren Generationen Ihrer Geschichte. Sie kennen aber auch die europäische Aufgabe, die Sie als Wien niemals entzogen hat.
Halten wir zusammen, kämpfen wir zusammen. Es geht nicht um uns, es geht nicht um die Partei, es geht um unser Land.
Heil unserem Führer!

Noch härterer Widerstand
Der Sowjetvorstoß und der Frontverlauf im Südosten

* Berlin, 2. April.

Der Feind ist in den letzten Tagen im Westen und im Südosten der weit weniger in allgemeiner Richtung Wiener Neustadt vordringenden feindlichen Truppen von den Verbänden der Wehrmacht nicht nur aufgehalten, sondern zerschlagen werden konnten. In besonderer Verbissenheit wird jetzt um die Fahnenjunkerschule Wiener Neustadt, die Ost- und West gerichtet ist, gekämpft. Ein Hauptwiderstand läuft in diesem Abschnitt jetzt etwa vom Ödenburg nach St. Peter, im Bogen nach Osten weit um Prottburg herum angreifend, bis nach Modern. Dort klafft eine geringe Frontlücke, und bei Sereth schwingt sich die zusammenhängende Linie durch die Slowakei bis etwa Neusohl. Der Feind hat die Lücke bei Modern benützt, um einen Vorstoß in Richtung Tyrnau zu machen.

Im nördlichen Abschnitt der Westfront, wo die Angriffe der englischen, kanadischen und amerikanischen Divisionen, die das Herz des Reiches gerichtet sind, setzte die feindliche Führung ihre Pläne fort, die zwischen dem Sieg im Süden und einer Linie im Norden etwa entlang der Reichsautobahn von Duisburg über Bottrop, Herten und Kamen stehenden deutschen Verbände einzuschließen. In diesem Plan, daß die deutschen Verbände zwischen Wesel und Emmerich nach Norden und Nordosten vorstoßenden feindlichen Verbände sich zum Teil nach Südosten wandten und bis zu Bottrop und an die Ruhr gelangten, dort toben zur Zeit heftige Kämpfe.

Der Bewegungskrieg im Westen hat eine gefährliche kritische Situation geschaffen. Wäre die Waffen strecken, so hätte der Gegner das gewonnen, was er in Frankreich im fast viel, nämlich die Sicherung seines Erfolges. Die deutschen Truppen aber kämpfen weiter, sich und verbissen, und geben dem Feind nicht, was er ebensowenig wie die deutsche Heimat, die in die Hand des Feindes zu geraten, der sie vernichten will.

Westlich des Neusiedler Sees aufgefangen
Erbitterter Widerstand zwischen den Kleinen Karpaten und der Waag

Führer-Hauptquartier, 2. April.
Das Oberkommando der Wehrmacht gibt bekannt:

Südwestlich des Plattensees und in der Grenzstellung südwestlich Steinamanger wehrten unsere Verbände heftige Angriffe der Bolschewisten ab. Im oberen Raabtal konnten die Sowjets dagegen nach Nordwesten Boden gewinnen. Westlich des Neusiedler Sees wurden feindliche Panzerspitzen in harten Kämpfen am Leithaabschnitt und am Südrand des Leithagebirges abgedrängt. Nördlich der Donau leisteten unsere Truppen zwischen dem Ostrand der Kleinen Karpaten und der Waag dem nach Nordwesten drängenden Gegner erbitterten Widerstand.

Erneute feindliche Durchbruchsversuche in Oberschlesien scheiterten zwischen Ratibor und Jägerndorf an der Standhaftigkeit unserer Divisionen, die in der zweiten Märzhälfte mit dem Abschuß von 952 Panzern einen bedeutenden Abwehrerfolg errangen. Die Besatzung von Breslau schlug starke von Pan-

zern und Schlachtfliegern unterstützte Angriffe ab.
Mit unvermindert starkem Kräfteaufwand setzten die Sowjets an der Danziger Bucht ihre Angriffe in der Oxhöfter Kämpe und gegen die westliche Weichselniederung fort. Sie konnten jedoch nur wenig Gelände gewinnen und verloren 39 Panzer.

Nordwestlich Doblen zerbrachen die mit neu aufgeführten Kräften geführten Angriffe des Feindes am entschlossenen Widerstand unserer Kurlandkämpfer.

Im Westen dauern die schweren Abwehrkämpfe in den holländischen Grenzgebieten und im Niederrhein und Ruhrgebiet an. Östlich Burgsteinfurt hielten unsere Truppen die Angriffe des Feindes an. Angriffe, östlich und südöstlich davon konnte der Gegner bis an die Ränder des Teutoburger Waldes beiderseits durchstoßen, wurde dann aber unter großen Panzer- und Menschenverlusten zum Stehen gebracht. Von Süden her vorgehend, haben die

Amerikaner den Raum Söst-Lippstadt erreicht. Am Nordrand des Industriegebietes sind um Recklinghausen heftige Kämpfe im Gange.

An der unteren und mittleren Sieg wurde durch harten Widerstand und im Gegenangriff im Vordringen des Feindes verhindert. An den Rothaargebirge und im Raum von Winterberg wurden zahlreiche Angriffe abgewiesen.

Eine weit im Rücken der Amerikaner stehende Kampfgruppe der Waffen-SS, durch eine Fahnenjunkerschule des Heeres verstärkt, hat in den letzten drei Tagen dem Gegner schwerste Verluste zugefügt und mehr als 35 Angriffe bis zu Regimentsstärke zurückgeschlagen. 35 Panzer und acht gepanzerte Fahrzeuge, zahlreiche Lastkraftwagen und Mannschaftstransportwagen wurden erbeutet oder vernichtet und mehrere hundert Amerikaner, darunter 50 Offiziere, als Gefangene eingebracht.

Angriffe auf Kassel scheiterten unter starken Panzerverlusten für den Feind. Zwischen der Werra und dem Kinzigtal hat sich der Druck des Gegners vor allem nördlich der Werra verstärkt. Im Spessart sowie zwischen der unteren Tauber und dem Maindreieck sind erbitterte Abwehrkämpfe entbrannt. Aus dem Gebiet zwischen Bad Mergentheim und der Jagstfront südlich Heidelberg drückt der Feind weiter nach Süden. In der Rheinebene wurden die Amerikaner ein Einbruch bis Buchsal, doch wurden ihnen die gewonnenen Angriffe auf die Stadt seitens blutig zurückgeschlagen.

Tag- und Nachtangriffe unserer Luftwaffe richteten sich mit nachhaltiger Wirkung gegen die feindlichen Nachschubverbindungen.

An der Westalpenfront konnte der Gegner nach siebenwöchigen starken Angriffen einen Stützpunkt am Kleinen Sankt Bernhard nehmen.

In Mittelitalien scheiterten zahlreiche Aufklärungsvorstöße der Amerikaner südwestlich Bologna.

Nach längeren schweren Kämpfen hat Kroatien in sowohl im Raum von Bihać wie in Ostbosnien eine Kampfpause eingetreten. Bei Angriffen amerikanischer Terrorverbänden gegen Orte in Südostdeutschland entstanden Personenverluste und schwere Häuserschäden, vor allem in der Stadtgebiet von Marburg an der Drau.

„Werwolf"

Berlin, 2. April.

Am Ostersonntag erklang es am Aether erstmalig der Ruf eines neuen Senders, der „Werwolf" nennt und als Organ einer Bewegung der nationalsozialistischen Freiheitskämpfer an die Öffentlichkeit tritt, die sich in den besetzten West- und Ostgebieten des Reiches gebildet hat. Das Hauptquartier dieser Bewegung wandte sich über das deutsche Volk, die fanatischen Willen deutscher Männer und Frauen, deutscher Jungen und Mädel in den besetzten Gebieten bezeigt, ihre festen, unverrückbaren, in einem feierlichen Eid bekräftigten Entschluß, mit allen Mitteln, Widerstand über Widerstandsgegenzusetzen, ihren unbändigen Haß und die unbändige Bequemlichkeit gegen den Feind und dessen Helfer. Jedes Mittel ist ihm recht, um den Feinden, die sie hassen gelernt, aus dem angehörigen unseres Volkes zuzufügen, aber Tod zu suchen.

Jedes Mittel ist ihm recht, um den Schaden zuzufügen. Er hat seine eigenen richtsbarkeit, die daher den Verfolgungsbestrebungen, die Feindes wie der Verräter an unserem „Unser Auftrag", so heißt es, weiter in der Proklamation, „unseren Freiheitswillen unseres Volkes zu erhalten, zehnfache Ehre der deutschen, also des deutschen Hüter vor, auf ein zu beruhen Völker, der Feind glaubt, daß er mit uns leicht haben werde und das dank unserer die rumänischen oder bulgarischen Hunnische oder Sklavendienste zusammenschließen könne, um es ins sibirische Tundren werke zu verschleppen, so soll dies ihm auch nicht so zurückweisen, und vor allem noch nicht."

"Each of us will do his duty to the utmost": on 3 April 1945, Commissar for the Defence of the Reich Schirach, supported by *SS-Oberstgruppenführer* Sepp Dietrich, addresses the people of Vienna one last time. *Neues Wiener Tagblatt*, 3 April 1945.

"Rather die than be cowardly": while his wife Henriette was already heading westward to safety, Schirach proclaimed the "toughest resistance" before his political leaders. *Völkischer Beobachter*, 6 December 1944.

The concrete monstrosity built by forced labourers and prisoners of war: the gun tower in the Augarten. Photo: Anna Saini.

He preferred retreat: Lothar Rendulic, supreme commander of the Army Group South.

Reasonably representative furnishings: the "Reichsleiter Room" in the basement of the "Schirach Bunker" on the Gallitzenberg hill. Schirach is said not to have appreciated staying at the "Gau Command Post".

"Youth's sacrifices guarantee victory": as early as 1940, Schirach referred to the "selfless loyalty" of the Hitler Youth; over 1,200 dead HJ leaders would serve as proof of this attitude. *Volks-Zeitung*, 5 September 1940. The commissar for the defence of the Reich didn't mind kneeling for a propaganda photo: military training for the Hitler Youth at a "defence training camp" in the Vienna Woods, summer 1944.

A stolen painting with a turbulent history from the collection of Cornelia, Marie and Philipp von Gomperz: *Mary with the Child on her Lap, Offering Him Grapes* by Lucas Cranach the Elder.

DER REICHSSTATTHALTER IN WIEN   WIEN, 18.Dezember 1942.

Herrn
Regierungspräsidenten Dr. D e l l b r ü g g e ,
W i e n .

Der Tisch aus dem Pietradurazimmer des Zeremonien-
appartements ist szt. auf meine Veranlassung dem
italienischen Minister des Äussern, Ciano, übergeben
worden, da er wiederholt während des Schiedsgerichts
diesen Tisch besonders lobte und darauf hinwies, dass
es nicht möglich wäre, in Italien ein solches Stück
aufzutreiben.

Schirach was generous with public property: he gave a precious eighteenth-century *pietra dura* table to Italy's foreign minister Count Ciano.

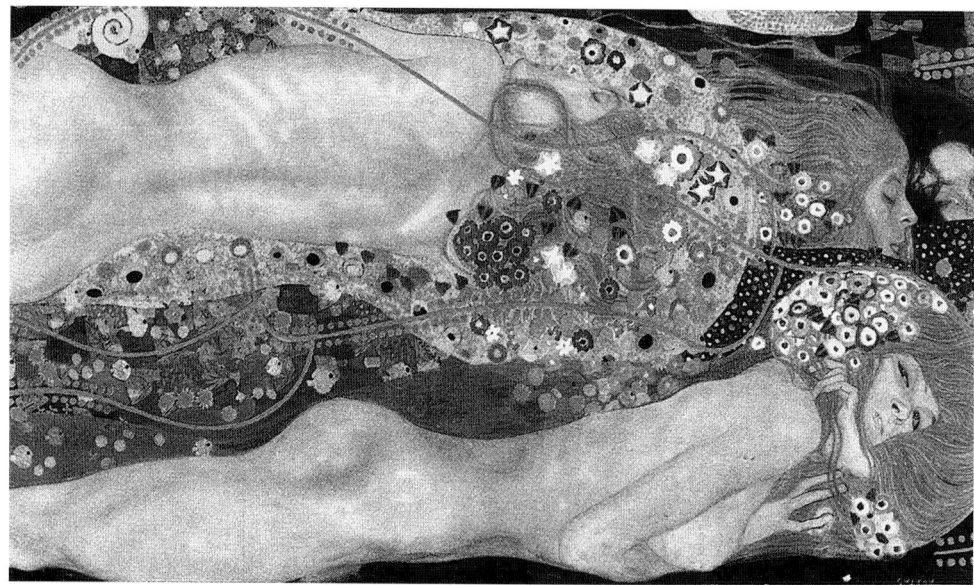

"Reserved" for the film director Gustav Ucicky upon Schirach's instruction: Gustav Klimt's painting *Water Snakes II* (*Girlfriends*). Ucicky, an illegitimate son of Klimt's, was able to buy the work for between 8,000 and 9,000 Reichsmark after it was confiscated from its Jewish owner, Jenny Steiner.

(1) Der grösste Massenmord und zugleich der grausamste, satanischste der Weltgeschichte ist nicht von Hoess begangen worden. Hoess war nur ein Henker.

Den Mord befohlen hat Adolf Hitler. Das steht in seinem Testament. Er und Himmler haben gemeinsam dieses Verbrechen veranlasst, das ein Schandfleck unserer Geschichte bleibt und jeden Deutschen mit Scham erfüllt.

Die deutsche Jugend trägt keine Schuld an dem Massenmord der Juden. Sie dachte antisemitisch, aber sie wollte nicht die Ausrottung des Judentums. Sie wusste und ahnte nichts davon, dass Hitler diese Ausrottung durch tägliche Morde an tausenden von unschuldigen durchführte.

(2) Nein, die jungen Menschen, die heute ratlos zwischen den Trümmern ihrer Heimat stehen, haben das nicht gewusst und nicht gewollt, was Hitler dem deutschen und dem jüdischen Volk angetan hat.

Ich habe diese Generation im Glauben an Hitler und in der Treue zu ihm erzogen. Die Jugendbewegung, die ich aufbaute, trug seinen Namen. Ich meinte einem Führer zu dienen, der unser Volk und die Jugend, gross, frei und glücklich machen würde.

Mit mir haben Millionen junger Menschen im Nationalsozialismus ihr Ideal gesehen. Im Glauben an dieses Ideal haben wir an der Gemeinschaft unserer Jugend gearbeitet und im Krieg gekämpft. Und diejenigen von uns,

(3) die gefallen sind, fielen im Glauben an dieses Ideal.

Meine Schuld, die ich fortan vor Gott und unserm Volk zu tragen habe, besteht darin, dass ich die Jugend unseres Volkes für einen Mann organisierte, der mir als Führer und als Staatsoberhaupt lange Jahre hindurch unantastbar schien, dass ich für diesen Mann eine Jugend bildete, die ihn so sah wie ich.

Und dieser Mann war ein millionenfacher Mörder.

Ich habe an diesen Mann geglaubt. Das ist meine Schuld, aber es ist nur meine Schuld. Nach dem Führerprinzip trug ich einst allein den Befehl und die

(4) Verantwortung für diese Jugend. Ich trage also auch allein die Schuld. Die Jugend ist schuldlos.

Die Jugend Deutschlands ist in einem antisemitischen Staat aufgewachsen. Die Gesetze des Staates waren antisemitische Gesetze. An diese Gesetze war die Jugend gebunden. Die Jugend verstand unter Rassenpolitik nichts Verbrecherisches. Wenn aber auf dem Boden der Rassenpolitik solche Verbrechen überhaupt möglich sind, wie sie von einem kleinen Kreis von Fanatikern ausgedacht und durchgeführt wurden, dann muss Auschwitz das Ende der Rassenpolitik, das Ende des Antisemitismus sein!

Hitler ist tot. Ich habe ihn nicht verraten, ich habe keinen Putsch und kein Attentat gegen ihn geplant. Kein Treue mit Untreue selbst als er meine Treue mit Untreue

(5) lohnte, blieb ich meinem Eid treu. Ich war kein Mitläufer. Ich war auch kein Opportunist. Ich war Nationalsozialist. So war ich auch Antisemit. Als solcher kann ich nach der Aussage des Hoess nur sagen:

Hitlers Rassenpolitik war ein Verbrechen. Diese Politik ist 5 Millionen Juden und allen Deutschen zum Verhängnis geworden.

Die Jugend ist ohne Schuld — wer aber nach Auschwitz noch an der Rassenpolitik festhält, der macht sich schuldig.

Seit frühester Jugend aus Überzeugung

BvS 24.5.1946

The handwritten introductory statement Baldur von Schirach prepared for his trial at Nuremberg. From the estate of the US forensic psychiatrist Gustave Mark Gilbert in Yad Vashem.

Baldur von Schirach's father-in-law and longstanding business partner: Heinrich Hoffmann, Hitler's personal photographer. Hoffmann was arrested by the US Army in April 1945 and sentenced to four years in 1946. His entire assets were confiscated.

The last station in his life: the run-down Pension Müllen in Kröv. Here, two former BDM leaders looked after Schirach, whose physical condition deteriorated rapidly.

The interview with British star journalist David Frost was held in tycoon Fritz Kiehn's villa in Trossingen.

a vague hint by asserting that "some of the spectators had behaved downright shamefully", that there was no excuse for this "attitude" and that they were a slap in the face to any "decent sportsman".[403] In the eyes of the spectators, the superior Admira had been cheated of victory in this "grand battle" by the refereeing of "Herrn Schulz from Dresden", who had disallowed what they claimed were two fair goals. The two teams eventually drew 1:1 before a crowd of 52,000. These transgressions were not so much anti-National Socialist in nature as born of resentment towards the 'Piefkes' (an Austrian anti-German slur), and Schirach personally saw to it that they resulted in severe political persecution and punishments.

Schirach established an "Asocials Committee", since he was of the opinion the state organs were not dealing strictly enough with the alleged "500,000 asocials" in Vienna.[404] The consequences for the people in question were horrific. For instance, Vienna's Steinhof psychiatric clinic was the site of a "Labour Education Institution for Asocial Women" (*Arbeitserziehungsanstalt für asoziale Frauen*). Patients were committed completely arbitrarily for political reasons. The inhumane "treatment methods" were revealed during the trial of the clinic's former director, Dr Alfred Hackl, in the People's Court (*Volksgericht*) in October 1946:

> The scientific methods this lead physician used for the female prisoners' "education" were taken from the catalogue of punishments in the German concentration camps: withdrawal of food, hours of outdoor exercise until the women collapsed, and incarceration in concrete cells with bread and water. Radical methods including apomorphine injections, to make renitent women obedient due to nausea and severe exhaustion, were part of the camp penal code, which was administered following prison methods.[405]

These brutal and inhumane treatments were Schirach's ultimate strategy for persecuting Vienna's "asocials".

Chapter 10

"Viennesed"

From Young "Crown Prince" to Potential Successor

Everything had begun so promisingly: in September 1940, Joseph Goebbels' aides praised the new man in Vienna for his ability to get the job done.[406] Schirach, who also enjoyed the support of "Reich Dramaturg" Rainer Schlösser, got to work. In September 1940, he used the inauguration of Heinrich Karl Strohm, who had already been announced the future head of the Vienna State Opera in December 1939,[407] to inform the public of his cultural policy in greater detail:

> Many may find it strange to assemble in an opera house in the middle of the war and introduce a new director while our soldiers are in battle. At a time when the victorious squadrons are flying over the British Isles […] Germany is more than a territory and more than a geographical concept […]. The Greater German Reich is also a political Reich, a Reich of music and a Reich of poetry. It is not just a political great power, but also a great power of the spirit, of the soul and of the mind; what's more, Germany is a cultural power […]. The sound of the Philharmonic Orchestra merges with the thunder of our long-barrel guns. My mission for him and everyone serving in this cultural institute of the Greater German Reich can only be to make the Vienna State Opera the foremost stage of the German Reich.[408]

Yet at the same time, he also interpreted this 'cultural imperialism' as serving Germany's expansionist military aims and subordinating the "Ostmark" into the "Third Reich" as a whole. In his latter aim, he was misunderstood by many in Vienna, however. For instance, only a few weeks later, the writer and philosopher Aurel Wolfram, cultural advisor to the Reich Propaganda Office, wrote in the *Neues Wiener Tagblatt* (New

Vienna Daily) of 29 September a "harsh article against Berlin, its way of living and its inhabitants" with the headline "Vienna – refuge of the German soul". Wolfram, who considered Vienna to be the "capital of the inner Reich", particularly criticised the gigantomania of the development plans for Berlin, contrasting them with the historic growth of the metropolis on the Danube.[409] There were consequences to his concerned appeal "Hands off, all ambitious city builders": he was released from his post, arrested and spent a short time in prison.

Schirach complained about the article to Goebbels, who cynically noted in his diary that he immediately gave him the

> executive power to remove the man from office and place him in custody for a few days. I can do without my own official organs in Vienna starting to stir things up publicly against the Reich and against Berlin. It's high time Vienna was sorted out again. Schirach is on the right path to doing so.[410]

For this reason, Goebbels also wanted to send a new *Reichspropagandaamtsleiter* to Vienna, and selected the young HJ journalist Günter Kaufmann for the task. Kaufmann had made a name for himself as editor-in-chief of Schirach's press organ *Wille und Macht*. With reference to Goebbels' announcement that the Reich Theatre Week should take place regularly in Vienna in peacetime, Kaufmann developed a series of focal points for cultural propaganda in the areas of theatre, Viennese film and radio programmes devoted to the subject of South-eastern Europe.[411]

The "new" task for those responsible for Vienna's culture became ever clearer: keeping up morale during the war. This also explains Goebbels' directive to make twenty performances at the opera and the Burgtheater available to Viennese workers "in battledress and civvies".[412] The political backdrop to this decision was the complete subordination of social life to warfare – which the *Neues Wiener Tagblatt* also saw through the rose-tinted spectacles of the party: such actions saw a "new and strong cultural awareness returned to Vienna".[413]

While Schirach gradually began to use Viennese culture to adapt to the traditional Austrian self-understanding as a "cultural great power", Goebbels, who completely rejected the idea of "Vienna's European mission", repeated *ad nauseam* by Schirach and his colleagues, attempted to intensify the pure entertainment value of Vienna's cultural scene in order to raise "morale": "Vienna must become a city of culture, of optimism, of music and conviviality. Radio must also be so oriented."[414]

Goebbels: No "Viennese rogues"

Two months later, however, during a joint visit to Linz on 14 March 1941, Hitler made it clear to Goebbels that he wanted to have "a new cultural centre" built there:

> As a counterweight to Vienna, which should be gradually neutralised. He doesn't like Vienna, for reasons of political expediency if nothing else. I tell him about some things from Vienna, directly hostile to the Reich, that deeply appal him. But Linz is his favourite [...]. He wants to rebuild St Florian at his own cost ... We spend a long time chatting to the people of Linz. Genuine German men. Not Viennese rogues.[415]

However, in the short term, Hitler and Goebbels were prepared to approve the high cultural budgets Schirach requested, since the immediate internal and external propaganda effect of Vienna's high cultural scene was more important to them than visions in the sphere of cultural policy. This also included appearances abroad by the State Opera and the Burgtheater in politically controversial regions, such as the performances by the State Opera and the Philharmonic in the "occupied" Netherlands in October 1940 or in the "Generalgouvernement" (General Governorate), where the State Opera provided the framework for celebrating the first anniversary of its existence in breach of international law. In both cases, their role in political propaganda as a 'fig leaf' masking the German war of aggression was patently obvious.[416]

Schirach's plans for developing his Viennese position were not motivated by a fundamental affinity to the "Ostmark" or the Austrians' special role as "better cultural Germans"; rather, it was all about visibly manifesting his claim to a central leadership role in the "Third Reich". Schirach sought to get back to the top and probably thought he could achieve it from Vienna. His conflicts with Hitler and Goebbels, who were also the main decision-makers in the cultural sphere, had yet to come.

However, from January 1941 onwards, Schirach increasingly placed accents on the Viennese cultural scene that were also audible and visible to Berlin without openly stating that they were thoroughly Austrian cultural symbols. An example of such efforts was a Grillparzer Week from 15 to 22 January marking the poet's 150th birthday. In his opening speech, he cannily sought to link Austrian cultural traditions and National Socialist ideas: "Grillparzer is a Viennese of the greater Reich [...] the ancient world celebrated its resurrection in Austria".[417]

In another speech at the second War Cantata Conference of German Booksellers, Schirach once again explained the military elements underlying his cultural offensive: "Every German person owns Mozart's *Zauberflöte* and Weimar. This is what we have to defend against the enemy, what we have to stand up for against him and what has to win in this present conflict."[418]

Contrary to the assumptions of many in Vienna, Schirach was not at all interested in putting up indirect resistance to Nazi Germany. Rather, he attempted to intensify military strength by providing additional cultural motivations, and made it perfectly clear that he identified with the National Socialist war of aggression. However, he reinterpreted it as a "defensive war" to protect Austrian or Viennese culture.

The headlines welcoming Schirach's "Viennese Cultural Programme" of 7 April 1941 signalled that he was on the right path. The newspapers ran headlines such as, "Vienna as the Reich's number-one city of theatre", "Prince Eugene's grave as a pilgrimage site", "Vienna's great mission", "The cultural centre Vienna", "Vienna – a capital city of work and art", "Vienna, the city of culture", "Vienna has received a new cultural mission", or "The great mission". Schirach's culture policy initiatives ranged from new literature prizes (the Grillparzer and Raimund Prizes of the City of Vienna) to the Mozart Week of the German Reich (from 28 November to 5 December 1941) and the reopening of closed theatres.

"Deserving party members" were repeatedly entrusted with these "achievements": the management of the Volksoper or the Burgtheater was placed in the hands of the "old" NSDAP cultural functionaries Oskar Jölli and Robert Valberg, the provincial head of the *Reichstheaterkammer*

(Reich Theatre Chamber); Hermann Stuppäck was one of the recipients of the first Raimund Prize, etc.

This "cultural initiative" of Schirach's also included the "Promotion of the State School of Arts and Crafts [*Staatliche Kunstgewerbeschule*] and the State Academy of Music and Performing Arts [*Staatsakademie für Musik und darstellende Kunst*] to the Reich University of Applied Arts or Music [*Reichshochschule für angewandte Kunst bzw. Musik*]" on 5 November 1941, in the Großer Musikvereinssaal (Great Hall of the Musikverein).[419] During the ceremony, Schirach showed his clever use of psychology in a speech primarily aimed at the student body. Pointing to the HJ camps and training, half a year's work in service of the Reich and at least two years' military service (in peacetime), his performance culminated in the claim "that while studying at the university, the German student will receive the freedom he needs to fully develop as a person. Academic freedom is not a catchword of liberalism. It is an achievement of the German spirit."[420] These words, with their subtle allusion to individualism ("The idea is lonely"), are certainly untypical of the terror regime of observation, censorship and discipline that also weighed on the era's cultural sphere. But there was no place for this ostensible liberalism in the covert or sometimes quite open climate of militarisation. Otherwise, Schirach's remarks increasingly resembled the pseudo-revolutionary visions of the Nazi cultural protagonists of the post-"Anschluss" "Ostmark". For instance, on the occasion of the Vienna Philharmonic's centenary, he declared that "all art is at home here in Vienna".[421] In Berlin, on the other hand, he was increasingly marginalising himself with his emphasis on "Viennese cultural imperialism", which in Hitler's eyes was "cultural opposition", and which Goebbels considered to be "Viennese cultural liberalism".[422]

Goebbels, who was keeping a watchful eye on events in Vienna, had identified the man he thought was to blame for the city's ambivalent cultural policy in 1942. His suspicions were fed by the crafty intrigues of Heinz Tietjen, the director general of the Prussian State Theatre company:

> In this context, Tietjen also reports to me on recurring attempts by the Viennese to increasingly force back Berlin as a cultural centre. Local General Culture Advisor [*General-Kulturreferent*] Thomas pursues a pretty unscrupulous policy and is ruthlessly exploiting

the emergency situation in which we find ourselves due to greater involvement in war work. Hence I will amplify my cultural-political line against Vienna, which was always reserved.[423]

Ultimately, Schirach's and Thomas's own depiction of their anti-Berlin cultural activities are only accurate in terms of mere details. It wasn't until Hitler ordered the closure of the exhibition on "Young Art in the German Reich" in 1943, leading to Thomas's dismissal, that things came to a head. In principle, Schirach adhered to the ideological framework, but he also attempted to push its boundaries to their limit. He did not shy away from internal party conflict, and hence he was vulnerable when it came to peripheral issues. What disturbed Goebbels and Hitler even more was that Vienna attracted prominent artists seeking to flee the air raids on Berlin.

To this day, Schirach's stubborn cultural policy is indirectly portrayed as a symptom of resistance to the "Third Reich" in Austria.[424] Certainly, Berlin was critical of the Gerhardt Hauptmann Week in Vienna in 1942, which had been organised by Cultural Advisor General Walter Thomas, but Hauptmann's significance for National Socialist propaganda in the field of German culture remained intact, despite some ideological criticism of the writer, as demonstrated by the fact that his works were performed throughout Germany and the "occupied territories".[425]

Subjectively, Schirach's ambivalent cultural policy and ostensible liberalism, which were also fed by his ambition, may have appeared to some people to be opposition to the "German occupiers". Vienna's cultural elite certainly appreciated the stance he took. As a societal phenomenon, however, it was this very understanding of culture that helped them suppress their own political responsibility for wars of aggressions and the Holocaust.

That the relevant authorities in Berlin were well aware of the importance of this specific type of cultural policy for the war effort – to keep up morale, as it were – is evident from the substantial budget Schirach received in the form of Reich subsidies from 1941 to 1943 even though he only indirectly administered Vienna's cultural institutions. In 1941, some 56,500 Reichsmark were made available for the written word, 275,500 for the visual arts and 409,400 for music.[426]

Clearly, Schirach was at pains to increase the promotion of the visual arts. A large amount of the funding was apportioned to the renovation of the Künstlerhaus or the acquisition of paintings to expand its inventory. Schirach's motivation for switching course when it came to subventions and promoting the visual arts probably owed not so much to his understanding of the genre as to the fact that he fancied himself as a patron of the arts. Moreover, the visual arts were far better suited to representation than literature, for instance. This image of the art patron was one Hitler too sought to cultivate.

In late 1944, Hitler made money from the "Führer's budgetary fund" available for the renovation of Professor Fritz Klimsch's apartment and studio; Klimsch's paintings had found favour with Hitler and Goebbels, and they both acquired a number of his pictures. (Hitler bought *Ötztaler Bäuerin* (Ötztal Peasant Woman), *Beim alten Getreidespeicher* (By the Old Grain Silo) and *Frühling im alten Gemäuer* (Springtime in the Old Walls), Goebbels *Die Stille im Raum* (Silence in the Room).[427]

In the musical sphere, the Society of Music Lovers (*Gesellschaft der Musikfreunde*) was promised a larger dedicated subsidy, and the Mozart Week also received the financial support it required. For 1942, Schirach obtained a total of 445,000 Reichsmark; 20,000 were for the written word, 197,000 for the visual arts and 228,000 for music. Funding to the tune of some 358,000 Reichsmark was available in 1943, following a similar breakdown; in the visual arts, the Society of Visual Artists (*Gesellschaft der bildenden Künstler*) was particularly favoured (receiving 100,000 Reichsmark in 1942 and 120,000 in 1943). These subventions were slightly more than those received by the Society of Music Lovers (80,000 Reichsmark in 1942 and 120,000 in 1943).[428] In 1941, Schirach had been able to use 800,000 Reichsmark in additional revenues from the state theatres for his cultural programme.[429]

For the budget of 1942, the Reich Ministry for the People's Enightenment and Propaganda made another 700,000 Reichmark available to the state theatres (201,000 for the State Opera, 134,000 for the Burgtheater, 22,000 for the Akademietheater, and the rest for decorations).[430]

The regular budget for the state theatres amounted to 9,051,600 Reichsmark in 1941; it would be cut to 7,484,350 in 1942. However, there were also theatre subventions for the Vienna Volksoper (1940: 150,000 Reichsmark, 1941: 117,673 Reichsmark, 1942: 150,000 Reichsmark), the Volkstheater and the Raimundtheater, the two *Kraft durch Freude*

(Strength through Joy) stages (400,000 Reichsmark per annum from 1940 to 1943) and the Theater in der Josefstadt (334,484 Reichsmark in 1940, 493,852 in 1941, and 400,000 in 1942).[431]

In the long term, however, the Grillparzer and Mozart Weeks, the rebuilding of the Künstlerhaus, the exhibition *Das schöne Wiener Frauen-Bildnis* (The Beautiful Image of the Viennese Woman), the Raimund Week and several prizes promoting young and "deserving national" artists could not stop people recognising their military defeat. From the National Socialist perspective, Schirach's cultural offensive did not pass the 'acid test'.

The revival of the 'classical Austrian cultural traditions' via "Viennese culture", which Schirach had successfully used to maintain National Socialist rule at least until 1943 and which was discontinued with the introduction of "total warfare" in 1944, had clear psychological consequences for Austria's failure to examine its political past. Due to the wartime pressures, the Austrian public developed a kind of latent Austrian identity by seeking refuge in "Old Austrian", usually conservative cultural traditions.

Every aspect of collaboration with National Socialist ideas and actions was suppressed, and hence after 1945 all forms of critical examination were rejected and National Socialism was reduced to a purely "Prussian German" problem for which, at the most, a few "illegal" National Socialists were to blame. To exaggerate slightly, one might say that Schirach's "Old Austrian high culture offensive" and the reinforcement of a – Vienna-centric – cultural awareness played a large role in preventing self-critical examination of Austria's own responsibility for Fascism, National Socialism, the Second World War and the Holocaust.

Not only did the conservative high culture create a number of niches in Austria itself, but it was also an essential element in preserving Austrian identity among émigrés. However, the fact that this "cultural tradition" enabled formerly National Socialist cultural figures to continue to work in the Second Republic without critically reflecting on their artistic production under the "Third Reich" is another mistake of Austrian cultural policy after 1945.

The Conflict Deepens

In March 1942, Schirach still enjoyed recognition as a young *Gauleiter*, even from the hypercritical propaganda minster Joseph Goebbels and despite initial negative debates within the party concerning his cultural policy. In particular, the protests in response to the premiere of Rudolf Wagner-Régeny's contemporary opera *Johanna Balk* at the Vienna State Opera in April 1941, which had seen the NSDAP and its 'old guard' try to outshout and provoke each other in the presence of the *Reichsstatthalter*, had also met with criticism in Berlin. Goebbels noted in his diary:

> Vienna's cultural policy is losing its way here and there. [Those determining it are] still too youthful and without experience. Schirach gained the bulk of his experience in the Hitler Youth. But he will soon grow out of this too. His advisor in matters of cultural policy, Thomas, is sometimes clumsy when it comes to personnel and business. The performance of [...] by Wagner-Régeny, for example, was a total blunder.[432]

Nevertheless, the propaganda minister was satisfied with the "announcement of the Anschluss" in Heldenplatz: "Vienna has indeed become a Reich city. Even if a few creases need ironing out here and there, that is of secondary importance. When push comes to shove, this city of two million will prove its loyalty to the Reich."[433] In principle, he also agreed with Schirach's strategy of developing the artistic and cultural sphere as a kind of surrogate for Vienna's loss of grandeur. This corresponded to Hitler's original aim, but Goebbels rejected Schirach's proximity to the composer and former president of the *Reichsmusikkammer* Richard Strauss, and issued him with a stern warning. At the same time, however, Berlin's status as "the" capital of the Reich was to remain unthreatened, including in the cultural sphere.[434]

Goebbels received a drip feed of irritating information about Schirach's activities, which could be interpreted as a kind of "interference" in the "leadership of German cultural policy"[435] – an example being his speech at the centenary celebrations of the Vienna Philharmonic. The Security Service (*Sicherheitsdienst*, SD) of the *Reichsführer-SS* also provided a constant stream of material, reporting, for instance, that Schirach had not mentioned the "Reich" when speaking during the jubilee festivities celebrating the Viennese poet Josef Weinheber. Only the poet himself, who had become an enthusiastic National Socialist, had mentioned the all-German perspective, the SD noted. Goebbels' political assessment of Vienna's cultural policy now read:

> The development in Vienna under Schirach gives cause for great concern. Schirach is not remotely a match for Viennese guile. He allows himself be flattered without knowing it and realising what the Viennese are really up to.[436]

Hitler also had the same concerns, but told Goebbels to "say nothing" about Schirach.[437] The telegram he sent to Schirach on his birthday on 9 May 1942 was misinterpreted by some people close to the *Reichsstatthalter* as a "crown prince telegram";[438] in fact, it was at this point that Hitler began to distance himself from Schirach personally and, ultimately, politically. Nevertheless, the *Völkischer Beobachter* reported the "Führer's warmly-worded congratulations".[439] However, the internal distance also became evident in the discussions on the potential successor to the position of *Gauleiter* in Munich, which was much more prestigious than that in Vienna.

Goebbels had already taken Schirach to task face-to-face in Berlin without causing a scandal. A week later, in May 1942, Hitler again took up the subject of Vienna and cultural policy:[440]

> Vienna should not be given preferential treatment to Linz and Graz, and hence he is also determined to break Vienna's cultural hegemony. He doesn't want the Reich to have two capitals competing with one another. Above all, Vienna should not take up a hegemonial position towards the Austrian Gau regions either. Vienna is just a city of one million like Hamburg, nothing more. Schirach is completely on the wrong path here. He has allowed himself to be very heavily influenced by the Viennese mood, the wine tavern atmosphere and the so-called Viennese "Hamur" [Viennese humour].[441]

There were a number of small conflicts between Schirach and Goebbels over this question of Vienna's cultural significance. Hitler got so involved in the cultural debate that he rejected the proposal that Schirach be sent to Munich as the successor to *Gauleiter* Adolf Wagner, who had suffered a heart attack, saying that Schirach had allowed himself to be influenced too much in Vienna.[442]

Schirach certainly benefited from his official visits to the Vienna Philharmonic, having been awarded the orchestra's ring of honour on 27 March 1942. For instance, Klaus von Schirach was given violin lessons by the orchestra's Karl Johannis.[443] On 15 December 1944, Schirach was also presented with a French violin from the State Opera's collection of instruments – it was never returned.[444] As many other examples show, the *Reichsstatthalter* had no qualms about gaining private advantage from public property.

The attempts by second violinist Johannis to use these private contacts to seek Göring's pardon for his brother-in-law, the lawyer Hans Wölfel from Bamberg,[445] who had been sentenced to death by the People's Court in Berlin for "undermining military morale" (*Wehrkraftzersetzung*), were in vain. Schirach is said to have made a personal phone call to Göring to discuss the matter.[446]

After US president Franklin D. Roosevelt gave a speech to the youth, Schirach was quickly tasked with giving a counter-speech to be broadcast on the radio news and via shortwave. Even Goebbels considered this speech "an extraordinarily effective and well-founded reply".[447] For a moment, the man who had Hitler's ear seemed satisfied. However, news of the European Youth Congress described above brought Schirach new criticism: above all, Goebbels feared that Schirach's many public pronouncements on the deportation of Jews from Vienna to the East could lead to criticism from the press in neutral states.[448]

Despite his Viennese cultural policy, Schirach still enjoyed plenty of respect in Berlin, especially due the good organisation of the *Erweiterte Kinderlandverschickung*.[449] But the particular Viennese honours bestowed on the writer and dramaturg Gerhart Hauptmann on the occasion of his eightieth birthday, which Goebbels considered to be "exaggerated adulation" contrary to his own strategy, moved the "Reich" propaganda minister to determine that "Schirach's extravagances in the cultural sector" were to be "prevented in future".[450]

Schirach was undeterred – he travelled to Breslau himself to collect Hauptmann and his wife Margarete. In the meantime, Henriette sent her cook, Rosa, by bus to Pressburg (today's Bratislava), where there was more to buy than in Vienna, and hosted an opulent breakfast for the Hauptmanns with "caviar, chickens and zander" at the "Aryanised" villa on the Hohe Warte. Richard and Pauline Strauss were also in attendance.[451] As a special treat, a small apartment had been set up for the Hauptmanns' eight-day visit, in the elegant townhouse Palais Pallavicini.

Goebbels, however, had only planned to honour the white-haired doyen of German literature in Breslau. Only one new production was planned for each theatre, and *Die Weber* (*The Weavers*) was banned.[452] As early as 1936, Goebbels had echoed Alfred Rosenberg's repeated pronouncements on the National Socialist regime's distance towards Hauptmann's works and their proximity to Modernism and social criticism, but had ultimately compromised in order to exploit his renown as a Nobel laureate. In 1942, however, Hauptmann was no longer a good fit for German culture's image of war and hence his birthday was meant to receive scant mention – and above all, quite in contrast to the period after 1933, he was not to "be termed an exponent of the National Socialist ideology".[453] At the same time, Adolf Bartels, the literary figure of the Weimar Group, to which Schirach's father and son also belonged, was praised to the heavens, since he happened to have been born on the same day of the same year as Hauptmann.[454] But Bartels was unknown in Vienna and Schirach wanted his public cultural policy to always be based on big names. Along with Gerhart Hauptmann and Richard Strauss, such figures included the up-and-coming artists Werner Egk, Carl Orff and Rudolf Wagner-Régeny, to name just three composers. The Reich Ministry for the People's Enlightenment and Propaganda knew that Hauptmann wasn't a Nazi, even if he certainly backed the regime publicly. Fittingly, Klaus Mann called him the "Hindenburg of German literature".

The Break with Hitler

In 1943, Hitler and Goebbels gradually broke with Schirach. The first cause of the growing discord was the above-mentioned exhibition on "Young Art in the German Reich" curated by art historian Wilhelm Rüdiger. Rüdiger had received his doctorate, written under Wilhelm Pinder, in Munich in 1932 and enjoyed a rapid rise despite his youth – not least due to having joined the NSDAP in 1930. In 1933, only eleven days after Hitler came to power in Germany, he had launched a severe attack on the exponents of Modernism in an article in the *Völkischer Beobachter* with the headline "Taking stock of the century: a cultural-political chamber of horrors".[455] In the art criticism he wrote for the *Völkischer Beobachter* or the journal *Die Kunst des Deutschen Reiches*, Rüdiger proved an uncompromising racist and anti-Semite: as early as 1933, during his brief stint as acting director of the Städtische Kunstsammlungen Chemnitz (Chemnitz Municipal Art Collections), he organised an exhibition on "degenerate art" entitled *Art That Does not Speak from Our Soul* (*Kunst, die nicht aus unserer Seele spricht*).[456]

In 1942, Rüdiger designed a controversial exhibition for the European Youth Meeting in Weimar, which was surreptitiously closed because it contained some works considered "degenerate".[457] Rüdiger was certainly open to "Aryan" artists, even if their works had been confiscated by the Nazi regime and categorised as "degenerate". This did not bother Schirach, who brought the exhibition to Vienna and had it expanded to include artists from the "Ostmark". On show were works by Josef Hegenbarth, Josef Henselmann, Hanna Nagel, Carl Moritz Schreiner, Milly Steger or Friedrich Vordemberge. A total of 582 pictures by 175 artists were exhibited in the Künstlerhaus.[458] Intelligence reports by the SD reached Goebbels, who for the time being did not wish to make a "big deal and state affair" out of it, even if the Vienna exhibition was perceived as a counterpoint to the annual grand exhibition in Munich.[459]

It was not until Hitler unexpectedly called a dinner on 21 March 1943 and unleashed a torrent of criticisms about Schirach that the exhibition in Vienna suddenly became a subject of any import. "He is extraordinarily indignant about the exhibition 'Young Art' that Schirach has put on in Vienna", noted Goebbels in his diary. He continued:

> He is giving me the task of keeping tabs on Vienna and, potentially, if such incidents should arise again, block Vienna's cultural subsidies. The Führer again emphasises how right he is to set Linz in competition with the city of Vienna. The greatest cheek is actually that Vienna goes against the Reich's official cultural policy while receiving the largest Reich subsidy for its [own] cultural policy. The Führer declares that if that doesn't change, he will disrobe Schirach of his sovereignty over cultural policy and have me install a cultural delegate in Vienna.[460]

One factor was that Adolf Ziegler, the president of the Reich Chamber of the Visual Arts (*Reichskammer der bildenden Künste*), had written a very negative report on the exhibition, discrediting it as a "moderate form of the art of decay". Architect and National Socialist Reich Stage Designer (*NS-Reichsbühnenbildner*) Benno von Arent had been sent to Vienna by Hitler personally, and reported with outrage on this "liberalistic disgrace".[461] Goebbels chimed in by sending Hitler a speech by Schirach on art policy that reflected the "tendencies" of the exhibition on Young German Art.[462] As outlined above, the exhibition was closed early, after just four weeks and 9,000 visitors. The concurrent Klimt exhibition attracted 24,000 people and demonstrated the breadth of Schirach's artistic taste. Hitler, however, was more annoyed by the fact that Josef Hegenbarth's painting entitled "Green Dog" (*Grüner Hund*) had been reproduced in black and white in the exhibition catalogue.

At the same time, when Schirach met with Hitler at the latter's private Bavarian refuge on the Obersalzberg, a second issue blew up: Schirach's attempts to prevent the movement of armament factories to Vienna.[463] Bormann, however, had passed on Hitler's instructions that all "total warfare" measures were to be implemented in Vienna too.[464]

Despite the dressing down he gave Schirach, Hitler still hesitated to break with him completely, even though he had opposed the concept of "total warfare" developed by Goebbels and Albert Speer, unlike the *Gauleiter* of "Oberdonau", Styria, and "Niederdonau" – August Eigruber, Sigfried Uiberreither and Hugo Jury. Schirach's cultural advisor, Walter Thomas, reviled by Goebbels, would serve as the sacrificial lamb for the cultural policy that was ultimately Schirach's responsibility. Thomas was to be sent to the Eastern Front. Thomas managed to avoid this 'death sentence', however; a military medical commission pronounced him unfit for service.[465] If Thomas is to be believed, Schirach had already realised in the winter of 1942–43 that he would no longer be able to continue his "special Viennese policy", which Hitler perceived to be "cultural opposition": "It has a provocative effect and only makes me more enemies."[466]

On 7 May 1943, an irritated Goebbels noted in his diary that Hitler was still considering sending Schirach to Munich as *Gauleiter* even though it was said that he had no ability to act politically.[467] But the very next day, the "Führer" shelved this plan, sharing Goebbels' stance entirely, as the latter noted, again in his diary:

> The Führer has a poor opinion of Schirach. Schirach has become Viennesed in Vienna. He has allowed himself to be too strongly infected by the Viennese atmosphere. He has not demonstrated any political instinct, nor is he a fully-fledged Nazi. Now he has suddenly started speaking with American inflection and rolling his Rs like an actor. He is dealing with too many artists, and it isn't doing him any good. At any rate, the Führer has no big plans for him. Sooner or later he would like to squeeze him out into a diplomatic career, which indeed is more suitable for Schirach.[468]

The very moment Goebbels had something positive to say about the signals coming from Vienna and was even planning to conclude "a working and friendship agreement", albeit one establishing clear subordination to Berlin,[469] matters came to a head. And yet the private dinner on Corpus Christi, 24 June 1943, to which Eva Braun had also invited the Schirachs, began convivially enough. In the teahouse, Heinrich Hoffmann, Goebbels and the Schirachs talked about the theatre and cultural issues. Marion Schönmann, Eva Braun's friend from Munich, also had plenty to say; according to Baldur von Schirach, she may have passed on rumours from Vienna to the "Führer".[470] Suddenly Hitler exploded, attacking not only Baldur, but also his wife, who had almost been like a godchild to him. However, she had "virtually brought the Führer to a rage" by "instantly" displaying "a somewhat childishly silly, teary manner, trying hard to be witty".[471] Hitler became increasingly aggressive, and Henriette, who was indeed close to tears, asked him to send her husband to Munich, allowing him to swap roles with Paul Giesler. Hitler categorically declined.[472] Over a month later, Hitler was still angry about this fireside gathering.

In her memoirs, Henriette would later describe what triggered this strong outburst: she had visited friends in Amsterdam and was woken by noise in the street. Jews were being rounded up and deported. A soldier from the SS had then offered her jewellery stolen from Jewish women. She reported her experience to Hitler at the Berghof. After a short silence, Hitler then shouted at her: "You're sentimental […] what have the Jews in Holland got to do with you? It's all sentimentality, humanity claptrap. You have to learn to hate …"[473] Henriette further claimed that she "let him shout" and ran to her room, whereupon an adjutant ran after her and ordered her to leave immediately. At five o'clock in the morning, the Schirachs took their sports car from the garage and drove off, not speaking a word on the way to Vienna. Henriette's insight after this turbulent night at the Berghof?: "And now I suddenly realised that it was precisely what we had performed, done, chosen that was unjust. Loved the wrong thing and hated the wrong thing."[474]

However, her criticism was probably only the last straw for Hitler, who was already in a foul mood; according to the "Führer's" *Luftwaffe* adjutant Nicolaus von Below, the conflict with Schirach was due to a "long and detailed conversation" the same day, in which Schirach had dared to "very unambiguously" point out that the war had to be stopped "some way or other". Hitler's response had been, "[...] He knows as well as I do that there is no longer any way, unless I put a bullet in my head." Hitler had been very agitated about this conversation with Schirach and had made it "clear" he no longer wanted anything to do with him.[475] Below was mistaken when he wrongly stated that this was Hitler's last encounter with Schirach, but it is true that from that day on, the *Gauleiter* of Vienna and his wife were no longer part of the "Führer's" inner circle. They were no longer welcome on the Obersalzberg after Corpus Christi 1943.

However, Schirach's words cannot have come as a surprise to the *Luftwaffe* adjutant: a few weeks earlier, in the early June of 1943, Below and his wife had holidayed in Vienna, where they had been received "extremely courteously and friendlily" by the Schirachs. Together, they went to see Shakespeare's *The Merchant of Venice* at the Burgtheater, and afterwards they had the opportunity to "talk openly and freely about the political and military situation":

> We spent at least an hour dealing with all the problems, and for my part, I gave him a clear picture of the development of the aerial situation. I told him that I considered it impossible to win the war with our forces. Schirach shared my views. He was just very annoyed that Ribbentrop, Keitel and other high-ranking officers weren't telling the Führer the whole truth. I had to contradict him there, for I knew that Ribbentrop and indeed many generals had clearly set out the difficulties of the war to the Führer and made their doubts clear to him. I had to tell Schirach very clearly that Hitler was the sole bearer of the war. He was now constantly referring to the Casablanca Conference, at which Roosevelt and Churchill had demanded

unconditional capitulation from us. Schirach did not consider this declaration to be so crucial, and thought that there was still enough time for a peace settlement.[476]

But Schirach had doubtlessly taken his still fresh impressions of this confidential conversation with von Below to the Obersalzberg; he had been determined to tell his idol the whole truth.

Goebbels, who had witnessed the conflict between Hitler and Schirach, could scarcely conceal his delight with this development in his diary:

> On the whole, it has been a very agitated and eventful evening in which all sorts of problems have been addressed. But due to the behaviour of Schirach and his wife, the evening takes on a certain tension. Frau von Schirach in particular behaves like a stupid turkey and will not accept the Führer's arguments in the slightest. But this does not bother the Führer at all. He puts all politeness aside and only elaborates on the matter in hand. Afterwards, Frau von Schirach encapsulates her entire unhappiness by saying she would like to return to Munich with her husband, and would the Führer send Giesler to Vienna to that end. The Führer categorically refuses. [He says] he won't even think about it. [He tells her] Schirach has to fulfil his mission for the party and the Reich in Vienna.[477]

Goebbels' remark that Henriette von Schirach brought up the idea of a swap with Paul Giesler, the *Gauleiter* of "München-Oberbayern" and "Westfalen-Süd", would suggest that the discussion also included detailed discussion of Baldur von Schirach's position and his 'performance' in Vienna. For Goebbels and probably for the other members of Hitler's entourage, it was certainly clear that following this scene, Schirach no longer held any political sway.

At the Nuremberg trials, Schirach received the opportunity to present his own detailed version of events at the Berghof in 1943. In fact, the conflict grew over the course of three evenings, culminating in the 'Vienna question'. If Schirach is to be believed, it was Goebbels who brought up the subject on the third evening, thus lighting the fuse once and for all:

I had intended – and I also carried out my intention – to mention at least three points during my visit. One was the policy toward Russia, the second was the Jewish question, and the third was Hitler's attitude toward Vienna.

I must state, to begin with, that Bormann had issued a decree addressed to me, and probably to all the other Gauleiters, prohibiting any intervention on our part in the Jewish question. That is to say, we could not intervene with Hitler in favor of any Jew or half-Jew. That too was stated in the decree. I have to mention this, since it makes matters clearer.

On the first evening of my stay at the Berghof, on what appeared to me a propitious occasion, I told Hitler that I was of the opinion that a free and autonomous Ukraine would serve the Reich better than a Ukraine ruled by the violence of Herr Koch. That was all I said, nothing more, nothing less. Knowing Hitler as I did, it was extremely difficult even to hazard such a remark. Hitler answered comparatively quietly but with pronounced sharpness. On the same evening, or possibly the next one, the Jewish question was broached according to a plan I made with my wife. Since I was forbidden to mention these things even in conversation, my wife gave the Führer a description of an experience she had had in Holland. She had witnessed one night, from the bedroom of her hotel, the deportation of Jewish women by the Gestapo. We were both of the opinion that this experience during her journey and the description of it might possibly result in a change of Hitler's attitude toward the entire Jewish question and in the treatment of the Jews. My wife gave a very drastic description, a description such as we can now read in the papers. Hitler was silent. All the other witnesses to this conversation, including my own father-in-law, Professor Hoffmann, were also silent. The silence was icy, and after a short time Hitler merely said, "This is pure sentimentality." That was all. No further conversation took place that evening. Hitler retired earlier than usual. I was under the impression that a perfectly untenable situation had now arisen. Then the men of Hitler's entourage told my father-in-law that from now on I would have to fear for my safety. I endeavored to get away from the Berghof as quickly as possible without letting matters come to an open break, but I did not succeed.

Then Goebbels arrived on the next evening and there, in my presence and without my starting it, the subject of Vienna was broached. I was naturally compelled to protest against the statements which Goebbels at first made about the Viennese. Then the Führer began with) I might say, incredible and unlimited hatred to speak against the people of Vienna. I have to admit, here and now, that even if the people of Vienna are cursing me today, I have always felt very friendly toward them. I have felt closely attached to those people. I will not say more than that Joseph Weinheber was one of my closest friends. During that discussion, I, in accordance with my duty and my feelings, spoke in favor of the people under my authority in Vienna.

At 4 o'clock in the morning, among other things, Hitler suddenly said something which I should now like to repeat for historical reasons. He said, "Vienna should never have been admitted into the Union of Greater Germany." Hitler never loved Vienna. He hated its people.[478]

In the months leading up to this tempestuous meeting on the Obersalzberg for which there are so many different versions, Hitler frequently criticised Schirach's inability to ensure Vienna was sufficiently protected against impending air raids, and considered replacing him as *Reichsstatthalter* and *Gauleiter*.[479] Baldur von Schirach's goose seemed to have finally been cooked; on 21 August 1943, following a conversation with Hitler, Goebbels noted in his diary: "The Führer doesn't want to know Schirach anymore. Schirach is a weakling, a windbag and an idiot when it comes to deep political matters. He would rather dismiss him from Vienna sooner than later, if only he had a successor."[480] This negative assessment, that Schirach was weak and that politically he was no National Socialist hardliner, was reinforced in the subsequent months.

In November 1943, Bormann was tasked with joining Goebbels in proposing specific successors to Schirach.[481] Once more, Goebbels and Hitler accused Schirach of failing to protect Vienna from air raids. Schirach responded with a suggestion that was rejected: in December 1943, he requested permission to evacuate some 300,000 women and children from the city.[482] The Allied bombing raids had reached the entire territory of the Reich.

That Schirach was not dismissed in the end was mainly due to the fact that potential candidates to succeed him, such as the *Gauleiter* of "Niederdonau", Hugo Jury, who was much admired by Hitler, declined. Day-to-day party work in Vienna increasingly fell to the long-serving deputy *Gauleiter* Karl Scharizer, who had been an SS brigade leader (*SS-Brigadeführer*) since 1941.

Baldur von Schirach, Goethe, the Hitler Youth and Art

Schirach's interest in Johann Wolfgang von Goethe, who along with Friedrich Schiller represented the central figure of German literature for the Weimar elite, was clearly influenced by the attempt to exploit symbolic personalities of bourgeois and aristocratic high culture for National Socialist purposes. Nazi cultural policy sought to gain political legitimation from the German classics – as long as the authors weren't figures of Jewish origin such as Heinrich Heine.

Schirach played an important role in the ideological instrumentalisation of German Classicism. Due to his experience in Weimar, discussed in depth in the earlier chapters, he considered himself particularly well suited to implementing this re-interpretation of Goethe as the ideologue of HJ training. While Goethe did write that "Youth educates itself in youth"[483] (*Maximen und Reflexionen* (*Maxims and Reflections*), volume 5, book 3, 1826), this line was ultimately of no real use as a *leitmotiv* to Schirach, who envisaged "youth's self-leadership" as a totalitarian educational principle. Hence Goethe had to be adapted to fit National Socialism.

The first step was thus to discredit the "falsifications" to which Goethe had allegedly been subjected. He addressed this in his opening speech at the Weimar Festival of German Youth (*Weimarer Festspiele für die deutsche Jugend*) on 14 June 1937:

> For what use was Goethe to us, Goethe the citizen of the world, the liberal prophet of so-called progress? Did he not place himself, the Olympian, above the fatherland and the nation, and free himself from the shackles of all ties to the fatherland to become a prophet of humanity? Such a Goethe, falsified as an idol of abstract aesthetehood and democratically left-wing fatherlandlessness, cannot be

reconciled with the marching columns of the youth of the "Third Reich", however. What nonsense to link, forcibly, as it were, a youth movement representing the revolutionary educational principle of self-leadership, putting everyone in uniform and communal education, with a personality that to some people embodies the ideal of a thoroughly individualistic education.[484]

Schirach went on to "prove" that it was possible to reconcile the HJ with Goethe the "intellectual leader". In the programme for the Weimar Festival of German Youth, the focus shifted from Schiller to Goethe, and even before Schirach's speech, the HJ *Reichsführer* youth camps of May 1937 had to discuss Goethe as the creator of Faust. Julius Petersen, the president of the Goethe Society (*Goethe-Gesellschaft*), was most enthusiastic: "Here we may perceive the "Third Reich's" acknowledgment of Goethe, Schiller and Weimar and the call to German youth to see in Weimar's heroes the symbols of German greatness and intellectual leadership."[485]

Ultimately, Schirach successfully ignored Goethe's concept of individuality, which was entirely contrary to the National Socialist ideal of the "people's community" ("Volksgemeinschaft").[486] The same went for Goethe's freemasonry, which was also played down and qualified. During National Socialism, Schirach no longer continued to pursue Goethe, but he was a co-founder of the University of Vienna's Central Institute of Theatre Studies (*Zentralinstitut für Theaterwissenschaft*), headed by Heinz Kindermann.[487]

However, Schirach's concept of art, which later brought him into open conflict with Hitler and Goebbels, was certainly based on ideas he had obtained from reading Goethe and on those of the nationalist cultural philosopher Houston Stewart Chamberlain.[488] During the opening of the exhibition on "Viennese Art in Düsseldorf" on 28 September 1941, he attempted to beat the drum for contemporary art, advancing the remarkable theory that "Art serves not reality, but the truth".[489] Schirach even went so far as to make the rebellious claim that pure realism – that is, the imitation of nature – was "degeneration" – a comment that was not reprinted by the National Socialist press, unsurprisingly. One of the few newspapers that reproduced Schirach's original speech was the *Kölnische Zeitung* (Cologne Newspaper): "It is just as much a degeneration of art if one paints two eyes on the cheek of a person depicted in profile as it is degeneration to paint objects, people or landscapes in such a way that they correspond to the truth of reality."[490]

Typically for Schirach, who unlike his father and sister had consciously remained a Protestant and had not left the Church, he invoked the deity: "God forbid that we lapse into a new art materialism and imagine we need only depict the real in order to be immediately true."[491] Here, he was describing a stylistic element that can be found not only in his prose but also in his poetry.[492]

The Düsseldorf newspaper *Der Mittag* (Noon) went so far as to quote this statement in a headline.[493] The Viennese edition of the *Völkischer Beobachters*, however, recognised that the statement was politically controversial and abbreviated the headline to read: "Art serves truth".[494] Schirach provided examples supporting his argument against a concept of art that recognised only "the truth of reality".[495]

Here, Schirach took up a debate primarily emanating from literature, and was attacking Hans Hagen, without naming him. Hagen had a doctorate in German, was a member of duelling fraternities, the SA and, later, the NSDAP, and an unsalaried lecturer at the Office for the Cultivation of the Written Word (*Amt für Schrifttumspflege*), which was part of the office of chief ideologue Alfred Rosenberg. Furthermore, he was a consultant to the executive editor of the new cultural propaganda magazine *Das Reich*, which had been initiated by Goebbels himself. In 1941, Hagen had been publicly accused by the "Reich" culture senator (*Reichskultursenator*) and National Socialist writer Eberhard Wolfgang Möller of writing a poem amounting to "aesthetic desecration of corpses", thereby triggering an art debate.[496] The lines Schirach cited above were taken from Hagen and were directed against Möller's alleged aestheticism.[497]

Schirach clearly had sufficient political influence to escape censure. However, Möller, whom he had supported during his HJ days, was sent to the front by order of the *Reichsführer-SS*. In contrast, Schirach's position was bolstered: his speeches in Düsseldorf attracted attention and he was elected president of the Bibliophile Society (*Gesellschaft der Bibliophilen*),[498] which printed two of his Düsseldorf addresses.[499] It is unclear with whom Schirach developed such questions on art theory or who drafted his speeches. It is unlikely it was his cultural advisor Günter Kaufmann, since his publishing remit was party political issues. At the art exhibition in Vienna, emphasis was placed on the role of the chairman of the Künstlerhaus, Rudolf Hermann Eisenmenger, and Cultural Advisor General Walter Thomas, who were all mentioned by name.[500] Thomas was Schirach's main advisor on cultural policy and the man who realised all projects in Vienna.

As already mentioned, Walter Thomas had not been Schirach's first choice; he would rather have taken Rainer Schlösser with him to Vienna. But as a dramaturg and aide to the renowned director and theatre manager Saladin Schmitt in Bochum, he did have something of a reputation in the art world. Thomas was a member of the NSDAP and made it unequivocally clear that after 1933 the Bochum stage had adapted to the "great ideological and political change".[501]

A few weeks after Schirach's opening speech at the Düsseldorf exhibition, Thomas explained how the former's extensive speech in the Burgtheater on 6 April 1941, in which he outlined the cultural programme,[502] would be implemented, with explicit reference to the Düsseldorf address.[503] In his memoirs, published under a pseudonym,[504] he played down Schirach's role in shaping Viennese cultural policy, but later apologised for doing so in a letter to Henriette von Schirach.[505] Due to his many functions, Baldur von Schirach was certainly not in a position to take care of day-to-day business in the cultural sphere, and Thomas also signed most of the correspondence that has survived. Schirach did attend most public events, however, and he and his wife Henriette took care of prominent guests such as the composer Richard Strauss or the writer Gerhard Hauptmann. He also enjoyed hosting breakfast or dinner in his "Aryanised" residence on the Hohe Warte.

With its strong emphasis on a local Viennese flavour and classical high culture, but also by supporting contemporary art and music, Schirach's cultural policy was certainly different to that of the other large metropolises under National Socialist influence. In his essay on the relationship between Schirach and the Vienna Philharmonic, Friedemann Pestel rightly speaks of symbiosis.[506] The orchestra remained relatively autonomous and also enjoyed Schirach's material and symbolic support. At the same time, he repeatedly instrumentalised the Philharmonic to make the central authorities in Berlin aware of Vienna's importance.

The post-war claims of the Vienna Philharmonic board, full of SS men, that Baldur von Schirach had been the orchestra's "saviour", do not reflect the truth. Rather, they are a myth. The decision to dissolve the orchestra as an association and subsume it under the Reich Ministry for Public Enlightenment and Propaganda had already been averted under *Gauleiter* Bürckel. Schirach was actually anything but a saviour: when on 25 January 1945 the board, in the presence of chief conductor Wilhelm Furtwängler, discussed the Viennese Reich radio station's suggestion of autumn 1944 to relocate the orchestra due to air raids,[507] Schirach rejected the proposal: the orchestra had to remain in Vienna – unlike its "protector" and "supporter", who fled the city shortly before its liberation by the Red Army. The members of the orchestra experienced the end of the war and Vienna's liberation in a cellar in the city centre's Tiefer Graben – with members of their family, instruments, scores and valuable archive documents. Originally, the orchestra was supposed to be deployed as a *Volkssturm* (People's Storm) unit to take care of the wounded; this was prevented, however, by a major by the name of Rudolf Marek,[508] not by Schirach.

As early as 19 April 1945, the Soviet occupying forces ordered the orchestra to return to rehearsals, under the conductor Clemens Krauss, whose political record was by no means without blemish. The programme included a Tchaikovsky symphony. The first concert took place in the Vienna Konzerthaus on 27 April 1945 – the same day Karl Renner's Provisional State Government was installed.

Chapter 11

Neither a Commander Nor a Hero

The End of the War and Flight from Vienna

"In the spring of 1945, there was no demand for heroes", wrote Henriette von Schirach in her memoirs – a sentence perfectly summing up her husband and his less-celebrated role in the Battle for Vienna. Baldur von Schirach was not only *Reichsstatthalter* and *Gauleiter* of Vienna, but also commissar for the defence of the Reich, tasked with "maximal mobilisation" of all resources. Berlin's demand that Vienna participate in 'total warfare' required efficient cooperation with the military leadership of the Defence District; however, the supreme command in "Greater Vienna" was not really up to the job. Alfred Streccius, the general in charge of Vienna's Defence District XVII, born in 1874 and socialised in the Prussian army, was already sixty-six years old on 25 October 1940.[509] Wounded during the brutal colonial war in German Southwest Africa against the Herero in 1904, like Schirach he attempted to overcome the "national differences" between the "Altreich Germans" and the former Austrian soldiers and officers.[510] But Goebbels had demanded Streccius's dismissal in March 1942,[511] which Hitler eventually pushed through in 1943.[512]

In 1943, Berlin already considered Schirach's defence strategy to be far too lax.[513] It was around this time that Schirach had his disagreement with Hitler and Goebbels regarding the exhibition "Young Art in the German Reich" (see Chapter 10), which Hitler soon had shut down, since he considered some works "degenerate". Goebbels accused Schirach of preventing the relocation of large armaments factories to Vienna despite Armament Minister Albert Speer's demands.[514] It was at this point that speculation arose concerning replacing Schirach, with Goebbels and Bormann repeatedly encouraging Hitler to remove him. Eventually, Hitler put a stop to this talk in the autumn of 1944 after Ernst Kaltenbrunner proposed Alfred E. Frauenfeld, who had already served as *Gauleiter* of Vienna in 1930–33 and was very unpopular in both Vienna and Berlin. Hitler's decision was probably due to a shortage of suitable candidates and because Schirach's deputy *Gauleiter*, Karl Scharizer, and the *Gauleiter* of "Niederdonau" Hugo Jury, defended Schirach and warned against replacing him during wartime.[515]

Schirach's relationship with Kaltenbrunner, the head of the Reich Security Main Office, was severely strained. For instance, the arrest of two Soviet agents, the Viennese Josef Angermann and his radio operator Georg Kennerknecht, whose mission was to liquidate Schirach, was not supposed to be made public. Schirach was number four on the Soviet death list behind Hitler and Göring – Criminal Counsellor (*Kriminalrat*) Johann Sanitzer, the former head of Section IV 2 at the Gestapo's Vienna control centre (*Leitstelle*) and a brutal interrogation specialist, confessed to the Americans in July 1945 that Kaltenbrunner was concerned that if the news got out, the *Reichsstatthalter* of Vienna would gain in popularity as a political figure.[516]

In the summer of 1944, *SS-Gruppenführer* (SS group leader) and *Oberbefehlsleiter* (supreme command leader) of the Munich party office Helmuth Friedrichs (1899–1945) was summoned by Martin Bormann for confidential discussions concerning a potential successor.

Despite critical undertones, Scharizer's assessment of Schirach was very positive. He did identify one weakness, however:

> Party Member V. Schirach is a decent and clean individual and above all a brave person too. He is not a leader of people, but will always respond in soldierly fashion under stress and take up a rifle if necessary to take on every internal and external enemy […] Party Member V. Schirach somehow lives [it is said] in a different world, in a high tower [playing on his Hohe Warte address – O.R.], as it were, pursuing his hobbies. He thinks about foreign policy and wants to sort it out […]. He would allow himself to be shot dead for the little man and fight as a National Socialist, but [says] he cannot understand this little man in terms of his development, in terms of his lifestyle. Without noticing, Schirach lives a life that is not in keeping with the times. He cannot empathize with the life and way of living of the common people.[517]

Schirach had blind faith in his deputy Scharizer when it came to party issues and also signed every submission he put before him. *SS-Brigadeführer* (SS Brigadier) Karl Scharizer (1901–56) himself was from Freistadt in Upper Austria, had passed his final exams at Austrian grammar school (*Matura*), and had been a crane operator for the Alpine Montangesellschaft mining company in Donawitz. He had also been National Socialist *Gauleiter* in Salzburg and a member of parliament in Vienna from 1932 before fleeing to Germany in 1933.[518] His interesting psychological profile of Schirach was probably quite accurate in some respects. There was one thing it got wrong, however; Schirach, even if he was "brave", ultimately did not defend Vienna to his last bullet.

After the spat between Hitler and Schirach in June 1943, criticism of Vienna's air defences intensified, as did Schirach's nervousness following the first air raid on Wiener Neustadt on 13 August 1943.[519] His proposal to evacuate around 300,000 women and children from Vienna was rejected, as mentioned above.[520] An investigation of Vienna's "air defence preparations" by the *Gauleiter* of "Westfalen-Süd", Albert Hoffmann, proved "relatively" unfavourable in its assessment.[521] In contrast, Schirach's former close aide Hartmann Lauterbacher insisted just short of six weeks later that much had been done to catch up in the field of air defence in Vienna, despite having been overlooked as his successor as *Reichsjugendführer*.[522] He was referring not least to the six flak towers constructed by foreign forced labourers and prisoners of war from 1942 onwards. Built in pairs following a Berlin prototype (one fire-control tower and one gun tower) at three locations and planned by the architect Friedrich Tamms, the concrete monstrosities served not only as military posts but also as air raid shelters for the civilian population.[523]

Goebbels blamed Schirach for the lack of air raid shelters and air defence systems, but they were a result of the excessively centralised German armament policy, since all financial and human resources were to be reserved for producing weapons and munitions. In the autumn of 1942, following raids by the British Royal Air Force on Reich territory, Hitler gave the order for work to begin on air defence in Vienna too. Paradoxically, in the summer of 1941, Göring, as Reich aviation minister and supreme commander of the *Luftwaffe*, had ordered that no new bunkers were to be built and that work that had begun on such shelters was to stop.[524]

After the Allies' devastating large-scale raids on Hamburg (25 July to 3 August 1943), during which firestorms reduced entire quarters to rubble and ashes and at least 34,000 people died,[525] Bormann ordered all *Gau* and district leaderships to create "contingency departments" (*Ausweichdienststellen*) on the edge of towns, equipped with telecommunications and office facilities.[526] Up to that point, the flak tower in Vienna's Arenbergpark had dedicated an entire floor with such communications to the *Gauleitung*.

Following this new order, Schirach initially sought to requisition a hotel on the Kahlenberg hill north of the city, but the *Wehrmacht* had already moved in with the *Luftwaffengaukommando* XVII (Air Force *Gau* Command). Second choice as a bunker site was a pre-existing observation tower on the Gallitzinberg hill to the north-west, since it was close to a viewing tower, the *Jubiläumswarte*, itself already 449 metres above sea level.

The local population was secretly critical of this project, since there were too few air raid shelters in the city, but Schirach nevertheless waded through rather bureaucratic financing efforts and recruited thirty-three miners from Bochum to realise the project. In the meantime, a provisional headquarters for the inner circle of the *Gauleitung* was set up in Josefsdorf on the Kahlenberg hill, in the former charterhouse of a disused hermitage of the Camaldolese Order. Josefsdorf could also be quickly reached from the Hohe Warte, where Schirach and his family had lived in an "Aryanised" state villa since 15 October 1940. Between 1942 and 1945, a tunnel, 16.5 metres long, 5 metres wide and 5 metres high, was dug for the two-storey "Gau Battle Post" (*Gaugefechtsstand*).[527] The tower housed not only the plush *Reichsleiter*'s room but also a command room with a frosted glass board on which to plot the flight paths of the Allied bombers and organise warning sirens (the "cuckoo signal") and announcements for the city's population, broadcast via Vienna's Reich radio station (*Reichssender Wien*).

Pupils from a local grammar were used as "messenger girls" on the Gallitzinberg together with five BDM leaders and had to live in a barracks in the grounds of the Wagner von Jauregg Sanatorium Am Steinhof and in a refuge.[528]

When the air raid warnings sounded, Schirach and his staff sped – in full sight of the population – from the Hohe Warte to the Gallitzinberg, and hence jocular whispers renamed Thaliastrasse "Heldenstrasse", Heroes' Street.[529] The dangers were very real, including for the direct environs: one of Schirach's closest aides, *HJ-Obergebietsführer* (Supreme Regional Leader) Herbert Müller, was killed during a strike on the *Gauhaus* when he ran back into the office to field a phone call following an air raid warning. Schirach's mother, Emma, burnt to death on 16 July 1944 when a plane crashed into her house in Wiesbaden and she attempted to rescue her Pekinese from the flames.[530]

The *Reichsstatthalter* had ensured his children, Angelika Benedikta (born 1933), Klaus (born 1935), Robert (born 1938) and Richard (born 1942), were out of harm's way in Schloss Aspenstein in Bavaria in 1944. He also attempted to move many children and adolescents from Vienna as part of the *Kinderlandverschickungen*. In practice, only 27,000 pupils could be evacuated in 1943–44; almost 50,000 remained to face the bombing in Vienna.[531] Overall, Schirach increasingly withdrew from the *Kinderlandverschickungen* in 1944–45,[532] but in September 1944, following the national uprising in Slovakia in August, he did organise military assistance under his own personal command, with the support of reservists, in order to return 2,000 children from what had suddenly become contested territory. Fifteen men fell during this operation.[533] This successful mission did not receive special praise from Berlin, however.

After heavy air raids on Vienna in the late autumn of 1944, Henriette von Schirach also left the villa on the Hohe Warte in the December for Schloss Aspenstein in Kochel am See. As she reports in her memoirs, her husband forbade her from taking too many things with her, since to do so would have been "downright obscene" and would have given the Viennese the impression she was fleeing. Hence she travelled with just one suitcase, the contents of which included a book of poems by Josef Weinheber and a meringue St Nicholas from the Demel confectionary.[534] However, their artworks, both their own and those they had bought cheaply from the property of dispossessed Jews, were shipped westwards.

That an assassination attempt was made on Schirach on the Gallitzinberg on 15 March 1945 was deliberate misinformation by the US–British command. In 1945, this fabricated story appeared in *Nachrichten für die Truppe* (News for the Troops), a publication in the style of a military newspaper, under the headline "Shots at Schirach to rescue

Vienna".⁵³⁵ The story was also reported by the paper *Neues Deutschland* in the Soviet Occupation Zone in 1946.⁵³⁶

Following the failed attempt to assassinate Hitler, Schirach briefly appeared to be back in favour with him, since he "applied to drop his aristocratic title",⁵³⁷ several members of the nobility having played a key role in the conspiracy along with the assassin Claus von Stauffenberg. However, Goebbels thwarted this proposal, informing Hitler that Schirach had not been in Vienna at the time of the putsch attempt of 20 July 1944; rather, he had been at a family gathering in Kochel with Carl von Schirach, Henriette and his children. But as early as 21 July 1944, he had returned to Vienna with his father and immediately made a show of vengeance by tearing the Golden Party Badge from the uniform of a general suspected of collusion with the plotters.⁵³⁸

In January 1945, even Goebbels changed his stance, conceding that Schirach had a "very clear and radical position on the war".⁵³⁹

"My hand is trembling, but my heart is not"

On 24 February 1945, during a memorable meeting with Hitler, Schirach witnessed his final orders to his *Gauleiter*, not all of whom were present. Together with Hugo Jury, the *Gauleiter* of "Niederdonau", Schirach had driven to Berlin in a VW, via the ruins of Dresden. Berlin's Wilhelmplatz presented itself to them as a field of rubble, and the Kaiserhof hotel, a popular haunt of Nazi dignitaries, was also a ruin. In the Reich Chancellery, which had gone almost unscathed, around thirty *Reichs-* and *Gauleiter* awaited the "eerie final roll call" in the *Mosaiksaal* (Mosaic Hall), although many from the occupied territories were absent. Schirach described this meeting, overshadowed by a "Nibelung atmosphere", in detail: "One of the giant doors opened, and Hitler entered the hall, accompanied by Bormann and Goebbels. A broken man. With great effort, he approached us, his shoulders drooping. One of his legs, apparently lame, dragged over the marble floor. His face was ashen grey. With trembling hand, he greeted each of us."

In his speech, Hitler tried to commit his assembled paladins to the final battle: "My party members, my hand is trembling but my heart is not. Just as it didn't tremble twenty-five years ago when I stood up with a small bunch of loyal followers in order to redress the injustice done to Germany."⁵⁴⁰ In his memoirs, Schirach claimed that he had wanted to spare Vienna the fate that befell Dresden. The following facts demonstrate, however, that at the time he was very impressed by Hitler's order to stand firm and his asking "Will the Viennese hold out?"

Vienna was to be held at any price. The "Spring Awakening" offensive of the Army Group South (*Heeresgruppe Süd*) on the Soviet troops in Hungary, which had been announced by Hitler himself, failed after just ten days on 16 March 1945. Schirach nevertheless adhered to Hitler's order and refused to declare Vienna a "free city", as recommended by Albrecht Schubert, the commander general of Defence District XVII, and Vienna's city commander, Lieutenant General Ludwig Merker. The city's Government President, Hans Dellbrügge, and the mayor, *SS-Brigadeführer* Hanns Blaschke, had also come to him with the same proposal.⁵⁴¹ Hitler responded swiftly, instructing Bormann to order Schirach to "conduct total warfare as is also the case on the rest of the Reich's territory".⁵⁴² Above all, Hitler pointed to the importance of the Greater Germany detachments stationed in Vienna, of which Schirach was also a member. The commissar for the defence of the Reich did not have much backing from the *Wehrmacht*, however; one officer of the *Wehrmacht* command later spoke of how the "Austrian soldiers" had sabotaged Schirach's orders, with the effect that "as the Red Army drew closer, the planned defence measures did not exist".⁵⁴³

On 4 April 1945, the armoured spearheads of the Red Army having already reached Hütteldorf on Vienna's western outskirts, Schirach and his staff abandoned the *Gau* Command Post (*Gaubefehlstand*) on the Gallitzinberg for the vaulted cellar under the Hofburg palace in the heart of the city. Here, two underground floors were used as a military hospital and facilities for the commissar for the defence of the Reich. Vienna-born *SS-Obersturmbannführer* and war criminal Otto Skorzeny,⁵⁴⁴ celebrated as a war hero after the liberation of Mussolini, described in his memoirs the apocalyptic mood in the final days before the liberation of Vienna by the Red Army; Schirach himself clearly still harboured illusions:

> On the floor lay splendid rugs, on the walls hung paintings of battles and portraits of generals from the eighteenth century. In the antechamber, people ate, drank and were noisy. I had to explain to the Gauleiter that I had not set eyes on a single German soldier in

the city and that the barricades were unmanned. I invited him to undertake a reconnaissance trip with me. He rejected this invitation, however, and explained to me, bent over his map, how they would rescue Vienna: two elite divisions were ready to attack. One would attack from the north and other from the west: the enemy would have to capitulate. Using a similar manoeuvre, he said, Prince Starhemberg forced the Turks to give up the siege of Vienna in 1683.[545]

Another contemporary witness, Karl Zischka, the technician responsible for the daily telecommunications with Berlin, confirms this absurd atmosphere:

There were jars of preserves and caviar, and the champagne flowed. Everything we hadn't seen for ages [...] I won't say there was binging, but they entertained themselves well, by and large. And everyone believed in victory. Everyone believed in the miracle weapon that was yet to be deployed somehow.[546]

Schirach was long since aware not only that the Red Army had also reached the suburbs of Vienna but also that a military resistance group led by Major Carl Szokoll had made contact with the Soviet detachments to discuss the possibility of their liberating Vienna together.

Around the same time that General Lothar Rendulic, an Austrian by birth, had given the order in the Army Group South's headquarters for all *Wehrmacht* units and the Second SS Armoured Corps (*SS-Panzerkorps*) to leave the inner city districts and withdraw via the Danube Canal, on 9 April 1945 Schirach also embarked on his sudden retreat from the contested metropolis. The fleeing *Reichsstatthalter*'s convoy left the city via the still intact Floridsdorf Bridge; Schirach himself had perched in an amphibious VW, followed by a Mercedes cabriolet containing four soldiers of the *Genesenen-Kompanie* (Convalesced Company; reservists who had recovered from wounding) of the Greater Germany Armoured Corps (*Panzer-Korps Großdeutschland*) equipped with submachine guns and a machine gun, the adjutant *SS-Obersturmführer* Fritz Wieshofer in a second amphibious VW, and two lorries with provisions.[547] Schirach moved into the Hempfling inn in Flandorf at the foot of the Bisamberg hill north-east of Vienna, where he tried to make himself useful as a liaison officer – with the rank of lieutenant – between the supreme commander of the Sixth SS *Panzer* Army (6. *SS-Panzerarmee*; armoured forces),[548] *SS-Oberst-Gruppenführer* (Colonel Group Leader) "Sepp" Dietrich and *SS-Obergruppenführer* (Upper Group Leader) Wilhelm "Willy" Bittrich, the commander of the Second SS Armoured Corps. Militarily, Schirach had long been an irrelevant figure, however, Goebbels mockingly writing in his diary:

> Uprisings[549] have occurred in the city in the formerly red suburbs, and these have taken on such dimensions that Schirach in his helplessness found himself moved to seek shelter among the troops. That is so typical of Schirach. First he lets things run as they are, and then he flees to the soldiers. I never expected anything else from him. Here too, the dire consequences of the Führer's lack of decisiveness in personnel policy show. For many years, Schirach was surplus to requirements and needed removing, but the Führer could not bring himself to send him into the wilderness. Now the toughest measures must be taken to sort things out in Vienna. The Führer remains determined to keep the city no matter what the situation.[550]

Nor did the Reich propaganda minister hold back regarding the Viennese population:

> The Führer has already got the Viennese right. They are a despicable bunch consisting of a mixture of Poles, Czechs, Jews and Germans. But I think that the Viennese would have been more easily reined in if a decent and above all an energetic political leadership had been at the helm there. Schirach was not the right man for the job. But how often did I say that, and how often did I go unheard![551]

However, it was not Schirach who had given up Vienna, but the military. Even the terrible war criminal "Sepp" Dietrich, sent by Hitler to Vienna to defend the city with the Sixth SS *Panzer* Army and the newly arrived Armoured Grenadier Division "Der Führer" (*Panzergrenadier-Division "Der Führer"*), concentrated on retreat. In his command post in a castle outside St Pölten, Dietrich's greatest concern was "that Adolf wants to have me removed because I didn't defend Vienna". For three weeks, Schirach served Dietrich as a liaison officer in the hinterland.

He also spent a few days in this function in Altmelon near Ottenschlag in the Waldviertel ("Forest Quarter") north of the Danube.[552] The Altmelon parish chronicle reports:

> Immediately thereafter [around 10 April, *sic*], the Reichsstatthalter Baldur von Schirach came, taking flight, one could say. He was initially supposed to be accommodated in the vicarage, but then he moved into the house of the merchant Wondraschek, who had a larger and nicer room. His two adjutants stayed at mine. It was a warm and beautiful time [i.e. the weather] then. A telephone connection was immediately put into the vicarage. The gentlemen sat in the garden; Schirach often appeared and gave orders etc. But after a few days the entire company departed west, to Upper Austria.[553]

The *Gauleiter* of "Niederdonau", Jury, with whom Schirach was well acquainted, was also in this area. A qualified doctor and an *SS-Obergruppenführer*, Jury would commit suicide in Zwettl in the night between 8 and 9 May 1945. Schirach, on the other hand, was still thinking about ways to escape the Red Army. He was joined in this endeavour by his three adjutants: Harald Döscher, first lieutenant and liaison officer for the Greater Germany Reserve Brigade (*Ersatzbrigade Großdeutschland*) in Cottbus from 1943 onwards; the former physical education teacher Gustav Höpken, a first lieutenant in the Luftwaffe and deputy director for the Central Office of the *Reichsstatthalterei*; and *SS-Obersturmführer* Fritz Wieshofer. On 1 May 1945, the four of them moved to Gmunden on the Traunsee lake, where there was a Naval Hitler Youth (*Marine-HJ*) radio post.[554]

Following the news of Hitler's suicide in Berlin, Schirach and Wieshofer fled westward in a VW Beetle driven by their chauffeur Franz Ram, towards the "Alpine Fortress" that had been planned but never realised. Via the Salzach Valley and Zell am See, the trio reached Schwaz in the Inn Valley, where Franz Ram's sister ran a tavern. When the Beetle, a gift from Robert Ley, suddenly broke down, they decided to remain in Schwaz. They now needed new identities: Schirach grew a moustache and was equipped with a typewriter in order to continue work on a new detective novel as the "crime writer Dr Richard Falk" in the Tyrolean idyll. Wieshofer, who had obtained a box of women's watches from the Greater Germany Regiment's inventory, bartered with the local farmers to ensure they had food.

On 4 June 1945, he and Wieshofer turned themselves in to American forces in the former Hotel Post, since he had heard that all HJ leaders were subject to automatic arrest and hence did not wish to avoid this internment. Beforehand, he wrote a letter to the local American command in Schwaz, delivered by Wieshofer, in which he explained his decision: "I, Baldur Benedikt von Schirach, voluntarily turn myself in to the occupying forces in order to be able to answer to an international court."[555]

Schirach initially received preferential treatment in the Rum prison camp outside Innsbruck, due to his good English and his openness in accepting his responsibility for building up the Hitler Youth. Hence he would also be allowed to see Henny for a few hours in June 1945, having been separated from her for half a year; an American jeep took her to Rum from her accommodation in a hotel in the mountains near Kufstein. She described this reunion in her memoirs: "In a large bare room, Baldur is standing by a table. I haven't seen him for half a year, I barely recognise him. A different person, with a different face in which one can see the terrible decision. His hair is brushed back smoothly, and I am not mistaken, it is grey."[556] She had taken with her 'proof of ancestry' documenting his American descent; she claimed a US officer in Rum turned out to be a "distant cousin".[557]

In August 1945, Schirach and Wieshofer were transferred to the US interrogation camp at Oberursel in the Taunus hills. There the former *Reichsjugendführer* signed a declaration stating that he was responsible for the "construction, organisation and leadership of the HJ from its foundation to the year 1940" and considered himself responsible for the organisation up to its collapse. On 10 September 1945, Schirach was eventually flown to Nuremberg; it is reported that at this point he had resigned himself to receiving the death penalty.[558]

"Youth's sacrifices guarantee victory"

A few weeks before the invasion of Poland, on 15 August 1939, Schirach established in an agreement with General Wilhelm Keitel, head of the *Wehrmacht* Supreme Command, that the entire HJ leadership had to receive training for their important future task – "defence training". Here too, Schirach pushed through his maxim of the Hitler Youth's self-organisation, although ultimately the training would be led by the HJ leadership cadres. By 1938, some 30,000 HJ leaders had received terrain and weapons training, although this figure was to be doubled.[559] In practice, however, this system was only marginally effective, and in 1942 only one in seven recruits from the HJ had received pre-military training.

Hence in March 1942, Hitler, in close consultation with the *Reichsjugendführung*, decreed that "Hitler Youth defence training camps" be established. These were three-week camps providing not only practical military training, but also ideological schooling. In practice, the camps were no longer led by HJ functionaries but by *Wehrmacht* officers. The trainers were wounded soldiers and non-commissioned officers, although efforts were increasingly made to enlist former HJ functionaries for the task. The consequences were often brutal military approaches to training; even *Reichsjugendführer* lodged an internal protest against the frequent "sadistic cruelty".[560] For instance, five adolescents who had fled from such a camp in Herrenhof near Eichgraben were forced to run the gauntlet by camp leader Erhart Mader, a wounded officer. Another boy had to jump around on all fours and constantly shout, "Woof woof, I'm the coal thief!",[561] thereby not only being subjected to physical humiliation but also being forced to denounce himself as a caricature public enemy deployed by Nazi wartime propaganda. The longer the war dragged on and the greater the losses at the fronts, the more fanatical the drill and the ideological brainwashing became; the youth were to be "raised for unconditional effort for victory".[562]

In 1944, those born in 1927 were the first year to undergo every stage of this training, and were hence considered a kind of "miracle weapon", including by the *Wehrmacht*. Heinrich Himmler, the supreme commander of the Reserve Army, but also *Reichsjugendführer* Axmann, who liked to keep close to Hitler in Berlin, tried to outdo each other with proposals to commit more and more members of the HJ to military training – eventually fifteen-year-olds too – in order to pitch them into the "final battle".

What was Schirach's attitude to this clear abuse of children and adolescents in the final years of the war?

At the Austrian Hitler Youth leaders' congress in Salzburg's Mozarteum on 17 May 1938, Schirach had precisely and unambiguously summed up the HJ's fundamental political aim: "The real, great educational act for a people lies in ingraining in youth blind obedience, unshakeable loyalty, unconditional comradeship and absolute reliability."[563] This is also the prerequisite for total obedience in war – be it in the *Wehrmacht* or on the home front.

As *Reichsleiter* for NSDAP Youth Education, the highest office he held, he further proclaimed the same heroic message he had repeatedly articulated in previous years: "German soldiers only ever die to become immortal."[564] As in the early days of the HJ, Schirach again alluded to the "fallen heroes" of Langemarck in 1914. The heroic epic of the First World War served as a bridge to the present and clearly called for new "heroism" – in death on the battlefield.[565] When he handed over his position to Artur Axmann, Schirach expressed similar ideological aims to the HJ *Führerkorps*, justifying the deaths of 1,200 *HJ-Führer*: "our army's above-average loss of blood sacrifices" corresponded to "the expected toughness, breeding and selfless loyalty of our community".[566] Schirach took up the watchword of the "days of struggle" before 1933 and the glorification of the "blood sacrifice", developing it further; he now demanded of the Hitler Youth total subordination and self-sacrifice in the war: "Toughened by the fate of war and accompanied by your dead comrades, you will return home after the war. You are certain to receive the recognition of the entire nation."[567]

In 1942, the European Youth Congress concluded with a carefully choreographed evening event in Vienna's Heldenplatz before the statues of Prince Eugen and Archduke Karl, attended by the delegates from fifteen nations and the entire Viennese Hitler Youth. Here too, symbols of the blood sacrifice were used: before the illuminated arcades of the Hofburg, "sacrificial flames blazed in commemoration of the heroes who fell for the future of Europe".[568] A year later, in the presence of the Romanian Fascist youth leader General Victor Iliescu, a demonstration was given of the strength of the *Nachrichten-HJ* (Signal HJ) – another opportunity for Schirach to proclaim the soldierly nature of the Hitler Youth: "You are the future and the hope of the Greater German Reich. Today, you are already National Socialist soldiers of our Führer, worthy of serving him."[569]

Schirach repeatedly used elements of psychological warfare to mentally prepare the members of the Hitler Youth for war and ultimately to demand of them total warfare and total self-sacrifice and subordination to Hitler's policies. But the aim was increasingly very specific pre-military training: in August 1944, Schirach opened the "War Volunteer Weeks of the Hitler Youth", in which "volunteers for the front" received training in "map reading, shooting, terrain exercises, throwing hand grenades and ideological schooling"[570] in the Vienna Woods. He appealed to the "enthusiasm" of the young lads, who would be sent to the front only a few months later, telling them that they were "worthy warriors of the National Socialist ideology" and that they represented "Hitler's young victorious guard" – a somewhat cynical idea given the military situation, but Schirach appears to have still meant it in all seriousness.

HJ leaders and members of the Hitler Youth received further ideological indoctrination and were recruited en masse by Axmann and Himmler for the "Third Reich's" final battle: as a result, fanatical adolescents kept fighting after the *Wehrmacht* and SS had retreated, thinking they had to embody the spirit of the Nazi ideology to the very end. In many cases, the seeds of this monstrous ideology led directly to murder and manslaughter; HJ functionaries were involved in numerous war crimes in the final phase of hostilities. To this day, there has yet to be a comprehensive survey of all the war crimes committed by members of the Hitler Youth in the German "Reich" and the occupied territories. Individual studies, such as those on the shooting of British and Canadian prisoners of war on the Western Front, document the brutality displayed by the young fanatics.[571] Were members of the Hitler Youth more prepared to commit murder due their ideological indoctrination than others who were less intensively influenced during their adolescence? This question cannot be answered here, but it must certainly be raised. While isolated internal statements by National Socialists on the status of the volunteers for the Twelfth SS Armoured Division "Hitler Youth" (*12. SS-Panzerdivision "Hitler-Jugend"*) reveal that the ideological indoctrination failed, the high death toll at the front undoubtedly shows an above-average commitment to self-sacrifice.[572] Schirach attempted to have the "Greater Germany" infantry division with which he was connected labelled a HJ division, but was unable to get the plan past Himmler and Axmann. As already discussed in detail in previous chapters, by 1943 Schirach no longer had any real influence over the central offices in Berlin.

Nevertheless, the many examples of war crimes committed by HJ leaders at the end of the war show that the ideological indoctrination that Schirach played a large role in shaping through his speeches, poems, songs and various publications had been most effective. Helmut Butterweck's study documenting all the public reports on trials at the Vienna People's Court between 1945 and 1955 provides ample evidence of the violence and brutality individual HJ leaders or members were still displaying in 1945. For instance, a fifteen-year-old schoolboy from the Göttweig National Political Education Institute (*Nationalpolitische Erziehungsanstalt*), also a member of the Hitler Youth, shot at three prisoners escaping from the prison in Stein an der Donau.[573] In Vienna's Döbling district, just five minutes from Schirach's villa, two "HJ lads" shot two Greek forced labourers after discovering weapons in their possession.[574] In March 1945, a twenty-five-year-old *HJ-Bannführer* (battalion leader) organised the execution of sixty Jews in Deutsch-Schützen deployed in the construction of the "South-east Wall". The execution was conducted by SS men, while members of the Hitler Youth aided and abetted the murder and buried the victims. A few days later, a survivor groaned in Hungarian that he had been "shot at by children".[575] Some HJ gangs committed executions themselves. For instance, on 15 April 1945, on the Kletschkahöhe summit near Reichenau an der Rax, a motorised HJ group shot the Supreme Regional Court (*Oberlandesgericht*) judge Dr Josef Thaller and his wife Maria Karasek. They were mercilessly liquidated as resistance fighters.[576] Towards the end of the war, the HJ defence training camps sent out brutal HJ detachments, as documented for the Neunkirchen camp. Of the 120 adolescents stationed here, some were transferred to the *Wehrmacht*, while twenty-five others formed a "Volkssturm-Sonderkommando der Kreisleitung Neunkirchen" (People's Storm Special Detachment of the District Administration of Neunkirchen).[577] This "special detachment" terrorised the local population, made numerous arrests, was also involved in executions and was utterly fanatical. Members of this gang repeatedly spoke of "killing, bumping off and shooting".[578]

These terrible "final phase crimes" committed by the HJ and its functionaries are not mentioned in the memoirs of former central leadership cadres such as Baldur von Schirach, Artur Axmann or

Hartmann Lauterbacher. The bloody reality of the war is suppressed; they prefer to write about the comradeship and idealism of an allegedly harmless youth organisation.

In contrast, Hilmar Hoffmann, one of the most important German cultural policymakers of the post-war period, comprehensively and self-critically considered his time in the Hitler Youth up to his military deployment as a parachutist. With subtle clarity and depth, Hoffmann describes how he was shaped as an adolescent, above all by the specific potency of Schirach's poems, texts and speeches.[579]

With his 'blood and soil' and sacrifice poetry, Schirach appealed not only to the HJ boys and adolescents but also to the BDM girls, for whom he also penned verses. Their pathos and metaphors may be unbearable today, but at the time they served their purpose:

Siehe es leuchtet die Schwelle, die uns vom Dunkel befreit,
hinter ihr strahlet die Helle herrlich kommender Zeit.
Die Tore der Zukunft sind offen dem, der die Zukunft bekennt
und im gläubigen Hoffen heute die Fackeln entbrennt.
Stehet über dem Staube, seid ihr Gottes Gericht.
Hell erglühe der Glaube An die Schwelle im Licht.

[Behold, the threshold that liberates us from darkness shines, behind it gleams the light of the splendid coming time. The future's gates are open to him who professes the future and burns the torches today in faithful hope. Stand above the dust, be God's judgment. May faith in the threshold in the light glow bright.]

Hoffmann, who had gone through all the stages in the life of a boy in National Socialism – from the *Deutsches Jungvolk* to membership of the NSDAP – quite correctly writes, for instance, of "strangely smarmy poetry" when describing Schirach's foreword to the BDM songbook *Wir Mädel singen* (We Girls Sing), for Schirach used to "help lend social expression to fascism, especially for the hearts of many naive young girls. At the time, I myself instinctively considered Baldur von Schirach more of a likeable poet than a dull ideologue."[581]

Schirach shaped German youth, boys and girls, for around a decade. He skilfully used all available means to ideologically influence the next generation. This was something he freely admitted at the Nuremberg trials, probably due to the influence of the American psychologists, with whom he had many conversations, and his defence lawyer Fritz Sauter. Whether this admission of guilt was genuine, we cannot know.

Two Smoking Rooms, Like in the Old Days – Back to Weimar

The father of Vienna's *Reichsstatthalter*, Carl von Schirach, was able to remain director of the Nassauisches Landestheater in Wiesbaden for a relatively long time, despite his old age. The contract he signed with Prussian prime minister Göring on 4 May 1934 included a clause allowing a year's extension if he wasn't dismissed.[582] Carl von Schirach received an annual salary of 17,000 Reichsmark. In 1936, another extension was discussed; in the Reich Ministry for Public Enlightenment and Propaganda, which was now responsible for the Wiesbaden theatre, it was pointed out that he held a Golden Badge of Honour of the NSDAP.[583] Subsequently, Carl von Schirach also sought to reduce his tax bill and asked the Propaganda Ministry for support. On 30 January 1938, Hitler appointed him director general (*Generalintendant*), and on 10 November 1938 Goebbels personally sent his felicitations on the occasion of his sixty-fifth birthday.

By express instruction of the propaganda minister, in 1938 Carl von Schirach was also given the status of "prominent artist", thus being entitled to pay a further 40 per cent less tax.[584] He was also allowed to write off at least 20 per cent in advertising costs. When the question of pensioning him off arose in 1940, Goebbels sought to discuss the matter directly with his son Baldur.[585] The minister and his officials sought to avoid sacking him, anticipating interventions and hoping the theatre would be taken over by the city administration instead, which would have meant the question of his dismissal would no longer have been a matter for Berlin.

But Carl von Schirach cleverly resisted, and in 1941 he even managed to secure a pay rise from 17,000 to 25,000 Reichsmark – approximately 102,500 euros in today's money.[586] He managed to hang on until he had served ten years in the role on 31 August 1943. Along with his retirement from the Weimar era, contested in court, of around 635 Reichsmark and a monthly contribution from Wiesbaden of 30 Reichsmark, he also received a monthly honorarium of 60 Reichsmark[587] and a one-off severance payment of 10,000 Reichsmark.[588]

A previously unknown letter Rosalind von Schirach wrote to her brother in 1967 provides good insights into their father's time in Weimar from 1945 to his death in 1948.[589] After the move from the destroyed house in Wiesbaden and the tragic death of his wife Emma, Carl von Schirach returned to the old villa in Weimar, which was now fitted out with furnishings from Vienna: "The former salon became a dining room with a grand piano. Two smoking rooms, like in the old days, above them two bedrooms and a drawing room."[590]

When Weimar was liberated by US troops, Schirach and his daughter were taken to the former concentration camp in Buchenwald on an open truck and photographed "before a huge pile of dead bodies reduced to skeletons. Our interrogation was broadcast around the world by the Luxemburg station, despite our requests to refrain from it. From above, the guards told us that the crowd would tear us to pieces if they knew who we were. Papa did not take in much and this is just a small al fresco picture. Neither of us ever spoke about it afterwards."[591] On 22 April 1945, Rosalind and Carl von Schirach had to clear the villa and were relocated to other apartments.

With the Soviet occupation, there followed various interrogations. Rosalind von Schirach faced them without her father and organised provisions. After an operation in 1948, he became increasingly weak, but did not wish to return to Wiesbaden, where he had been offered an apartment. Carl von Schirach died on 11 July 1948. After heavy debates with the city administration, the urn holding his ashes was eventually buried among the theatre's graves of honour near the princely vault. In 1950, his daughter travelled to Berlin to visit her brother in the "Allies' prison" in Berlin-Spandau and remained in the West thereafter, thus bringing to a close the long chapter of 'the Schirach family and Weimar'.

Chapter 12

A Cranach for the *Reichsleiter*

Art Theft and "Aryanisation"

> "I possess a great collection of paintings and I am convinced that none are from Jewish property."[592]

The Russians, Henriette von Schirach relates in her memoirs, placed the pictures the Schirachs had not been able to take with them from their villa in 1944 in the garden and used them for target practice. She claims the caretaker told her this during her visit to Vienna after the war, in 1955; she found it "original" of them "to shoot at a Dutch landscape".[593] However, this nice little anecdote does not tell the whole truth, and the subject of how assets and artworks stolen from Jews were dealt with was not even mentioned during the Nuremberg trials in 1946. The state villa in the refined district of Döbling, at Hohe Warte 52, which Schirach had taken over from his predecessor Josef Bürckel, was originally built by the architect Julius Mayreder, as a country home for the transport tycoon Gottfried Schenker (1842–1901). The generous garden was presumably created by the renowned German garden philosopher Karl Foerster from Bornim.[594] Schirach held court here, and Hitler himself visited twice in 1941, admiring the garden's ginkgo tree and a small bench that had belonged to Prince Eugen – this too has been missing since 1945.[595] Well-known women were also frequently invited, such as the Burgtheater and film star Maria Holst or *Obergauführerin* (Supreme *Gau* Leader) Annemarie Kaspar, delegate for the BDM section *Glaube und Schönheit* (Faith and Beauty) in the *Reichsjugendführung*. Kaspar spent an evening with the "Führer" and the Schirachs, with chamber music performed by musicians from the Vienna Philharmonic.

To entertain Hitler, Henriette von Schirach also invited "celebrated young Viennese artists".[596] Actively supported by Henriette, who managed their staff, the *Reichsstatthalter* also enjoyed hosting guests of state who happened to be in Vienna, such as Italian foreign minister Gian Galezzo or General Andrei Vlasov, Romanian dictator Ion Antonescu or the grand mufti of Jerusalem, Amin al-Husseini.[597]

But the Hofburg, the city hall and the Belvedere palace also served as reception venues. As in many dictatorships, large hunts were popular: Schirach liked to invite celebrated figures from the "Altreich", such as "Party Comrade" *SS-Obergruppenführer* Rudolf Querner, who took part in the "Riegeljagd"[598] on 11 December 1943 in Vienna's Lainz reserve, shooting wild boars and fallow deer.[599] A pheasant hunt followed the next day. Then the Schirachs hosted a "dinner in the house Hohe Warte 52", attended by Querner and his wife[600] Querner had been a higher SS and police leader for the Danube region (*Höherer SS- und Polizeiführer Donau*) since 1943,[601] and had accompanied Heinrich Himmler on a trip to Byelorussia in October 1941 to inspect the Mogilev labour camp, which was to be converted into a death camp. He knew full well, then, that Jews were being murdered in the East.

Despite enjoying these absurd leisure activities while war crimes and the mass murder of the Shoah were taking place on a daily basis, Schirach and Querner did not neglect their ideological work: among other things, they attempted to get adolescents reluctant to fight to serve in the war. One such individual was Alfred Hrdlicka, who would later achieve renown as a sculptor:

> During the final event on the Marswiese, a large sports ground in the 17th District, those who refused to sign up from all the defence training camps were paraded before everyone. An SS general, called Querner, if I'm not mistaken, and Baldur von Schirach sat down before us and levelled the most bitter accusations at us, or to put it better, they talked big, blathered about the final victory and the great honour of being allowed to die for the Führer, the people and the fatherland.[602]

The Schirachs' villa was situated on a large plot of land, almost 11,000 square metres, immediately next to what used to be Nathaniel von Rothschild's gardens. Before the "Anschluss", the "mighty stone wardrobe" to which Henriette von Schirach initially took a dislike[603] had belonged to the builder Arnold Spritzer, who fled to Zurich. It was he who had the building's 372 square metre interior completely rebuilt in 1927 as well as adding a gardener's house, a garage and a conservatory. The luxurious building, described in detail when it was confiscated, had a basement with a maid's room, a laundry with an ironing room, a cellar antechamber, four cellars, two rooms for storing garden furniture, a linen room, a gasometer room, a central heating system, a room for the oil tank and a buffer space, a room for coke and coal, a larder and a toilet. The upper ground floor consisted of a stairwell, a hall, reception, dining, smoking and music rooms, a kitchen, a study, a toilet, a larder and an upper and lower terrace. On the first floor, there was another hall, a library, a breakfast room, a bedroom and a guestroom, two bathrooms, two taprooms, a broom cupboard, a servant's room and two toilets. The second floor contained an apartment with an antechamber, four rooms, two cabinets, two servant's rooms, a chamber, a bathroom, a "passage" and two toilets with their own antechamber.[604] The entire villa and its grounds were estimated to be worth 410,000 Reichsmark. The wealthy entrepreneur Arnold Spritzer, who was of Jewish origin, retained net assets of 1,729,217 Reichsmark even after the deduction of *Reichsfluchtsteuer* (tax for having fled the "Reich"). Whether at least part of this sum was ever transferred to him in exile remains unclear. He certainly demanded considerable restitution after 1945, which would indicate massive seizure of his assets under National Socialism.

The Schirachs were not interested in the issues of "Aryanisation" and deprivation of material rights, neither during the Nazi era nor after 1945. Although there is currently no inventory – unlike for the Schirachs' property in Kochel near Bad Tölz – nine works of art have been found that were taken from confiscated Jewish collections and purchased by Schirach or his wife at low cost.[605] Along with furniture, rugs and other works of art from the former imperial furniture collection (*Hofmobiliendepot*), which he was allocated as *Gauleiter* for his official dwelling, Schirach also procured rugs and tapestries from the confiscated Palais Schwarzenberg or the extensive collection of Oscar Bondy (1870–1944), an entrepreneur of Jewish origin who had fled to the USA via Switzerland.

It is implausible that Schirach knew nothing of the former owners, since Hitler had decreed on 18 June 1938 that all confiscated collections were subject to "Führer's proviso" (*Führervorbehalt*) concerning their use, i.e. they were actually intended for the "Führermuseum" planned for

Linz. Special permission was required to even be allowed to purchase these paintings.

The Vienna Gestapo reported extensively on the great personal interest Schirach took in the collection seized from the Gomperz family:

> The Reichsleiter and Reichsstatthalter in Vienna, Baldur von Schirach, has taken note of the securing of the Gomperz collection of paintings and has personally taken a look at them and arranged for specialists from the Kunsthistorisches Museum [Museum of Art History] in Vienna to produce slides. In his letter of 24.6.1943 from the Führer headquarters, he informed me that he had spoken to the Führer. As far as I can further ascertain from this letter, the Führer has determined that part of the collection is to go to the Linz museum, part of it can be bought by the Österreichische Galerie [Austrian Gallery] and the Kunsthistorisches Museum.[606]

One of the works Schirach chose was originally entitled *Maria mit dem Kind auf dem Schoße, demselben einen Weintrauben reichend* (*Mary with The Child on Her Lap, Offering Him Grapes*) from the confiscated collection of Cornelia, Marie and Philipp Gomperz.[607] Schirach obtained permission to acquire the painting by a "decision of the Führer" in June 1943, for an estimated price of 30,000 Reichsmark. He also bought two Persian tiles from the nineteenth century for 500 Reichsmark.

This "Aryanised" painting had a somewhat adventurous history after the end of the war in 1945: following the air raids on Vienna, Schirach's valuable artworks from the villa on the Hohe Warte were taken to Bavaria, to Schloss Aspenstein, in 1944. Under interrogation in 1948, Schirach claimed, however, that he had acquired the work from an art dealer or art historian and that it had been destroyed by the Red Army after the liberation of Vienna – which would fit with Henriette's version of events outlined at the beginning of this chapter. As far as *Mary with the Child on Her Lap* is concerned, Henriette and her lover, the film merchant Alfred H. Jacob, told a different story in various interrogations: Jacob, who lived in Urfeld am Walchensee, claimed that he had purchased the painting in 1944. He had subsequently kept it in a safe he had rented at the Bayerische Vereinsbank in 1949–50 and it was later sold to the American Siegfried Thalheimer, who resold it in the USA. Following the restitution settlement, in Munich Gomperz's heirs received 1,000 marks. In 1999, the picture was discovered in the Museum of Art in Raleigh, North Carolina, by the Jewish World Congress's Commission for Art Recovery and returned to heirs of Philipp von Gomperz, Cornelia and Marianne Hainisch – the grandchildren of former Austrian Federal President Michael Hainisch, incidentally. In turn, they sold the painting to the museum in North Carolina for 600,000 US dollars.

Another detective story vividly demonstrates how Baldur and Henriette von Schirach attempted to hide all traces of their art possessions after 1945 and also managed to hide "Aryanised" possessions from restitution, despite the USA's intensive efforts and various investigations by the German and Austrian authorities. In December 1955, Henriette reported to the police station in Innsbruck that towards the end of the war, her husband's adjutant, First Lieutenant (*Oberleutnant*) Gustav Höpken, had taken a suitcase containing valuable artworks last located in Schloss Aspenstein – including Pieter Brueghel the Younger's painting *The Good Shepherd* – to a farmer in Bramberg in the Upper Pinzgau.[608] They had agreed that the works would be collected and that the code word "Doktor Faust" would be used. A certain Gerhard Schulze had then opened the suitcase and stolen its contents. When on 17 October 1946 Ingeborg Hubich tried to pick up the suitcase using the code word on behalf of Edith Kaufmann, the wife of Schirach's former press officer Günter Kaufmann, all it contained was six books and two newspapers. An Interpol investigation was unable to locate the mysterious stranger by the name of Gerhard Schulze. It remains unclear whether the suitcase did contain the painting by Brueghel and possibly a second by Puvis de Chavannes. The fact is that Brueghel's painting was from the confiscated collection of Ernst Pollack and appeared at an auction in Cologne in 2003 before being withdrawn due its provenance. Three years later, however, the painting *The Good Shepherd* by Pieter Brueghel the Younger, confiscated in 1942, appeared at Christie's in New York. It was stated to have come from "heirs of Ernst and Gisela Pollack" and was sold for 688,000 US dollars. One should be cautious here, since there are three versions of this painting, but there are a number of indications it was the painting Schirach's adjutant Herbert Müller collected from Vienna's Dorotheum auctioneers on 17 September 1942 and which Schirach was subsequently able to purchase for its starting price of 24,000 Reichsmark.[609] In this case, too, the "Führer's proviso" was relinquished.

Ernst and Gisela Pollack were deported to Theresienstadt concentration camp (Terezín) on 18 June 1942. They died the same year.[610] Shortly before their deportation, on 5 June 1942, Baldur von Schirach had given his speech declaring he would make Vienna "free of Jews" (see Chapter 9).[611]

Schirach not only attempted to purchase "Aryanised" artworks himself but also supported others, such as the film director Gustav Ucicky. On Schirach's instructions, in 1940 Gustav Klimt's painting *Wasserschlagen II (Freundinnen)* (*Watersnakes II (Girlfriends)*) was removed from the Dorotheum so that Ucicky, who claimed to be Klimt's illegitimate son and whose greatest cinematic hit was the anti-Polish and anti-Semitic film *Heimkehr* (*Homecoming*) starring Paula Wessely, could acquire the work for 8,000 to 9,000 Reichsmark.[612]

Wasserschlangen II (Freundinnen) belonged to the collection of Jenny Steiner, who had been able to escape from the National Socialists, initially via Paris and then to Brazil in 1940. With an interest in the family silk factory, Jenny Steiner was an important patron of Vienna's Secession gallery and Gustav Klimt. Her assets were confiscated in October 1938.[613]

In 2013, Ursula Ucicky, the director's widow, sold the painting privately through Sotheby's for a reported 112 million US dollars plus premium following a settlement with Steiner's heirs, with whom she shared the proceeds.[614] The new owner of this most valuable painting, the Swiss businessman Yves Bouvier, sold it to the Russian millionaire Dmitri Rybolovlev for 183 million US dollars the day after the settlement had been realised.

Incidentally, in relating her memorable encounter on the Obersalzberg in 1943, Henriette von Schirach mentions her host during her visit to The Hague, the banker and art dealer Alois Miedl, who confirmed the brutal deportation of Jewish women.[615] What Frau von Schirach does not mention is that Miedl was one of the most active art dealers, selling stolen treasures to Hitler and Göring, but also to Baldur von Schirach.[616] At the same time, he threw generous banquets for visitors to his moated castle: "Indians in white turbans served delicious ingredients with rice on exquisite Chinese porcelain, accompanied by caviar, lobster, genever, Champagne [...] At our receptions in the Hofburg in Vienna, the servers wore livery from the time of Emperor Franz Joseph, but on the silver platters they brought in were flat slices of bread with sardine paste and a caper blossom as a garnish."[617]

Miedl, who, as Henriette writes, told her to speak to Hitler personally about the deportations of Jews, gave the Schirachs a Renaissance painting entitled *Tobias and the Angel* by an unknown Italian artist.[618] The picture's provenance, possibly a looted Jewish collection, was of no concern to her. The Schirachs bought around twelve paintings from Miedl, who was also well acquainted with Heinrich Hoffmann.[619] Another dealer important for Göring but also for Schirach was Pieter de Boer, who sold the latter at least twenty paintings. At the Mühlmann Agency in the Netherlands, twenty-five purchases by Schirach amounting to over 244,000 Reichsmark are documented – although he sold most of them on at a profit.

The *Reichsstatthalter*'s taste in art was wide ranging. His interest was also piqued by "Aryanised" jewellery collections – for instance that of publisher Paul Zsolnay: Hitler had received ten items from this collection for his birthday from the special delegate for the "Führermuseum" in Linz, Hans Posse. Schirach "acquired" four pieces.[620]

As a prolific author of prefaces and forewords, Schirach also considered setting up his own publishing house. His press officer Günter Kaufmann thus instructed Wilhelm Hofmann, the escrow for the confiscated house Paul Zsolnay Verlag, to establish "how high the purchasing price will be if the press is taken over by Herrn Reichsstatthalter".[621] Ultimately, the renowned publishing house went to Karl Heinrich Bischoff, specialist consultant to the Reich Literature Chamber in the special unit for "Monitoring Harmful and Undesirable Literature", in the autumn of 1941.

In connection with the "Aryanisation" of Universal Edition, which was to remain in Vienna, Schirach also intervened personally in the music publishing business: he initially blocked its sale to the C.F. Peters press via the Länderbank Wien (Vienna Regional Bank), already approved by his predecessor, Bürckel, before eventually permitting it – presumably only after speaking to Goebbels.[622]

Despite the frequent resistance of subordinate authorities, Schirach gave people public property as gifts – for instance a *pietra dura* table from the mid-eighteenth century, which had been exhibited in the Belvedere gallery to mark the signing of the Second Vienna Award negotiated by Ribbentrop and Ciano on 30 August 1940. Since this sumptuous example of Florentine stone carving marvelled the Italian foreign minister,

Schirach presented it to him as a gift.[623] When the relevant administrators enquired about it, he gave them his personal confirmation that he had given the valuable ornate table away. If it hasn't been destroyed or resold, it remains in Italy to this day; the Republic of Austria has never demanded restitution. In the president's office, a sign still declares it missing.

On the basis of a temporary export licence (November 1940–February 1941), Schirach sent his Italian friend Renato Ricci, the former youth leader, then the minister of corporations, an Italian Renaissance box made of black wood with ivory inlays and a matching table from the seventeenth century. Their whereabouts is not documented in the files of the Federal Furniture Administration (*Bundesmobilienverwaltung*).

Schirach also played a role in the National Socialist plunder of Jewish art collections, and was certainly aware the original owners were Jewish. He was repeatedly involved in the internal debates on artworks stolen from Jews for the public collections in Vienna, since he made several attempts to revoke the "Führer's proviso". At the instigation of various museum directors in Vienna, he repeatedly sought to persuade Hitler to rescind his decision so that the stolen paintings could remain in the city's museums.[624]

Ecclesiastical collections were also affected by Schirach's instructions. The Canon Monastery (*Chorherrenstift*) of Klosterneuburg, for instance, was requisitioned for an Adolf Hitler school, but the "Gau Wien" (Vienna *Gau*) claimed the monastery's artworks for itself. Here the "Führer's proviso" initially prevented the *Reichsstatthalter* from gaining direct access.[625]

Schirach himself was even interested in items Jews had taken with them during deportation and which were stored in Trieste for seizure by the German Reich. He wanted to have these possessions relocated to Vienna in 1943, since there were fears they would be destroyed by bombing raids.[626]

In the final days of the war, Schirach, who was ultimately responsible for the relocation of artworks, gave the order via General Cultural Advisor Hermann Stuppäck, who was present in person, for 184 paintings – including works by Rembrandt, Pieter Bruegel the Elder, Titian and Velázquez – and forty-nine bags containing Gobelin tapestries to be moved further west, from the secure repository in the Lauffen mine near Bad Ischl to Bramberg in Salzburg's Pinzgau.[627] As outlined above, this area also played a role for Schirach's private collection. We do not know what Schirach was planning to do with these pictures after the war. Nevertheless, the mere fact that the most valuable paintings were concentrated in the Pinzgau by direct order of Baldur von Schirach is worth noting.

A study financed by his grandson, the writer and former criminal defence lawyer Ferdinand von Schirach, has enabled the partial reconstruction of Baldur and Henriette von Schirach's art collection:

> A total of 132 *objets d'art* and seventy items of furniture and ornaments could be established. Additionally, ca. 490 books and their titles were recorded, which admittedly only represented a fraction of the Schirachs' library. Clear confiscation as a result of National Socialist persecution could be established for at least five items. Additionally, the provenance of forty-five items is at least concerning, since Schirach acquired them in the occupied territories of the German Reich.[628]

In the period from December 1942 to June 1943 alone, Baldur von Schirach purchased stolen artworks with a reported total value of 42,092 Reichsmark via the euphemistically named Gestapo Administrative Department for Jewish Relocation Property (*Verwaltungsstelle für jüdisches Umzugsgut der Gestapo – Vugesta*).

Like many other Nazi potentates, Schirach intervened for third parties during acts of "Aryanisation" – for instance on behalf of Major Theodor von Hoffmann-Ostenhof of the *Waffen-SS* Battalion for Special Deployment (*Bataillon der Waffen-SS z. b. V.*).[629] The major wanted to buy the villa of the expatriated chemist Johann Wilhelm (Jean) Billiter in St Gilgen on Lake Wolfgang.[630] Incidentally, the villa went to the widow of Reich Minister for Church Affairs Hanns Kerl, who had died in 1941.

In large-scale "Aryanisation cases", the *Reichsstatthalter* also had a right of veto, as demonstrated by the complex case of the Bunzl & Biach AG conglomerate. The sale of this large company, renamed "Kontropa Kontinentale Rohstoff und Papierindustrie AG" (Kontropa Continental Raw Materials and Paper Industry AG), to a consortium led by the general agent of Opel in Berlin, Eduard Winter, was blocked by Schirach after he had been informed of the pending deal by Walther Kastner, the managing director of the Österreichische Kontrollbank für Industrie und Handel (Austrian Control Bank for Industry and Trade), which was in charge of the Aryanisation of large companies in Austria.[631] Eventually, the company was taken over by a Viennese banking consortium comprising the Creditanstalt-Bankverein, the Länderbank, Schoeller & Co. and E. v. Nicolai (the "Aryaniser" of S. M. v. Rothschild). Nevertheless, the case shows the extent of Schirach's involvement in "Aryanisation policy" and his detailed knowledge of the seizure of Jewish assets beyond looted art.

As mentioned above, no concrete figures have been produced to date concerning Schirach's private worth during the Nazi era. One piece of the puzzle is provided by a case brought before a Vienna People's Court senate on 28 May 1949, held in Schirach's absence. The proceedings revolved around "two accounts with the Länderbank" that had been seized[632] by the Republic of Austria and consisted of a package of shares in Polish industries and "various savings books and life insurance policies held in Jewish names".[633] While the villa on the Hohe Warte had been "Aryanised", as a state villa it was not Schirach's property. In this legal battle of 1949, his trustee, the lawyer Ernst Jahoda, unsuccessfully argued that since extradition proceedings were under way, his assets could not be confiscated by the state. It is unclear whether the Republic of Austria then attempted to establish who these assets' owners or heirs were – although in the light of asset seizure policy, I very much doubt it.

It is also unclear whether the two accounts in question were private or party accounts. Schirach's predecessor Bürckel had opened an account under Schirach's name holding 850,000 Reichsmark, most likely stolen assets, at the Länderbank.[634] Schirach instructed the bank that only he should have access to the account. Bürckel was nevertheless able to persuade the relevant board member, manager Wilhelm Lehr, to transfer 150,000 Reichsmark from this Schirach account to the account of *SS-Gruppenführer* Ernst Kaltenbrunner. Schirach actually wanted Lehr to be sacked from the board of the Länderbank, which was owned by the Dresdner Bank. The bank itself was reliant on good relations with the *Reichsstatthalter* and *Gauleiter* and hence Schirach received a generous loan for the Hitler Youth[635] – apparently as consolation, since Lehr remained on the board. Schirach was also given a loan of over one million Reichsmark in order to buy looted artworks in the occupied territories.

He never really made use of this loan, however, and in 1944 it was used for other activities supporting members of the *Wehrmacht* instead.[636] The board of the Dresdner Bank even raised it to 1.5 million Reichsmark on 30 May 1944 for "the purchase of provisions to be forwarded to the divisions under Schirach's charge in return for payment".[637]

On 30 January 1945, the minutes of the Dresdner Bank board meeting contained a reference to the "prolongation of the cash loan of 1 million Reichsmark until 31.1.1946".[638] Due to a lack of sources, it is unclear whether this was a different loan, but it is reasonable to assume that the sum was intended for looted art. Whether Schirach withdrew the money in cash is also unknown due to the sparse source material, and it was not touched on during his trial in Nuremberg either. Nevertheless, what is clear is that Baldur von Schirach had no qualms about exploiting his political position in order to get his hands on "Aryanised" items – and at favourable prices whenever possible.

A difficult issue is determining who the legal owners of the artworks really were, a question that has also vexed Theresa Sepp of the Central Institute of Art History (*Zentralinstitut für Kunstgeschichte*) in Munich. While Henriette von Schirach was financially well-off due to her father Heinrich Hoffmann, the land registry listed Baldur von Schirach as the sole owner of Schloss Aspenstein, even though by her own account her dowry only amounted to around 100,000 Reichsmark.[639] The large payments Baldur von Schirach received from the royalties for the many publications he edited, mostly as *Reichsjugendführer* and together with his father-in-law Heinrich Hoffmann, have not been fully documented. Hoffmann's companies, which had around 300 employees at their peak – with a branch on Vienna's Opernring, incidentally – had an enormous turnover of 58 million Reichsmark in 1943.[640] His art purchases in the years 1940 to 1944 were made with income from royalties along with his salary as *Reichsstatthalter* and *Gauleiter*.

In the post-war years, the traces revealing artworks' provenance remained largely covered, and hence Henriette von Schirach managed to regain thirty-four of the sixty works confiscated by the US occupying authorities without having to offer anything in return. She was able to buy back nineteen of the items cheaply without their provenance being established. Sixty-eight pieces of furniture taken from Schloss Aspenstein were also returned to her.[641] Most of these items she sold on immediately.

His grandson Ferdinand von Schirach succinctly summed up the moral aspect of this way of dealing with the stolen assets of Jews:

> It is ultimately the case that Henriette and some of my family brought guilt upon themselves a second time after 1945, repeating their theft from these families by demanding repossession of these artworks.[642]

Chapter 13

I Alone Bear the Guilt

Nuremberg 1946

Henriette von Schirach, who had found a place to live in the Nuremberg suburb of Erlenstegen, attempted to find her husband an English lawyer, but Baldur von Schirach had already chosen one from a list that had been presented to him: Dr Fritz Sauter from Munich, "a big, jolly, somewhat boisterous man who had made a name for himself defending poachers and completely hopeless cases". Dr Sauter was a pragmatist and made this quite clear to Henriette: "'What we need', he said while filling his pipe, 'is exonerating material. You must provide whatever you can get hold of.'"[643] Henriette supplied him with information about her husband's American relatives and his early career in the "time of the struggle", and Dr Sauter quickly found the key points for a promising line of defence he could present to his client.

Baldur von Schirach's strategy during the Nuremberg trials was ultimately very different to those of many of his co-defendants, such as the case advanced by Hermann Göring. On the one hand, he openly admitted to being a former anti-Semite and the creator of the myth of the "Führer" Adolf Hitler for children and adolescents, while on the other hand he pointed to the influence of the American car manufacturer Henry Ford and his racist publications as reading that had shaped his anti-Semitic attitudes. He said nothing about his family home or his personal environment in Weimar, despite the fact that an aggressively anti-Semitic and anti-democratic mood had prevailed in the town during the 1920s. The stance he took during his trial gave the impression that Ford's theories had made him an anti-Semite. However, if we consider the political atmosphere in Weimar and the values and ideals of the youth organisations of which Schirach was a member, his statements are in no way convincing.

He did not see the Hitler Youth as a paramilitary organisation, repeatedly comparing it to the British and international Boy Scouts. He did not deny the murder of six million Jews and declared the genocide to have been just that:

> It is the greatest, the most devilish mass murder known to history. But that murder was not committed by Hoess; Hoess was merely the executioner. The murder was ordered by Adolf Hitler, as is obvious from his last will and testament. The will is genuine. I have held the photostat copy of that will in my hands. He and Himmler jointly committed that crime which, for all time, will be a stain in the annals of our history. It is a crime which fills every German with shame.
>
> The youth of Germany is guiltless. Our youth was anti-Semitically inclined, but it did not call for the extermination of Jewry. It neither realized nor imagined that Hitler had carried out this extermination by the daily murder of thousands of innocent people. The youth of Germany who, today, stand perplexed among the ruins of their native land, knew nothing of these crimes, nor did they desire them.[644]

Schirach had worked on this statement intensively, as demonstrated by his handwritten version for the psychologist Dr Gustave M. Gilbert of 24 May 1946, dated to the second day of proceedings.[645]

What is remarkable is Gilbert's assessment that Göring had subsequently attempted to "turn" Schirach. A dedicated "Youth Lunchroom" was set up with Albert Speer, Hans Fritzsche, Schirach and Walther Funk around a table in order to remove Schirach and Funk from Göring's influence.[646] Gilbert considered Schirach a "narcissist",[647] noting an "essential moral weakness" clearly manifested in the way "he has subdued his indignation at the 'betrayal' of German youth by Hitler under the influence of Göring's aggressive cynicism, nationalism, and pose of heroic romanticism".[648]

Ultimately, however, Schirach followed the line of the former minister for armament, Albert Speer, in conceding political guilt, but he rejected legal responsibility for the crimes of the National Socialist regime and the accusation he had militarised the Hitler Youth.

For the main hearing, he prepared the above-cited statement, which was somewhat radical in comparison to the opening statements of his co-defendants. It had perhaps been prepared in consultation with his lawyer

Sauter and was potentially influenced by the months of conversations with American psychologists such as Gustave M. Gilbert and Douglas M. Kelley. Schirach also asked Gilbert to show his handwritten statement to his former adjutants Gustav Höpken and Fritz Wieshofer, feeling that if they saw it was genuine, they would ensure that German youth learnt of what their former boss had said.[649]

It can be assumed that Höpken and Wieshofer received Schirach's statement before 28 May 1946, the day they gave their own witness statements. Höpken, who had been interned by the Americans since 19 May 1945, was questioned by defence counsel Fritz Sauter about Schirach's attitude towards the churches, especially the Catholic Church, after 1933. Höpken responded that Schirach had been monitored by Martin Bormann and hence was unable to make direct contact with Cardinal Innitzer, but apologised to the latter in writing when he was harassed by HJ leaders during a mass in the winter of 1944/45.[650] Schirach also entrusted Höpken with establishing direct contact with the dean of the Evangelical Faculty, Gustav Entz.[651] Entz was an active anti-Semite and supporter of the National Socialist regime but nevertheless tried to prevent anti-Church measures via several written submissions, with the effect that his own home was raided in 1944.[652]

Höpken's aim was to exonerate Schirach from the accusation that he had seen Heydrich's reports about German war crimes against Jews, partisans and civilians in the occupied territories of the Soviet Union.[653] This he denied on the basis of his experience as head of Schirach's Central Bureau, saying that in accordance with the mailing list, these reports had been sent to Dr Felber at the office of (Vienna) Government President Dellbrügge and to Supreme Government Councillor (*Oberregierungsrat*) Dr Fischer at the office of the commissar for the defence of the Reich. However, given Schirach's high positions of office and his proximity to Heydrich, it seems unlikely Schirach was not informed about them.

Wieshofer, born in Vienna in 1914, became Schirach's personal adjutant after being transferred from the Office of Foreign Affairs in October 1940. Like Höpken, he exonerated Schirach in every respect – including the deportation of Vienna's Jews, blaming the Reich Security Main Office and "SS-Obersturmführer" (*sic*; *Hauptsturmführer*) "Dr. [*sic*] Alois Brunner". He claimed that interventions on behalf of individual Jews made by the Central Bureau under Schirach as *Reichsstatthalter* had also been negotiated with Brunner, in two such cases by Wieshofer himself.[654] Wieshofer also made the seemingly absurd claim that Schirach had told him about a visit to Mauthausen concentration camp, where he had attended a symphony concert.[655] In fact, Schirach did go to Mauthausen and its satellite camp of Gusen on 16 February 1943, where there was indeed an inmates' orchestra that also had to play during executions. Even Hartmann Lauterbacher, whom Schirach had not proposed as his successor as *Reichsjugendführer*, decided not to remain silent and lent him his support.[656] Lauterbacher had been flown in from a British prison for the trial. He pointed to a speech by Schirach to the HJ regional leaders (*Gebietsführer*) on 15 November 1938 in which he distanced himself from the November pogrom. Lauterbacher claimed that on 10 November, Schirach had instructed him by telephone to forbid members of the Hitler Youth to participate in these pogroms.[657] In fact, however, the destruction and looting had already taken place the night before, with the active and brutal participation of many members of the Hitler Youth throughout the entire German "Reich", as documented in detail by several regional studies.[658]

Perhaps Schirach's intention behind this speech was to regain control over the regional organisations, since the lust for destruction had spiralled out of control and the Hitler Youth's looting ultimately meant losses for the "Reich", since the plan was to confiscate Jewish assets. Even before the pogrom, there had been repeated isolated incidents of members of the Hitler Youth looting from Jewish shops.[659] However, in this speech, Schirach was ultimately concerned only about discipline, not turning around anti-Jewish National Socialist policy.

Lauterbacher also recalled a confidential conversation with Schirach in March 1943 in which the latter told him the war was lost and Bormann was denying him access to Hitler.[660]

The other co-defendants' reactions to Schirach's portrayal of his open break with Hitler were mixed: Hans Frank and Joachim von Ribbentrop criticised both Schirach and Göring. Albert Speer, on the other hand, welcomed his stance, Göring having originally sent Schirach to warn him not to say anything against Hitler during the hearing. Now Speer and Schirach were even on familiar terms with each other. Admiral Dönitz too supported Schirach's version of events, emphasising, however, that he did not subscribe to Schirach's denial of the HJ's anti-Church policy.[661]

In his statement, Schirach concentrated on the murder of millions of Jews, leaving other groups such as Roma and Sinti, victims of euthanasia, prisoners of war etc. unmentioned, and declared Adolf Hitler the sole central perpetrator – supported by Heinrich Himmler. There was no truth, however, to his claim that an order for the mass murder was also contained by Hitler's testament, in which he further demanded "merciless resistance to the poisoner of all peoples of the world, international Jewry".[662]

On the whole, the extant literature assessing the Nuremberg trials underestimates the role played by the two American psychologist-psychiatrists. Particularly in the case of Schirach, whom they described as someone who could be influenced, it is likely that these intensive interviews lasting several weeks left their mark. At the same time, Schirach was very cautious not to incriminate himself in his statements concerning what he knew about the Shoah and his own involvement in it.

Schirach subsequently wrote a defence of the Hitler Youth on 21 August 1946.[663] In it, he suppressed the prehistory of the HJ and the BDM and avoided in-depth analysis of the indoctrination of German youth via National Socialist education. Nor did he mention how all the other youth organisations had been done away with.

Schirach's thesis that he had merely built up a self-administered youth organisation similar to the Boy Scouts is disproven by, for instance, a decree of the "Führer on the military deployment of German Youth"; Schirach was forwarded the draft version by Artur Axmann on 30 March 1942.[664]

He had good reason not to mention his personal involvement in the "Aryanisation" of Jewish property discussed in the previous chapter. He said he was guilty of having "educated this generation in faith and loyalty to Hitler [...] a man whom I for many long years had considered unimpeachable [...] a man who murdered by the millions".[665]

Confronted with the deportation of the Jews from Vienna in 1941–42, he blamed the Reich Security Main Office.[666] From the detailed interviews, one could have gained the impression that all information about deportations, but also murders and violence, was communicated via other channels in Vienna, since Schirach stated he had neither read nor signed any of these reports.[667] When the American prosecutor Thomas Dodd presented him with fifty-five reports by Reinhard Heydrich[668] that had been made available to the Reich Defence Council

(*Reichsverteidigungsausschuss*) in Vienna, on which Schirach had served, he said he could not remember having read these reports, since they were addressed to Dr Fischer.⁶⁶⁹ These reports documented the murder of Jews. Schirach claimed it was only much later that he had learnt that Jews had been shot.

In contrast, he was unable to deny having sent the following telegram to Bormann after Heydrich's assassination in the occupied "Protectorate of Bohemia and Moravia", but he was able to secure an adjournment when Dodd overran:

"Dear Martin Bormann,
"I request that the following be submitted to the Führer:
Knowing the Czech population and its attitude in Vienna as well as in the Protectorate, I would draw your attention to the following:

"The enemy powers and the British cliques around Benes have for a long time felt bitter about the co-operation generally found among the Czech workers and their contribution to the German war economy. They are seeking for a means to play off the Czech population and the Reich against each other. The attack on Heydrich was undoubtedly planned in London. The British arms of the assailant suggest parachuted agents. London hopes by means of this murder to induce the Reich to take extreme measures with the aim of bringing about a resistance movement among Czech workers. In order to prevent the world from thinking that the population of the Protectorate is in opposition to Hitler, these acts must immediately be branded as of British authorship. A sudden and violent air attack on a British cultural town would be most effective and the world would have learned of this through the headline 'Revenge for Heydrich.' That alone should induce Churchill to desist immediately from the procedure begun in Prague of stirring up revolt. The Reich replies to the attack at Prague by a counterattack on world public opinion. [...]"⁶⁷⁰

One of the biggest problems besetting the prosecution was the scant evidence. Since comprehensive research could not be conducted so soon after the war, many documents were only available as fragments, and the prosecution relied on reports and information. For instance, the legal department of the US forces in Austria received from the mayor of Vienna, Theodor Körner, a transcript of Schirach's speech of 6 June 1942 at a councillors' meeting of the City of Vienna[671] in which he announced that "already in the latter part of summer or in the fall of this year all Jews would be removed from the city, and that the removal of the Czechs would then get under way, since this is the necessary and right answer to the crime committed against the Deputy Reich Protector of Bohemia and Moravia".[672]

Schirach repeatedly dropped in statements intended to support his claims that there had been growing opposition to Hitler. For example, he described in detail the conflict between his wife Henriette and Hitler at the Berghof in 1943 concerning the issue of deportations (see Chapter 10) or brought up Hitler's heavy criticism of his cultural policy in Vienna.[673] In his autobiography, Albert Speer later verified the argument at Hitler's residence, writing that it was the only time he had witnessed an open challenge to National Socialist policy towards Jews.[674]

It is striking that in his very detailed closing speech, defence counsel Fritz Sauter, of whom Schirach makes no mention in his memoirs, banked entirely on Schirach's supposedly open and honest examination of National Socialism, claiming that the former *Gauleiter* and *Reichsstatthalter* was "perhaps the one defendant who not only clearly realised his mistakes, however they may be regarded, but who confessed to them most honestly and who through his plain speaking prevented the creation of a Hitler legend in the future. Such a defendant must be given consideration for trying to repair as far as he can the damage which he caused in good faith."[675]

Sauter, a very well-known defence lawyer from Munich who had left the NSDAP in 1940 but nevertheless joined the National Socialist Motor Corps (*Nationalsozialistisches Kraftfahrkorps*) in 1941,[676] defended both Schirach and the former Reich economics minister Walther Funk. Later, he also represented some other defendants at Nuremberg. In Schirach's case, he consistently adhered to an individual strategy; his arguments were regarded very positively by British prosecutor David Maxwell-Fyfe, but negatively by Telford Taylor, the legal advisor to the American chief prosecutor Robert H. Jackson. While Sauter certainly also considered

"Nuremberg" a site for critical examination of the history of National Socialism,[677] his client's interests were always his main focus.

An important piece of the puzzle in Schirach's defence strategy was his close family ties to the USA. That this was well-received by American citizens is evident in the assessment of Schirach by the American psychiatrist Dr Douglas M. Kelley.[678] Kelley spent five months working at the military prison in Nuremberg, interviewing one of the twenty-two main defendants almost every day. In addition to medical examinations, he also used the Rorschach test developed by the Swiss psychiatrist Hermann Rorschach, which was then a modern method in the USA. The subject's interpretation of ten symmetrical inkblots was supposed to allow insights into his personality. Reaction time also played a role in this assessment related to social and intellectual personality traits. Kelley's assistant, Captain Dr Gustave M. Gilbert, who served as an interpreter and clerk during the interviews, also conducted a Wechsler–Bellevue intelligence test. Schirach did relatively well in this test taken by the defendants; he displayed an IQ of 130. The highest IQ was 143, recorded by the former president of the Reichsbank and economics minister Hjalmar Schacht, while Julius Streicher, *Gauleiter* of Franken and editor of the anti-Semitic smear-sheet *Der Stürmer*, came in last, with 106. Hermann Göring impressed the American psychologists with a score of 138.

Schirach employed a remarkably clever strategy in order to win Kelley over, untruthfully stating that as a boy he had not been interested in politics but had been devoted entirely to literature, especially poetry. At the age of seventeen, he had then discovered the book by the great American car manufacturer Henry Ford, *The International Jew*, which had made a deep impression and opened up a new world to him (so much so that he seems to have forgotten its title, confusing it with the legend of the "Eternal Jew").[679] Julius Streicher subsequently made him enthusiastic about politics and turned him into an anti-Semite. "Then I met Hitler. I was young and impressionable, filled with an eager zeal to destroy Germany's enemies and restore my Fatherland to its rightful greatness. Hitler, in his speeches and his person, inspired me profoundly. I wanted only to be near him, to serve him and, thereby, serve Germany. That was all I thought of, all I dreamed."[680]

Both in his conversations with Kelley and before the court, Schirach admitted to having been an anti-Semite. Although he had approved "in one speech, the evacuation of Vienna's Jews", he distanced himself from his remarks by saying he had made them "only at Hitler's suggestion".[681] He also told Kelley about the dispute with Hitler at the Berghof on the Obersalzberg that had led to their falling out, but dated the incident to 1942 instead of 1943. Kelley also refers to a remarkable proposal that Schirach made after his arrest; the former *Reichsjugendführer* suggested that "all youth leaders be called together for a re-education programme".[682] On 27 October 1945, Schirach even told Gilbert he wanted to set up a re-education camp at the former Buchenwald concentration camp.[683] Later, attempts were indeed made by representatives of the French authorities and former HJ leaders to develop a catalogue of values for the integration of former National Socialists.[684]

Kelley's assessment was quite clear: "Schirach was good material gone wrong".[685] Consequently, the psychiatrist was most enthusiastic about the hard-working way he had gone about his work as *Reichsjugendführer*, completely forgetting the team he had had around him and the large organisational operation; the rise of the Hitler Youth became a one-man show. Schirach made, then, a lasting impression on the American: "Finally, he was of good family, well educated, and handsome, a young man of keen imagination, and considerable creative and literary ability. Moreover, he was – second to Hess – the Nazi without a vice."

Kelley dismissed the rumours about Schirach's alleged homosexuality; quite on the contrary, Schirach violently prevented homosexuality in the Hitler Youth while cautiously promoting heterosexual relations between HJ boys and BDM girls. Within the HJ, Schirach intensified the persecution of homosexuals via an internal observation apparatus from 1935 onwards.[686]

In his daily interviews with Schirach, which went on for several months, Kelley received the impression that the "feelings of guilt" expressed by Hitler's former paladin were "profound. But his convictions were still those of a romantic easily led".[687] The psychiatrist nevertheless thought that it would "require years of re-education before the basic doctrines of Nazi philosophy can be eradicated from the minds of youthful Germans".[688]

In his cell, Schirach "looked gaunt and haggard", quite in keeping with the cliché of the "prison poet"; Kelley had him write a poem entitled "Dem Tod" ("To Death"), which he dedicated to his psychiatrist:

> *Your dark eye I have so often seen,*
> *That you have become like an old friend to me.*
> *When the bullets scourged, you stood at the mark,*
> *And looked at me. To the left and right fell*
> *My neighbor. Yet you turned away.*
> *I greeted each grave later, all alone.*
> *When the bombs burst from the sky,*
> *You drew to me the house's silent guest*
> *Yet you have not done your work on me.*
> *I know, my friend, that your eye is on me.*[689]

In the context of these conversations, Schirach claimed on 27 October 1945 that he had intervened on behalf of individual Jews at great risk to his own person in order to protect them from imprisonment in a concentration camp. In some cases, this was true, but these efforts did not involve any personal danger to Schirach himself. He usually had the president of the government in Vienna, Dellbrügge, or his aides take care of these matters. He even claimed to have hidden his efforts to intervene from his defence counsel Sauter: "But in view of the great mass of murdered victims, he did not wish to lower himself to seek clemency because of a few people he had spared, making a pitiful spectacle of defense like some of the others", Kelley wrote in his papers.[690]

Contemporary observers thought that US prosecutor Thomas Dodd's[691] cross-examination of Schirach[692] was not enough to penetrate his defence strategy, which ultimately made Hitler solely responsible for all the crimes of National Socialism.[693] A graduate of Yale, Dodd had previously served as an assistant to five US Departments of Justice, but had never actively prosecuted anyone in court. Hence he got bogged down, for instance, in analysing anti-Catholic and anti-Semitic content in the Hitler Youth's songbook *Blut und Ehre* (Blood and Honour), which Schirach had edited. On the whole, in letters from Nuremberg to his family in the USA he did not seem particularly committed to prosecuting Schirach.[694] As the journalist Walter Cronkite, yet to achieve world renown, reported, Schirach clearly attempted to curry favour with Dodd on the basis of their faith (Dodd was a Catholic, Schirach a Protestant)[695] and the fact that the prosecutor had run the National Youth Administration in the USA. Dodd's response to his personal approach was curt. "We're nothing alike."[696]

Under National Socialism, however, Schirach had always stressed that "the Hitler Youth was neither Protestant nor Catholic, but German".⁶⁹⁷ In July 1939, he reasserted this stance, saying that "service to Germany, which is also religious service, stands above service in any particular confession, and our youth must not be someone who does not unconditionally belong to Germany".⁶⁹⁸ He had ultimately broken the independence of the Catholic and Protestant youth organisations via the monopoly of the Hitler Youth and had either integrated the associations – such as the Protestant ones – into the HJ or dissolved them. Private worship remained possible, however.

The Soviet prosecution had little success against Schirach either, partly due to severe problems with translation and a witness statement concerning the massacre of Jews by members of the Hitler Youth in Lviv in the summer of 1941 that was submitted too late.⁶⁹⁹

Ultimately, Schirach and Sauter's defence strategy of distancing himself from National Socialism, and especially Adolf Hitler, and expressing remorse for the mass murder of European Jews proved effective. In this context, the American psychologist Gilbert played a particularly important role for Schirach; Gilbert also helped him escape the influence of Hermann Göring by allowing him to take his meals at a different table. Despite the many conversations they had, Schirach does not mention Gilbert in his memoirs either.

Originally, Schirach was charged with both "crimes against peace" and "crimes against humanity", defined by the charter of the International Military Tribunal of 1 August 1945 according to three categories:

(a) **CRIMES AGAINST PEACE**: namely, planning, preparation, initiation or waging of a war of aggression, or a war in violation of international treaties, agreements or assurances, or participation in a common plan or conspiracy for the accomplishment of any of the foregoing;

(b) **WAR CRIMES**: namely, violations of the laws or customs of war [...].

(c) **CRIMES AGAINST HUMANITY**: namely, murder, extermination, enslavement, deportation, and other inhumane acts committed against any civilian population, before or during the war;

or persecutions on political, racial or religious grounds in execution of or in connection with any crime within the jurisdiction of the Tribunal, whether or not in violation of the domestic law of the country where perpetrated.

Leaders, organizers, instigators and accomplices participating in the formulation or execution of a common plan or conspiracy to commit any of the foregoing crimes are responsible for all acts performed by any persons in execution of such plan.[700]

Baldur von Schirach was ultimately sentenced to twenty years in prison for crimes against humanity, but not for crimes against peace. However, the judges discussed this verdict. On the US side, the legal experts Henry Wechsler of Columbia Law School in New York and James Rowe internally opposed what they considered an excessively mild sentence.[701]

Regarding the military and aggressive character of the Hitler Youth, the court came to the following conclusion, despite plenty of evidence of ideological and concrete preparation for war within the organisation itself:

Despite the warlike nature of the activities of the Hitler Jugend, however, it does not appear that Von Schirach was involved in the development of Hitler's plan for territorial expansion by means of aggressive war, or that he participated in the planning or preparation of any of the wars of aggression.[702]

In the case of crimes against humanity, on the other hand, the court followed the argument that Schirach was clearly guilty:

The Tribunal finds that Von Schirach, while he did not originate the policy of deporting Jews from Vienna, participated in this deportation after he had become Gauleiter of Vienna. He knew that the best the Jews could hope for was a miserable existence in the ghettos of the East. Bulletins describing the Jewish extermination were in his office.

While Gauleiter of Vienna, Von Schirach continued to function as Reichsleiter for Youth Education and in this capacity he was informed of the Hitler Jugend's participation in the plan put into effect in the fall of 1944 under which 50,000 young people between the ages of 10 and 20 were evacuated into Germany from areas recaptured by the Soviet forces and used as apprentices in German industry and as auxiliaries in units of the German Armed Forces. In the summer of 1942, Von Schirach telegraphed Bormann urging that a bombing attack on an English cultural town be carried out in retaliation for the assassination of Heydrich which, he claimed, had been planned by the British.

The court concluded "that Von Schirach is not guilty on Count One. He is guilty under Count Four."[703]

The sentences were pronounced in the Nuremberg *Justizpalast* (Palace of Justice) on 1 October 1946. In the witness house, a villa run by the German–Hungarian Countess Ingeborg Kálnoky and a temporary home to around a hundred important witnesses, irrespective of whether they were former high-ranking National Socialists, followers (*Mitläufer*), concentration camp prisoners or resistance fighters, Henriette von Schirach reacted with a scream of delight when she heard that Baldur had received a twenty-year prison sentence and not the death penalty.[704] She could be heard throughout the entire building.[705] It would appear she had reckoned with his execution. Baldur von Schirach's defence strategy – declaring himself morally guilty and confessing to having been an anti-Semite while nevertheless denying early knowledge of the Shoah and personal involvement in the deportation and persecution of Jews – had worked. His massive criticism of Adolf Hitler in connection with the genocide against Europe's Jews had ultimately persuaded the court not to punish him with death by hanging.

The Price of Glory

After her internment in Bad Tölz until March 1946, Henriette von Schirach visited her father Heinrich Hoffmann at the witness house in the May of that year. American policy concerning the wives of high-ranking National Socialist functionaries was brutal and bore clear vestiges of Nazi *Sippenhaft* (relatives' guilt by association). For Schirach's children, too, this was an extremely tough time; they were often away from both parents. In his book *Der Schatten meines Vaters* (My Father's

Shadow, 2005), Richard von Schirach, the youngest son, provides a striking and vivid description of the sometimes traumatic experiences the four children underwent in the immediate post-war years.[706]

Angelika von Schirach was twelve years old in 1945, Klaus was ten, Robert was seven and Richard was three. The children had to leave Schloss Aspenstein, where they had lived in the annex below the stables following the building's confiscation by US troops. On Christmas Eve 1945, they were taken by lorry to a forester's lodge in the remote Jachenau.[707] Their mother protested strongly when they were brought to Bad Tölz.

Their cousins Heidi and Susi were already in Jachenau, under the care of their grandmother from Graz. Made their carer by the authorities, she struck them with a bundle of wooden rods, especially the littlest, Richard, in order to beat bed-wetting out of him. She was generally extremely violent towards them until she was replaced by a nanny known as "Beidau". In the March, Henriette von Schirach returned from the prison in Bad Tölz, where she had shared a cell with eight women. What followed, Richard von Schirach writes, was an emotional roller coaster: "agitation, being startled, relief, demands, hot and cold, but the evenings are nevertheless unforgettable".[708] From the forester's lodge, the family then moved to an inn in the village. Shortly before Christmas 1946, Henriette was arrested again and taken to the women's prison in Göggingen near Augsburg pending prosecution before a German *Spruchkammer* (a court set up for "de-Nazification"). There she was charged with having been an early member of the NSDAP in 1932 and a "favourite" of Hitler.[709] Other wives of prominent National Socialists, such as Emmy Göring, Ilse Hess, Elisabeth Kaltenbrunner, Luise Funk and Margarete Frick, were imprisoned there too. Conditions in the prison were anything but pleasant; Henriette told the American journalist and war reporter Marguerite Higgins, "You will make Nazis out of people who were never Nazis before. Please tell your General Clay[710] I hope he will not treat me in such a fashion that my children will grow up to hate America."[711] She also complained about being in a camp with SS wives in which former concentration camp prisoners were used as guards. The Bad Tölz lawyer Dr Karl Katzenberger defended her in the *Spruchkammer* case and acted as her children's legal guardian.

In the case against Henriette von Schirach, in which the defence called well-known witnesses such as the writers Hans Carossa, Kasimir

Edschmid and Waldemar Bonsels, the latter a self-confessed anti-Semite, the former "old party member" was deemed a "lesser offender" (*minderbelastet*) and was fined 200 marks.[712]

Ultimately, Robert and Richard von Schirach found a temporary home with nanny Beidau's parents at the foot of the Aspenstein mountain. The two elder siblings, Angelika and Klaus, stayed at Beidau's house in Kochel, travelling to school on an open truck.

For a time, the confiscated Schloss Aspenstein served as the headquarters of the Americans' Tenth Armoured Division before housing displaced persons the Nazis had taken from all over Europe. In 1948, the Bavarian branch of the German Social Democratic Party (*Sozialdemokratische Partei Deutschlands*, SPD) rented it on a five-year lease at 400 marks a month from the Free State of Bavaria's trust administration (*Vermögensverwaltung*). In 1951, the party then acquired it as restitution for its loss of assets during the Nazi era. From 1948 onwards, the stately home also served as a venue for educational courses in democracy in the newly established Georg von Vollmar School. Since 1968, the legal title-holder has been the Georg von Vollmar Academy.[713]

The last co-owner, Elsa Dessauer, whose husband was stigmatised as a "one-quarter Jew", had sold the property to Baldur von Schirach in 1936. Her attempt to have it returned to her was unsuccessful, since her lawyer could not provide any documentation. Henriette von Schirach was not recorded as a co-owner in the land registry and did not submit a formal application for the building's return, but she repeatedly laid claim to its contents and also repeatedly forced her way in to take items away with her.[714]

After many applications and several internments, Henriette von Schirach was able to rent from the Free State of Bavaria the wooden house in Urfeld am Walchensee that Baldur had bought in 1939 with its grounds amounting to one hectare. The house in which Colin Ross and his wife Elisabeth had taken their own lives in the late April of 1945 had also been confiscated by the Bavarian state as a "direct party asset" of the NSDAP.[715] Henriette moved into this house with her new partner, Alfred H. Jacob,[716] a film screenwriter and director, and her youngest son, Richard.[717] Richard was often left to his own devices and suffered under his mother's new relationship, while his twelve-year-old brother Robert was sent to a boarding school in Kaufbeuren.

In 1949, Henriette filed for divorce from Baldur von Schirach. In a custody case, her partner Jacob ultimately lost his status as the children's guardian, since it was alleged that he "used to punish the boys [...] with hard beatings that were not always called for".[718] Legal custodianship of the children was transferred to the Bad Tölz youth welfare department; only Richard remained with his mother and her partner, later moving to Munich with them. The couple also suffered professional setbacks: Jacob's film projects, for instance a portrait of Richard Strauss in 1949, on which Henriette also worked, turned out to be a financial disaster.

Henriette's later life was casually summarised by the *Süddeutsche Zeitung* newspaper:

> Henriette von Schirach now lives in Schwabing, under her less conspicuous maiden name Hoffmann. The parties at her villa are attended by artists, curators and the Munich set. She sometimes operates as a film producer, sometimes as a journalist, sometimes as a writer. That she occasionally calls herself Henriette Richards, that she lets it be known she has divorced the film producer Alfred Jacob, to whom she was married, that she is being sentenced for perjury, that in her memoirs she flirts with the notion that she sold her old clothes to GIs as the "last clothes of Eva Braun" – none of this bothers anyone: in the mid-fifties, she can buy back her confiscated country home on the Kochelsee from the Free State at the ridiculously low price of 45 marks per square metre, immediately selling it again for twice as much. Now she wants art and furniture back.[719]

Despite her "business successes", she was always short of money and lived modestly in the end.

Henriette von Schirach's eldest son, Klaus, wrote an afterword to the ninth edition of his mother's memoirs *Der Preis der Herrlichkeit* (*The Price of Glory*), adding to her depiction of late post-war Munich high society and providing more accurate context. Taking up the incident at the Berghof in which she had confronted Hitler, whom she had known well during her childhood in Munich, with the brutal deportations of Jews in the Netherlands, Klaus von Schirach writes:

My mother's courage was a result of childlike instinct – throughout her life, she remained a creative child, highly talented as an artist and (as this book demonstrates) as a writer, acting on instinct. She was brilliant, bursting with ideas that she usually did not realise because she was already taken with another one. And like a child, she opened up to the boom of the fifties, established a company, with which she imported the first Italian and French art films (Fellini, Rosselini, Cocteau etc.), published a *Film Revue*, and if something went wrong with her enterprises (actually, everything went wrong), she did not open unpleasant letters, hiding them. When she was to be arrested in 1946 to be taken to the Nazi wives' camp, she initially simply ran into the woods.[720]

And "Henny" was extremely industrious, despite the many business flops she experienced, some of them with Jacob, for whom she had sent the divorce papers to Baldur in his prison cell in Spandau. As well as coping with day-to-day problems, with the help of Eberhard Hanfstaengl, the director of the Bavarian State Painting Collections (*Bayerische Staatsgemäldesammlungen*), she was able to regain unchecked works from the confiscated property of Baldur von Schirach, despite the fact that some of them were from collections belonging to dispossessed Jews. She was also able to buy back artworks at a good price. Incidentally, Hanfstaengl was a cousin of Ernst "Putzi" Hanfstaengl, who as chief foreign press officer had been part of Hitler's inner circle before fleeing to Britain. His cousin Eberhard was initially well-disposed to Henriette Hoffmann, formerly von Schirach: "As early as 4 June 1949, he gives the 'most esteemed Mrs. Hoffmann', formerly von Schirach, forty-four pieces of furniture, pictures and rugs and thirteen other items. All of them 'without value', as Hanfstaengl asserts."[721] In 1948, she had already had an affidavit signed by her father Heinrich Hoffmann and his housekeeper Anna Ollert confirming "that the entire furnishings of Aspenstein House, that is, furniture, rugs, bedding and table cloths, pictures and all 'other works of art […]' had already been in the possession of Heinrich Hoffmann and were transferred to Henriette upon her marriage".[722] After the US authorities had handed over responsibility for the works of art securely held at the Central Collection Point in Munich to the Bavarian State Ministry for Education and Culture in 1949, this authority entrusted its administration to Director Hanfstaengl. Hanfstaengl initially favoured Henriette von Schirach even when proof of ownership was dubious, but he was increasingly subjected to internal criticism before finally receiving an official warning. State Commissar for Victims of Racial, Religious and Political Persecution Philipp Auerbach produced a severe written attack on Director Hanfstaengl, accusing him of a "particular act of gallantry towards ladies of war criminals".[723]

Schirach's father-in-law, Heinrich Hoffmann, who had acquired a large fortune during the Nazi era due to his exclusive position as Hitler's personal photographer and had been sentenced to four years' imprisonment in 1946, also made energetic attempts to regain artworks after his release.[724] Always in financial difficulty, his daughter Henriette continued these efforts after his death. In a class action with the Texan entrepreneur Billy F. Price and her brother Heinrich Hoffmann jr, she sued the United States for compensation of 41 million US dollars. For this law suit, she used the more well-known name von Schirach.

On the basis of the Trading with the Enemy Act, the US forces had confiscated four watercolours by Hitler and Hoffmann's entire photo archive, today located in the US National Archives in College Park, Maryland,[725] and a small collection of Hoffmann photos employees of Time Inc. had taken from Germany to the US. Price had been trying to secure restitution of the items to the Hoffmann/Schirach family since 1982 so that he could buy Hitler's watercolours.

In 1995, the United States Court of Appeals, Fifth Circuit, dismissed his application due to lack of jurisdiction. At the same time, the court overturned an earlier ruling by the District Courts for the Southern District of Texas, which had partially found in favour of the litigants, granting them eight million US dollars in compensation in 1989.[726]

In 2003, Robert H. Hoffmann, heir to Heinrich Hoffmann jr, and a group of heirs from the Schirach family attempted to bring the same claim before a District Court in the District of Columbia, despite having been unsuccessful in 1999 following Billy T. Price's exclusion as a litigant.[727] The class action group comprised Robert H. Hoffmann, Heidemarie Krüger, Susanne Hustadt and the executor of Henriette von Schirach, Klaus von Schirach. This action too was unsuccessful, all relevant points being dismissed.

Chapter 14

I Believed in Hitler

The Perfect Myth?

After Baldur von Schirach had been transferred to the vast Allied Prison in Berlin Spandau on 18 July 1947 to serve his twenty-year sentence, it was ultimately only his four children who looked after him. In 1949, Henriette informed her husband that she wanted a divorce.

Whereas conservative circles intervened on behalf of the former foreign minister and *Reichsprotektor* of Bohemia and Moravia, Konstantin von Neurath, and veterans' associations supported the former grand admirals (*Großadmirale*) Erich Raeder, supreme commander of the navy until 1943, and Karl Dönitz, who had been Hitler's successor as *Reichspräsident* and supreme commander of the *Wehrmacht*, Schirach, in prison slang the "number one" in Spandau, did not have any lobby at all. Neurath, Raeder, Dönitz and Funk were released early in the 1950s. With financial support from the British newspaper *The Daily Mail*, Henriette von Schirach attempted to secure her ex-husband's release in March 1958.

Henriette's efforts proved counterproductive however, since she had been divorced since 1950.[728] Margarete Speer, the wife of Albert Speer, made a better impression in London the same year. Klaus von Schirach, who in the meantime had become a lawyer, severely criticised the conditions in which his father was remanded. In 1963, he had to be transferred to the British military hospital for two weeks in order to undergo medical treatment. For the first time, a representative of the Federal Government also expressed concern about the state of Schirach's health. Two years later, his sons Klaus (aged twenty-nine) and Robert (twenty-six), then a printer's merchant, visited their father after an eye operation in the military hospital; they reported that the surgery had been unsuccessful and that they had not been able to secure better conditions for him.[729] In February 1965, Schirach again had to be taken to the military hospital.

Klaus sent a telegram to the embassies of the USA, the Soviet Union, France and Britain, again requesting less severe conditions – in vain. The sons' efforts did mean that their father's prison sentence again became a subject of public discussion, however.

Exactly twenty years after their sentences were pronounced in Nuremberg, in the night of 1 October 1966 the Spandau prison gates were opened for Baldur von Schirach and Albert Speer. Prior to his release, the journalist Jochen von Lang had already made contact with the Schirach family, presumably with Klaus, to secure the rights to a series of articles in the magazine *Stern* and to his memoirs. A similar series on Speer was supposed to appear, but this project fell through.[730] Speer told an anecdote that is not atypical of Schirach's hunger for what he considered the lifestyle that befitted him: when asked what suits the prisoners should have made for their release, Speer estimated costs of 400 to 500 marks, Schirach 1,000 marks. He spoke about wanting to order five suits, a dinner jacket, three coats, leisure suits, smoking jackets, bespoke shirts, a dress coat, an evening coat and brogues, at an estimated cost of around 20,000 marks, reckoning with well over a million marks in proceeds from, among things, three planned book projects.[731]

Stern, under editor-in-chief Henri Nannen, who had secured exclusive rights to the interviews, had perfectly organised his collection by his three sons: a room had been reserved in the Hilton and a chartered plane was at the ready, and their own photographer was also constantly on hand.

In 1989, Jochen von Lang shared with the Austrian radio station Ö1 his perspective on the conditions under which the *Stern* interviews and the memoirs were produced.[732] Lang, editor of Germany's biggest magazine, said he thought Schirach's remorse was genuine. They got in touch with Schirach via secret messages smuggled into Spandau, while Schirach entrusted his son Klaus with the preliminary contracts. Schirach would speak to *Stern* on the condition that there would be no commentary on his statements. Lang said that Schirach's behaviour following his release was "blinkered by his aristocratic origins". Lang himself had fought as an infantryman at Leningrad and in the battle for Berlin, and also saw this memoirs project as an important contribution to coming to terms with the past. These interviews held over several months produced 1,500 pages of transcripts, which a colleague of Lang's used to compile the volume of memoirs *Ich glaubte an Hitler* (I Believed in Hitler, 1967).

This colleague remains unidentified to this day. Sales of the volume were initially good, but soon tailed off. In 1988, Lang published a biography of Schirach entitled *Der Hitler-Junge* on the basis of these 1,500 pages of interview transcripts. Today they are kept in the archive of the Institute of Contemporary History in Munich.

The interviews took place in the wooden house in Urfeld that had been sold by Henriette von Schirach but bought back by their son Robert. Together with Schirach, a secretary and a ghost writer worked on the interviews and transcripts. The weekly pre-print series in *Stern* was produced in this same stressful atmosphere.[733] The front cover presented Schirach as an elderly, elegant gentleman, "In a bespoke double-breasted suit, fine flannel by Knize, a tie with a Windsor knot, a Stetson and raw leather gloves in his right hand, a picture like in the film 'The Great Gatsby'."[734]

There was conflict over the question as to what Schirach knew about the "extermination of the Jews" before the end of the war – a subject that was also discussed when Lang interviewed him for television. The journalist also described a scene during the interview in which Schirach labelled the Nuremberg trials a "show trial". Asked whether his admission of guilt had also been pretend, he got up to leave, and it took much persuasion for him to continue the interview.

After the media storm surrounding his release in October 1966 and the hectic production of the memoirs by the *Stern* staff, Schirach also spoke to the British star journalist David Frost.[735] In an interview lasting almost forty minutes, Schirach showed another side to himself, being less critical of the past and Hitler than one would have expected from his statements at Nuremberg. Frost, an experienced interviewer, was well prepared for this interview in the villa of industrial tycoon Fritz Kiehn in Trossingen in the Black Forest.[736] The opening sequence shows a friendly, elegant white-haired man with a pipe, wearing a tie despite the private setting, accompanied by two dogs and kissing a small boy, possibly his grandson. Later, in his autobiography, Frost wrote of a "lady friend"[737] who was present. Perhaps he meant Gretl Wieshofer Kiehn, the former wife of Fritz Wieshofer.

At the beginning of this interview, which he gave in polished English, Schirach described his first encounters with Hitler in Weimar, saying he had become his "political father". Asked by Frost how he would describe

Hitler in a single sentence, he replied that he was "a man without measure [i.e. without any sense of measure – O.R.], a man with great gifts, a man who in some ways could be considered a genius" – a disturbing remark that revealed how fascinated the former *Reichsjugendführer* was with his "boss". There was no longer any talk of "a man who murdered by the millions".

Schirach also displayed great self-satisfaction in answering the question as to whether he had "made it", saying he had built up a youth movement. When he said he had sought to create "a new Germany of the future without any difference in classes", Frost pointed out that one class had been powerfully excluded – the Jews. Schirach replied that it had been Hitler that wanted this, not him. He said he had not had any objection to Jews in the government and recalled that Jews had also been "welcome guests" at his parents' house. Here, he completely departed from the line he had taken at the Nuremberg trials in 1946, when he declared himself an anti-Semite. When Frost put it to him that he had supported a quota for Jewish students at the universities as early as 1933, he said he had been "absolutely wrong" to do so – but "the whole generation was wrong".

Frost also asked him if he had ever heard Hitler use the term "final solution". Schirach said that he hadn't, but that he must have used it only "inside a certain group" consisting of Hitler, Himmler, Bormann and the "substitutes that did the dirty business", although he only mentioned the Gestapo. He claimed that he himself had only heard about the National Socialist extermination policy from his friend Colin Ross in 1944, since Ross, as an advisor to the Office of Foreign Affairs, was able to read foreign newspapers. However, as has been demonstrated, Schirach had already received clear indications as to the brutal extermination policy in the cynical speech Arthur Greiser had given before the *Führerkorps* of the Vienna *Gau* on 12 May 1942 – not to mention Heydrich's reports.

With respect to his shared responsibility for the deportations of the Jews who remained in Vienna, the excuse Schirach presented was quite absurd: he had supported their deportation fearing they would be killed by the Viennese. He claimed Kaltenbrunner had assured him they would be treated well in the ghettos.

Incidentally, the latest studies on the Gestapo control centre (*Leitstelle*) in Vienna document very clearly that Schirach was also personally involved in the deportation system and was privy to precise information:

"Besides Baldur von Schirach as the driving force, Huber was the second local protagonist of the deportation and annihilation of Vienna's Jewish population."[738] From Munich, Franz Josef Huber was in charge at the Gestapo control centre in Vienna, the largest in the Reich, from 1938 onwards. As an *SS-Brigadeführer*, a police major general and a Security Police (*Sicherheitspolizei*) and Security Service (*Sicherheitsdienst*, SD) inspector, he was directly responsible for the deportation of Jews. He was also Schirach's deputy as commissar for the defence of the Reich in Defence District XVII and a consultant to the *Reichsstatthalterei* based at the Gestapo headquarters in Hotel Metropol. That Huber remained loyal to Schirach, at least in 1941, became evident in the conflict between the *Reichsstatthalter* and the head of the SD Main Department for Vienna (*SD-Leitabschnitt Wien*), *SS-Sturmbannführer* Friedrich Polte, who had attempted to spy on Schirach via one of his secretaries.[739] That Schirach emerged from this conflict the victor demonstrates the strength of his position in Vienna in 1941.

Since Frost did not stop asking him what he knew about the fate of Vienna's Jews, Schirach finally placed all the blame on the SS. In the interview with Frost, Baldur von Schirach presented himself as an elegant, friendly and well-read former National Socialist, without a hint of his self-critical reflections in Nuremberg. The "I believed in Hitler" myth was perfect.

Despite the PR coup of the first few months after his release, Schirach's memoirs would not become a bestseller. The much livelier and more fantastical memoirs of Henriette, *The Price of Glory*, appealed much more to readers, as the number of print runs and translations demonstrate. The fees he received from *Stern* and for his memoirs were extremely generous, as Klaus von Schirach also confirmed; his publishing and contract negotiations earned him the best commission he had received in his career as a lawyer.[740] While the memoirs of Albert Speer also became an international bestseller, interest in Baldur von Schirach soon ebbed away, whereupon he withdrew to private life.

We have very little information on the last years of Schirach's life. Most of the sources are in private collections. Mention must be made here of the excellent study by Hartmut Berghoff and Cornelia Rauh-Kühne on the industry tycoon Fritz Kiehn (1885–1980), with whom not only local former NSDAP functionaries but also former employees of Schirach found work as well as having private contact. A key figure in Schirach's post-war network is Fritz Wieshofer, a former personal adjutant from Austria, a most loyal character and clearly a charming one too. As described above (see Chapter 11), he was involved in the Schirachs' flight from the battle for Vienna in 1945 and their arrest by US troops in Schwaz. Wieshofer was born in Vienna in 1914; his father Friedrich worked on the Vienna tramway. According to his CVs,[741] after passing his *Matura* (Austrian grammar school final exams) he briefly studied geopolitics at the University of Vienna before receiving training in civilian air raid protection and working as an expert instructor and state trainer in this field in Carinthia.[742] Even then, he was active for the forbidden NSDAP; suspected of having committed assassinations using explosives, he was arrested but not convicted. The work in radio he listed in his CV turned out to be employment for the *Gauleitung* (*Gau* Administration) in Carinthia, where he performed propaganda activities for the NSDAP in 1938–39.[743] Following the "Anschluss", he entered the Civil Service, where his last role was that of legation secretary in the protocol department between May and October 1940.

In his CVs, Wieshofer kept quiet about his membership of the Waffen-SS from 26 June 1940 and the general SS from 1939 onwards, calling himself a 'captain in the German Wehrmacht' who had been wounded three times on the "Russian front". In fact, he had held the rank of *SS-Obersturmführer*.[744] From 3 October 1940 onwards, he served as an adjutant to Baldur von Schirach and was head of the Central Bureau (*Zentralbüro*) of the *Reichsstatthalterei* (the office of the *Reichsstatthalter*). Schirach also outfitted him "with the shiny silver adjutant's aiguillettes (or monkey's swing, as it was called)"[745] in order to lend stronger emphasis to his own high rank as *Reichsstatthalter*. In 1944, Wieshofer was appointed a *Bannführer* (district leader) of the Hitler Youth despite never having been a member of the organisation. Between 5 June 1945 and 10 December 1947, Fritz Wieshofer was interned in various camps and after a short spell working for the Bandag factories in Wels he went to Germany, where he briefly managed a hotel restaurant in Berlin before concentrating on financial media as a freelance editor. From 1 July 1954 onwards, after a brief training period he was made manager of the cigarette paper manufacturers Efka-Werke Fritz Kiehn GmbH due to his liaison with the daughter of the company's founder, Gretl Kiehn, whom he later married. Here he took care of the company's entwinement with politics, as demonstrated by his membership of various economic associations. Here he undertook activities important to the company's patriarch Kiehn, such as establishing beneficial contacts with local functionaries of the conservative Free Democratic Party (*Freie Demokratische Partei*, FDP), but also with former HJ leaders such as the former *SS-Obersturmführer* Siegfried Zoglmann, who was very active on the party's right-wing periphery.[746] Wieshofer also used other ties to ensure Kiehn was made an "honorary citizen" (*Ehrenbürger*) of the University of Innsbruck following the appropriate "donations".[747]

After divorcing, he had to leave the company, but he received a lifelong monthly pension of 1,300 marks and one of his later jobs was as secretary to the writer Gerhard Hermann Mostar.

Today, Fritz Wieshofer, who also published a successful handbook on good manners in the series Knigge up to Date (Up to Date Guide), would be termed a job-hopper and skilful networker who was long able to adeptly exploit his old contacts from his time under Baldur von Schirach for professional gain. Wieshofer is a prime example of the importance of Nazi networks in the economic sector of the German Federal Republic in the post-war era.

Father-in-law Fritz Kiehn, a Swabian provincial bourgeois, had joined the NSDAP as early as 1930[748] and successfully went into local politics in Trossingen in 1931. In 1932 he gained a seat in the *Reichstag* as a representative of the NSDAP. This could also have been when he had contact with Schirach in person. As an *SS-Hauptsturmführer*, in 1943 Kiehn even became a member of Himmler's personal staff and was involved in "Aryanisation". In 1949, he returned from French internment, was quickly "de-Nazified" and rebuilt the Efka works, which became the world's leading company for cigarette papers and tubes. In June 2020 the Trossingen factory, which had been taken over by the British company Imperial Tobacco, was closed due to lack of business.

Gustav Höpken, the former physical education instructor, HJ functionary and adjutant to Schirach, soon also found work for Kiehn, becoming head of the "Zentralbüro" (Central Bureau), a curious terminological throwback to their days in Vienna.[749] Three other former aides of Schirach's were employed at the Efka factory: Heinz Diesing as sales manager, Herbert Gasser as a manager of a subsidiary firm and Richard Heil as a salesman for smoking paraphernalia. Heil was promoted to managing director in 1972. Schirach's second-eldest son Robert, known as "Bobby" as a boy, was also employed by Höpken, and married Kiehn's granddaughter Elke, from his first marriage to Gretl.[750] As early as 1968 – not yet thirty years old – Robert von Schirach was made managing director for the mail order household goods department. He divorced in 1970.

After his release from prison in 1966, Baldur von Schirach found his first, highly representative accommodation at the Stubenrauch villa at Werneckstrasse 18 in Munich,[751] which his son Robert had rented for him.[752] But he also spent some of his time in Urfeld working on the *Stern* series and his memoirs. Two years later, he moved to Trossingen, to Fritz Kiehn's villa in Deibhalde with its spacious grounds with a park, a swimming pool and corresponding outbuildings. For a time, he was looked after by the ex-wife of his former adjutant Fritz Wieshofer, Gretl Kiehn, before she left following a quarrel. But in 1968 Schirach was very much the object of her desire and sent her a card on her fiftieth birthday.[753] They also visited Ischia in the Gulf of Naples together.

Two years previously, however, there had been considerable conflict between Schirach and Fritz Wieshofer himself, who had managed his assets during his time in prison. In a letter of 9 December 1966, Schirach attempted to placate him. "I would be really sorry if there were no longer a way for two old friends like us to meet in person again […] My hand remains outstretched, whereby I gratefully look back on our erstwhile collaboration and the willingness to help and loyalty you so often showed during my long years of imprisonment."[754] However, it appears the breach could not be mended. Two years later, Wieshofer told his friend Katinka Mostar: "You didn't need to open my eyes to the Nazis anymore. But you have to the Schirach clique."[755]

Schirach's actual financial situation remains unclear to this day, since he and his sister Rosalind also owned assets in the USA following the death of their father Carl in 1948. His mother Emma's property in the USA had already been seized in 1944, including the land in Philadelphia and various insurance policies, shares and mortgages.[756] After the war, Carl von Schirach's US assets were confiscated in 1947 pursuant to the Trading with the Enemy Act; as a German citizen, he had to give up his life insurance and various shares and other securities.[757] Following their father's death, Baldur and Rosalind inherited this fortune, which continued to be managed by the US Custodian of Enemy Property, however.[758]

Consequently, Rosalind von Schirach also played a role in managing the family's assets, although she is only mentioned in passing in the memoirs of both Baldur and Henriette von Schirach. Rosalind was an opera singer and performed under the stage name Rosa Lind at the start of her career. She joined the party in 1932 and never left the Evangelical Church.[759] After engagements at the opera house in Leipzig and the National Theatre in Mannheim, she went to the Deutsche Oper in Berlin in 1930 and sang at the Bayreuth Festival in 1931. In 1933, her career seemed to have passed its zenith, at least according to Theodor Front, a Jewish artist who was able to perform until the mid March despite the National Socialist takeover. Paul Breisach, the conductor, shared this assessment.[760] Her career nevertheless continued for some years; in 1935, for instance, she made a guest appearance at the Royal Opera House in London's Covent Garden.[761] It is certainly to her credit that she warned "Putzi" Hanfstaengl, who had fallen out with Hitler, that the Nazi leadership sought revenge,[762] but it does not make her an opponent of the regime. In the early 1950s, Rosalind von Schirach and Schirach's brother-in-law, Heinrich Hoffmann jr, also looked after the children of the Spandau prisoner financially, and especially took care of their schooling.[763]

In 1971, his eyesight failing him, Baldur von Schirach moved to the more modest Pension Müllen, the former Montroyal hotel in Kröv an der Mosel – run by two former BDM leaders,[764] the sisters Ida and Käthe Müllen. Under National Socialism, Käthe had been the local leader (*Ortsführerin*) of the BDM in Kröv; she was thus known in the village as "Hitler-Kätchen".[765]

Käthe Müllen painted a quite different portrait of Schirach, who in 1946 had personally confessed his guilt and harshly criticised Hitler for murdering millions of European Jews. It would seem that in the early 1970s, none of these views remained: "Nothing about the family. That always tore his heart apart. He couldn't [talk about] that. The whole war, that didn't interest him, what the people went through in the war. I went through it all as well."[766]

In an interview, Jochen von Lang revealed the reason for Schirach's poor mental and physical condition: excessive alcohol consumption.[767] His miserable life in the remote boarding house reflected the total decline of Schirach, who had ultimately fallen out with those who had been close to him.

On 8 August 1974, Schirach died of heart failure in Kröv. The eulogy was given by his former press adjutant Günter Kaufmann, who now worked in the media.[768] Kaufmann praised his deceased former boss as a "person tossed to and fro and tested by fate" who had done time in Spandau as a "symbolic figure of the youth and their leaders".[769] Besides his sons, the mourners included his former deputy Hartmann Lauterbacher, who had made his peace with him but criticised both his comments on Hitler in Nuremberg and the *Stern* series after 1966.[770] For many HJ leaders, Schirach's partial confession was wrong and did not match their view of history. In this respect, he certainly made something of a contribution to a critical picture of history, even if he remained extremely defensive regarding the Hitler Youth and his knowledge of the Shoah.

Gretl Wieshofer-Kiehn, Klaus von Schirach and other members of his family also attended the funeral in Kröv. What followed was rather cringeworthy correspondence between Gretl Wieshofer-Kiehn and Klaus von Schirach, who took care of the inheritance proceedings. For instance, she demanded an old black-and-white television set and part of the costs of the hotel and flights for the above-mentioned holiday to Ischia in 1968. She had also acted as a guarantor for a loan from the Deutsche Bank. On the other hand, she contested a claim by Baldur von Schirach against Elke, Robert von Schirach's ex-wife, for 60,000 marks from the sale of the house in Urfeld. Klaus von Schirach rejected the claims, since insufficient funds remained from the estate settlement.[771] According to the fragmentary documentation available to date, Schirach did not leave a large fortune.

In the years after 2000, Schirach's grave repeatedly became the subject of discussions. One point of concern came from Jewish visitors, who were worried it could become a site of pilgrimage for neo-Nazis. The epitaph, "I was one of you", was chosen by Käthe Müllen. According to Klaus von Schirach it was engraved without context, although Baldur von Schirach's other children were against this: Käthe Müllen herself said in an interview, "I fear we must leave this puzzle uninterpreted and leave it to the visitor to think what he will."[772] Her remarks make it quite clear that towards the end of his life, Schirach was no longer interested in a critical examination of the National Socialist past. His attempt to stylise himself as a simple German and completely draw a line under what he had done raises the question as to just how genuine his self-critical statement at Nuremberg in 1946, his partial confession, his version of events and his memoirs *Ich glaubte an Hitler* really were.

In 2014, the family did not extend the lease of the burial plot, and hence the gravestone was finally levelled.

The questions raised regarding Schirach's reflections on National Socialism and the Shoah following the media storm surrounding his interviews and memoirs will perhaps be answered when his sons transfer his correspondence written after his release from Spandau to a public archive, thus rendering it freely accessible. The 1968 interview with David Frost differs considerably from his statements in Nuremberg with respect to his political guilt and sections of his memoirs which stress that Hitler bore the main responsibility for the war and the genocide.

The few fragments that can be found with correspondence partners do not document any interest in National Socialism, the Shoah or the Second World War, or at least he did not display any outwardly. The media paid particular attention to a passage in Richard von Schirach's book *Der Schatten meines Vaters*: on page 308 he writes of a "secret emissary of the Vienna Philharmonic" who as a "professor from Vienna" gave him the "ring of honour of the Vienna Symphonic [*sic*] and a record of Schubert's later quartets" as thanks for his support during the war. Schirach's first ring from 1942 was taken from the safe in Kochel am See by a US officer in 1945.[773] Neither Richard nor Klaus von Schirach were prepared to reveal the messenger's identity. Following the public discussion in Austria concerning the gift of this second ring, a contemporary witness, Wilhelm Bettelheim, wrote in a letter to the author dated 19 January 2013: "The person who presented Baldur von Schirach with the ring of honour of the Vienna Philharmonic was Helmut Wobisch. Professor Wobisch had been an SS man and managing director of the Vienna Philharmonic in 1966. Professor Krips, an old friend of the family, told me this fact in the grounds of the old Vienna General Hospital in the Alserstrasse in 1968." Josef Krips was stigmatised as a "half-Jew" under National Socialism, was banned from performing and had to work in an armament factory.

In the meantime, correspondence between Schirach and the former chairman of the Vienna Philharmonic Wilhelm Jerger, a member of the

SS and the NSDAP, has surfaced in the archive of Vienna's Musikverein. However, it does not contain any indications concerning the ring.[774] Silvia Kargl and Friedemann Pestel have brought some arguments suggesting it could have been Jerger who presented it to him, but the question remains: why does the otherwise complete collection of correspondence not contain a letter by Schirach thanking him? Or is there a third member of the Philharmonic, such as Otto Strasser, who in 1963, then chairman, sent greetings to Hermann Stuppäck, Schirach's former general cultural advisor, on the occasion of his sixtieth birthday, thanking him for protecting the orchestra during the National Socialist era?[775] The answer can only come from Schirach's estate from the period between 1966 and 1974.

Selected Bibliography

(In chronological order)

Wille und Weg des Nationalsozialistischen Deutschen Studentenbundes, Munich 1929.

Die Feier der neuen Front, 2nd edition, Munich 1929.

Heinrich Hoffmann (ed.), *Hitler wie ihn keiner kennt. 100 Bild-Dokumente aus dem Leben des Führers*, with a foreword by Baldur von Schirach, Berlin 1932.

Kurt Maßmann, *Wir Jugend! Ein Bekenntnisbuch der deutschen Nachkriegsgeneration*, with a foreword by Baldur von Schirach, Berlin 1933.

Rudolf Ramlow, *Herbert Norkus? – Hier! Opfer und Sieg der Hitler-Jugend*, with a foreword by Baldur von Schirach, Stuttgart 1933.

Die Pioniere des 'Dritten Reiches', Essen 1933.

Die Fahne der Verfolgten, Berlin 1933.

Baldur von Schirach, *Das Manifest der Jugend. (Zum Todestage von Herbert Norkus vom Reichsjugendführer der NSDAP herausgegeben und am Sonntag, den 29. Jänner 1933, allen Gefolgschaften der Hitler-Jugend durch ihre Führer verkündet.)*, Munich 1933.

Der Tag von Potsdam. 100 Bilddokumente vom größten Jugendaufmarsch der Welt, Munich 1933.

Baldur von Schirach (ed.), *Blut und Ehre. Lieder der Hitler-Jugend*, score, Berlin 1933.

Baldur von Schirach (ed.), *Blut und Ehre. Lieder der Hitler-Jugend*, edition without score, Berlin 1933.

Heinrich Hoffmann, *Der Triumph des Willens. Kampf und Aufstieg Adolf Hitlers und seiner Bewegung*. With a foreword by Baldur von Schirach, Berlin 1933.

Heinrich Hoffmann, *Der Parteitag des Sieges. 100 Bild-Dokumente vom Reichsparteitag zu Nürnberg 1933*. With a foreword by Baldur von Schirach, Berlin 1933.

Martin Lezius, *Das deutsche Heldenbuch. Von deutscher Ehre und Mannentreue*, with a foreword by Baldur von Schirach, Berlin 1933.

Erich Beier-Lindhardt, *Das Buch vom Führer für die deutsche Jugend*. With a foreword by Reichsjugendführer Baldur von Schirach, Oldenburg 1933.

Reichsjugendführung der NSDAP (ed.), *Uniformen der H.J. Vorschrift und Vorbild für die Bekleidung und Ausrüstung der Hitler-Jugend, des Deutschen Jungvolks in der H. J., des Bundes Deutscher Mädel in der H.J. und der Jungmädel im B.D.M. in der H.J. Amtlich herausgegeben von der Reichsjugendführung der NSDAP*, with a foreword by Baldur von Schirach, Hamburg 1934.

Walter Frank, *Kämpfende Wissenschaft*. With a foreword by Baldur von Schirach, Hamburg 1934.

Heinrich Hoffmann (ed.), *Jugend um Hitler. 120 Bilddokumente aus der Umgebung des Führers*, with a foreword by Baldur von Schirach, Berlin 1934.

Arnold Littmann, *Herbert Norkus und die Hitlerjungen von Beusselkietz*. With a foreword by Baldur von Schirach, Berlin 1934.

Die Hitler-Jugend. Idee und Gestalt, Berlin 1934.

Heinrich Hoffmann, *Der Parteitag der Macht, Nürnberg 1934*. With a foreword by Baldur von Schirach, Berlin 1934.

Abt.. I [Willi-Botho Bicker] (ed.), *Bekleidung und Ausrüstung der Hitler-Jugend: Amtl. Bekleidungsvorschrift d. Reichsjugendführung d. NSDAP*. With a foreword by Baldur von Schirach, Berlin 1934.
Bekenntnisse deutscher Mädels zum Nationalsozialismus. With a foreword by Baldur von Schirach, Berlin 1934.
Der Staat der Arbeit und des Friedens. Ein Jahr Regierung Adolf Hitler. With a foreword by Baldur von Schirach, Altona-Bahrenfeld 1934 (collection card album).
Reichsjugendführung (ed.), *Reif werden – rein bleiben! Gesundheitsaktion der Hitler-Jugend*. With a foreword by Baldur von Schirach, Berlin 1935.
Heinrich Hoffmann (ed.), *Jugend um Hitler. 120 Bilddokumente aus der Umgebung des Führers*. With a foreword by Baldur von Schirach, Berlin 1935.
Helmut Stellrecht, *Die Wehrerziehung der deutschen Jugend*. With a foreword by Reichsjugendführer Baldur von Schirach, Berlin 1937.
Heinrich Hoffmann (ed.), *Hitler in seinen Bergen. 86 Bilddokumente aus der Umgebung des Führers*. With a foreword by Baldur von Schirach, Munich 1935, second edition Berlin 1938.
Baldur von Schirach (ed.), *Das Lied der Getreuen. Verse ungenannter österreichischer Hitler-Jugend aus den Jahren der Verfolgung 1933–37*, Leipzig 1938.
Baldur von Schirach, *Revolution der Erziehung. Reden aus den Jahren des Aufbaus*, Munich 1938.
Baldur von Schirach (ed.), *Adolf Hitler an seine Jugend*, Munich 1939.
Heinrich Hoffmann (ed.), *Das Antlitz des Führers*. With a foreword by Baldur von Schirach, Berlin 1939.
Eberhard Wolfgang Möller, *Der Führer. Das Weihnachtsbuch der deutschen Jugend*. Ed. by Baldur von Schirach, Munich 1938.
Alfred Thon, *Weimars klassische Stätten. Zehn farbige Tafeln nach Aquarellen*. With a foreword by Baldur von Schirach, Berlin 1938.
Günter Kaufmann (ed.), *Langemarck. Das Opfer der Jugend an allen Fronten*. With an introduction by Generalfeldmarschall Hermann Göring, Reichsjugendführer Baldur von Schirach and Reichskriegsopferführer Oberlindober, Stuttgart 1938.
Baldur von Schirach (ed.), *Das Reich Adolf Hitlers. Ein Bildbuch vom Werden Großdeutschlands 1933 bis 1940*, Munich 1940.
Baldur von Schirach, *Das Wiener Kulturprogramm. Rede des Reichsleiters Baldur von Schirach im Wiener Burgtheater am Sonntag, dem 6. April 1941*, Vienna 1941.
Baldur von Schirach, *Kantatrede*, Weimar 1941.
Baldur von Schirach, *Rede zur Feier des 250-jährigen Bestehens der Wiener Akademie der Bildenden Künste*, 24 October 1942, Vienna 1942.
Baldur von Schirach, *Goethe an uns. Ewige Gedanken des großen Deutschen*, Berlin 1942.
Egbert Mannlicher (ed.), *Wegweiser durch die Verwaltung unter besonderer Berücksichtigung der Verwaltung im Reichsgau Wien sowie in den Reichsgauen Kärnten, Niederdonau, Oberdonau, Salzburg, Steiermark und Tirol mit Vorarlberg*. With a foreword by Reichsleiter und Reichsstatthalter Baldur von Schirach, Berlin/Leipzig/Vienna 1942.
Baldur von Schirach, *Zwei Reden zur deutschen Kunst*, Weimar 1942.
Baldur von Schirach, *Junge Kunst im Deutschen Reich. Februar–März 1943 im Künstlerhaus Wien*, Vienna 1943.
Baldur von Schirach, *Rede zur Eröffnung der Mozart-Woche, gehalten in Wien am 28. November 1941*, Weimar 1943.
Baldur von Schirach, *Den Freunden in Feldgrau. Gedichte*, no year (= Schriftenreihe des Kriegsbetreuungsdienstes, book 2).
Baldur von Schirach, *Ich glaubte an Hitler*, Hamburg 1967.

Selected Bibliography

Rüdiger Ahrens, *Bündische Jugend. Eine neue Geschichte 1918–1933*, Göttingen 2015.
Gabriele Anderl/Edith Blaschitz/Sabine Loitfellner/Mirjam Triendl/Niko Wahl, *Arisierung von Mobilien*, Vienna/Munich 2004 (Veröffentlichungen der Österreichischen Historikerkommission, Volume 17).
Alfred Andreesen, *Hermann Lietz. Der Schöpfer der Landerziehungsheime*, Munich 1934.
Artur Axmann, *Hitler-Jugend. Das kann doch nicht das Ende sein. Erinnerungen des letzten Reichsjugendführers Artur Axmann*, Erlangen 1995.
Claus-Ekkehard Bärsch, *Die politische Religion des Nationalsozialismus. Die religiösen Dimensionen der NS-Ideologie in den Schriften von Dietrich Eckart, Joseph Goebbels, Alfred Rosenberg und Adolf Hitler*, 2nd, revised edition, Munich 2002.
Bodo-Michael Baumunk, *Colin Ross. Ein deutscher Revolutionär und Reisender 1885–1945*, corrected edition, Berlin 2015 (PDF online).
Nicolaus von Below, *Als Hitlers Adjutant 1937–45*, Mainz 1980.
Hartmut Berghoff/Cornelia Rauh-Kühne, *Fritz K. Ein deutsches Leben im 20. Jahrhundert*, Munich 2000.
Udo Bermbach, Houston Stewart Chamberlain. *Wagners Schwiegersohn – Hitlers Vordenker*, Stuttgart 2015.
Helmut Berding, *Moderner Antisemitismus in Deutschland*, Frankfurt am Main 1988.
Bertrand Perz/Verena Pawlowsky/Ina Markova/Parlamentsdirektion (eds.), *Inbesitznahmen. Das Parlamentsgebäude in Wien 1933–1956*, Salzburg 2018.
Klaus E. Bohnenkamp (ed.), *Hugo von Hofmannsthal, Rudolf Kassner und Rainer Maria Rilke im Briefwechsel mit Elsa und Hugo Bruckmann 1893–1941*, Göttingen 2014.
Fred Borth, *Nicht zu jung zum Sterben. Die 'Hitler-Jugend' im Kampf um Wien 1945*, Vienna 1988.
Gerhard Botz, *Nationalsozialismus in Wien. Machtübernahme, Herrschaftssicherung, Radikalisierung, Kriegsvorbereitung, 1938/1939*, revised and expanded edition, Vienna 2018.
Robert Bouchal/Johannes Sachslehner, *Das nationalsozialistische Wien: Orte – Täter – Opfer*, Vienna 2015.
Karl Dietrich Bracher, *Die deutsche Diktatur. Entstehung, Struktur, Folgen des Nationalsozialismus*, Frankfurt am Main/Berlin/Vienna 1979.
Werner Brill, *Pädagogik der Abgrenzung. Die Implementierung der Rassenhygiene im Nationalsozialismus durch die Sonderpädagogik*, Bad Heilbrunn 2011.
Christopher R. Browning, *Der Weg zur 'Endlösung'. Entscheidungen und Täter*, Berlin 1998.
Theodor Brückler (ed.), *Kunstraub, Kunstbergung und Restitution in Österreich 1938 bis heute*, Vienna 1999.
Michael Buddrus, *Totale Erziehung für den totalen Krieg. Hitler-Jugend und nationalsozialistische Jugendpolitik* (Texte und Materialien zur Zeitgeschichte 13), Munich 2003.
Hellmut Butterweck, *Nationalsozialisten vor dem Volksgericht Wien. Österreichs Ringen um Gerechtigkeit 1945–1955 in der zeitgenössischen öffentlichen Wahrnehmung*, Innsbruck 2016.
Holger Dainat, 'Zur Berufungspolitik in der Neueren deutschen Literaturwissenschaft 1933–1945', in: Holger Dainat/Lutz Danneberg (eds.), *Literaturwissenschaft und Nationalsozialismus*, Tübingen 2003.
Christopher Dodd/Larry Bloom, *Letters from Nuremberg: My Father's Narrative of a Quest for Justice*, New York 2007.
Max Domarus, *Hitler. Reden und Proklamationen 1932–1945. Kommentiert von einem deutschen Zeitgenossen.* Part 1: *Triumph*, Volume 2: 1935–1938, Leonberg 1988.
Boguslaw Drewniak, *Das Theater im NS-Staat: Szenarium deutscher Zeitgeschichte 1933–1945*, Düsseldorf 1983.

Selected Bibliography 205

Milan Dubrović, *Veruntreute Geschichte*, Vienna 1985.
Albrecht Dümling/Peter Girth (eds.), *Entartete Musik. Dokumentation und Kommentar zur Düsseldorfer Ausstellung von 1938*, 3rd, revised and expanded edition, Düsseldorf 1993.
Jack El-Hai, *The Nazi and the Psychiatrist: Hermann Göring, Dr. Douglas M. Kelley, and a Fatal Meeting of Minds at the End of WWII*, New York 2013.
Albert Elmar, 'Der 'Schirachbunker' im Gallitzinberg', in: *Wiener Geschichtsblätter* 34 (1979), 133 ff.
Helmut Engelbrecht, 'Wien und die sogenannte Kinderlandverschickung', in: *Studien zur Wiener Geschichte. Jahrbuch des Vereins für Geschichte der Stadt Wien*, Volume 57/58, Vienna 2002.
Gerald D. Feldman, *Austrian Banks in the Period of National Socialism*, Washington D.C./Cambridge 2015.
Nils Fiebig, *Alois Miedl. Der Bankier und die Raubkunst. Geschäfte im Schatten der Macht*, Würzburg 2020.
Florian Freund/Bertrand Perz and Mark Spoerer, *Zwangsarbeiter und Zwangsarbeiterinnen auf dem Gebiet der Republik Österreich 1939–1945* (Veröffentlichungen der Österreichischen Historikerkommission, Volume 26/1). Vienna 2004.
Carl Freytag, *Deutschlands 'Drang nach Südosten'. Der Mitteleuropäische Wirtschaftstag und der 'Ergänzungsraum Südosteuropa' 1931–1945*, Göttingen 2012 (Zeitgeschichte im Kontext, Volume 7).
Dirk Gelhaus/Jörn-Peter Hülter, *Die Ausleseschulen als Grundpfeiler des NS-Regimes*, Würzburg 2003.
Gustave M. Gilbert, *Nuremberg Diary*, London 1948.
Joseph Goebbels, *Die Tagebücher von Joseph Goebbels*, ed. by Elke Fröhlich by commission of the Instituts für Zeitgeschichte and with the support of the Russian State Archive Service, Munich 1987 ff.
Alexander Graf, Mütze, *Band und Braunhemd – Marburger Studentenverbindungen und der Nationalsozialistische Studentenbund während der Weimarer Republik*, Marburg 2012.
Thomas R. Grischany, *Der Ostmark treue Alpensöhne. Die Integration der Österreicher in die großdeutsche Wehrmacht, 1938–45*, Göttingen 2015.
Alexander Haide, *Der Schirach Bunker*, Vienna 2004.
Murray G. Hall, *Der Paul Zsolnay Verlag: Von der Gründung bis zur Rückkehr aus dem Exil*, Volume 1, Tübingen 1994.
Ernst Hanfstaengl, *Zwischen Weißem und Braunem Haus. Memoiren eines politischen Außenseiters*, Munich 1970.
Susanne Heim (ed.), *Die Verfolgung und Ermordung der europäischen Juden durch das nationalsozialistische Deutschland 1933–1945*, Volume 6: *Deutsches Reich und Protektorat Böhmen und Mähren Oktober 1941–März 1943*, Berlin 2019.
Jutta Held (ed.), *Kunstgeschichte an den Universitäten im Nationalsozialismus* (Kunst und Politik, Volume 5), Göttingen 2003.
Rudolf Herz, *Hoffmann & Hitler*, Munich 1994.
Adolf Hitler, *Mein Kampf*, Volume 1, *Eine Abrechnung*, Munich 1933.
Adolf Hitler, *Reden, Schriften, Anordnungen: Februar 1925 bis Jänner 1933. Außenpolitische Standortbestimmung nach der Reichstagswahl Juni–Juli 1928*, Munich 1994.
Karin Hartewig, *Kunst für alle! Hitlers ästhetische Diktatur*, Norderstedt 2018.
Hilmar Hoffmann, *Generation Hitler-Jugend, Reflexionen über eine Verführung*, Frankfurt am Main 2018.
Roman Horak, 'Germany versus Austria. Football, Urbanism and National Identity', in: Alan Tomlinson, Christopher Young (eds.), *German Football: History, Culture, Society and the World Cup 2006*, London 2005.

Andreas Huber/Linda Erker/Klaus Taschwer, *Der Deutsche Klub. Austro-Nazis in der Hofburg*, Vienna 2020.

Stefanie Hundehege, 'Baldur von Schirach. Der "Sänger der Bewegung"', in: Rolf Düsterberg (ed.), *Dichter für das 'Dritte Reich'. Biografische Studien zum Verhältnis von Literatur und Ideologie*, Volume 3, Bielefeld 2015, 209–245.

Stefanie Hundehege, *Modernizing Fate? Die Ahnfrau and the Grillparzer-Festwoche in Vienna, 1941*, in: Austrian Studies 25 (2018), 81–87.

Internationaler Militärgerichtshof, *Der Prozess gegen die Hauptkriegsverbrecher vor dem Internationalen Militärgerichtshof, Nürnberg 14. November 1945–1. Oktober 1946*, Nuremberg 1948.

International Military Tribunal. *Trial of the Major War Criminals Before the International Military Tribunal. Nuremberg 14 November 1945 – 1 October 1946*. Nuremberg 1948.

Ingeborg Kálnoky/Ilona Herisko, *The Witness House: A Nuremberg Memoir of Countess Kálnoky*, London 1975.

Silvia Kargl/Friedemann Pestel, *Ambivalente Loyalitäten. Beziehungsnetzwerke der Wiener Philharmoniker 1938–1970*, März 2017 (PDF online)

Michael H. Kater, 'Der NS-Studentenbund von 1926 bis 1928. Randgruppe zwischen Hitler und Strasser', in: *Vierteljahrshefte für Zeitgeschichte*, 22:2 (1974), Issue 2, 148–190.

Michael H. Kater, *Hitler-Jugend*, Darmstadt 2005.

Günter Kaufmann, *Baldur von Schirach. Ein Jugendführer in Deutschland. Richtigstellung und Vermächtnis*, Füssen 1993.

Franz-Werner Kersting, *Militär und Jugend im NS-Staat. Rüstungs- und Schulpolitik der Wehrmacht*, Wiesbaden 1989.

Douglas M. Kelley, *22 Cells in Nuremberg*, London 1947.

Holm Kirsten, *Weimar im Banne des Führers. Die Besuche Adolf Hitlers 1925–1940*, Cologne 2001.

Christiane Kohl, *Das Zeugenhaus. Nürnberg 1945: Als Täter und Opfer unter einem Dach zusammentrafen*, Munich 2005.

Albert Krebs, *Tendenzen und Gestalten der NSDAP. Erinnerungen an die Frühzeit der Partei*, Munich 1959.

Martin Krist/Albert Lichtblau, *Nationalsozialismus in Wien: Opfer. Täter, Gegner*, Innsbruck 2017.

Christoph Kühberger, 'Europa als "Strahlenbündel nationaler Kräfte". Zur Konzeption und Legitimation einer europäischen Zusammenarbeit auf der Gründungsfeierlichkeit des "Europäischen Jugendverbandes" 1942', in: *Journal of European Integration History* 2/2009, 17.

Jochen von Lang, *Der Hitler-Junge. Baldur von Schirach. Der Mann, der Deutschlands Jugend erzog*, Hamburg 1988.

Eleonore Lappin, 'Ungarische Jüdinnen und Juden in Niederösterreich 1944/45', in: Eleonore Lappin/Susanne Uslu-Pauer/Manfred Wieninger, *Ungarisch-jüdische Zwangsarbeiterinnen und Zwangsarbeiter in Niederösterreich*. St Pölten 2006, 7–102 (Studien und Forschungen aus dem Niederösterreichischen Institut für Landeskunde, Volume 45).

Eleonore Lappin, *Ungarische Zwangsarbeiter und Zwangsarbeiterinnen in Österreich 1944–45. Arbeitseinsatz – Todesmärsche – Folgen*, Vienna/Münster 2010.

Hartmann Lauterbacher, *Erlebt und mitgestaltet. Kronzeuge einer Epoche 1923–1945. Zu neuen Ufern nach Kriegsende*, Preußisch Oldendorf 1984.

Joachim Lilla, 'Die Erörterungen zur Neubesetzung der Gauleiterstelle in Wien 1939/40 und 1943/44', in: Studien zur Wiener Geschichte. Jahrbuch des Vereins für Geschichte der Stadt Wien, Volume 57/58, Vienna 2002, 113–124.

Selected Bibliography 207

Sophie Lillie, *Was einmal war. Handbuch der enteigneten Kunstsammlungen Wiens*, Vienna 2003.
Peter Longerich, *Hitler. Biographie*, Munich 2015.
Stephan Malinowski, *Vom König zum Führer. Sozialer Niedergang und politische Radikalisierung im deutschen Adel zwischen Kaiserreich und NS-Staat*, Berlin 2003.
Wolfgang Martynkewicz, *Salon Deutschland. Geist und Macht 1900–1945*, Berlin 2009.
Bernadette Mayrhofer/Fritz Trümpi, *Orchestrierte Vertreibung. Unerwünschte Wiener Philharmoniker. Verfolgung, Ermordung und Exil*, Vienna 2014.
Christian Merlin, *Die Wiener Philharmoniker. Das Orchester und seine Geschichte*, Volume 1, Vienna 2017.
Imo Moszkowicz, *Der grauende Morgen: Erinnerungen*, reprint Münster 2004.
Harald Oelrich, *Sportgeltung, Weltgeltung. Sport im Spannungsfeld der deutsch-italienischen Außenpolitik von 1918 bis 1945*, Münster 2003.
Martin Pabst, *Couleur und Braunhemd. Deutsche Studenten in der Weimarer Republik*, Munich 1993.
Bertrand Perz, *Verwaltete Gewalt. Der Tätigkeitsbericht des Verwaltungsführers im Konzentrationslager Mauthausen 1941–1944*, Vienna 2013 (Mauthausen-Studien, Volume 8).
Henry Picker (ed.), *Hitlers Tischgespräche im Führerhauptquartier 1941–1942*, Stuttgart 1977.
Alessio Ponzio, *Shaping the New Man: Youth Training Regimes in Fascist Italy and Nazi Germany*, Madison 2015.
Hugo Portisch/Sepp Riff, Österreich II: Die Wiedergeburt unseres Staates, Volume 1, Vienna 1985.
Manfried Rauchensteiner, *Der Krieg in Österreich 1945*, Vienna 1984.
Mathias Rösch, *Die Münchener NSDAP 1925–1933. Eine Untersuchung zur inneren Struktur der NSDAP in der Weimarer Republik*, Munich 2002.
Thomas Rösner, 'Adolf Bartels', in: Uwe Pruschner, Walter Schmit und Justus H. Ulbricht, *Handbuch zur 'Völkischen Bewegung' 1871–1918*, Munich 1999.
Klaus Rüffler, *Vom Landfriedensbruch bis zum Mord von Potempa. Der 'Legalitätskurs' der NSDAP*, Frankfurt am Main 1994.
Hans Safrian, *Die Eichmann-Männer*, Vienna/Zurich 1993.
Harald Sander, *Hitler – Das Intinerar. Aufenthaltsorte und Reisen von 1889 bis 1945*, Volume 1: *1889–1927*, Berlin 2016.
Henriette von Schirach, Der Preis der Herrlichkeit, Berlin 1975.
Max von Schirach, *Geschichte der Familie von Schirach*, Berlin 1939, reprint 2016.
Richard von Schirach, *Der Schatten meines Vaters*, Munich 2005.
Renato Schirer, *Der Schirachbunker. Die Errichtung eines bombensicheren und unterirdischen Befehlsstandes für die Wiener Gauleitung der NSDAP* (PDF online).
Detlef Schmiechen-Ackermann/Marlis Buchholz/Bianca Roitsch/Christiane Schröder (eds.), *Der Ort der 'Volksgemeinschaft' in der deutschen Gesellschaftsgeschichte*, Paderborn 2018.
Peter Stitz, *Der CV 1919–1938. Der hochschulpolitische Weg des Cartellverbandes der katholisch deutschen Studentenverbindungen (CV) vom Ende des 1. Weltkrieges bis zur Vernichtung durch den Nationalsozialismus*, Munich 1970.
Harald Scholtz, *Erziehung und Unterricht unterm Hakenkreuz*, Göttingen, Neuausgabe 2009.
Birgit Schwarz, *Geniewahn: Hitler und die Kunst*, Vienna/Cologne/Weimar 2009.
Anna Maria Sigmund, *Die Frauen der Nazis*, Vienna 1998.
Otto Skorzeny, *Meine Kommandounternehmen*, Rastatt 1981.
Bradley F. Smith/Agnes F. Peterson (eds.), *Heinrich Himmler. Geheimreden 1933 bis 1945 und andere Ansprachen*, Frankfurt am Main 1974.
Susan Sontag, 'Fascinating Fascism', in: *New York Review of Books*, 6 February 1975, n. p.

Albert Speer, *Der Sklavenstaat. Meine Auseinandersetzungen mit der SS*, Munich 1981.

Markus Stumpf, "'Ich erteile deshalb den mir nachgeordneten Dienststellen des Staates und der Partei den Befehl, nach der erfolgten Evakuierung der Juden sämtliche Tschechen aus dieser Stadt zu entfernen.'" Das "Gaupresse"-Archiv Wien anhand ausgewählter Reden Baldur von Schirachs', in: Lucile Dreidemy/Richard Hufschmied/Agnes Meisinger/Berthold Molden/Eugen Pfister/Katharina Prager/Elisabeth Röhrlich/Florian Wenninger/Maria Wirth (eds.), *Bananen, Cola, Zeitgeschichte: Oliver Rathkolb und das lange 20. Jahrhundert*, Volume 1, Vienna/Cologne/Weimar 2015, 330–345.

Vanessa Stürz, Elite und Diktatur. Die Rolle der Eliteschulen im Nationalsozialismus und ihre Bedeutung für das Regime, Hamburg 2013.

Tagung der Südosteuropa-Gesellschaft und der Deutschen Gesellschaft der Wirtschaft in Böhmen und Mähren, Prague 1942.

Walter Thomas, *Bis der Vorhang fiel. Aufzeichnungen aus den Jahren 1940 bis 1945*, Dortmund 1947.

Justus H. Ulbricht, '*Deutsche Religion*' *und* '*Deutsche Kunst*'. *Intellektuelle Sinnsuche und kulturelle Identitätskonstruktionen in der* '*Klassischen Moderne*', doctoral thesis, University of Jena 2006.

Das Urteil von Nürnberg. With a foreword by Jörg Friedrich, Munich 2005.

Volker Weiß, *Moderne Antimoderne. Arthur Moeller van den Bruck und der Wandel des Konservatismus*, Paderborn 2012.

Uwe Werner, *Anthroposophen in der Zeit des Nationalsozialismus (1933–1945)*, Munich 1999.

Matthias Wieben, *Studenten der Christian-Albrechts-Universität im* '*Dritten Reich*'. *Zum Verhaltensmuster der Studenten in den ersten Herrschaftsjahren des Nationalsozialismus*, Frankfurt am Main 1994.

Birgit Witamwas, *Geklebte NS-Propaganda, Verführung und Manipulation durch das Plakat*, Berlin/Boston 2016.

Michael Wortmann, *Baldur von Schirach. Hitlers Jugendführer*, Cologne 1982.

Notes

1. Ferdinand von Schirach, 'Du bist, wer du bist. Warum ich keine Antworten auf die Fragen nach meinem Großvater geben kann', in: *Der Spiegel* 36, 2011, 142.
2. Walter Thomas, *Bis der Vorhang fiel. Aufzeichnungen aus den Jahren 1940 bis 1945*, Dortmund, 1947, 213.
3. Baldur von Schirach's foreword to the volume of photographs *Hitler in seinen Bergen*, Berlin 1935.
4. Universität Wien/Fachbereichsbibliothek Zeitgeschichte, "Gaupresse"-Archiv Wien: 'Baldur v. Schirach' [nine-page typed curriculum vitae], www.ns-pressearchiv.at/archiv/akte/k187-7-m001-a007, accessed 28 February 2020.
5. On the process of working on his memoirs, see Richard von Schirach, *Der Schatten meines Vaters*, Munich 2005, 360 f. The transcripts of the questions Jochen von Lang put to Baldur von Schirach and a brief series of questions he put to Henriette von Schirach can be found in the archive of the Institut für Zeitgeschichte (IfZ) in Munich and are also available online; see www.ifz-muenchen.de/archiv/zsa/ZS_A_0030_01.pdf (plus three other sections).
6. Max von Schirach, *Geschichte der Familie von Schirach*, Berlin 1939.
7. Hermann, the musically gifted brother of Friedrich Karl, retired as a colonel of the *1. Badischen Leib-Grenadier-Regiment* in Karlsruhe in 1900. He lived at his brother's until his death in 1920.
8. Richard von Schirach, *Der Schatten*, 25.
9. Cf www.hhhistory.com/2015/07/the-slaves-of-middle-place-plantation.html, accessed 1 March 2020.
10. George McMillan, 'South Carolina's Great Colonial Garden', in: *The New York Times*, 30 March 1986.
11. Cf. the entry on Henry Middleton, www.middletonplace.org/explore/stories, accessed 1 March 2020.
12. Richard von Schirach, *Der Schatten*, 24.
13. *Reports of the Committees of the Senate of the United States for the Third Session of the Forty-Fifth Congress 1878–79*, Washington 1979, 475; cf. too *Official Army Register for 1896*, 317, and Francis B. Heitman, *Historical Register and Dictionary of the United States Army: From its Organization, September 29, 1789 to March 2, 1903*, Volume 1, Washington 1903, 989.
14. Max von Schirach, *Geschichte*, 153.
15. Baldur von Schirach, *Ich glaubte an Hitler*, 8.
16. Henriette von Schirach, *Der Preis der Herrlichkeit, Erfahrene Zeitgeschichte*, Munich, 7th edition 2007, 155 and 180. For a self-critical analysis and assessment of Henriette von Schirach's self-presentation, see Johanna Gehmacher, *Im Umfeld der Macht. Populäre Perspektiven auf Frauen der NS-Elite*, in: Elke Frietsch/Christian Herkommer (eds.), *Nationalsozialismus und Geschlecht: Zur Politisierung und Ästhetisierung von Körper, 'Rasse' und Sexualität im 'Dritten Reich' und nach 1945*, Bielefeld 2009, 49–69.
17. Ingrid Czaika, *Arthur Rösel. Leben und Werk des Weimarer Komponisten*, Munich 2015, 47.

18. As Walter Thomas related in his memoirs, Schirach especially admired *Buddenbrooks* as a "masterpiece". Thomas, *Bis der Vorhang fiel*, 213.
19. As related by the composer Hugo Wolf, who called Vignau an "old friend and admirer of my art", in: Heinz Nonveiller (ed.), *Hugo Wolf, Briefe an Heinrich Potpeschnigg*, Stuttgart 1923, 211.
20. Reinhard R. Doerries (ed.), *Erika von Watzdorf-Bachoff. Im Wandel und in der Verwandlung der Zeit. Ein Leben von 1878 bis 1963*, 154.
21. *Prager Tagblatt*, 21 July 1908, 9.
22. Cf. in detail Justus H. Ulbricht, *'Deutsche Religion' und 'Deutsche Kunst'. Intellektuelle Sinnsuche und kulturelle Identitätskonstruktionen in der 'Klassischen Moderne'*, doctoral thesis, Universität Jena 2006, 129–136.
23. *Der Kunstwart*, vol. 13, part 1, 1900, 438.
24. Volker Wahl, 'Gustav Kiepenheuers Anfänge', in: Siegfried Lokatis/Ingrid Sonntag (eds.), *100 Jahre Kiepenheuer-Verlage*, 34.
25. Cit. Ulbricht, *'Deutsche Religion' und 'Deutsche Kunst'*, 130.
26. Jochen Golz/Justus H. Ulbricht (eds.), *Goethe in Gesellschaft: Zur Geschichte einer literarischen Vereinigung vom Kaiserreich bis zum geteilten Deutschland*, Vienna 2005, 3.
27. *Ibid.*, 6.
28. Holm Kirsten, *Weimar im Banne des Führers. Die Besuche Adolf Hitlers 1925–1940*, Cologne 2001, 117 f.
29. *Ibid.*, 118.
30. *Ibid.*, 112.
31. Irene Lucke-Kaminiarz, 'Der Fall Dr Ernst Praetorius. Seine Hintergründe und Wirkungen', in: Helen Geyer/Maria Stolarzewicz (eds.), *Verfolgte Musiker im nationalsozialistischen Thüringen. Eine Spurensuche*, Vienna/Cologne 2020, 97.
32. Landesarchiv Thüringen – Hauptstaatsarchiv Weimar, shelf no. 58, 'Matrikel des Wilhelm-Ernst-Gymnasiums: Aufnahme des Herrn Baldur von Schirach Ostern 1916' (fol. 219); shelf no. 70, 'Abgangszeugnisse des Wilhelm-Ernst-Gymnasiums: Abgangszeugnis von Baldur von Schirach im März 1918' (fol. 194).
33. Schirach, *Ich glaubte an Hitler*, 10.
34. Cf. *Militär-Wochenblatt: Unabhängige Zeitschrift für die deutsche Wehrmacht*, vol. 6.
35. Peter Dudek, *'Liebevolle Züchtigung'. Ein Missbrauch der Autorität im Namen der Reformpädagogik*, Bad Heilbrunn 2012, 29.
36. Cit. Jürgen Oelkers, '"Reformpädagogik": Ein deutsches Schicksal?' (talk given at the University of Wuppertal, 13 July 2010), 7.
37. Cf. Rainer Marwedel, *Theodor Lessing 1872–1933. Eine Biographie*, Darmstadt/Neuwied 1987, 71–74.
38. Cit. Uwe Werner, *Anthroposophen in der Zeit des Nationalsozialismus (1933–1945)*, Munich 1999, 95. Alfred Andreesen ran the Lietz schools from 1919 to 1944.
39. Alfred Andreesen, *Hermann Lietz. Der Schöpfer der Landerziehungsheime*, Munich 1934.
40. *Neue Bahnen*, vol. 46, 1935, 62.
41. Schirach, *Ich glaubte an Hitler*, 11 f.
42. Gerhard Lingelbach, 'Weimar 1919 – Demokratie von oben oder von unten?', in: Walter Pauly (ed.), *Wendepunkte – Beiträge zur Rechtsentwicklung der letzten 100 Jahre* (Jenaer Schriften zum Recht 41), Hanover 2009, 19.
43. IfZ Munich, ZS A30, vol. 1, J. v. Lang, Interview mit Baldur von Schirach, 9 November 1966, 20–21.
44. See the transcript at: www.uni-marburg.de/de/icwc/dokumentation/dokumente/protokolle-nuernberg/ntvol14.pdf, accessed 10 June 2021.
45. Carl Alexander Krethlow, *Generalfeldmarschall Colmar Freiherr von der Goltz Pascha. Eine Biographie*, Paderborn 2012, 407–416; Frank Becker, 'Massengesellschaft – Massensport – Massenritual. Carl Diem und die Herausforderungen der Moderne',

in: Michael Krüger (ed.), *Der deutsche Sport auf dem Weg in die Moderne: Carl Diem und seine Zeit*, Münster 2009, 41. Cf. also Colmar Freiherr von der Goltz, *Das Volk in Waffen. Ein Buch über Heerwesen und Kriegsführung unserer Zeit*, Berlin 1899.
46. Cf. www.deutsche-biographie.de/sfz21654.html, accessed 1 March 2020.
47. Schirach, *Ich glaubte an Hitler*, 14.
48. *Ibid.*, 15.
49. Richard von Schirach, *Der Schatten*, 30–35.
50. Schirach, *Ich glaubte an Hitler*, 13.
51. *Ibid.*, 127.
52. Institut für Zeitgeschichte, Universität Wien, Archiv der Österreichischen Gesellschaft für Zeitgeschichte, 'Personalakt Baldur von Schirach, SA Führerfragebogen' – copy from the Berlin Document Center (today: Bundesarchiv Berlin).
53. *Ibid.*
54. 'Herbert Gottwald, Preußenbund (PB) 1913–1934', in: Dieter Fricke et al. (eds.), *Lexikon zur Parteiengeschichte. Die bürgerlichen und kleinbürgerlichen Parteien und Verbände in Deutschland (1789–1945)*, vol. 3, Cologne 1985, 594–598. For a fundamental study of the role played by the aristocracy after 1918–19, cf. Stephan Malinowski, *Vom König zum Führer. Sozialer Niedergang und politische Radikalisierung im deutschen Adel zwischen Kaiserreich und NS-Staat*, Berlin 32003, 257 f.
55. Klaus Rüffler, *Vom Landfriedensbruch bis zum Mord von Potempa. Der 'Legalitätskurs' der NSDAP*, Frankfurt am Main 1994, 147; for Weimar, cf. also Kirsten, *Weimar im Banne des Führers*, 23, 188 and a critical examination in *Die Glocke*, vol. 8, 1922, 598.
56. Schirach, *Ich glaubte an Hitler*, 16.
57. *Ibid.*, 17.
58. Baldur von Schirach, *Die Hitler-Jugend. Idee und Gestalt*, Leipzig 1936, 17.
59. Harald Sander, *Hitler – Das Intinerar. Aufenthaltsorte und Reisen von 1889 bis 1945*, vol. 1, 1889–1927, Berlin 2016.
60. Schirach, *Ich glaubte an Hitler*, 19.
61. *Ibid.*, 20.
62. *Ibid.*, 22.
63. Cit. *ibid.*, 22.
64. *Ibid.*, 24.
65. For a biography of Eckart, see www.dhm.de/lemo/biografie/dietrich-eckart, accessed 4 April 2020. For a more detailed study, see Claus-Ekkehard Bärsch, *Die politische Religion des Nationalsozialismus. Die religiösen Dimensionen der NS-Ideologie in den Schriften von Dietrich Eckart, Joseph Goebbels, Alfred Rosenberg und Adolf Hitler*, 2nd, revised edition, Munich 2002.
66. Schirach, *Ich glaubte an Hitler*, 23.
67. *Idid.*, 22 f.
68. Pallmann wrote the music to numerous NS songs but also had to answer to countless party tribunals (including within the SA) and had been a leader of the Young German Order. For a comprehensive study, see K. Prieberg, *Handbuch Deutsche Musiker 1933–1945*, CD-Rom version 1.2-3/2005, 5082–5126.
69. Schirach, *Ich glaubte an Hitler*, 23.
70. *Ibid.*, 26.
71. *Ibid.*, 28.
72. *Ibid.*, 29.
73. *Ibid.*, 31.
74. *Ibid.*, 28.
75. Bundesarchiv Berlin (BArch), R 55, Sig. 24529, RK020, 'Reichsministerium für Volksaufklärung und Propaganda, Personalakten Carl von Schirach, Intendant am deutschen Theater in Wiesbaden, Ergänzungsfragebogen'.
76. *Ibid.*, 'An den Reichsminister [Goebbels]', 14 October 1938.

77. Schirach, *Ich glaubte an Hitler*, 34.
78. IfZ Munich, Interviews Jochen Lang mit Baldur von Schirach, ZS-A 30/01-44, 9 November 1966.
79. Schirach, *Ich glaubte an Hitler*, 33.
80. Student record on 'Baldur von Schirach', Thüringisches Landesmusikarchiv. I am indebted to Esther Schönberger for kindly bringing this to my attention.
81. Bruno Hinze-Reinhold, *Lebenserinnerungen und Lebensbeichte*, Typoskript im Thüringischen Landesarchiv, Zweiter Teil, 91.
82. *Ibid.*, 37.
83. *Ibid.*, 38 f.
84. Thomas Neumann (ed.), *Quellen zur Geschichte Thüringens. 'Wir müssen eine Welt zum Tönen bringen …'. Kultur in Thüringen 1919–1949*, Weimar 1998, 133, cf. www.lzt-thueringen.de/files/huerkultur_19-49_1.pdf, accessed 4 March 2020.
85. Neumann (ed.), *Quellen zur Geschichte Thüringens*, 149–150.
86. *Ibid.*, 144.
87. *Ibid.*, 166. The original version of this simply malicious brochure, *Entartete Musik – Eine Abrechnung* by Staatsrat (State Councillor) Dr H. S. Ziegler, bursting with the worst anti-Semitic and racist attacks and accusations, can be viewed at https://archive.org/details/EntarteteMusik_758/page/n31/mode/2up8, accessed 4 March 2020. Cf. the comprehensive critical studies in Albrecht Dümling/Peter Girth (eds.), *Entartete Musik. Dokumentation und Kommentar zur Düsseldorfer Ausstellung von 1938*, 3rd, revised edition, Düsseldorf 1993.
88. Cf. Thomas Rösner, 'Adolf Bartels', in: Uwe Pruschner, Walter Schmit and Justus H. Ulbricht, *Handbuch zur 'Völkischen Bewegung' 1871–1918*, Munich 1999, 874–896.
89. Cf. Schirach's statements before the International Military Tribunal, www.uni-marburg.de/de/icwc/dokumentation/dokumente/protokolle-nuernberg/ntvol13.pdf, accessed 10 June 2021.
90. *Boy's Life*, February 1935, 16.
91. Cf. Tim Jeal, *Baden-Powell: Founder of the Boy Scouts*, New Haven 2001, the intense debate on an earlier edition of the book *The Boy-Man: The Life of Lord Baden-Powell*, New York 1990, in: *New York Review of Books*, Ian Buruma, 'Boys Will Be Boys', 15 March 1990, Michael Rosenthal's riposte 'A Bad Scout?' and Buruma's response, 28 June 1990.
92. See the collections of letters *Houston Stewart Chamberlain, Briefe 1882–1924 and Briefwechsel mit Kaiser Wilhelm II.*, vol. 2, https://archive.org/details/ChamberlainHoustonBriefe18821924UndBriefwechselMitKaiserWilhelmII.Band11928121S.Text/page/n1/mode/2up/search/Juden, accessed 6 March 2020. The many anti-Semitic statements in the correspondence between Chamberlain and Kaiser Wilhelm II are immediately apparent.
93. Helmut Berding, *Moderner Antisemitismus in Deutschland*, Frankfurt am Main 1988, 150.
94. For a comprehensive study see Udo Bermbach, *Houston Stewart Chamberlain. Wagners Schwiegersohn – Hitlers Vordenker*, Stuttgart 2015.
95. Adolf Bartels, 'Heinrich Heine. Auch ein Denkmal', Dresden/Leipzig 1906, cit. in: *Geständnisse. Heine im Bewußtsein heutiger Autoren*, ed. by Wilhelm Gössmann with Hans Peter Keller and Hedwig Walwei-Wiegelmann, Düsseldorf 1972, 22.
96. Kurt Tucholsky, 'Herr Adolf Bartels', in: *Die Weltbühne*. 1922, 18. no. 12, 291–294.
97. Cf. www.verbrannte-buecher.de/?page_id=1680w.
98. *Ibid.*
99. Cf. www.deutsche-biographie.de/sfz2104.html, accessed 6 March 2020.
100. Cit. Volkhard Knigge, 'Professor Bartels' Bücher', in: *Die Zeit*, 11 November 2004.
101. *Ibid.*

102. On the broader context of anti-Semitic, racist and sometimes religious nationalist movement before 1918, cf. Uwe Puschner, *Die völkische Bewegung im wilhelminischen Kaiserreich. Sprache – Rasse – Religion*, Darmstadt 2001 and Puschner/Schmitz/Ulbricht (ed.), *Handbuch zur 'Völkischen Bewegung'*, Munich 1996.
103. Knigge, 'Professor Bartels' Bücher'.
104. Michael Wortmann, *Baldur von Schirach. Hitlers Jugendführer*, Cologne 1982, 34.
105. Schirach, *Ich glaubte an Hitler*, 40.
106. BArch, 'Akte Baldur von Schirach' – copy held in the Archiv der Österreichischen Gesellschaft für Zeitgeschichte, Vienna, 'Personalakte Schirach, Baldur von'.
107. See Stefanie Hundehege, 'Baldur von Schirach: Der "Sänger der Bewegung"', in: Rolf Düsterberg (ed.), *Dichter für das 'Dritte Reich'*, vol. 3, 209–245, 226.
108. Schirach, Ich glaubte an Hitler, 40.
109. Cf. Jutta Held, 'Kunstgeschichte im "Dritten Reich": Wilhelm Pinder und Hans Jantzen an der Münchner Universität', in: Jutta Held (ed.), *Kunstgeschichte an den Universitäten im Nationalsozialismus* (Kunst und Politik 5), Göttingen 2003, 17–59.
110. Holger Dainat, 'Zur Berufungspolitik in der Neueren deutschen Literaturwissenschaft 1933-1945', in: Holger Dainat/Lutz Danneberg (eds.), *Literaturwissenschaft und Nationalsozialismus*, Tübingen 2003, 84.
111. Andreas Huber/Linda Erker/Klaus Taschwer, *Der Deutsche Klub. Austro-Nazis in der Hofburg*, Vienna 2020, 144.
112. Schirach, *Ich glaubte an Hitler*, 40.
113. Maximilian Schreiber, Walther Wüst, *Dekan und Rektor der Universität München 1935–1945* (Beiträge zur Geschichte der Ludwig-Maximilians-Universität München 3) Munich 2008, 155.
114. 'Bayerische Stimme gegen den Judenhass' in: *Abwehrblätter. Mitteilungen aus dem Verein zur Abwehr des Antisemitismus* 40, 1930, 56.
115. *Jahrbuch der Deutschen Shakespeare-Gesellschaft*, Neue Folge Band 1 (vols 59–60), Jena 1924, 14 and 200. Cf. Gerhard J. Bellinger, Brigitte Regler-Bellinger, *Schwabings Ainmillerstrasse und ihre bedeutendsten Anwohner. Ein repräsentatives Beispiel der Münchner Stadtgeschichte von 1888 bis heute*, 2nd, revised edition, Norderstedt 2013, 152 f., and Frank-Rutger Hausmann, *Anglistik und Amerikanistik im 'Dritten Reich'*, Frankfurt am Main 2003, 248.
116. Cf. Gerhard J. Bellinger, Brigitte Regler-Bellinger, *Schwabings Ainmillerstrasse und ihre bedeutendsten Anwohner. Ein repräsentatives Beispiel der Münchner Stadtgeschichte von 1888 bis heute*, 2nd, revised edition, Norderstedt 2013, 152 f., and Frank-Rutger Hausmann, *Anglistik und Amerikanistik im 'Dritten Reich'*, Frankfurt am Main 2003, 248.
117. Victor Klemperer, *Man möchte immer weinen und lachen in einem. Revolutionstagebuch 1919*. With a foreword by Christopher Clark and a historical essay by Wolfram Wette, Berlin 2015, 97. The Romance scholar Klemperer, who wrote his *Habilitation* under Karl Vossler, was appointed professor at the Technische Universität Darmstadt in 1920. The work describes with linguistic precision anti-Semitism and the difficulties he encountered as a converted in Jew in 1919. His diaries from 1933–1945 are some of the most important eye-witness accounts of the National Socialist era.
118. Christoph Studt, 'Oncken, Karl Hermann Gerhard', in: *Neue Deutsche Biographie* 19 (1999), 538 f.
119. Maurin Johannes Schunke, 'Friedrich in Weimar. Wandel und Wirksamkeit der politischen Klassikrezeption 1914–1933', in: Walter Pauly/Klaus Ries (ed.), *Politisch-soziale Ordnungsvorstellungen in der Deutschen Klassik. Staatsverständnisse*, Baden-Baden 2018, 260 f.
120. *Ibid.*, 260.
121. Studt, 'Oncken'.

122. Alfred Grimm, 'Spiegelberg, Wilhelm', in: *Neue Deutsche Biographie* 24 (2010), 682–684.
123. Hans-Albert Walter, *Deutsche Exilliteratur 1933–1950*, vol. 1: *Die Vorgeschichte des Exils und seine erste Phase* and vol 1.2: *Weimarische Linksintellektuelle im Spannungsfeld von Aktionen und Repressionen*, Stuttgart 2017, 401.
124. Cf. the comprehensive study by Wolfgang Martynkewicz, *Salon Deutschland. Geist und Macht 1900–1945*, Berlin 2009.
125. Cf. the splendidly edited correspondence and the excellent introduction in Klaus E. Bohnenkamp (ed.), *Hugo von Hofmannsthal, Rudolf Kassner und Rainer Maria Rilke im Briefwechsel mit Elsa und Hugo Bruckmann 1893–1941*, Göttingen 2014
126. Katrin Hillgruber, 'Salon Bruckmann. Die unselige Freitagsgesellschaft', in: *Der Tagesspiegel*, 10 January 2010.
127. Otto Gritschneder/Lothar Gruchmann/Reinhard Weber (eds.), *Der Hitlerprozess 1924*. Vol 3: *12.–18. Verhandlungstag*. K. G. Munich 2000, 1090–1093.
128. Schirach, *Ich glaubte an Hitler*, 46.
129. Cit. Wortmann, *Baldur von Schirach*, 76.
130. Cf. Hundehege, *Schirach*, 218.
131. Mathias Rösch, *Die Münchener NSDAP 1925–1933. Eine Untersuchung zur inneren Struktur der NSDAP in der Weimarer Republik*, Munich 2002, 134 f. On the National Socialist Students' League as a whole, cf. Michael H. Kater, 'Der NS-Studentenbund von 1926 bis 1928; Randgruppe zwischen Hitler und Strasser', in: *Vierteljahrshefte für Zeitgeschichte*, 22 (1974), no. 2, 148–190.
132. Rösch, *Münchner NSDAP*, 136.
133. *Ibid.*, 201.
134. Wortmann, *Baldur von Schirach*, 56.
135. Alfred E. Norris, a partner of Parrish & Co. with the prestigious address of 25 Broadway, was suspected smuggling alcohol during the prohibition era. Cf. Ernest Knaebel, *United States Reports: Cases Adjudged in the Supreme Court at October Term, 1929*, vol. 281, Washington, D.C. 1930, 621.
136. Alexander Graf, *Mütze, Band und Braunhemd – Marburger Studentenverbindungen und der Nationalsozialistische Studentenbund während der Weimarer Republik*, Marburg 2012, 40.
137. Matthias Wieben, *Studenten der Christian-Albrechts-Universität im 'Dritten Reich'. Zum Verhaltensmuster der Studenten in den ersten Herrschaftsjahren des Nationalsozialismus*, Frankfurt am Main 1994, 33.
138. Wortmann, *Baldur von Schirach*, 82.
139. Schirach, *Ich glaubte an Hitler*, 123 f.
140. Rösch, *Münchner NSDAP*, 333.
141. NSDStB-Organisationsleiter Dr Reinhard Sunkel.
142. Adolf Hitler, *Reden, Schriften, Anordnungen: Februar 1925 bis Jänner 1933. Außenpolitische Standortbestimmung nach der Reichstagswahl Juni-Juli 1928*, 1994, 352–356.
143. Cf. Wortmann, *Baldur von Schirach*, 80 and 239.
144. Martin Pabst, *Couleur und Braunhemd. Deutschen Studenten in der Weimarer Republik*, Munich 1993, 41.
145. Peter Stitz, *Der CV 1919–1938. Der hochschulpolitische Weg des Cartellverbandes der katholisch deutschen Studentenverbindungen (CV) vom Ende des 1. Weltkrieges bis zur Vernichtung durch den Nationalsozialismus*, Munich 1970, 59.
146. Hitler, *Reden*, 294.
147. Cit. Jochen von Lang, *Der Hitler-Junge*, 48.
148. Cit. Wortmann, *Baldur von Schirach*, 84 f.
149. Contrary to Schirach's claims, the house did not belong to the Bruckmanns. See Klaus E. Bohnenkamp (ed.), *Hugo von Hofmannsthal, Rudolf Kassner und Rainer Maria*

Rilke im Briefwechsel mit Elsa und Hugo Bruckmann, 1893–1941, Göttingen 2014, 67 (note 42).
150. *Regierungsblatt für Mecklenburg-Schwerin, Jahrgang 1933*, 33.
151. Birgit Schwarz, *Geniewahn: Hitler und die Kunst*, Vienna/Cologne/Weimar 2009, 151.
152. Cit. Wortmann, *Baldur von Schirach*, 81.
153. Wortmann, *Baldur von Schirach*, 83. Cf. also Albert Krebs, *Tendenzen und Gestalten der NSDAP. Erinnerungen an die Frühzeit der Partei*, Munich 1959, 232.
154. Krebs, *Tendenzen*, 232.
155. Baldur von Schirach, 'Des Daseins Sinn', in: *Nationalsozialistische Monatshefte* 1/May 1930, 1; here the second and third strophes.
156. Cit. Bohnenkamp, *Hofmannsthal*, 106.
157. Goebbels, *Tagebücher*, 7 August 1928. Originally published in: *Die Tagebücher von Joseph Goebbels*. Ed. by Angela Hermann and Elke Fröhlich by commission of the Institut für Zeitgeschichte and with the support of the Russian State Archive Serviceausgegeben von Elke Fröhlich. Digital edition in: *Nationalsozialismus, Holocaust, Widerstand und Exil 1933–1945*. Online-Datenbank De Gruyter, 2 July 2020.
158. *Ibid.*, 4 July 1929.
159. *Ibid.*, 6 July 1929.
160. Birgit Witamwas, *Geklebte NS-Propaganda. Verführung und Manipulation durch das Plakat*, Berlin/Boston 2016, 57–75.
161. *Der unbekannte S.A. Mann. Ein guter Kamerad der Hitlersoldaten!*, no author, Munich 1930, 38.
162. Schirach, *Der Preis der Herrlichkeit*, Frankfurt am Main, 184.
163. Goebbels, *Tagebücher*, 5 July 1930.
164. *Ibid.*, 24 July 1930.
165. *Ibid.*, 20 July 1930.
166. Ernst Hanfstaengl, *Zwischen Weißem und Braunem Haus. Memoiren eines politischen Außenseiters*, Munich 1970, 221.
167. *Ibid.*, 248 f.
168 *Ibid.*, 360.
169. The NSDAP obtained more than double the votes it received in the *Reichstag* elections of 1930, to become the strongest parliamentary group with 37.3 per cent.
170. *Neues Wiener Tagblatt*, 7 August 1938, 29.
171. Jochen von Lang, *Der Hitler-Junge. Baldur von Schirach, der Mann, der Deutschlands Jugend erzog*, Hamburg 1988, 64.
172. Jean Pierre Faye, *Totalitäre Sprachen: Kritik der narrativen Vernunft, Kritik der narrativen Ökonomie*, Berlin 1977, 301.
173. Speech by Kurt Gruber in May 1931, cit. André Postert, *Hitlerjunge Schall: Die Tagebücher eines jungen Nationalsozialisten*, DTV Digital 2016.
174. This was the umbrella term used for all bourgeois and non-confessional youth groups and associations from 1923 onwards. The largest group were the associations belonging to the *Wandervogel* movement, followed by the various *Pfadfinder* organisations.
175. Michael H. Kater, *Hitler-Jugend*, Darmstadt 2005, 19.
176. Goebbels, *Tagebücher*, 22 November 1931.
177. Werner Brill, *Pädagogik der Abgrenzung. Die Implementierung der Rassenhygiene im Nationalsozialismus durch die Sonderpädagogik*, Bad Heilbrunn 2011, 159.
178. Munich address book for 1932, http://wiki-de.genealogy.net/w/index.php?title=Datei:Muenchen-AB-1932-2.djvu&page=823, accessed 29 March 2020.
179. Schirach, *Ich glaubte an Hitler*, 116.
180. *Ibid*.
181. Rüdiger Ahrens, *Bündische Jugend. Eine neue Geschichte 1918–1933*, Göttingen 2015, 308 f.

182. Baldur von Schirach, *Die Fahne der Verfolgten*, Berlin 1935, 10.
183. Baldur von Schirach, 'Gedenkansprache für den Hitlerjungen Herbert Norkus', original speech available at https://archive.org/details/19350124BaldurVonSchirach GedenkanspracheFuerDenHitlerjungenHerbertNor- kus14m28s, accessed 29 March 2020.
184. Heinz Reif, *Adel im 19. und 20. Jahrhundert* (Enzyklopädie Deutscher Geschichte 55), Munich 2012, 88.
185. *Tagblatt*, 1 June 1932, 11.
186. *Ibid.*
187. Hohlwein also designed a poster for the NSDAP's campaign ahead of the Reichstag elections of 6 November 1932. He joined the NSDAP himself on 1 May 1933 (as member number 2945937). Cf. www.arthistoricum.net/themen/textquellen/gebrauchs-und-reklamegrafik/zeitschrift-gebrauchsgraphik/literatur/ludwig-hohl-wein-zum-140-geburtstag, accessed 5 April 2020.
188. Witamwas, *Geklebte NS-Propaganda*, 130–134. Altogether, Hohlwein designed around forty posters for the NSDAP and its organisations as well as the advertising posters for the Olympic Games held in Berlin in 1936.
189. Schirach, *Ich glaubte an Hitler*, 155 f.
190. *Völkischer Beobachter*, 4 October 1932.
191. Schirach, *Ich glaubte an Hitler*, 160.
192. http://db-saur-de.uaccess.univie.ac.at DGO/basicFullCitationView.jsf?documentId=PS03508 document ID: PS03508 Originally in: *Nürnberger Dokumentenkartei. Erschließungskartei zu den Beweisdokumenten der Nürnberger Kriegsverbrecherprozesse aus dem Institut für Zeitgeschichte*. Munich.
193. Goebbels, *Tagebücher*, 2 March 1934.
194. *Ibid.*, 12 August 1934.
195. *Ibid.*, 7 May 1934.
196. *Ibid.*, 19 October 1934.
197. Paul Meier-Benneckenstein (ed.), *Dokumente der Deutschen Politik*, vol. 1, Berlin 1939, 65 f. and 393.
198. Document 2229-ps; *The reich youth leader at work* – Issue 423, 22 June 1933, of the NSK. National Socialist Party Press Agency, [NSK, *Nationalsozialisitsche Parteikorrespondenz*, the official press agency of the NSDAP]. Edited by Wilhelm Weiss. Responsible for communications of the Reich Press Office. Dr Otto Dietrich, Reich Press chief. Published by Franz Eher Successor, Munich. Important order of baldur von schirach NSK Berlin [*sic*], 22 June, https://avalon.law.yale.edu/imt/2229-ps.asp, accessed 5 April 2020).
199. Baldur von Schirach, *Die Hitler-Jugend*, Berlin 1934, 69.
200. Schirach, *Ich glaubte an Hitler*, 175.
201. On the genesis of the Hitler Youth's song 'Vorwärts, vorwärts', see https://jugend1918-1945.de/portal/archiv/album.aspx?root=6380&id=6380&redir=%2fpor%20tal%2fJugend%2fthema.aspx%3fbereich%3darchiv%26root%3d26636%26id%3d4927, accessed 17 May 2020.
202. Fred K. Prieberg, *Handbuch Deutsche Musiker 1933–1945*, Version 1.2-3/2005, Auprès des Zombry 2005, CD-Rom, 8164 f. After 1945, he turned his attention to anti-fascist music and composed the score for the film *Nuremberg: Its Lesson for Today* (www.nurembergfilm.org/film_bio_hans_borgmann.shtml, accessed 17 May 2020).
203. Goebbels, *Tagebücher*, 6 September 1933.
204. *Ibid.*, 20 September 1933, in: *ibid.*, 272.
205. Wilhelm Schepping, *'Menschen seid wachsam'. Widerständisches Liedgut der Jugend in der NS-Zeit. Liedtexte*, Munich 1993, 5 f., www.hf.uni-koeln.de/data/musikeume/File/Oppositionelles%20Lied/Menschen%20seid%20wachsam.pdf, accessed 17 May 2020.

206. Schirach, *Ich glaubte an Hitler*, 112. Incidentally, Hitler stopped paying any tax after 1935, following a number of controversies with the Munich tax office and tax decrees. See Sven Felix Kellerhoff, '"Mein Kampf" brachte Hitler Millionen. Steuerfrei', in: *Die Welt*, 25 September 2015, www.welt.de/geschichte/zweiter-weltkrieg/article146837543/Mein-Kampf-brachte-HitlerMillionen-Steuerfrei.html, accessed 28 May 2020.
207. Cf. the search results in the catalogue of the Deutsche Nationalbibliothek, with 91 entries for 'Baldur von Schirach', although the list includes individual speeches.
208. Baldur von Schirach, *Die Hitler-Jugend. Gestalt und Idee*, Leipzig 1934, 16. On the subject of tax, cf. Ralf Banken, *Hitlers Steuerstaat: Die Steuerpolitik im Dritten Reich*, Berlin 2018, 242, with reference to Schirach's tax return in 1934. As *Reichsjugendführer*, Schirach received a basic salary of 8,400 Reichsmark, with total earnings of 14,880 Reichsmark, the equivalent of around 61,000 euros today.
209. Originally published in: Max Domarus, *Hitler. Reden und Proklamationen 1932–1945. Kommentiert von einem deutschen Zeitgenossen*. Part 1: *Triumph*. Vol. 2: 1935–1938, Leonberg 1988, 465–560.
210. Adolf Hitler, *Mein Kampf*, vol. 1, *Eine Abrechnung*, Munich 1933, 392.
211. Susan Sontag, 'Fascinating Fascism', in: *New York Review of Books*, 6 February 1975, n. p., available at http://marcuse.faculty.history.ucsb.edu/classes/33d/33dTexts/Sontag FascinFascism75.htm, accessed 18 June 2021.
212. Peter Longerich, *Hitler. Biographie*, Munich 2015, 254.
213. Cf. 'Gesetz über die Hitler-Jugend' (1 December 1936), http://ghdi.ghi-dc.org/sub_document.cfm?document_id=1564&language=german, accessed 28 May 2020.
214. *Ibid.*
215. Michael Buddrus, *Totale Erziehung für den totalen Krieg. Hitler-Jugend und nationalsozialistische Jugendpolitik* (Texte und Materialien zur Zeitgeschichte 13), Munich 2003, 268 f.
216. *Ibid.*, 270.
217. *Ibid.*, 11.
218. Buddrus, *Totale Erziehung*, 265.
219. The 98 rifle, a repeating rifle manufactured by Mauser with an integrated magazine holding five cartridges, was the standard weapon of the German infantry during the First World War.
220. Helmut Stellrecht, *Soldatentum und Jugendertüchtigung* (Schriften der Deutschen Hochschule für Politik I/16), Berlin 1935, 19.
221. Hartmann Lauterbacher, *Erlebt und mitgestaltet. Kronzeuge einer Epoche 1923–1945. Zu neuen Ufern nach Kriegsende*, Preussisch Oldendorf, 122 ff.
222. Karl Heinz Jahnke/Michael Buddrus (eds.), *Deutsche Jugend 1933–1945. Eine Dokumentation*, Hamburg 1989, 328 f.
223. 'Unter Verweis auf eine Äußerung Hitlers über die Bestrafung von …' (Regest 11540),' in: *Nationalsozialismus, Holocaust, Widerstand und Exil 1933–1945*. Online-Datenbank. De Gruyter. 2 July 2020.
224. *Ibid.*
225. Goebbels, *Tagebücher*, 28 January 1937.
226. *Ibid.*, 16 February 1935.
227. https://archive.org/details/1935-03-20-UfA-Tonwoche-Nr.237, accessed 11 June 2020.
228. Margarete Götz, *Die Grundschule in der Zeit des Nationalsozialismus: eine Untersuchung der inneren Ausgestaltung der vier unteren Jahrgänge der Volksschule auf der Grundlage amtlicher Maßnahmen*, Bad Heilbrunn/OBB 1997, 33.
229. Cit. Karl Dietrich Bracher, *Die deutsche Diktatur. Entstehung, Struktur, Folgen des Nationalsozialismus*, Frankfurt am Main/Berlin/Vienna 1979, 287.
230. Buddrus, *Totale Erziehung*, 875.

231. Vanessa Stürz, *Elite und Diktatur. Die Rolle der Eliteschulen im Nationalsozialismus und ihre Bedeutung für das Regime*, Hamburg 2013, 43. Cf. in detail Dirk Gelhaus/Jörn-Peter Hülter, *Die Ausleseschulen als Grundpfeiler des NS-Regimes*, Würzburg 2003.
232. Franz-Werner Kersting, *Militär und Jugend im NS-Staat. Rüstungs- und Schulpolitik der Wehrmacht*, Wiesbaden 1989, 202.
233. *Ibid.*, 210.
234. Harald Scholtz, *Erziehung und Unterricht unterm Hakenkreuz*, Göttingen, new edition, 2009, 158.
235. Ingeborg Wiemann-Stöhr, *Die pädagogische Mobilmachung. Schule in Baden im Zeichen des Nationalsozialismus*, Bad Heilbrunn 2018, 261 f.
236. Sven Reichardt, *Beteiligungsdiktaturen in Italien und Deutschland*. Cf. the observations on the 'Volksgemeischaft' debate in: Detlef Schmiechen-Ackermann/Marlis Buchholz/Bianca Roitsch/Christiane Schröder (eds.), *Der Ort der 'Volksgemeinschaft' in der deutschen Gesellschaftsgeschichte*, Paderborn 2018, 122.
237. Harald Oelrich, *Sportgeltung, Weltgeltung. Sport im Spannungsfeld der deutsch-italienischen Außenpolitik von 1918 bis 1945*, Münster 2003, 277.
238. Goebbels, *Tagebücher*, 2 May 1937.
239. Oelrich, *Sportgeltung*, 370.
240. www.standard.co.uk/news/uk/scout-leader-robert-baden-powell-controversial-a4466376.html, accessed 14 June 2020. Lauterbacher's claims in his memoirs that Lord Baden-Powell attended NSDAP's Reich Party Congress of 1937 can be neither verified nor disproven (Lauterbacher, Erlebt, 136).
241. https://kval.com/news/nation-world/mi5-papers-show-britain-feared-nazi-spyclists-11-12-2015, accessed 14 June 2020.
242. www.telegraph.co.uk/news uknews/7393468/MI5-suspected-Nazi-Youth-of-organising-cycling-tours-as-cover-for-spying.html, accessed 14 June 2020.
243. Lóránt Tilkovszky, *Teufelskreis. Die Minderheitenfrage in den deutsch-ungarischen Beziehungen 1933–1938*, trans. by Johanna Till, Budapest 1989, 88 and 126.
244. Goebbels, *Tagebücher*, 12 January 1938.
245. Schirach, *Ich glaubte an Hitler*, 223–228.
246. Goebbels, *Tagebücher*, 16 December 1937.
247. Cf. *Das Archiv. Nachschlagewerk für Politik, Wirtschaft, Kultur*, issues 43–45 (1937), 1057; *Metaxas – Hitler: Griechisch-deutsche Beziehungen während der Metaxas-Diktatur 1936–1941*, Berlin 2006, 60.
248. Peter Wien, *Iraqui Arab Nationalism. Authoritarian, Totalitarian, and Pro-Fascist Inclinations, 1932–1941*, New York 2006, 96.
249. *Akten zur deutschen auswärtigen Politik, 1918–1945: 1937–1945*, series D., vol. 5, 1953, 682.
250. Richard Flower, *Die Entwicklung von Sadeq-e Hedayât in seinen literarischen Werken unter Berücksichtigung des Inhaltlichen und Formalen*, inaugural dissertation, Freie Universität Berlin 1969, 46.
251. Zhand Shakibi, *Pahlavi Iran and the Politics of Occidentalism: The Shah and the Rastakhiz Party*, London 2020, 112.
252. *Ibid.*, 113.
253. Günter Kaufmann, *Baldur von Schirach. Ein Jugendführer in Deutschland. Richtigstellung und Vermächtnis*, Füssen 1993, 55.
254. Volker Weiß, *Moderne Antimoderne. Arthur Moeller van den Bruck und der Wandel des Konservatismus*, Paderborn 2012, 453.
255. Oelrich, *Sportgeltung*, 370.
256. Alessio Ponzio, *Shaping the New Man: Youth Training Regimes in Fascist Italy and Nazi Germany*, Madison 2015, 174.
257. Boris Celovsky, *Das Münchener Abkommen von 1938*, Stuttgart 1958, 244.
258. Wortmann, *Baldur von Schirach*, 181.

259. Cf. here Dirk Böttcher/Klaus Mlynek/Waldemar R. Röhrbein/Hugo Thielen, *Hannoversches biographisches Lexikon: Von den Anfängen bis in die Gegenwart*, Hanover 2002, 224.
260. Buddrus, *Totale Erziehung*, 21.
261. Schirach, *Ich glaubte an Hitler*, 262.
262. Universität Wien/Fachbereichsbibliothek Zeitgeschichte, "Gaupresse"-Archiv Wien: www.ns-pressearchiv.at/archiv/akte/k187-1-m003-a001, accessed 14 June 2020 (prior registration required).
263. Raffael Scheck, *Hitler's African Victims. The German Army Massacres of Black French Soldiers in 1940*, Cambridge 2006, 124–126, 154–157.
264. 'Air Force interrogation report: SRA [Special Report Air Force – O.R.] 3576, 22 January 1943A 713 – (Fighter Pilot: F.W.190) Captured 18 Dec 42A 1172 – Unteroffizier (Bomber Observer: Ju. 88, 3E+GK, 2/K.G.6) Captured 18 Jan 43)'. On this source, cf. also Sönke Neitzel/Harald Welzer, Soldaten. Protokolle vom Kämpfen, Töten und Sterben, Frankfurt am Main 2011. My thanks to Dr Richard Germann (Vienna) for pointing me towards this information and the quotation.
265. Schirach, *Ich glaubte an Hitler*, 263.
266. Schirach, *Preis der Herrlichkeit*, 203.
267. Goebbels, *Tagebücher*, 6 September 1939.
268. Cit. Buddrus, *Totale Erziehung*, 81.
269. Wortmann, *Baldur von Schirach*, 185.
270. *Kleine Volksblatt*, 8 August 1940, 1.
271. Henry Picker (ed.), *Hitlers Tischgespräche im Führerhauptquartier 1941–1942*, Stuttgart 1977, 360.
272. Lois Weinberger, *Tatsachen, Begegnungen und Gespräche. Ein Buch um Österreich*, Vienna 1948, 84.
273. Goebbels, *Tagebücher*, 4 June 1939.
274. Hans Safrian, *Die Eichmann-Männer*, Vienna/Zurich 1993.
275. Universität Wien/Fachbereichsbibliothek Zeitgeschichte, "Gaupresse"-Archiv Wien: […], www.ns-pressearchiv.at/archiv/akte/k187-1-m003-a001, accessed 14 June 2020.
276. NSDAP Gauleitung Wien Gaupresseamt-Archiv, 'Reichsleiter Baldur von Schirach. Tätigkeit als Reichsstatthalter und Gauleiter in Wien August 1940 – November 1942. Chronik der Pressemeldungen mit Sach- und Namensregister', cf. www.ns-pressearchiv.at/reichsleiter-baldur-von-schirach-taetigkeit-als-reichsstatthalter-und-gauleiter-wien-august-1940.
277. *Völkischer Beobachter*, Vienna edition, 11 August 1940, 1.
278. *Neues Wiener Tagblatt*, 11 August 1940, 1.
279. *Völkischer Beobachter*, Vienna edition, 11 August 1940, 34.
280. Schirach, *Ich glaubte an Hitler*, 63.
281. Goebbels, *Tagebücher*, 27 October 1940.
282. Universität Wien/Fachbereichsbibliothek Zeitgeschichte, "Gaupresse"-Archiv Wien: 'Ansprache des Reichsleiters Baldur von Schirach im Zimmer des Gauleiters (Parlamentsgebäude). 13. August 1940', www.ns-pressearchiv.at/archiv/akte/k185-1-m004-a002, accessed 14 June 2020. For a comprehensive history of the *Gauhaus* from 1940–1945, see Bertrand Perz/Verena Pawlowsky/Ina Markova/Parlamentsdirektion (eds.), *Inbesitznahmen. Das Parlamentsgebäude in Wien 1933–1936*, Salzburg 2018, 185–252.
283. Gerhard Botz, *Nationalsozialismus in Wien. Machtübernahme, Herrschaftssicherung, Radikalisierung, Kriegsvorbereitung, 1938/1939*, revised and expanded edition, Vienna 2018, 593.
284. 'Durch Bormann übermittelte Weisung Hitlers an den Wiener Reichsstatthalter' (Regest 15406), in: *Nationalsozialismus, Holocaust, Widerstand und Exil 1933–1945*. Online-Datenbank. De Gruyter. Accessed 22 June 2020.

285. NSDAP Gauleitung, Reichsleiter, 9.
286. *Ibid.*, 15.
287. Goebbels, *Tagebücher*, 17 September 1940. Heinz Drewes was a conductor and head of Department X (music) in the Reich Ministry for the People's Enlightenment and Propaganda in Berlin.
288. *Ibid.*, 27 September 1940.
289. *Ibid.*, 4 October 1940.
290. *Ibid.*, 27. October 1940. On the history of the building and the political procedures, see Manfred Matzka, *Die Staatskanzlei. 300 Jahre Macht und Intrige am Ballhausplatz*, Vienna 2017.
291. Heike B. Görtemaker, *Eva Braun: Leben mit Hitler*, Munich 2010, 116.
292. Schirach, *Ich glaubte an Hitler*, 268.
293. *Der Montag*, 6 October 1941, 1.
294. Buddrus, *Totale Erziehung*, 884.
295. *Das Kleine Volksblatt*, 8 August 1940, 4.
296. Cit. Buddrus, *Totale Erziehung*, 900, fn. 204.
297. *Ibid.*, 899.
298. Cit. Walter Thomas, *Bis der Vorhang fiel*, 207.
299. *Ibid.*, 206.
300. Cf. Axmann, *Das kann doch nicht das Ende sein*, 298 f.
301. *Neues Wiener Tagblatt*, 16 September 1942, 3.
302. GIL translates as 'The Italian Youth of Victory'.
303. Oelrich, *Sportgeltung*, 543.
304. *Neues Wiener Tagblatt*, 18 September 1942, 3.
305. *Ibid.*
306. *Ibid.*, 16 September 1942, 3.
307. Cf. Toni Morant i Ariño, 'Die Gründung des "Europäischen Jugendverbands" und die Frauen- und Jugendorganisation der Falange (Vienna, September 1942)', in: *Themenportal Europäische Geschichte*, 2012, www.europa.clio-online.de/essay/id/fdae-1574, accessed 20 June 2020.
308. *Neues Wiener Tagblatt*, 15 September 1942, 2.
309. *Ibid.*
310. Universität Wien/Fachbereichsbibliothek Zeitgeschichte, "Gaupresse"-Archiv Wien: www.ns-pressearchiv.at/archiv/akte/k119-4-m002-a017, accessed 20 June 2020.
311. 'Reichsleiter Baldur von Schirach als Ehrenpräsident des Europäischen Jugendverbandes auf der Terrasse der Neuen Burg zu Wien am Freitag, den 18. September 1942, 20 Uhr 55 Minuten', in: *Rede Baldur von Schirach*, 18.09.1942, URL: www.ns-pressearchiv.at/archiv/akte/k185-2-m004-a002, accessed 20 June 2020.
312. Cit. Oelrich, *Sportgeltung*, 547.
313. Goebbels, cit. *ibid.*, 550.
314. Goebbels, *Tagebücher*, 25 September 1942.
315. Cit. Peter Longerich, *Propagandisten im Krieg: Die Presseabteilung des Auswärtigen Amtes unter Ribbentrop*, Munich 1987, 97.
316. *Ibid.*
317. Oelrich, *Sportgeltung*, 551.
318. 'Telegramm von Martin Bormann aus dem Führerhauptquartier an Reichsleiter Rosenberg, 9. 9. 1942. Einstellung einer geplanten Vortragsfolge zum Thema "Europa", aufgrund eines …' (Regest 26682), in: *Nationalsozialismus, Holocaust, Widerstand und Exil 1933–1945*. Online-Datenbank. De Gruyter. Accessed 21 June 2020.
319. Josef Stummvoll, *Geschichte der Österreichischen Nationalbibliothek*, vol. 2, Vienna 1968, 136.
320. *Akten zur Deutschen Auswärtigen Politik 1918–1945*, series E: 1941–1945, vol. III, Göttingen 1974, 488.

321. Cit. Christoph Kühberger, 'Europa als "Strahlenbündel nationaler Kräfte". Zur Konzeption und Legitimation einer europäischen Zusammenarbeit auf der Gründungsfeierlichkeit des "Europäischen Jugendverbandes" 1942', in: *Journal of European Integration History* 2/2009, 17.
322. Goran Miljan, '"The Brotherhood of Youth". A Case Study of the Ustaša and Hlinka Youth Connections and Exchanges', in: Arnd Bauerkämper, Grzegorz Rossoliński-Liebe (ed.), *Fascism without Borders, Transnational Connections and Cooperation between Movements and Regimes in Europe from 1918 to 1945*, New York 2017, 123 f. The author mistakenly speaks of a second congress in Madrid, but it was only a work meeting (Universität Wien/Fachbereichsbibliothek Zeitgeschichte, "Gaupresse"-Archiv Wien: www.ns-pressearchiv.at/archiv/akte/k119-4-m002-a008, accessed on 27 June 2020).
323. *Neues Wiener Tagblatt*, 28 February 1944, 3.
324. *Völkischer Beobachter*, 13 December 1941.
325. 'Neue Presse-Ära im neuen Europa', in: *Völkischer Beobachter*, Vienna, 14 December 1941.
326. *Völkischer Beobachter*, 9 May 1942.
327. *Ibid.*, 20 September 1942.
328. *Ibid.*, 22 Juni 1943.
329. Universität Wien/Fachbereichsbibliothek Zeitgeschichte, "Gaupresse"-Archiv Wien: www.ns-pressearchiv.at/archiv/akte/k119-4-m002-a007, accessed 20 June 2020.
330. Bodo-Michael Baumunk, *Colin Ross. Ein deutscher Revolutionär und Reisender 1885–1945*, corrected edition, Berlin 2015, 96, see http://colinrossproject.net/fileadmin/user_upload/baumunk_colin-ross_online2015. pdf, accessed 18 July 2020.
331. His books, published in many runs by the Leipzig press F. A. Brockhaus, include: *Im Banne des Eises* (1911), *Im Balkankrieg* (1913), *Das ABC der wissenschaftlichen Betriebsführung* (1917), *Südamerikanisches Auswanderer-ABC* (1921), *Der Weg nach Osten. Reise durch Rußland, Ukraine, Transkaukasien, Persien, Buchara und Turkestan* (1923), *Mit dem Kurbelkasten um die Erde* (1926), *Mit Kind und Kegel in die Arktis* (1928), *Mit Kamera, Kind und Kegel durch Afrika* (1928), *Der Balkan Amerikas. Mit Kind und Kegel durch Mexiko zum Panamakanal* (1937), Vier Jahre am Feind (1938), *Die 'Westliche Hemisphäre' als Programm und Phantom des amerikanischen Imperialismus* (1941).
332. Cf. the project funded by the Austrian Science Fund (FWF) in Vienna, *Welterkundung zwischen den Kriegen. Die Reisefilme des Colin Ross*, conducted by the Ludwig Boltzmann Institut für Geschichte und Gesellschaft and the Austrian Film Museum, which holds his film estate (https://scilog.fwf.ac.at kulturgesellschaft/7643/die-vermessung-des-herrn-ross and www.colinrossproject. net).
333. Bayerisches Hauptstaatsarchiv, NL Colin Ross, no date, 'Politische Prognose. I. Was heißt Weltkrise?, II. Warum Weltkrise?, III. Der Weg aus der Krise', cit. Baumunk, *Colin Ross*, 79 f.
334. Bundesarchiv Koblenz, NL Haushofer, vol. 27, Ross to Haushofer, Chicago 24.11.1933, cit. Baumunk, Colin Ross, 84.
335. Colin Ross, 'Die Vollendung der Jugend. Gedanken zum Weimarer Reichsführerlager', in: *Fränkische Zeitung*, 2 June 1938, 1–2.
336. Baumunk, *Colin Ross*, 100.
337. *Ibid.*, 105.
338. Klaus P. Fischer, *Hitler and America*, Philadelphia 2011, 27–29. Klaus Kipphan, *Deutsche Propaganda in den Vereinigten Staaten 1933–1941*, Heidelberg 1971, 13.
339. *Kronen-Zeitung*, 17 March 1940.
340. Christopher R. Browning, *Der Weg zur 'Endlösung'. Entscheidungen und Täter*, Berlin 1998, 24.
341. Goebbels, *Tagebücher*, 30 April 1942.

342. *Kleine Volkszeitung*, 29 May 1942.
343. *Neues Wiener Tagblatt*, 17 September 1942, 3.
344. *Völkischer Beobachter*, Vienna edition, 17 September 1942, 3.
345. Wolfgang Schumann/Walter Bartel (eds.), *Deutschland im Zweiten Weltkrieg*, vol. 4, Cologne 1981, 301.
346. IfZ Munich, transcripts of Jochen Lang's interviews with Baldur von Schirach.
347. Schirach, *Ich glaubte an Hitler*, 301.
348. Baumunk, *Colin Ross*, 133–134. Baumunk challenges the melodramatic portrayal of their last dinner together as featured in the memoirs of Henriette von Schirach.
349. Records of Werner Heisenberg, cit. Richard von Schirach, *Der Schatten meines Vaters*, 108 f.
350. Imo Moszkowicz, *Der grauende Morgen: Erinnerungen*, reprint Münster 2004, 53.
351. The former Major Egon Keutmann. Registration information of the Wiener Stadt- und Landesarchiv, 7 July 2020, Käthe Keutmann, née Dobbs.
352. I thank Prof. Dr Peter Roessler for various archive materials relating to Katharina Dobbs from the archive of the Max Reinhardt Seminar. From the materials for the period 1941–1943 we know that 'Käthe Dobbs' received top grades in early 1941 and the second highest grades in all her courses in 1942. She left on 30 January 1943.
353. *Oberdonau Zeitung*, 17 August 1943, 3.
354. www.hebrewsurnames.com/arrival_ MENDOZA_1948-02-28, accessed 29 July 2020.
355. Information provided by telephone by a friend of the Dobbs family, Renate Moszkowicz, Munich, 29 July 2020.
356. *Trial of the Major War Criminals before the International Military Tribunal, Nuremberg 14 November 1945 – 1 October 1946*, vol. 14. One Hundred and Thirty-Ninth Day, Monday 27 May 1946, Morning Session. www.uni-marburg.de/de/icwc/dokumentation/dokumente/protokolle-nuernberg/ntvol14.pdf, accessed 10 June 2021.
357. *Ibid*.
358. Dokumentationsarchiv des Österreichischen Widerstandes, Zl. 8919/1, copy of the People's Court (*Volksgericht*) file Baldur von Schirach. 'Verfahren des Landesgerichts für Strafsachen Wien gegen Josef Bachmayer, Albrecht Neumann und Baldur von Schirach' (Vg. 2d Vr 6137/46).
359. In the morning session of 24 May 1946, Schirach stated: 'Dr. Colin Ross came to Vienna in 1944 and told me that he had received information, via the foreign press, that mass murders of Jews had been perpetrated on a large scale in the East. I then attempted to find out all I could. What I did discover was that in the Warthegau executions of Jews were carried out in gas vans.' He claimed that it was only somewhat later that he had learnt of the shootings in the east and that he had known nothing about the 'organized annihilation'.
360. Cf. Roman B. Kremer, *Autobiographie als Apologie. Rhetorik der Rechtfertigung bei Baldur von Schirach, Albert Speer, Karl Dönitz und Erich Raeder*, Göttingen 2017, 90.
361. Bradley F. Smith/Agnes F. Peterson (eds.), *Heinrich Himmler. Geheimreden 1933 bis 1945 und andere Ansprachen*, Frankfurt am Main 1974, 169 f.
362. Wortmann, Baldur von Schirach, 205.
363. Universität Wien/Fachbereichsbibliothek Zeitgeschichte, "Gaupresse"-Archiv Wien, 'Vortrag des Gauleiters des Warthelands Arthur Greiser in Wien, 12. Mai 1942', shelf mark K145_3-M021-A001.
364. Letter from Arthur Greiser to Heinrich Himmler. See Harvard Law School Library Nuremberg Trials Project, http://nuremberg.law.harvard.edu/documents/1500-letter-to-heinrich-himmler?q=%2AGreiser#p.1, accessed 28 June 2020.
365. Letter from Heinrich Himmler to Herbert Greiser, see Harvard Law School Library Nuremberg Trials Project, http://nuremberg. law.harvard.edu/documents/1520-letter-to-herbert-greiser?q=%2AGreiser#p.1, accessed 28 June 2020.

366. Wortmann, *Baldur von Schirach*, 206.
367. *Trial of the Major War Criminals before the International Military Tribunal, Nuremberg 14 November 1945 – 1 October 1946*, vol. 11, *Proceedings*, One Hundredth and Sixth Day, Friday, 12 April 1946, Afternoon Session. See www.uni-marburg.de/de/icwc/dokumentation/dokumente/protokolle-nuernberg/ntvol11.pdf, accessed 10 June 2021.
368. Eleonore Lappin, 'Ungarische Jüdinnen und Juden in Niederösterreich 1944/45', in: Eleonore Lappin/Susanne Uslu-Pauer/Manfred Wieninger, *Ungarisch-jüdische Zwangsarbeiterinnen und Zwangsarbeiter in Nieder*österreich. St Pölten 2006, 7–102 (Studien und Forschungen aus dem Niederösterreichischen Institut für Landeskunde, vol. 45).
369. *Trial of the Major War Criminals before the International Military Tribunal, Nuremberg 14 November 1945 – 1 October 1946*, vol. 14, *Proceedings*, One Hundredth and Thirthy-Eighth Day, Friday, 24 May 1946, Morning Session. See www.uni-marburg.de/de/icwc/dokumentation/dokumente/protokolle-nuernberg/ntvol14.pdf, accessed 10 June 2021.
370. Eleonore Lappin, *Ungarische Zwangsarbeiter und Zwangsarbeiterinnen in Österreich 1944–45. Arbeitseinsatz – Todesmärsche-Folgen*, Vienna/Münster 2010, 161.
371. *Trial of the Major War Criminals before the International Military Tribunal, Nuremberg 14 November 1945 – 1 October 1946*, vol. 14, *Proceedings*, One Hundredth and Thirty-Eighth Day, Friday, 24 May 1946, Morning Session. See www.uni-marburg.de/de/icwc/dokumentation/dokumente/protokolle-nuernberg/ntvol14.pdf, accessed 10 June 2021.
372. As Walter Thomas calls the head of the "legalised pogroms" in his memoirs. Thomas, *Bis der Vorhang fiel*, 51.
373. Susanne Heim (ed.), *Die Verfolgung und Ermordung der europäischen Juden durch das nationalsozialistische Deutschland 1933–1945*, vol. 6: *Deutsches Reich und Protektorat Böhmen und Mähren Oktober 1941–März 1943*, Berlin 2019, 492.
374. *Ibid.*, 273 f.
375. Archiv der Wiener Philharmoniker, Depot Staatsoper, 'Personalmappe Wilhelm Jerger, Schreiben Jerger an Thomas', 23 October 1941. For the entire history of the banishment and murder of members of the Vienna Philharmonic, see Bernadette Mayrhofer/Fritz Trümpi, *Orchestrierte Vertreibung. Unerwünschte Wiener Philharmoniker. Verfolgung, Ermordung und Exil*, Vienna 2014.
376. On the case of Alice Strauss, see www.usmbooks.com/strauss_jewish.html, accessed 27 June 2020.
377. Eva Humperdinck, *Der unbekannte Engelbert Humperdinck im Spiegel des Briefwechsels mit seinen Zunftgenossen: 1884–1893*, vol. 1, Koblenz 2004, 214
378. Thomas, *Bis der Vorhang fiel*, 228.
379. Klaus Mann, 'Three Masters', manuscript for the US soldiers' newspaper *Stars and Stripes*. Schirach was incorrectly spelt "Schierach", however (www.monacensia-digital.de/mann/content/pageview/130781, 5, accessed 14 August 2020).
380. *Rheinisch Westfälische Zeitung*, 11 March 1940.
381. Carl Freytag, *Deutschlands 'Drang nach Südosten'. Der Mitteleuropäische Wirtschaftstag und der 'Ergänzungsraum Südosteuropa' 1931–1945* (Zeitgeschichte im Kontext, Volume 7), Göttingen 2012, 290. Here Freytag uses an unverified source. However, the study by Andreas Huber/Linda Erker/Klaus Taschwer, *Der Deutsche Klub. Austro-Nazis in der Hofburg*, Vienna 2020, p. 187 and footnote 424, states a much lower figure: "His assets of 25,830.35 Reichsmark went to the Vienna *Gauleitung* of the NSDAP." (= Cf. 'Bekanntmachungen', *Wiener Zeitung*, 24 October 1939, 2).
382. Cf. Andreas Huber/Linda Erker/Klaus Taschwer, *Der Deutsche Klub. Austro-Nazis in der Hofburg*, Vienna 2020.
383. 'Die Rede Baldur von Schirachs: "Wien bleibt seiner europäischen Sendung treu"', in: *Völkischer Beobachter*, Vienna, 2 September 1940.
384. *Völkischer Beobachter*, 16 August 1940.

385. *Tagung der Südosteuropa-Gesellschaft und der Deutschen Gesellschaft der Wirtschaft in Böhmen und Mähren*, Prague 1942.
386. *Ibid.*, 29.
387. Cf. in detail Freytag, *Deutschlands Drang*, 289–292.
388. *Ibid.*, 297.
389. Cit. *Ibid.*, 298, fn. 1221.
390. *Völkischer Beobachter*, Vienna, 22 September 1941.
391. Universität Wien/Fachbereichsbibliothek Zeitgeschichte, "Gaupresse"-Archiv Wien: 'Großappell der DAF im Konzerthaus', in: 'Rede Baldur von Schirach, 05. 06. 1942', www.ns-pressearchiv.at/archiv/akte/k185-1-m027-a003,2, accessed 22 June 2020.
392. *Ibid.*, 3.
393. Botz, *Nationalsozialismus in Wien*, 613.
394. Martin Krist/Albert Lichtblau, *Nationalsozialismus in Wien: Opfer. Täter, Gegner*, Innsbruck 2017.
395. Thomas, *Bis der Vorhang fiel*, 203.
396. *Trial of the Major War Criminals before the International Military Tribunal, Nuremberg 14 November 1945 – 1 October 1946*, vol. 14, *Proceedings*, One Hundredth and Fortieth Day, Tuesday, 28 May 1946, Morning Session. See www.uni-marburg.de/de/icwc/dokumentation/dokumente/protokolle-nuernberg/ntvol14.pdf, accessed 10 June 2021.
397. Cit. Freytag, *Deutschlands Drang*, 310.
398. Cf. Florian Freund/Bertrand Perz/Mark Spoerer, *Zwangsarbeiter und Zwangsarbeiterinnen auf dem Gebiet der Republik Österreich 1939–1945* (Veröffentlichungen der Österreichischen Historikerkommission, vol. 26/1), Vienna 2004.
399. Bertrand Perz, *Verwaltete Gewalt. Der Tätigkeitsbericht des Verwaltungsführers im Konzentrationslager Mauthausen 1941–1944* (Mauthausen Studien, vol. 8), 130.
400. Cit. Perz, 131.
401. Morning session of 24 May 1946, www.uni-marburg.de/de/icwc/dokumentation/dokumente/protokolle-nuernberg/ntvol14.pdf
402. Cf. Roman Horak, 'Germany versus Austria. Football, Urbanism and National Identity', in: Alan Tomlinson, Christopher Young (eds.), *German Football: History, Culture, Society and the World Cup 2006*, London 2005.
403. *Völkischer Beobachter*, Vienna edition, 18 November 1940, 29. Kevin E. Simpson, *Soccer under the Swastika: Stories of Survival and Resistance during the Holocaust*, Lanham et al. 2016, 121 f.
404. Hellmut, Butterweck, *Nationalsozialisten vor dem Volksgericht Wien, Österreichs Ringen um Gerechtigkeit 1945–1955 in der zeitgenössischen öffentlichen Wahrnehmung*, Innsbruck 2016.
405. *Neues Österreich*, 22 October 1946, 3.
406. Goebbels, *Tagebücher*, vol. 4, 317.
407. *Völkischer Beobachter*, Vienna edition, 14 December 1939.
408. *Neues Wiener Tagblatt*, 19 September 1940.
409. Goebbels, *Tagebücher*, 6 October 1940.
410. *Ibid.*, 6 October 1940. The version of events presented by Milan Dubrović, *Veruntreute Geschichte*, Vienna 1985, 276, namely that Schirach protected Wolfram from Goebbels, does not reflect the facts.
411. *Ibid.*, 4 October 1940, *Neues Wiener Tagblatt*, 28 October 1940.
412. *Völkischer Beobachter*, 4 January 1941.
413. *Neues Wiener Tagblatt*, 4 January 1941.
414. Goebbels, *Tagebücher*, 19 January 1941.
415. *Ibid.*, 13 March 1941.
416. *Völkischer Beobachter*, 18 October 1940; *Wiener Neueste Nachrichten*, 29 October 1940.
417. *Illustrierte Kronen-Zeitung*, 16 January 1941.
418. *Ibid.*, 12 May 1941.

419. *Völkischer Beobachter*, 6 November 1941.
420. Universität Wien/Fachbereichsbibliothek Zeitgeschichte, "Gaupresse"-Archiv Wien: 'Rede des Reichsleiters Baldur v. Schirach aus Anlass der Erhebung der Kunstgewerbeschule zur Reichshochschule für angewandte Kunst und der Akademie für Musik und darstellende Kunst zur Reichshochschule für Musik und Darstellende Kunst am 5. Nov. 1941 im Großen Musikvereinssaal', manuscript.
421. *Das Kleine Volksblatt*, 29 March 1942.
422. Drewniak, *Theater im NS-Staat*, 23.
423. BA, NL Goebbels/46, 5 June 1942.
424. Cf. e.g. Dubrović, *Veruntreute Geschichte*, 186 ff.
425. Cf. Drewniak, *Theater im NS-Staat*, 195 ff.
426. Bundesarchiv Berlin-BDC, 'Personalakt Thomas, Walter', 11 June 1942 (exhibition).
427. BA, R 55, Bd. 99, 104 f.
428. *Ibid.*, 5 March 1943.
429. *Ibid.*, Schirach to Goebbels, 6 May 1941.
430. *Ibid.*, 16 March 1942.
431. *Ibid.*, 8 June 1942.
432. Goebbels, *Tagebücher*, 14 March 1942.
433. *Ibid.*
434. Goebbels, *Tagebücher*, 15 March 1942.
435. *Ibid.*, 8 April 1942.
436. *Ibid.*, 14 April 1942.
437. *Ibid.*, 24 May 1942.
438. Wortmann, *Baldur von Schirach*, 207.
439. *Völkischer Beobachter*, 10 May 1942, 1.
440. Goebbels, *Tagebücher*, 30 May 1942.
441. *Ibid.*
442. *Ibid.*, 23 June 1942.
443. Silvia Kargl and Friedemann Pestel, *Ambivalente Loyalitäten. Beziehungsnetzwerke der Wiener Philharmoniker 1938–1970*, March 2017, cf. http://wphdata.blob.core.windows.net/documents/Documents/pdf/NS/ns_kargl_ pestel_ambivalente_loyalitaeten_de_v02.pdf, 18, accessed 3 August 2020.
444. Cf. *Wiener Staatsoper, Inventarbuch Musikinstrumente, Orchesterinspektion*.
445. For more on his biography, see www.foerderkreis-hans-woelfel.de/materialien.html, accessed 3 August 2020.
446. Kargl/Pestel, *Ambivalente Loyalitäten*, 18. Cf. also Christian Merlin, *Die Wiener Philharmoniker. Das Orchester und seine Geschichte*, vol. I, Vienna 2017, 52.
447. *Ibid.*, 5 and 6 September 1942.
448. *Ibid.*, 15 September 1942.
449. *Ibid.*, 4. November 1942.
450. *Ibid.*, 9. December 1942.
451. Schirach, *Preis der Herrlichkeit. Erlebte. Zeitgeschichte*, Frankfurt am Main, 190.
452. Forr Gerhart Hauptmann's biography, see www.gerhart-hauptmann.de/index.php?page=43&language=1&id=141&os=0, accessed 6 July 2020.
453. Cit. Thomas Eicher, 'Spielplanstrukturen 1929–1944', in: Thomas Eicher/Barbara Panse/Henning Rischbieter (eds.) *Theater im 'Dritten Reich'. Theaterpolitik, Teil II*, Seelze-Velber 2000, 378.
454. Wolfgang Leppmann, *Gerhart Hauptmann. Eine Biographie*, reprint of the Bern edition *of 1986*, Berlin 2007, 368 f.
455. Cit. Christoph Zuschlag, 'Kunst, die nicht aus unserer Seele kam. Chemnitz, Städtisches Museum, 14. Mai bis Juni 1933', in: *'Entartete Kunst'. Ausstellungsstrategien im Nazi-Deutschland*, Wernersche Verlagsgesellschaft, Worms 1995, 94 f.

456. Kerstin Drechsel, *Städtische Kunstsammlungen Chemnitz*, Leipzig 1996, 17; Sander L. Gilman, *Difference and Pathology. Stereotypes of Sexuality, Race, and Madness*, New York 1985, 235.
457. Karin Hartewig, *Kunst für alle! Hitlers ästhetische Diktatur*, Norderstedt 2018, 100.
458. *Völkischer Beobachter*, 9. February 1943, 3.
459. Goebbels, *Tagebücher*, 25 February 1943.
460. *Ibid.*, 21 March 1943.
461. Hartewig, *Kunst für alle*, 101.
462. *Ibid.*
463. Goebbels, *Tagebücher*, 3 April 1943.
464. *Ibid.*, 5 April 1943.
465. Thomas, *Bis der Vorhang fiel*, 374 f.
466. *Ibid.*, 217 f.
467. Goebbels, *Tagebücher*, 7 May 1943.
468. *Ibid.*, 10 May 1943.
469. *Ibid.*, 22 June 1943.
470. Schirach, *Ich glaubte an Hitler*, 268.
471. *Ibid.*, 10 August 1943.
472. *Ibid.*, 25 June 1943.
473. Schirach, *Preis der Herrlichkeit*, 215.
474. *Ibid.*, 222.
475. Nicolaus von Below, *Als Hitlers Adjutant 1937–45*, Mainz 1980, 340.
476. *Ibid.*, 338 f.
477. Goebbels, *Tagebücher*, 24 June 1943.
478. Statement by Schirach on 24 May 1946 during the morning session in Nuremberg. *Trial of the Major War Criminals before the International Military Tribunal, Nuremberg 14 November 1945 – 1 October 1946*, vol. 14, *Proceedings*, One Hundredth and Thirty-Eighth Day, Friday, 12 1946. See www.uni-marburg.de/de/icwc/dokumentation/dokumente/protokolle-nuernberg/ntvol14.pdf, accessed 10 June 2021.
479. Goebbels, *Tagebücher*, 14 August, 15 August, 20 August, 21 August, 28 August, 23 September 1943.
480. *Ibid.*, 21 August 1943.
481. *Ibid.*, 30 November 1943.
482. *Ibid.*, 14 Dezember 1943.
483. Johann Wolfgang Goethe, *Maximen und Reflexionen*, Berlin 2016, 2nd edition, 37.
484. Baldur von Schirach, 'Goethe an uns. Rede gehalten am 14. Juni 1937 of 14 June 1937 zur Eröffnung der Weimar-Festspiele der deutschen Jugend', in: *Wille und Macht* 5,1937, 5.
485. Cit. W. Daniel Wilson, *Der Faustische Pakt: Goethe und die Goethe-Gesellschaft im 'Dritten Reich'*, Munich 2018, 156.
486. Cf. the comprehensive study by Dirk Kemper, 'Goethes Individualitätsbegriff als Rezeptionshindernis im Nationalsozialismus', in: Werner Keller (ed.), *Goethe-Jahrbuch*, Stuttgart 2000, 129–143.
487. Birgit Peter, Martina Payr (ed): *'Wissenschaft nach der Mode'? Die Gründung des Zentralinstituts für Theaterwissenschaft an der Universität Wien 1943*, Vienna 2008.
488. Cf. Houston Stewart Chamberlain, *Die Grundlagen des Neunzehnten Jahrhunderts*, vol. 2, Munich 1922, 1110 f., and Thomas Mathieu, *Kunstauffassungen und Kulturpolitik im Nationalsozialismus. Studien zu Adolf Hitler, Joseph Goebbels, Alfred Rosenberg, Baldur von Schirach, Heinrich Himmler, Albert Speer, Wilhelm Frick*, Saarbrücken 1997, 245.
489. Cit. Mathieu, *Kunstauffassungen*, 244. Incidentally, Schirach made generous purchases of 70,000 Reichsmark in paintings and sculptures from the 'counter-exhibition' on 'Rhine Art' organised in Vienna for the city's Galerie der Neuzeit (Gallery of Modernism).

490. Universität Wien/Fachbereichsbibliothek Zeitgeschichte, "Gaupresse"-Archiv Wien: 'Wien – Düsseldorf. Die Eröffnung der Ostmärkischen Kunstausstellung', in: *Der Mittag*, Düsseldorf, 28 September 1941.
491. Ibid.
492. Ralf Georg Czapla, 'Erlösung im Zeichen des Hakenkreuzes. Bibel-Ursupation in der Lyrik Joseph Goebbels' und Baldur von Schirachs', in: Ralf Georg Czapla/Ulrike Rembold (eds.), *Gotteswort und Menschenrede. Die Bibel im Dialog mit Wissenschaften, Künsten und Medien*, Bern 2006, 319–326.
493. Universität Wien/Fachbereichsbibliothek Zeitgeschichte, "Gaupresse"-Archiv Wien: 'Die Kunst dient nicht der Wirklichkeit, sondern der Wahrheit!', in: *Der Mittag*, Düsseldorf, 29 September 1941.
494. 'Die Kunst dient der Wahrheit!', in: *Völkischer Beobachter*, Vienna, 30 September 1941.
495. Ibid.
496. Stefan Busch, *'Und gestern, da hörte uns Deutschland': NS-Autoren in der Bundesrepublik. Kontinuität und Diskontinuität bei Friedrich Griese, Werner Beumelburg, Eberhard Wolfgang Möller und Kurt Ziesel*, Würzburg 1998, 166.
497. Busch, *Und gestern*, 169.
498. Wilhelm Haefs, Buchherstellung und Buchgestaltung, in: Ernst Fischer and Reinhard Wittmann (eds.), *Geschichte des deutschen Buchhandels im 19. und 20. Jahrhundert. Drittes Reich, Teil 1*, Berlin 2015, 250.
499. Baldur von Schirach, *Zwei Reden zur deutschen Kunst*, Weimar, no year (1942).
500. 'Wahrheit, Wirklichkeit, Natur. Baldur von Schirach sprach in Düsseldorf', in: *Wiener Mittag*, 29 September 1941.
501. Walter Thomas, 'Bochum, eine westdeutsche Bühne', in: *Völkischer Beobachter*, Vienna, 15 January 1941.
502. 'Wiens Kulturauftrag eine Verpflichtung! Baldur von Schirachs richtunggebende Weisungen an die Kulturschaffenden unserer Stadt', in: *Völkischer Beobachter*, Vienna, 7 April 1941.
503. 'Das Wiener Kulturprogramm', in: *Völkischer Beobachter*, Vienna, 16 October 1941.
504. There is another edition of this book by Walter Thomas under the pseudonym Th. W. Anderman. Extensive research in a section of his estate in the Stadt- und Landesbibliothek Dortmund that was first opened for this project did not produce any leads for this book manuscript or said notes. The book's publisher, Karl Schwalvenberg Verlag Dortmund, no longer exists.
505. Retired lawyer Dr Klaus von Schirach in interview with the author, 19 December 2019.
506. Friedemann Pestel, '"Special Years"?: The Vienna Philharmonic, Baldur von Schirach, and Nazi Cultural Politics in Vienna', in: *Musical Quarterly*, 2019, 289.
507. Archiv Wiener Philharmoniker, F 22a Furtwängler, Wilhelm, Aktenvermerk Jerger, 20 January 1945, 2.
508. *Tagebuchblätter* April 1945, in: http://az413597.vo.msecnd.net/static/upload/files/CMSEditor/Tagebuch_Barylli_de.pdf, accessed 16 August 2020.
509. www.lexikon-der-wehrmacht.de/Personenregister/S/StrecciusAlfred-R.htm, accessed 30 July 2020.
510. Thomas R. Grischany, *Der Ostmark treue Alpensöhne: die Integration der Österreicher in die großdeutsche Wehrmacht, 1938–45*, Göttingen 2015, 168.
511. Goebbels, *Tagebücher*, 16 March 1942.
512. Ibid., 10 August 1943.
513. Ibid., 13 March 1943.
514. Ibid., 3 April 1943.
515. Cf. in detail, on all potential candidates, Joachim Lilla, 'Die Erörterungen zur Neubesetzung der Gauleiterstelle in Wien 1939/40 und 1943/44', in: *Studien zur*

Wiener Geschichte. Jahrbuch des Vereins für Geschichte der Stadt Wien, vol. 57/58, Vienna 2002, 113–124.
516. www.cia.gov/library/readingroom/docs/SANITZER%2C%20JOHANN%20%20%20VOL.%201_0014.pdf, accessed 14 August 2020.
517. *Ibid.*, 124.
518. www.parlament.gv.at/WWER/PAD_01594/index.shtml, accessed 30 July 2020.
519. Goebbels, *Tagebücher*, 15 August 1943.
520. *Ibid.*, 16 December 1943.
521. *Ibid.*, 19 December 1943.
522. *Ibid.*, 3 February 1944.
523. www.geschichtewiki.wien.gv.at/Flakt%C3%BCrme, accessed 31 July 2020.
524. Renato Schirer, *Der Schirachbunker. Die Errichtung eines bombensicheren und unterirdischen Befehlsstandes für die Wiener Gauleitung der NSDAP*.
525. www.zeit.de/politik/deutsch-land/2018-07/gedenkveranstaltung-ham-burg-luftangriffe-opfer-75-jahrestag-sankt-michaelis, accessed 31 July 2020.
526. Schirer, *Der Schirachbunker*, 35.
527. Albert Elmar, 'Der 'Schirachbunker' im Gallitzinberg', in: *Wiener Geschichtsblätter* 34 (1979), 133 ff. Cf. also Alexander Haide, *Der Schirach Bunker*, Vienna 2004.
528. *Ibid.*, 53.
529. Robert Bouchal, Johannes Sachslehner, *Das nationalsozialistische Wien: Orte-Täter-Opfer*, Vienna 2015, 103.
530. Schirach, *Preis der Herrlichkeit*, 14; on Herbert Müller, 225.
531. Helmut Engelbrecht, 'Wien und die sogenannte Kinderlandverschickung', in: *Studien zur Wiener Geschichte. Jahrbuch des Vereins für Geschichte der Stadt Wien*, vol. 57/58, Vienna 2002, 90.
532. Martha Schlegel, *Von der Nordseeküste in die Kinderlandverschickung, 1940–1945*, Oldenburg 1996, 17 f.
533. Lang, *Hitler-Junge*, 361.
534. Schirach, *Preis der Herrlichkeit*, 227.
535. https://books.google.at/books?hl=de&id=KapEAQAAIAAJ&dq=Das+Attentat+wurde+gegen+Gauleiter+von+Schirach+und+eine+Gruppe+reichsdeulscher+Parteif%C3%BChrer+vci%C3%BCbt.+als+sie+den&focus=searchwithinvolume&q=Schirach, 71, accessed 31 July 2020.
536. https://books.google.at/books?hl=de&id=PeJVAAAAYAAJ&dq=Neues+deutschland+attentat+auf+schirach+wien&focus=searchwithin-volume&q=+Schirach+fehlte, accessed 31 July 2020.
537. Goebbels, *Tagebücher*, 3 August 1944.
538. Lang, *Hitler-Junge*, 360.
539. Goebbels, *Tagebücher*, 14 January 1945.
540. Schirach, *Ich glaubte an Hitler*, 308.
541. Cf. Manfried Rauchensteiner, *Der Krieg in Österreich* 1945, Vienna 1984, 155. Schirach, *Ich glaubte an Hitler*, 237 and 'Volksgerichtsakt Baldur von Schirach. Verfahren des Landesgerichts für Strafsachen Wien gegen Josef Bachmayer, Albrecht Neumann und Baldur von Schirach' (Vg. 2d Vr 6137/46), cit. Markus Reisner, 'Schirachs Wiener Hitler-Jugend – "Treu bis zum Ende"' (published seminar paper, Universität Wien 2012, www.ns-pressearchiv.at/sites/default/files/markus_reisner_seminararbeit_2012_schi- rachs_wiener_hitler-jugend_0.pdf, accessed 30 July 2020).
542. Goebbels, *Tagebücher*, 5 April 1943.
543. Statement by Oskar Schlegelhofer on 11 October 1945 during questioning at the Vienna Landgericht (State Court) in the criminal case against Baldur von Schirach, Geschäftszahl [court file no.] Vg3 cVr1920/45.
544. Gentile, Carlo, Skorzeny, Otto, in: *Neue Deutsche Biographie* 24 (2010), 491–492 [online version]; URL: www. deutsche-biographie.de/pnd118614886.html#ndbcontent.

545. Otto Skorzeny, *Meine Kommandounternehmen*, Rastatt 1981, 308.
546. Hugo Portisch, Sepp Riff, Österreich *II: Die Wiedergeburt unseres Staates*, vol. I, Vienna 1985, 102.
547. Lang, *Hitler-Junge*, 392.
548. Fred Borth, *Nicht zu jung zum Sterben. Die 'Hitler-Jugend' im Kampf um Wien 1945*, Vienna 1988, 218.
549. Here Goebbels was perhaps referring to the public execution of the military resistance fighters Major Karl Biedermann, Hauptmann Alfred Huth and Oberleutnant Rudolf Raschke in the square Am Spitz in Floridsdorf, Vienna, on 8 April 1945. There was no far-reaching resistance among the population.
550. Goebbels, *Tagebücher*, 8 April 1945.
551. *Ibid.*, 9 April 1945.
552. www.ilsekrumpoeck.at/geburtstags-gruesse-fuer-ottenschlag, accessed 31 July 2020.
553. Cit. Isolde Spannagl, *Der politische Bezirk Zwettl im Jahr 1945, Diplomarbeit*, Vienna 2008, 185.
554. Lang, *Hitler-Junge*, 399.
555. *Ibid.*, 406.
556. Schirach, *Preis der Herrlichkeit*, 54.
557. Lang, *Hitler-Junge*, 408.
558. *Ibid.*, 408 f.
559. Buddrus, *Totale Erziehung*, 186.
560. *Ibid.*, 210.
561. Butterweck, *Nationalsozialisten*, 204 f.
562. Buddrus, *Totale Erziehung*, 221.
563. 'Schirach über die HJ-Arbeit der Ostmark. Arbeitstagung der HJ in Salzburg', in: *Salzkammergut Zeitung*, Gmunden, 26 May 1938.
564. 'Deutsche Soldaten sterben nur, um unsterblich zu sein. Von Brauchitsch und Baldur von Schirach bei der Feierstunde in Langemarck', in: *Neues Wiener Tagblatt*, 10 November 1940.
565. *Ibid.*
566. 'Opfer der Jugend garantieren den Sieg. Das Vorbild der gefallenen 1200 HJ-Führer. Eine Botschaft Schirachs', in: *Volks-Zeitung*, 5 September 1940.
567. *Ibid.*
568. 'Europas Jugend ehrt Europas tote Helden. Weihevoller Ausklang der Europäischen Jugendtagung', in: *Das Kleine Blatt*, Vienna, 19 September 1942.
569. 'Arbeiten – kämpfen – siegen. Schirach und Axmann vor der Jugend'/'Der rumänische Staatsjugendführer Gast der HJ', in: *Kleine Volks-Zeitung*, Vienna, 27 September 1943.
570. 'Geist der Jugend – Bürgschaft des Sieges. Reichsleiter Baldur von Schirach eröffnete die Kriegsfreiwilligenwochen der Wiener Hitler-Jugend', in: *Kleine Volks-Zeitung*, Vienna, 19 August 1944.
571. Peter Lieb, *Konventioneller Krieg oder NS-Weltanschauungskrieg? Kriegsführung und Partisanenbekämpfung in Frankreich 1943/44*, Munich 2007, 162 f.
572. Wortmann, *Schirach*, 223 f.
573. Butterweck, *Nationalsozialisten vor dem Volksgericht Wien*, 143.
574. *Ibid.*, 156.
575. *Ibid.*, 217.
576. *Ibid.*, 612.
577. *Ibid.*, 45.
578. *Ibid.*, 160.
579. Hilmar Hoffmann, *Generation Hitler-Jugend, Reflexionen über eine Verführung*, Frankfurt am Main 2018, 105.
580. Reichsjugendführung (ed.), *Wir Mädel singen. Liederbuch des Bundes Deutscher Mädel*, Wolfbüttel/Berlin 1936, foreword by Baldur von Schirach.

581. Hoffmann, *Reflexionen*, 105.
582. Bundesarchiv Berlin, R 55, Zl. 24529, 'Personalakt Carl von Schirach', microfilm, 384 ff.
583. *Ibid.*, 390.
584. *Ibid.*, 418–420.
585. *Ibid.*, 422.
586. *Ibid.*, 436.
587. *Ibid.*, 642.
588. *Ibid.*, 654 f.
589. Bayerische Staatsbibliothek, Handschriftensammlung, Nachlass Gerhard Mostar, ANA, 802. H V, Rosalind von Schirach to Baldur von Schirach, San Marino, California, 5 April 1967.
590. *Ibid.*, 1.
591. *Ibid.*, 2.
592. National Archives (NA), Microfilm Collection 1926, Record Group (RG) 260 Roll 15, OMGUS Property Division, Restitution Branch, MFA & A Section, Transcript of Interrogation Baldur von Schirach, Spandau, 9 April 1948, 4.
593. Schirach, *Preis der Herrlichkeit*, 235.
594. *Ibid.*, 234.
595. *Ibid.*, 235.
596. Anna Maria Sigmund, *Die Frauen der Nazis*, Vienna 1998, 211.
597. Schirach, *Preis der Herrlichkeit*, 234.
598. A driven hunt with few beaters, usually without dogs.
599. Bundesarchiv Berlin, 'Parteikanzlei Korrespondenz, Schirach. Baldur von', microfilm, 290, Schirach to Querner, 24 November 1943.
600. *Ibid.*, 294.
601. On Rudolf Querner, see Towiah Friedman (ed.), *SS-Obergruppenführer Querner Rudolf, höherer SS- und Polizeiführer in Hamburg und Wien 1940–45*, Haifa 2005.
602. Alfred Hrdlicka, 'Als die Freiheit anfing', in: Jochen von Lang (ed.), *Vom Reich zu Österreich. Kriegsende und Nachkriegszeit in Österreich, erinnert von Augen- und Ohrenzeugen*, Munich 1985, 272.
603. *Ibid.*, 234.
604. Cf. the survey in the Archiv der Republik, Finanzen, AdR/06/BMfF/VVST/VA/FLD, Vermögensanmeldung 8120, box 70, Arnold Spritzer.
605. Unpublished project study by the Zentralinstitut für Kunstgeschichte in Munich: Theresa Sepp, *Vorstudie zur Rekonstruktion des Besitzes von Kunst- und Kulturgut, über das Baldur von Schirach und seine Ehefrau Henriette zwischen 1933 und 1945 verfügten – unter besonderer Berücksichtigung der Aktivitäten Henriette von Schirachs zur Aushändigung von Gegenständen, die nach dem Ende der nationalsozialistischen Herrschaft konfisziert worden waren*, Munich 2018, 12. I thank project co-leader Dr Christian Fuhrmeister for making this study available to me.
606. Cit. Gabriele Anderl/Edith Blaschitz/Sabine Loitfellner/Mirjam Triendl/Niko Wahl, *Arisierung von Mobilien*, Vienna/Munich 2004 (Veröffentlichungen der Österreichischen Historikerkommission, Volume 17), 155.
607. All three Gomperz siblings were able to flee – Marie von Gomperz died in 1940 in Brno/Brünn (then the occupied Protectorate of Bohemia and Moravia), Cornelia von Gomperz in 1944 in Bern and Philipp von Gomperz in 1948 in Montreux in Switzerland. Cf. *Ibid.*, 76. Cf. also Sophie Lillie, *Was einmal war. Handbuch der enteigneten Kunstsammlungen Wiens*, Vienna 2003, 416–419.
608. Project study by the Zentralinstituts für Kunstgeschichte in Munich, 72. Cf. also Lillie, *Was einmal war*, 838–842.
609. *Ibid.*, 71.
610. Cf. www.lexikon-provenienzforschung.org/pollack-ernst, accessed 18 July 2020.

611. Cf. also Markus Stumpf, "'Ich erteile deshalb den mir nachgeordneten Dienststellen des Staates und der Partei den Befehl, nach der erfolgten Evakuierung der Juden sämtliche Tschechen aus dieser Stadt zu entfernen." Das "Gaupresse"-Archiv Wien anhand ausgewählter Reden Baldur von Schirachs', in: Lucile Dreidemy/Richard Hufschmied/Agnes Meisinger/Berthold Molden/Eugen Pfister/Katharina Prager/Elisabeth Röhrlich/Florian Wenninger/Maria Wirth (eds.), *Bananen, Cola, Zeitgeschichte: Oliver Rathkolb und das lange 20. Jahrhundert*, vol. 1, Vienna/Cologne/Weimar 2015, 330–345.
612. Hubertus Czernin, *Die Fälschung. Der Fall Bloch-Bauer und das Werk Gustav Klimts*, Vienna 1999, 476.
613. Sophie Lillie, *Was einmal war. Handbuch der enteigneten Kunstsammlungen Wiens*, Vienna 2003, 1245 ff.
614. Cf. www.derstandard.at/story/2000038649219/gustav-klimts-wasserschlangen-ii-schneller-60-millionen-profit, accessed 18 July 2020.
615. Schirach, *Preis der Herrlichkeit*, new, expanded edition 2016, 18 f.
616. Nils Fiebig, Alois Miedl. *Der Bankier und die Raubkunst. Geschäfte im Schatten der Macht*, Würzburg 2020.
617. Schirach, *Preis der Herrlichkeit*, new, expanded edition 2016, 19.
618. Jonathan Petropoulos, *Art as Politics in the Third Reich*, Chapel Hill 1996, 224. Schirach, *Preis der Herrlichkeit*, new, expanded edition 2016, 229.
619. Zentralinstitut für Kunstgeschichte, *Vorstudie* [pilot study], 115 f.
620. Lillie, *Was einmal war*, 1364.
621. Murray G. Hall, *Der Paul Zsolnay Verlag: Von der Gründung bis zur Rückkehr aus dem Exil*, vol. 1, Tübingen 1994, 687.
622. Sophie Fetthauer, *Musikverlage im 'Dritten Reich' und im Exil*, Neumünster 2004, 203 f.
623. I thank Ministerialrätin Dr Eva Ottillinger for this information and for pointing me the corresponding file: document enclosed with a letter by the head of the Federal Furniture Administration (Federal Furniture Administration) to the ÖPK of 8 July 1949, code 5447/1949 re. 'Prunktisch Schirach-Ciano'.
624. Cf. Schwarz, *Hitlers Sonderauftrag*.
625. *Ibid.*, 148–153.
626. Anderl et al., *Arisierung*, 198.
627. Herbert Haupt, 'Die Rolle des Kunsthistorischen Museums bei der Beschlagnahme, Bergung und Rückführung von Kunstgut in den Jahren 1938–1945', in: Theodor Brückler (ed.), *Kunstraub, Kunstbergung und Restitution in Österreich 1938 bis heute*, Vienna 199, 70 f. On Bramberg under National Socialism, cf. Rudolf Leo, *Der Nationalsozialismus im Pinzgau (Land Salzburg) 1930 bis 1945 – Widerstand und Verfolgung*, doctoral thesis, Vienna 2012 (= https://othes.univie.ac.at/23576/).
628. Project study by the Zentralinstitut für Kunstgeschichte in Munich, 4.
629. "Zur besonderen Verwendung" – "for special use".
630. Albert Lichtblau, *'Arisierungen', beschlagnahmte Vermögen, Rückstellungen und Entschädigungen in Salzburg* (Veröffentlichungen der österreichischen Historikerkommission, Volume 17/2), Vienna/Munich 2004, 124.
631. Gerald D. Feldman, *Austrian Banks in the Period of National Socialism*.
632. *Wiener Kurier*, 30 May 1949, 3.
633. *Neues Österreich*, 29 May 1949, 2. Cf. also Hellmut Butterweck, *Verurteilt und begnadigt: Österreich und seine NS-Straftäter*, Vienna 2003, 257.
634. Feldman, *Austrian Banks*, 484 f.
635. *Ibid.*, 485.
636. *Ibid.*, 486.
637. 'Auszug aus dem Protokoll über Vorstandssitzung der Dresdner Bank Kreditantrag des …' (NID-13798) cit. *Nationalsozialismus, Holocaust, Widerstand und Exil 1933–1945*. Online database. De Gruyter. 14 June 2020.

638. 'Auszug aus dem Protokoll über Vorstandssitzung der Dresdner Bank Kreditantrag des …' (NID-13799) cit. *Nationalsozialismus, Holocaust, Widerstand und Exil 1933–1945*. Online-Datenbank. De Gruyter. 14 June 2020.
639. *Ibid.*, 10.
640. Rudolf Herz, *Hoffmann & Hitler*, Munich 1994, 50.
641. 'Auszug aus dem Protokoll über Vorstandssitzung der Dresdner Bank Kreditantrag des …' (NID-13799) cit. Nationalsozialismus, Holocaust, Widerstand und Exil 1933–1945. Online-Datenbank. De Gruyter. 14. 06. 2020, 41.
642. www.deutschlandfunk.de/ns-raubkunst-baldur-von-schirachs-kunstsammlung.691.de.html?dram:article_id=446210, accessed 20 July 2020.
643. Henriette von Schirach, *Der Preis der Herrlichkeit*, 92.
644. *Trial of the Major War Criminals before the International Military Tribunal, Nuremberg 14 November 1945 – 1 October 1946*, vol. 14, *Proceedings*, One Hundredth and Thirty-Eighth Day, Friday, 24 March 1946, Morning Session. See www.uni-marburg.de/de/icwc/dokumentation/dokumente/protokolle-nuernberg/ntvol14.pdf, accessed 27 July 2021.
645. Cf. https://documents.yadvashem.org/index. html?language=en&&TreeItemId=9257574, accessed 5 August 2020.
646. Gilbert, *Nuremberg Diary*, London 1948, 93 f.
647. *Ibid.*, 81.
648. *Ibid.*
649. *Ibid.*, 215.
650. IMT, vol. 14, 566, www.uni-marburg.de/de/icwc/dokumentation/dokumente/protokolle-nuernberg/ntvol14.pdf, accessed 5 August 2020.
651. *Ibid.*, 571.
652. Roman Pfefferle/Hans Pfefferle, *Glimpflich entnazifiziert. Die Professorenschaft der Universität Wien vor 1944 in den Nachkriegsjahren*, Göttingen 2014, 249–252.
653. IMT, vol. 14, 574ff., www.uni-marburg.de/de/icwc/dokumentation/dokumente/protokolle-nuernberg/ntvol14.pdf, accessed 5 August 2020. *Ibid.*, 571.
654. *Ibid.*, 587.
655. *Ibid.*, 588.
656. Lauterbacher, *Erlebt und mitgestaltet*, 167 f.
657. *Ibid.*, 543 f.
658. E.g. Uwe Schellinger, *Gedächtnis aus Stein. Die Synagoge in Kippenheim 1852–2002*, Heidelberg 2002, 85.
659. Edith Raim, *Justiz zwischen Diktatur und Demokratie, Wiederaufbau und Ahndung von NS-Verbrechen in Westdeutschland 1945–1949*, Oldenburg 2013, 689, on the HJ's looting in Mellrichstadt, 853: 'Massive Plünderung durch 20 HJ-Angehörige in Usingen'. On the HJ's attacks on "Jewish shops", see Hans Safrian/Hans Witek, *Und keiner war dabei. Dokumente des alltäglichen Antisemitismus in Wien 1938*, Vienna 1988, 43. On Würzburg, for instance, see Hans Steidle, *Jakob Stoll und die Israelitische Lehrerbildungsanstalt. Eine Spurensuche*, Würzburg 2002, 81. On the November pogrom in Vienna, see Kurt Schmid/Robert Streibel, *Der Pogrom 1938: Judenverfolgung in Österreich und Deutschland. Dokumentation eines Symposiums der Volkshochschule Brigittenau*, Vienna 1990, 18. Mahn- und Gedenkstätte Düsseldorf (ed.), *Novemberpogrom 1938 in Düsseldorf*, Essen 2008, 122 and 185. Cf. also www.fritz-bauer-institut.de/fileadmin/editorial/download/publikationen/PM-03_Novemberpogrome-1938.pdf, 70, 82, accessed 5 August 2020.
660. IMT, vol. 14, 550, www.uni-marburg.de/de/icwc/dokumentation/dokumente/protokolle-nuernberg/ntvol14.pdf, accessed 5 August 2020.
661. Gilbert, *Nuremberg Diary*, 217–220.
662. Facsimile of Adolf Hitler's political testament, siehe www.ns-archiv.de/personen/hitler/testament/faksimile-1945-2/index.php?img=0#thumbs, accessed 5 August 2020.

663. Cf. https://documents.yadvashem.org/index. html?language=en&&TreeItemId=9257574, document 8 ff., accessed 5 August 2020.
664. IMT, vol. 33, Nuremberg 1949, 557–559, document 3933-PS, www.uni-marburg.de/de/icwc/dokumentation/dokumente/protokolle-nuernberg/ntvol33.pdf, accessed 5 August 2020.
665. IMT, vol. 14, 433, www.uni-marburg.de/de/icwc/dokumentation/dokumente/protokolle-nuernberg/ntvol14.pdf, accessed 5 August 2020.
666. *Ibid.*, 425.
667. *Ibid.*, 453.
668. Cf. the examples in IMT, vol. 33, 287–296, document 3876-PS, www.uni-marburg.de/de/icwc/dokumentation/dokumente/protokolle-nuernberg/ntvol33.pdf, accessed 5 August 2020.
669. IMT, vol. 14, 417, 490 f., www. uni-marburg.de/de/icwc/dokumentation/dokumente/protokolle-nuernberg/ntvol14.pdf, accessed 5 August 2020.
670. IMT, vol. 33, 297 f. document 3877-PS, www.uni-marburg.de/de/icwc/dokumentation/dokumente/protokolle-nuernberg/ntvol33.pdf, accessed 5 August 2020. In this "teletype" written only in lower case, upper case was rendered by spaces for emphasis in the note: "e x p r e s s – u r g e n t – immediate attention". The translation presented here is the one read out by prosecutor Dodd during the trial: IMT, vol. 14, 492 f., www.uni-marburg.de/de/icwc/dokumentation/dokumente/protokolle-nuernberg/ntvol14.pdf
671. Wiener Stadt- und Landesarchiv, Bürgermeisteramt der Stadt Wien, no. A6/6, BA 349/46
672. IMT vol. 14, 497, www.uni-marburg.de/de/icwc/dokumentation/dokumente/protokolle-nuernberg/ntvol14.pdf; IMT, vol. 33, 530 f., document 3886-PS, www.uni-marburg.de/de/icwc/dokumentation/dokumente/protokolle-nuernberg/ntvol33.pdf, accessed 5 August 2020.
673. IMT, vol. 14, 427 f., https://www.uni-marburg.de/de/icwc/dokumentation/dokumente/protokolle-nuernberg/ntvol14.pdf, accessed 5 August 2020.
674. Albert Speer, *Der Sklavenstaat. Meine Auseinandersetzungen mit der SS*, Munich 1981, 346.
675. United States. Office of Chief of Counsel for the Prosecution of Axis Criminality, International Military Tribunal, United States. War Department, and United States. Department of State, Nazi Conspiracy and Aggression. Supplement AB, Washington 1947/1948, 694.
676. Hubert Seliger, *Politische Anwälte? Die Verteidiger der Nürnberger Prozesse*, Baden-Baden 2016, appendix 550.
677. Seliger, *Politische Anwälte*, 526.
678. Douglas M. Kelley, *22 Cells in Nuremberg*, London 1947, 71–76.
679. *Ibid.*, 72.
680. *Ibid.*
681. *Ibid.*, 73.
682. *Ibid.*
683. Gilbert, *Nuremberg Diary*, 16.
684. Cf. Kerstin von Lingen, '"… unsere Fahne ist die neue Zeit"? Kontinuitätslinien zwischen Hitler-Jugend und "Jugendsozialwerk" in der französischen Besatzungszone, 1945–1949', in: *Jahrbuch für Historische Bildungsforschung*, vol. 16, 2010, 241–265.
685. Kelley, *22 Cells*, 74.
686. Kathrin Kollmeier, *Ordnung und Ausgrenzung: die Disziplinarpolitik der Hitler-Jugend*, Göttingen 2007, 162–177.
687. *Ibid.*, 76.
688. *Ibid.*
689. Jack El-Hai, *The Nazi and the Psychiatrist. Hermann Göring, Dr Douglas M. Kelley, and a Fatal Meeting of Minds at the End of WWII*, New York 2013, 56.

690. *Ibid.* The manuscript of the interview is held at the Holocaust Memorial Museum, Washington D.C.
691. Cf. from Dodd's estate, 'Closing Brief Against Baldur von Schirach', 31 July 1946, https://collections.ctdigitalarchive.org/islandora/object/20002:1917#page/28/mode/2up, accessed 3 August 2020. Cf. also the affidavits and depositions in favour of Schirach: https://connecticuthistoryillustrated.org/islandora/object/20002%3A1915#page/16/mode/2up, accessed 3 August 2020.
692. Cf. a nine-minute film excerpt: www.roberthjackson.org/nuremberg-event/von-schirach-ii.
693. According to Alan Bullock discussing the book of the Nuremberg trial court records, in: International Affairs, vol. 25/1, January 1949, 87.
694. Christopher J. Dodd/Larry Bloom, *Letters from Nuremberg: My Father's Narrative of a Quest for Justice*, New York 2007, 4 and 307.
695. Friedrich Zipfel, *Kirchenkampf in Deutschland 1933–1945. Religionsverfolgung und Selbstbehauptung der Kirchen in der nationalsozialistischen Zeit*, Berlin 1965, 135 (on the basis of *Reichstag* documents).
696. Dodd, *Letters*, 307.
697. Rolf Schieder, *Religion im Radio. Protestantische Rundfunkarbeit in der Weimarer Republik und im 'Dritten Reich'*, Stuttgart/Berlin/Cologne 1995, 140.
698. Cit. Johann Neuhäusler, *Kreuz und Hakenkreuz. Der Kampf des Nationalsozialismus gegen die katholische Kirche und der kirchliche Widerstand*, Munich 1946, 255.
699. IMT vol. 14, 445, www.uni-marburg.de/de/icwc/dokumentation/dokumente/protokolle-nuernberg/ntvol14.pdf.
700. *Charter of the International Military Tribunal*, 8 August 1945, www.uni-marburg.de/de/icwc/zentrum/pdfs/imtcenglish.pdf, accessed 6 August 2020.
701. Kim Christian Priemel, *The Betrayal. The Nuremberg Trials and German Divergence*, Oxford 2016, 147.
702. ITM vol. 22, 564, in www.uni-marburg.de/de/icwc/dokumentation/dokumente/protokolle-nuernberg/ntvol22.pdf; *Das Urteil von Nürnberg*. With a foreword by Jörg Friedrich, Munich 1996, 230 f.
703. *Ibid.*, 566, in www.uni-marburg.de/de/icwc/dokumentation/dokumente/protokolle-nuernberg/ntvol22.pdf., *Das Urteil von Nürnberg*, 232 f.
704. Cf. Christiane Kohl, *Das Zeugenhaus. Nürnberg 1945: Als Täter und Opfer unter einem Dach zusammentrafen*, Munich 2005.
705. Ingeborg Kálnoky/Ilona Herisko, *The Witness House: A Nuremberg Memoir of Countess Kálnoky*, London 1975, 228.
706. Richard von Schirach, *Der Schatten*, 51–124.
707. Around 28 kilometres south of Bad Tölz and 30 kilometres south of Kochel.
708. Richard von Schirach, *Der Schatten*, 60.
709. *Ibid.*
710. Lucius D. Clay was a US four-star general and military governor of the American Occupation Zone in Germany from 1947–1949.
711. Cf. 'Germany: The Women', in: *Time*, 28 July 1947, 23, http://content.time.com/time/subscriber/article/0,33009,887431,00.html, accessed 19.9.2021.
712. Anna Maria Sigmund, *Die Frauen der Nazis*, vol. 1, Vienna 1998, 216.
713. Cf. www.historisches-lexikon-bayerns.de/Lexikon/Georg-von-Vollmar-Akademie, accessed 4 August 2020.
714. Project study by the Zentralinstitut für Kunstgeschichte in Munich, 24 f.
715. *Ibid.*, 29.
716. Cf. www.filmportal.de/person/alfred-h-jacob_11f3f3ce8d-6b422c8b811e042851292a.
717. Richard von Schirach, *Der Schatten*, 97.
718. *Ibid.*, 101.

719. *Süddeutsche Zeitung*, 24 June 2016, cf. www.commartrecovery.org/docs Suddeutsche EmmyGoring20160624.pdf, accessed 6 August 2020.
720. Schirach, *Preis der Herrlichkeit*, new, expanded edition 2016, 312.
721. David Klein, *Die Kunst der toten Juden*, in www.bazonline.ch/kultur/kunst/die-kunst-der-toten-juden/story/30852155, accessed 8 August 2020.
722. Project study by the Zentralinstitut für Kunstgeschichte in Munich, 26.
723. *Ibid.*
724. *Ibid.*, 37.
725. Sebastian Peters is currently writing a doctoral thesis on this subject: Sebastian Peters, *Heinrich Hoffmann. Hitlers Fotograf und seine Netzwerke zwischen Politik, Propaganda und Profit*, cf. www.ifz-muenchen. de/forschung/ea/forschung/heinrich-hoffmann-hitlers-fotograf-und-seine-netzwerke-zwischen-politik-propaganda-und-profit/, accessed 8 August 2020.
726. See the ruling of the Court of Appeals, Fifth Circuit, www.ca5.uscourts.gov/opinions/pub/93/93-02564.CV0.wpd.pdf, accessed 8 August 2020. See additional information in Christina Irrgang, *Hitlers Fotograf: Heinrich Hoffmann und die nationalsozialistische Bildpolitik*, Bielefeld 2020, 94.
727. Cf. www.courtlistener.com/opinion/2516585/hoffmann-v-united-states, accessed 8 August 2020). Cf. also the estate of the lawyer of Billy F. Price, Robert I. White, https://archon.library.tamu.edu/?p=collections/findin-gaid&id=1136&q=&rootcontentid=33645, accessed 8 August 2020.
728. On Schirach's situation in the Allied Military Prison in Spandau, cf., Norman J. W. Goda, *Tales from Spandau. Nazi Criminals and the Cold War*, Cambridge 2007, 215 f.
729. *Der Spiegel*, 24 February 1965 (www.spiegel.de/spiegel/print/d-46169605.html, accessed 8 August 2020).
730. Magnus Brechtken, *Albert Speer. Eine deutsche Karriere*, Berlin 2017, 372 f.
731. *Ibid.*, 482.
732. www.mediathek.at/journale/suche/treffer/atom/0B1D50B6-067-0009B-00000468-0B1C6A5B/vol/67075/pool/BWEB, accessed 9 August 2020.
733. Richard von Schirach, *Der Schatten meines Vaters*, 360.
734. *Ibid.*, 369.
735. *Frost on Friday – Baldur von Schirach*, London Weekend Television, 13 September 1968 (www.dailymotion.com/video/xs8tlm, accessed 8 August 2020).
736. Willi Frischauer, *David Frost*, London 1972, 191. Cf. also Frost's memoirs, David Frost, *An Autobiography: Part One. From Congregations to Audiences*, New York 1993, 373–380, 383 f.
737. David Frost, *An Autobiography: From Congregations to Audiences, Part 1*, London 1993, 374.
738. Elisabeth Boeckl-Klamper/Thomas Mang/Wolfgang Neugebauer, *Gestapo-Leitstelle Wien 1938–1945*, Vienna 2018, 146. Cf. also Wolf Gruner, *Zwangsarbeit und Verfolgung. Österreichische Juden im NS-Staat 1938–1945*, Innsbruck 2000, 190, 199.
739. *Ibid.*, 185.
740. Retired lawyer Dr Klaus von Schirach in interview with the author in Munich, 19 December 2019.
741. Four CVs personally compiled by Fritz Wieshofer, Bayerische Staatsbibliothek, Handschriftensammlung, Nachlass Gerhard Hermann Mostar, 802.H.V.
742. *Ibid.*
743. Cf. Wieshofer's statement in: *Trial of the Major War Criminals before the International Military Tribunal, Nuremberg 14 November 1945 – 1 October 1946*, vol. 14, Proceedings, One Hundredth and Fortieth Day, Tuesday, 28 May 1946, Morning Session. See www.uni-marburg.de/de/icwc/dokumentation/dokumente/protokolle-nuernberg/ntvol14.pdf.

744. Hartmut Berghoff/Cornelia Rauh-Kühne, *Fritz K. Ein deutsches Leben im 20. Jahrhundert*, Munich 2000, 287.
745. Jochen von Lang, *Der Hitler-Junge. Baldur von Schirach. Der Mann, der Deutschlands Jugend erzog*, Hamburg 1991, 291.
746. Berghoff/Rauh-Kühne, *The Respectable Career of Fritz K.: The Making and Remaking of a Provincial Nazi Leader*, New York 2015, 262.
747. Cf. the highly critical biography: www.uibk.ac.at/universitaet/profil/geschichte/ehrungen-biografien/kiehn.html, accessed 9 August 2020.
748. Hartmut Berghoff/Cornelia Rauh-Kühne, *The Respectable Career of Fritz K.*, 28. Cf. also Hartmut Berghoff, *Zwischen Kleinstadt und Weltmarkt. Hohner und die Harmonika 1857–1961. Unternehmensgeschichte als Gesellschaftsgeschichte*, Paderborn et al., second edition 2006, 592.
749. *Ibid.*, 263.
750. *Ibid.*, 264 f.
751. www.spiegel.de/spiegel/print/d-46414495.html, accessed 8 August 2020.
752. Christine von Unruh, who had a relationship with Robert von Schirach, in a telephone call with the author, 19 August 2020.
753. Berghoff/Rauh-Kühne, *The Respectable Career of Fritz K.*, 293.
754. Münchener Hauptstaatsbibliothek, Nachlass Gerhard Mostar, December 1968.
755. *Ibid*, I.2, Wieshofer to Katinka Mostar.
756. *Federal Register*, 20 April 1944, 4258 f.
757. *Federal Register*, 15 October 1947, 6779 f. During the period from 25 January to 2 May 1941, Carl von Schirach bought 37,573.70 US dollars in thirteen transactions and sold shares with a total value of 42,913.74 US dollars. Bayerische Staatsbibliothek, Handschriftensammlung, Nachlass Gerhard Hermann Mostar, Ana 802, H. I.
758. Jack Fishman, *The Seven Men of Spandau*, New York 1954, 73.
759. BArch, R/9361/II, Mikrofilm PK P 77, 'Akten zu ihrer Mitgliedsnummer in der NSDAP', R/9361/V, Mikrofilm RKJ 98, 'Rosalind von Schirach, Reichsfilmkammerakten'.
760. Theodore Front, 'Events and Friends', in: Darwin F. Scott, *For the Love of Music: Festschrift in Honor of Theodore Front on his 90th Birthday*, Lucca 2002, 246.
761. Rudolf Vierhaus (ed.), *Deutsche Biographische Enzyklopädie*, 2nd edition, vol. 8, Munich 2007, 876.
762. Ernst Hanfstaengl, *The Unknown Hitler. Notes from the Young Nazi Party*, London 2005, 295 f.
763. Fishman, *The Seven Men*, 261.
764. Lauterbacher, *Erlebt und mitgestaltet*, 168.
765. https://rpb.lbz-rlp.de/cgi-bin/wwwalleg/srchrnam.pl?db=rnam&recnums=0005635, accessed 8 August 2020.
766. www.volksfreund.de/region/mosel-wittlich-hunsrueck/keine-erinnerung-mehr-an-ehemaligen-reichsjugend-fuehrer-baldur-von-schirach-in-kroev_aid-5839466, accessed 8 August 2020.
767. www.mediathek.at/journale/suche/treffer/atom/0B1D50B6-067-0009B-00000468-0B1C6A5B/vol/67075/pool/BWEB, accessed 9 August 2020. This was confirmed as a fact by Christine von Unruh (in a telephone call of 19 August 2020), who had visited him in Kröv with Robert von Schirach, with whom she was then in a relationship.
768. Heinrich Riedel, *Kampf um die Jugend: Evangelische Jugendarbeit, 1933–1945*, Munich 1976, 282 f.
769. Kaufmann, *Baldur von Schirach* 113 f., with the text of the eulogy.
770. Lauterbacher, *Erlebt*, 168.
771. Bayerische Staatsbibliothek, Handschriftensammlung, Nachlass Gerhard Hermann Mostar, 802. H1, letters by Gretl Wieshofer-Kiehn to Klaus von Schirach, 6 September 1974 and reply by Klaus von Schirach, 11 September 1974.

772. *Ibid.*
773. Schirach, *Preis der Herrlichkeit*, 77.
774. Silvia Kargl/Friedemann Pestel, *Ambivalente Loyalitäten: Beziehungsnetzwerke der Wiener Philharmoniker zwischen der Nachkriegszeit, 1938–1970*, March 2017 (http://wphdata.blob.core.windows.net/documents/Documents/pdf/NS/ns_kargl_pestel_ambivalente_loyalitae-ten_de_v02.pdf, accessed 9 August 2020).
775. *Ibid.*, 42 f.

Index

Academy of Music and Performing Arts 107
Adrian von Renteln, Theodor 45
Alfieri, Dino, 66
American Civil War 4
Anacker, Heinrich 42
Andermann, Wilhelm 44
Andreesen, Alfred 12, 204, 210
Art
   Beim alten Getreidespeicher 124
   Die Stille im Raum 124
   Die Weber 129
   Frühling im alten Gemäuer 124
   Maria mit dem Kind auf dem Schoße, demselben einen Weintrauben reichend 163
Ashley River, Garden, USA 4
Aspang station 2
Aspenstein, Schloss 61, 146, 163–4, 170, 185–6
Atatürk, Kemal 67, 68
Athens 68
Auschwitz concentration camp 29
Austrian Control Bank for Industry and Trade 169
Austrian National Library 89
Axmann, Artur 1, 62, 70, 75, 83–4, 153–6, 176, 204, 220, 230

Bad Tölz 162, 184–5, 187, 236
Baden-Powell, Robert 14, 24–5, 67, 212, 218
Badisches Leib-Dragoner-Regiment 15
Baghdad 68
Bagrianoff, Ivan 110
Baily Norris, Elisabeth 2, 4–5, 97, 185–6, 208, 232, 237
Balk, Johanna 126
Balkan War 93
Barlani Dini, Piero 85
Bartels, Adolf 6, 18, 22, 24–7, 129, 207, 212–13
Barton, Waltraud 104
Baumann, Hans 57
Bavarian Field Artillery 92
Bavarian People's Party 29
Benedikta, Angelika 42, 146
Bibliophile Society 139
Black Forest 72, 192
Black Sea 26
Blagovchina woods 104
Blaschke, Hanns 104–105, 148
Blunck, Hans Friedrich 57
Blut und Ehre 181, 202
Boer, Pieter de 166

Bohemia 83, 85, 110, 177–8, 190, 231
Bohle 85
Bondy, Oscar 162
Bonsels, Waldemar 186
Boothby, Robert 43
Borcherdt, Hans Heinrich 29
Borgmann, Hans-Otto 55
Bormann, Martin 72, 78, 81, 89, 90, 99, 113, 131, 135–6, 142–3, 145, 147–8, 174–5, 177, 184, 193, 220–1
Bouvier, Yves 165
Boy Scouts 13–14, 24–5, 67, 173, 176, 212
Bracht, Fritz 85
Brauchitsch, Manfred von 62
Braun, Eva 46, 80, 132, 187, 220
Brazil 98, 165
British Expedition Corps 71
British Royal Air Force 144
Brown revolution 1
Bruckmann, Elsa 22, 28, 31, 40
Bruckmann, Hugo 31–2, 38, 204, 214–15
Bruegel the Elder, Pieter 167
Brueghel the Younger, Pieter 164
Brunner, Alois 107, 174, 175
Bucharest 68–9
Buenos Aires 98
Bulgaria 69, 91, 93, 110, 114
Bull Run, Virginia 4
Bündische Jugend 41, 45–6, 204, 216
Bürckel, Josef 72–3, 75–81, 109, 141, 160, 166, 169

Campaign Plan for the Ideological War 96
Cantacuzène, Theodor, Prince 31
Carossa, Hans 185
Catholic Church 52, 174
Catholic Hitler Youth 52
Central European Economic Conference 111
Central Institute of Art History xi, 170
Chamberlain, Eva 23
Chamberlain, Houston Stewart 23–5, 138, 204, 212–13, 227
Charleston 4
Chemnitz Municipal Art Collections 130
Chestnut Hill 2–4
Chicago 93, 222
Churchill, Winston 43
Ciano, Galeazzo 66, 69, 110, 166, 232
Colin, Ralph 92, 93, 96

Index 239

Columbia Law School, New York 183
Corps Franconia 35
Council of Ministers for the Defence of the Reich 65, 70
Croatia 85, 91, 92
Cross of Honour Second Class 71
Csáky, István, Count 110
Czechoslovakia 69

Dachau concentration camp 114
Dadieu, Armin 97
Damascus 68
Dambrone, Gabriele 98
Danube 83, 111, 119, 149, 151, 161
De Pillecyn, Filip 85
Defence District XVII 75, 142, 148, 194
Defregger, Franz 38
Degeyter, Pierre 54
Dellbrügge, Hans 100, 104–105, 108, 148, 174, 181
Denmark 69, 85
Department of Contemporary History 102
Der braune Buchring 44
Dessau Court Theatre 7
Dessauer, Elsa 186
Deutsche Bank 18, 199
Deutscher Klub, Vienna 29, 109
Diem, Carl 88, 211
Dietrich, Josef ("Sepp") 18, 91, 150–1, 204, 211, 217–18
Dobbs, Katharina 97, 98, 222
Dobbs, William 98
Dodd, Thomas 176–7, 181, 205, 234–5
"Doktor Faust" 164
Dollfuss and Schuschnigg regime 78
Dollfuss, Engelbert 59
Donndorf, Hans 18, 37–8
Dresden 25, 34, 117, 147, 148, 213
Duesterberg, Theodor 21
Dunkirk 71
Düsseldorf 24, 138, 139, 140, 205, 212, 213, 227, 228, 234
Dux, Fanny 107
Dux, Margarethe 107

Eckart, Dietrich 18, 204, 211
Edschmid, Kasimir 185
Egk, Werner 129
Egyptology 31
Eigruber, August 114, 131
Eisenmenger, Rudolf Hermann 140
Endemann, Emil 10, 12
England iv, 25, 30, 67, 69, 91
Entz, Gustav 174
Estonia 85
Eugen, Prince 73, 154, 160
European Youth Association 83–4, 87–8, 90, 92
European Youth Congress ix, 83, 88, 90, 112, 128, 154
Evangelical Pedagogium 11
Extended Relocation of Children to the Countryside 81

Felber, Oberregierungsrat, Innere Verwaltung, Reichsgau Wien 174
Feldherrnhalle, Munich 17
Finland 69
First Continental Congress 3–4
First Reich Youth Day 50
Ford, Henry 24, 27, 172, 179
Förster, Max 28
France 29, 39, 67–9, 71, 91–3, 191
Francke, Otto 7
Frank, Hans 99, 175
Franz Joseph, Emperor 165
Franz Liszt Society 9
Frauenfeld, Alfred E. 142
Free Democratic Party 196
Free State of Saxe-Weimar-Eisenach 8
Freischar Junge Nation 53
Frick, Margarete 185
Frick, Wilhelm 17, 227
Friedrichs, Helmuth 143
Fritzsche, Hans 173
Frković, Ivica 112
Führer's Delegate for the Entire Intellectual and Ideological Education of the NSDAP 74
Funk, Luise 185
Funk, Walther 109–110, 173, 178

Gardes Cuirassiers Regiment 7
Gardes du Corps No. 1 3
Gašpar, Tido J. 85
General Military Service 59
Georg von Vollmar Academy 186
Georg von Vollmar School 186
George Washington 4
George, Heinrich 55
German Fatherland Party 11
German Labour Front 60, 112
German National People's Party 16, 21, 47
German National Writers' Union 25
German Nationalist Protection and Defiance Federation 6
German Neoclassicism 23
German Scouts Association 53
German Shakespeare Society 8, 9, 30
German Social Democratic Party 186
German Students' Conference 37
German Wandervogel movement 14
German Youth Movement 74
German–Italian Institute for Youth Leadership 66
Gestapo Administrative Department for Jewish Relocation Property 168
Gestapo ix, 46, 57, 65, 108, 135, 143, 163, 168, 193, 194, 237
Giesler, Paul 132, 134
Gilbert 173–4, 179–80, 182, 205, 233–5
Gilbert, Gustave M. 173–4, 179, 205
Giovanni, Don 80
Glattauer, Moritz 107
Goebbels, Joseph x, 34, 41, 45, 50, 55, 79, 118, 126, 204–205, 211, 215, 227

Goethe, Johann Wolfgang von vii, x, 18–19, 23, 29, 94, 137–8, 203, 210, 227
Goetz, Walter 26
Golden Badge of Honour 20, 21, 158
Golden Party Badge 21, 147
Gomperz, Philipp von 164, 231
Göring, Emma ("Emmy") 185
Göring, Hermann x, 50–1, 55, 65, 74, 78, 96, 98, 128, 143–4, 158, 165–6, 172–3, 175, 179, 182, 203, 205, 235
Göttweig National Political Education Institute 156
Grand Ducal Museum of Arts and Crafts 7
Grand Ducal Treasury 37
Grand Duchy and Court Theatre vii, 2, 8, 23
Great Assembly Hall 102
Great Britain iv, 68, 93, 95
Great Hall of the Musikverein 122
Greater Germany Armoured Corps 149
Greater Germany Regiment 152
Greater Germany Reserve Brigade 151
Greece 69, 86
Greifswald 35
Greiser, Arthur 102, 104, 193, 223
Grimm, Hans 57
Gruber, Kurt 41, 44, 45, 216
Guards Cuirassiers viii, 2, 5
Gusen satellite camp 114

Habilitation 30, 214
Habsburg Empire 25, 109
Hácha, Emil 110
Hackl, Alfred 117
Hainisch, Cornelia 164
Hainisch, Marianne 164
Hainisch, Michael 164
Hamburg 25, 36, 39, 41, 81, 127, 145, 202–204, 206, 208, 215, 218, 231, 237
Hanfstaengl, Eberhard 43, 188–9, 198, 205, 215, 238
Hanfstaengl, Ernst "Putzi" 43, 188
Hanke, Karl 85
Hassell, Ulrich 111
Hatzimichalis 112
Hauberrisser, Georg 38
Haupt, Joachim 34
Hauptmann, Gerhard ix, 123, 128, 129, 140, 226, 230
Hegenbarth, Josef 130–1
Heimatkunst 6
Heimsoth, Karl-Günther 46
Heine, Heinrich 6, 25, 137, 213
Heinrichsbauer, August 114
Heisenberg, Werner 97, 222
Hellingrath, Norbert von 32
Henselmann, Josef 130
Hess, Rudoph 19, 20, 28, 36–7, 50, 78, 180, 185
Heydrich, Reinhard 74, 99–101, 110, 112, 174, 177, 184, 193
Higgins, Marguerite 185
Himmler, Heinrich x, 74, 79, 96, 101–102, 104, 106, 153, 155, 161, 173, 176, 193, 196, 208, 223, 227

Hinze-Reinhold, Bruno 21, 212
Hofburg palace 73, 148
Hoffmann, Heinrich viii, 19, 35, 42–4, 46, 48, 50, 81, 111, 132, 135, 144, 157, 166, 168, 170, 184, 187–9, 198, 202–203, 205–206, 230–1, 233, 236
Hoffmann, Henny 35, 42, 44, 46, 152, 188
Hofmann, Wilhelm 166
Hofmannsthal, Hugo von 31–2, 204, 214–15
Hohe Warte hill ix
Holocaust x, 97, 123, 125, 215, 218, 220–1, 225, 233, 235
Holst, Maria 160
Holzschuher, Wilhelm von 35
Höpken, Gustav 113, 151, 164, 174, 196, 197
"Horst-Wessel-Lied" 53, 54
Hotel Post und Jäger 62
Hrdlicka, Alfred 161, 231
Huber, Franz Josef 165, 194
Hubich, Ingeborg 164
Hugenberg, Alfred 21
Hungarian Jews 96, 104–106, 114
Hungary 67, 69, 85, 91, 110, 148

Infantry Demonstration Regiment 70
Innsbruck 152, 164, 196, 204, 206, 224–5, 237
Institute for History of Theatre 29
Institute for Newspaper Studies 92
International Military Court 5
Iran 68–9, 219
Iraq 68–9
Iron Cross First Class viii
Isaria München fraternity 37
Italian Fascist ix, 32, 66
Italy 66–7, 69–70, 79, 84, 90–1, 110, 167, 207, 219
Izbica 104

Jacob, Alfred H. 163, 186, 187, 188
Jerger, Wilhelm 107, 200, 224
Johannis, Karl 128
Johst, Hanns 57
Jölli, Oskar 121
Junghans, Frau 15
Jury, Hugo 131, 137, 143, 147

K'oseivanov, Georgi 68
Kahr, Gustav von 33
Kaltenbrunner, Ernst 104, 142, 143, 169, 185, 193
Kaspar, Annemarie 160
Kassner, Rudolf 32, 204, 214–15
Kastner, Walther 169
Kaufmann, Edith 164
Kaufmann, Günter xi, 69, 79, 80, 88, 113, 119, 139, 164, 166, 199, 203, 206, 219, 238
Keitel, Wilhelm, General 152
Kelley, Douglas M. 174, 179, 205–206, 234–5
Kennerknecht, Georg 143
Kerl, Hanns 168
Kessler, Harry Graf 7, 23, 32
Keutmann, Egon 98, 222
Keyserling, Hermann Graf 32

Kiehn, Fritz 192, 194–7, 237
Klages, Ludwig 32
Klemperer, Victor 30, 213–14
Klimsch, Fritz 124
Klimt, Gustav 165
Klotz, Helmuth 46
Knabe, Herbert 34
Kontropa Kontinentale Rohstoff und Papierindustrie AG 168
Kozich, Thomas 78
Krauss, Clemens 107, 141
Krebs, Albert 39, 206, 215
Krips, Josef 107, 200
Krosigk, Johann Ludwig ("Lutz") Graf Schwerin von 112
Künstler, Wilhelm 98
Kuscheff, Dmitri 112

Lammers, Heinrich 72, 90, 99
Lang, Jochen von 96, 104, 191, 198, 206, 209, 215, 231, 237
Langenbeck, Curt 57
Latvia 85
Lauterbacher, Hartmann 61, 66–7, 69–71, 75, 90–1, 144, 157, 175, 199, 207, 218, 233, 238
"Law Remedying the Plight of the People and the Reich" 53
League of German Girls vii, 48, 56
Lebrun, Albert 93
Leipzig German Students' Union 26
Ley, Robert 50–1, 62–4, 85, 88, 110, 151
Liebmann, Mayer August 28
Lienau, Walter 36–7
Lietz, Hermann 10–12, 14, 204, 210
Lincoln, Abraham 4
Linz 39, 98, 106, 114, 120, 127, 130, 163, 166
Littman, Max 7
LMU 28, 30
Lower Bavarian 18
Ludendorff, Erich, General 16–17, 21, 33, 76
Luftwaffe 133, 144, 151
Luftwaffengaukommando XVII 145

Mader, Erhart 153
Manhattan 34
Mann, Klaus xii, 108, 128–9, 146, 185–7, 189–91, 194, 199–200, 204, 206–207, 211, 213–15, 219, 222, 224, 228, 237–8
Mann, Thomas 6
Manoilescu, Mihail 110
Martersteig, Max 7
Maxims and Reflections 137
Maxwell-Fyfe, David 178
Mayreder, Julius 160
Medrický, Gejza 112
Mercedes Kompressor 17
Metaxas, Ioannis 68
Mexican Civil War 93
MI5 67, 218
Middleton, Arthur 4
Middleton, Henry 3–4, 209

Middleton, Lynah Tillou, Emma 2–3
Miedl, Alois 165–6, 205, 232
Militant League for German Culture viii, 9, 22, 29, 34
Ministry of the Interior 16–17, 104
Minsk 99–101, 104
Möckel, Helmut 82
Moravia 83, 85, 110, 177–8, 190, 231
Moscow 68
Moszkowicz, Imo 97–8, 207, 222
Mozart Week of the German Reich 121
Mozart, Wolfgang Amadeus ix
Mühlmann Agency 166
Müller, Herbert 146, 164, 229
Museum of Arts and Crafts 7, 23
Mussolini, Benito 32, 66–7, 69–70, 84–85, 89, 148

Nagel, Hanna 130
National Festival for German Youth 7
National Holiday of the German People 66
National Socialist People's Welfare 82
National Theatre 6, 19–20, 22, 24, 64, 198
National Youth Administration 181
National Youth Organisation 68
Nationalist Socialist Teachers' League 65, 82
Netherlands ix, 69, 92, 110, 120, 166, 187
Neubacher, Hermann 110
Neurath, Konstantin 67
New City Hall 38
New Reich Chancellery 94
New York 30, 34, 94, 164, 183, 205, 208–209, 212, 217, 219, 221, 226, 235, 237
Norkus, Herbert 47–8, 55, 202, 216
Norris, Alfred E. 34, 214
Norris, Richard 4
Norway 69, 85, 91, 92, 104
Nuremberg ix, 2, 5–6, 13, 19, 22, 24–5, 57, 59, 69, 96, 99, 101, 106, 108, 113–14, 134, 152, 158, 160, 170, 172, 176, 178–9, 181, 191–4, 199–200, 205–206, 217, 223–5, 227, 233–5, 237
Nuremberg trials ix, 2, 6, 13, 24, 96, 99, 101, 114, 134, 158, 160, 172, 176, 192, 193, 235
Nuremberg *Justizpalast* 184

Office for the Cultivation of the Written Word 139
Office of Foreign Affairs 69, 83, 88—90, 92, 96, 111, 174, 193
Oncken, Hermann 29–31, 214
Opera Nazionale Balilla 66, 70
Ottoman Empire 93

Palazzo Venezia 67
Papen, Franz von 51
Paris 68, 165
Pathfinder 13, 14
Paul, Crown Prince 68
Paul, Prince Regent of Yugoslavia 69
Paul Zsolnay Verlag 166, 205, 232 166, 205, 232
People's Court 66, 105, 117, 128, 156, 169, 223
Perard-Petztl, Luise 81
Pestel, Friedemann 140, 201, 206, 226, 228, 238

Philadelphia iv, 2, 34, 197, 222
Pia, Jack 58
Pinakothek museum 28
Pinder, Wilhelm 28, 29, 129, 213
Poland 26, 65, 78, 101, 152
Pollack, Ernst 164
Pollack, Gisela 164, 165
Portugal 69, 85
Posse, Hans 166
Potsdam viii, 48, 49, 50, 202
Price, Billy F. 189, 236

Querner, Rudolf 161, 231

Raimund Prize 122
Ram, Franz 151
Ravensbrück concentration camp 114
Red Army ix, 2, 106, 141, 148, 149, 151, 163
Red Cross 96
Reich Centre for Urban Children's Rural Stays 81
Reich Chamber of Culture 107
Reich Chamber of Music 80
Reich Chamber of the Visual Arts 131
Reich Committee of German Youth Leagues 52
Reich Foreign Ministry 90
Reich Industrial Group 111
Reich Labour Service 60
Reich Ministry for Education 65
Reich Ministry for Public Enlightenment 20, 68, 141, 158
Reich Music Days 24
Reich Party Congress 22, 48, 69, 218
Reich Propaganda Office 80, 118
Reich Security Main Office 104, 106, 143, 174, 176
Reich Theatre Chamber 98, 122
Reich Theatre Week 119
Reich Vocational Games 62, 63
Reich Youth Day 48
Reich Youth Party Congress viii
"Reichskommissariat Ostland" 69
Rendulic, Lothar, General 149
Reventlow, Ernst Graf zu 52
Ribbentrop, Joachim von 67, 83, 88–9, 92, 94, 96, 110, 133, 166, 175, 221
Ricci, Renato 66, 70, 79, 84, 87, 89, 167
Riefenstahl, Leni 57–8
Rilke, Rainer Maria 32, 204, 214, 215
Rintelen, Emil von 90
Robitschek, Viktor 107
Röhm, Ernst 43
Romania 69, 91, 110
Romanian state youth 69
Rome 66, 67, 84, 86
Rommel, Erwin 60–1
Roosevelt, Franklin D. 128
Rosenberg, Alfred 22, 34, 52, 69, 74, 89, 129, 139, 204, 211, 221, 227
Ross, Colin 92–3, 95–7, 101, 186, 193, 204, 222–3
Ross, Lisa 92
Rossleben Evangelical boarding school 15

Rothschild, Nathaniel von 161
Rousseau, Jean Jacques 14
Rowe, James 183
Rüdiger, Wilhelm 129, 130, 204, 216
Rum prison camp 152
Russia 135
Rust, Bernhard 62, 64, 73
Rybolovlev, Dmitri 165

Saale station 17
Saar Referendum 52
Sahm, Heinrich 69
Sander, Harald 17, 62, 151, 207, 211, 218–19
Sauter, Fritz 158, 172, 174, 178, 181, 182
Schacht, Hjalmar 32, 179
Scharizer, Karl 137, 143, 144
Schell, Adolf von 112
Schenker, Gottfried 160
Schick, Josef 29–30
Schick, Mary 30
Schiller, Friedrich vii, x, 7, 18, 19, 23, 138
Schirach, Carl Baily Norris von 2–3, 5
Schirach, Carl von x, 4, 6–8, 20–3, 147, 158–9,
Schirach, Ferdinand von xi, xii, 168, 171, 209
Schirach, Friedrich Karl von 2, 4, 209
Schirach, Henriette von 20, 116, 124, 134, 165, 183, 184
Schirach, Karl Benedikt von 2, 15
Schirach, Klaus von xii, 128, 187, 189–90, 194, 199–200, 228, 237–8
Schirach, Max von 3, 207, 209
Schirach, Richard von 15, 185–6, 200, 207, 209, 211, 222, 236
Schirach, Rosalind von 5, 15, 159, 197, 198, 231, 237
Schirmer, Gustav 17, 197, 212, 231, 237
Schlemmer, Eva 30
Schleswig-Holstein 6
Schlösser, Rainer 26, 79, 118, 140
Schmidt, Paul 92
Schmitt, Saladin 140
Schönmann, Marion 81, 132
Schreiner, Carl Moritz 130
Schulerm, Alfred 32
Schulze, Gerhard 164
Schütz, Franz 107
Schweitzer, Hans 42
Second Reich Party Congress 22
Seldte, Franz 21
Sepp, Theresa xi, 170, 231
Severus, Ziegler Hans 6, 8, 17–18, 24, 38
Shah, Reza 68
Sherman, General 4
Simmel, Georg 32
Sixth SS Panzer Army 150
Skorzeny, Otto 148, 208, 229
Slovakia 69, 79, 85, 91, 114, 146
Society of Artists 8
Society of Music Lovers 124
Society of Visual Artists 124
Sontag, Susan 58, 208, 217

Index 243

South Carolina 3, 4, 209
Spain 69, 84, 91, 93
Spalding Rotary Club 67
Speer, Albert x, 114, 131, 142, 173, 175, 178, 190, 191, 194, 208, 223, 227, 234, 236
Spiegelberg, Wilhelm 29, 31, 214
Spritzer, Arnold 161–2, 231
St Petersburg 4
Starace, Achille 69–70
Starkmann, Max 107
State Academy of Music and Performing Arts 98, 122
State Library 18
State School of Arts and Crafts 122
Stauffenberg, Claus Philipp Maria Justinian Schenk Graf von 147
Steger, Milly 130
Steiner, Jenny 165
Stellrecht, Helmut 65, 74, 203, 218
Stojadinović, Milan 69
Strasser, Gregor 43, 50
Strasser, Otto 34, 43, 50–2, 201, 206, 214
Strasser, Robert 50
Strauss, Alice 107–8, 224
Strauss, Pauline 129
Strauss, Richard ix, 108, 126, 129, 140, 187
Streccius, Alfred 142
Streicher, Julius 22, 179
Střítež, Caroline Deym von, Countess 31
Strohm, Heinrich Karl 80, 118
Stuppäck, Hermann 122, 167, 201
Stwertka, Julius 107
Sunkel, Reinhard 36, 215
Supreme Reich Authority 59
Switzerland 93, 110, 162, 231

Tamms, Friedrich 144
Tanner, Väinö 112
Tassinari, Giuseppe 92
Taylor, Telford 178
Tchaikovsky 80, 141
Teleki, Pál, Count 110
Tempel, Wilhelm 33
Thalheimer, Siegfried 163
The Hague 165
Third Reich 1, 42, 94, 118, 120, 123, 125, 138, 155, 232
Thomas, Walter 79, 83–4, 107–108, 113, 123, 131, 140, 208–10, 220, 224, 228
Thuringian Public Education Ministry 23
Tietjen, Heinz 122
Titian 167
Tobias and the Angel 166
Treaty of Versailles 23, 39, 59
Tucholsky, Kurt 25, 213
Turkey 67, 68, 69, 110
Twelfth SS Armoured Division 155
Tyroler, Armin 107

Ucicky, Gustav 165
Ucicky, Ursula 165

Uiberreither, Siegfried 85, 131
Undersecretary of State 90, 112
Union of National Journalists' Associations 91
Universities
  Cologne 39
  Columbia, New York 30
  Erlangen 35, 204
  Jena 38, 208
  Munich 28, 31, 48
  Music Franz Liszt 21
  Reich University of Applied Arts or Music 122
  Vienna 30, 102, 138, 195
Unruh, Christine von xii, 98, 237–8
Urfeld am Walchensee 61, 96, 163, 186
USA iv, ix, 2–4, 34, 91–2, 94–5, 97, 99–100, 162–4, 179, 181, 191, 197

Valberg, Robert 121
Van de Velde, Henry 7
Velázquez 167
Verlag des Waisenheims an der Ilse 12
Vienna Autumn Trade Fair 109, 111
Vienna Philharmonic 80, 107, 118, 122, 126, 128, 140, 160, 200, 224, 228
Vienna State Opera 80, 118, 126
Vignau, Hippolyt von 7
Vordemberge, Friedrich 130
Vossler, Karl 29, 30, 31, 214

Waffen-SS Battalion for Special Deployment 168
Wagner, Adolf 62, 128
Wagner, Robert 72, 75
Wagner-Régeny, Rudolf 126, 129
Wagner, Winifred 23
Wandervogel movement 14
Wechsler, Henry 183
Weimar Festival of German Youth 137, 138
Weimar railway station 19
Weimar Republic vii, x, 8, 12, 15, 19, 23, 30, 36, 39, 47, 50, 53, 93
Weimar via Isserstedt 17
Weinheber, Josef 127, 146
Weiß, Wilhelm 91
Western Allies 106
Weygand Line 71
Wieser, Charlotte 105
Wieshofer, Fritz 149, 151–2, 174–5, 192, 195–7, 199, 237–8
Wilhelm II, Kaiser 5, 25, 212
Wilhelm Ernst, Grand Duke of Saxe-Weimar-Eisenach 6
Wilhelm, Friedrich 32, 76
Wilhelm, Johann 168
Wilhelmine Empire 12
Wilmowsky, Tilo 114
Winter, Eduard 168
Wobisch, Helmut 200
Wölfel, Hans 128
Wölfflin, Heinrich 32
Wolfram, Aurel 118

Wolfram, Wette 118, 119, 213, 225
Wolfskehl, Karl 32

Young Art in the German Reich 123, 129, 142
Young German Order 16
Young Socialist Workers 45
Young Trade Unionists 45
Youth and Family Consortium 90
Youth Around Hitler 44, 50

Youth in the Reich 82
Yugoslavia 69

Ziegler, Adolf 6–8, 17–20, 24, 38, 131, 212
Ziegler, Hans Severus 6, 8, 17–18, 24, 38
Ziereis, Franz 106
Ziesché, Hermogenes 52
Zimmer, Arthur 81